W9-AVA-529

# Introduction to the Principalship

The latest leadership textbook from respected author team Kaplan and Owings explores how principals can effectively build a culture around student achievement. *Introduction to the Principalship* helps aspiring principals understand how to develop a vision for improvement, make decisions and manage conflict, build teachers' capacity, communicate, monitor the organization's performance, and create a school climate of mutual respect. This important book provides readers with various leadership concepts to inform their practice, as well as the cognitive and practical tools to evaluate and prioritize what leadership actions to take. Each chapter offers opportunities for readers to create personal meaning and explore new ways of doing leadership to advance a positive, person-focused environment. Providing both the theoretical framework and skills for effective practice, *Introduction to the Principalship* addresses the issues most urgent and relevant for educational leadership graduate students learning how to build a school culture that promotes every student's success.

Special features include:

- Learning objectives—chapter openers introduce the topic and initiate student thinking.
- Reflections and relevance—interactive exercises, role plays, class activities, and assignments help readers think about content in personally meaningful ways, facilitate understanding of chapter content, and help transfer leadership thinking to action in their own schools.
- ISLLC Standards—each chapter is aligned to the 2015 Interstate School Leadership Licensure Standards.
- Companion website—includes links to supplemental material, additional readings, and PowerPoints for instructors.

**Leslie S. Kaplan** is a retired school administrator, a full-time education writer, and an Adjunct Research Professor at Old Dominion University, USA.

**William A. Owings** is Professor of Educational Leadership at Old Dominion University, USA.

# Introduction to the Principalship

## Theory to Practice

Leslie S. Kaplan and
William A. Owings

NEW YORK AND LONDON

Visit the companion website for this title at www.routledge.com/cw/Kaplan

First published 2015
by Routledge
711 Third Avenue, New York, NY 10017

and by Routledge
2 Park Square, Milton Park, Abingdon, Oxon, OX14 4RN

*Routledge is an imprint of the Taylor & Francis Group, an informa business*

© 2015 Taylor & Francis

The right of Leslie Kaplan and William Owings to be identified as author of this work has been asserted by him/her in accordance with sections 77 and 78 of the Copyright, Designs and Patents Act 1988.

All rights reserved. No part of this book may be reprinted or reproduced or utilised in any form or by any electronic, mechanical, or other means, now known or hereafter invented, including photocopying and recording, or in any information storage or retrieval system, without permission in writing from the publishers.

*Trademark notice*: Product or corporate names may be trademarks or registered trademarks, and are used only for identification and explanation without intent to infringe.

*Library of Congress Cataloging in Publication Data*
Kaplan, Leslie S.
Introduction to the principalship: theory to practice/Leslie S. Kaplan, William A. Owings.
  pages cm.
  Includes bibliographical references and index.
  1. School principals—United States. 2. School management and organization—United States. 3. Educational leadership—United States. I. Owings, William A., 1952– II. Title.
  LB2831.92.K36 2015
  371.2′0120973—dc23                               2014030557

ISBN: 978-1-415-74195-8 (hbk)
ISBN: 978-1-415-74196-5 (pbk)
ISBN: 978-1-315-81496-4 (ebk)

Typeset in Sabon and Helvetica
by Florence Production Ltd, Stoodleigh, Devon, UK

SFI Certified Sourcing
www.sfiprogram.org
SFI-00453

Printed and bound in the United States of America
by Edwards Brothers Malloy

*This book is dedicated to the aspiring principals who will make a difference—one school at a time.*

# Contents

# Detailed Contents

# Figures

# Tables

# About the Authors

**Leslie S. Kaplan, Ed.D.** is a retired school administrator in Newport News, VA and is currently a full-time education writer. She has provided middle and high school instructional and school improvement leadership as an assistant principal for instruction as well as central office leadership as a director of program development. Before becoming a school administrator, she was a middle and high school counselor, and these insights continue to infuse her leadership perspective. Her professional interests focus on teacher quality, principal quality, school culture, school finance, and educational foundations and their relationship to school improvement and increasing student achievement. She has co-authored several books and monographs with William Owings, including *Culture Re-Boot: Reinvigorating School Culture to Improve Student Outcomes*; *American Public School Finance* (2nd edition); *Educational Foundations* (2nd edition); *Leadership and Organizational Behavior in Education: Theory into Practice*; *The Effective Schools Movement: History, Analysis, and Application*; *Teacher Quality, Teaching Quality, and School Improvement*; *Best Practices, Best Thinking, and Emerging Issues in School Leadership*; and *Enhancing Teacher and Teaching Quality*. Kaplan's scholarly publications, co-authored with Owings, appear in numerous peer-reviewed professional journals. Kaplan is co-editor of the *Journal for Effective Schools* and serves on the NASSP *Bulletin* Editorial Board. She is a past president of the Virginia Counselors' Association and the Virginia Association for Supervision and Curriculum Development and is presently the Board Secretary of Voices for Virginia's Children in Richmond, VA.

**William A. Owings, Ed.D.** is currently a professor of educational leadership at Old Dominion University in Norfolk, VA. Owings has worked as a public school teacher, an elementary and high school principal, assistant superintendent, and superintendent of schools. His professional interests are in school finance, principal quality, and teacher quality as they relate to school improvement and student achievement. In addition, his scholarly publications co-authored with Leslie Kaplan include articles in the National Association of Secondary School Principals (NASSP) *Bulletin*, *Journal of School Leadership*, *Journal of Education Finance*, *Journal of Effective Schools*, *Phi Delta Kappan*, the *Teachers College Record*, and the *Eurasian Journal of Business and Economics*. Owings has served on the state and international board of the Association for Supervision and Curriculum Development (ASCD), is currently the editor of the

*Journal for Effective Schools*, and is on the *Journal of Education Finance* Editorial Advisory Board.

Kaplan and Owings are frequent presenters at state and national conferences on topics including educational leadership, school finance, school culture, and instructional improvement. Owings and Kaplan share the 2008 Virginia Educational Research Association Charles Edgar Clear Research Award for Consistent and Substantial Contributions to Educational Research and Scholarship. Recently, they were each named as 2014 Distinguished Research and Practice Fellows of the National Education Finance Academy.

# Preface

*Introduction to the Principalship: Theory into Practice* is designed to help aspiring principals understand the human and leadership components of a successful school. It describes what the effective principalship looks like from the inside, providing a working model of instructional leadership in action. Most importantly, this book identifies how principals can make students, and their learning to high levels, their top priority and improve student outcomes.

Most teachers enter education to make the world a better place one classroom at a time. Most aspiring principals seek leadership positions to make the world a better place one school at a time—a way to benefit more children. Yet although teachers see their principals at work every day, most teachers—and many assistant principals—do not fully understand the role's complexities, subtleties, or scope. When they start their first leadership positions, they are often surprised. They wonder, "Where do I begin?"; "How can I focus on what's important, not simply on what's urgent?"; "How do I effectively manage a school with countless moving parts—and all these people?"

Many introductory textbooks for future principals don't help answer these questions. Instead, they take an outsider's view, briefly surveying educational leadership "topics" such as school administration, governance, finance, law, public relations, and other areas as if observing leadership from an altitude of 10,000 feet. In contrast, this book views the principalship from inside the principal's office, walking the school's corridors and visiting its classrooms, identifying the priorities and organizational dynamics that actual leaders must address effectively as they work to promote every student's success.

With this in mind, the authors have written an introduction to the principalship that meets professors' needs for scholarly work and conceptual challenge and graduate education students' need for practical professional relevance and personal meaning. This book can advance the following common goals:

- To use a textbook that adult students and their professors will find readable, interesting, scholarly, practical, and immediately relevant.
- To address what future principals will need to know, understand, and be able to do as their school's instructional leader.
- To identify student learning as the principal's priority by providing a rationale and strategies for establishing a student-centered learning culture in every classroom and throughout the school.

- To enable future principals to develop their philosophy of education and their philosophy of leadership by considering contemporary perspectives.
- To help future principals develop a social justice philosophy of educational leadership by considering equity, equality, and fairness in education.
- To illustrate how principals as change agents can shape and leverage school culture to change school norms, expectations, and behaviors in ways that enhance student learning and teacher satisfaction.
- To examine how leaders can understand, initiate, develop, and sustain organizational change.
- To explain the importance of principals developing ethical behaviors and trust in their schools and with teachers, parents/guardians, and community members.
- To show future principals the advantages of developing teachers' professional capacity for instruction and leadership.
- To describe how principals can effectively use decision making and problem solving as leadership tools to improve their schools.
- To give future principals a perspective on how to use data for informed decision making about school issues and their role in teacher and principal evaluation.
- To highlight best practices for school improvement supported by the professional literature.
- To "keep it real" by infusing successful practitioners' orientations from two authors with over 50 years of combined K-12 school leadership.
- To cultivate reflective practitioners by providing on-going opportunities to discuss educational ideas with peers and professors.
- To facilitate learning and frequent occasions to generate personal meaning, workplace relevance, and networking by applying the content in appropriate contexts, generating feedback, and reflecting on its implications.
- To enable graduate students to build their own leadership skills as they apply the book's concepts to advance teaching and learning in their current schools.
- To help future principals identify coursework and field experiences to help them become more effective leaders.
- To enable the transfer of learning and practice from graduate classrooms into teacher leader, assistant principal, or principalship positions.
- To accommodate adult students' varied learning styles with auditory, graphic, and interpersonal learning activities.

## FEATURES OF *INTRODUCTION TO THE PRINCIPALSHIP: THEORY INTO PRACTICE*

This text offers special features to help future principals learn each chapter's content:

• *ISLLC Standards.* The Interstate School Leadership Licensure Consortium (ISLLC) Standards help define the broad, high-priority themes that educational leaders must address to promote every student's success. A matrix of the refreshed 2015 research-based ISLLC Standards and related leadership functions by chapter (in DRAFT form as of this writing) follows this Preface. Likewise, each chapter opens by noting the standards it discusses. The standards affirm that the school leader's primary responsibility is to improve teaching and learning for all children. State education leadership policies and the School Leaders Licensure Assessment (SLLA) that future principals take to earn their principalship certificates are based in these standards. ISLLC 2015 Standards, and discussion of their leadership functions, can be found at a variety of locations, including the Council of Chief State School Officers (http://www.ccsso.org/Resources/Programs/Developing_and_Supporting_School-Ready_Leaders.html).

Briefly, the draft version of the 11 ISLLC Standards call for *an educational leader who promotes the academic success and personal wellbeing of every student by:*[1]

1. *Vision and mission. Ensuring the development, articulation, implementation, and stewardship of a child-centered vision of high quality schooling that is shared by all members of the school community.* Leadership functions to perform this standard include: collaboratively develops, implements, and promotes a shared vision and mission for quality teaching and learning; collects and uses data to identify goals, assess organizational effectiveness, and promote organizational learning; creates and implements plans to achieve goals; promotes continuous and sustainable improvement; monitors and evaluates progress and revises plans; and acts in ways that consistently reflect the school's/district's vision, mission, and values.

2. *Instructional capacity. Enhancing instructional capacity.* Leadership functions to perform this standard include: recruits and hires instructionally effective teachers and other professional staff; develops individual and collective knowledge, skills, and dispositions of instructional staff; ensures on-going and differentiated professional learning based on knowledge of adult learning and development; supports staff with human, financial, and technological resources; employs research-anchored and valid systems of supervision and evaluation; protects teaching and learning from disruptive forces; and provides motivational support to staff teachers and other professional staff.

3. *Instruction. Promoting instruction that maximizes student learning.* Leadership functions to enact this standard include: maintains a culture of high expectations and challenge; ensures that instruction is authentic and relevant to students experiences and futures; ensures that instruction is anchored on best understandings of child development and effective pedagogy; ensures student strengths-based approaches to teaching and learning; ensures the use of effective differentiated pedagogy and student supports to reduce learning gaps; provides on-going, salient, informative, and actionable feedback to teachers and other professional staff; ensures the use of pedagogy that treats students as individuals and promotes constructive sense of self; ensures the presence of culturally responsive pedagogy that affirms student identities; monitors instruction and instructional time; employs technology in the service of teaching and learning.

4. *Curriculum and assessment. Promoting robust and meaningful curricula and assessment programs.* Leadership functions to perform include: ensures academic rigorous and well-rounded curricular and assessment programs; ensures culturally relevant curricula and assessments; direct curricula and assessments to maximize opportunity for student learning; ensures authentic learning and assessment experiences; emphasizes assessment systems congruent with understandings of child development and technical standards of measurement; ensures the use of learning experiences that enhance both the enjoyment of and success in learning; uses assessment data in ways that are appropriate to their intended uses and within their technical limitations.

5. *Community of care for students.* Promoting the development of an inclusive school climate characterized by supportive relationships and a personalized culture of care. Leadership functions to enact this standard include: ensures the formation of a culture defined by trust; ensures that each student is known, accepted and valued, respected, and feels a sense of belonging; ensures that students are enmeshed in a safe, secure, emotionally protective, and healthy environment; ensures that each student has adequate, relevant and sustained academic and social support; ensures that each student is an active member of and takes responsibility for the school; provides student with academic and social support that are congruent with the community's cultures and languages.

6. *Professional culture for teachers and other professional staff.* Promoting professionally normed communities for teachers and other professional staff. Leadership functions to carry out this standard include: develops and supports productive and trusting working relationships; nurtures a commitment to shared goals; provides for collaborative work; facilitates shared ownership; develops collaborative leadership skills; promotes a climate of collective efficacy; monitors and nurtures a culture of shared accountability for colleagues, for students, and for the school as a whole.

7. *Communities of engagement for families.* Promoting communities of engagement for families and other stakeholders in the school's community. Leadership functions to carry out this standard include: promotes understanding, appreciation, and use of the community's diverse cultural, social, and intellectual resources; nurtures a sense of approachability and welcome and sustains positive relationships with families and caregivers; builds and sustains productive relationships with community partners in the government, non-profit, and private sectors; advocates for policies and resources for the community; is present in, understands, and engages with community needs, priorities, and resources, communicates regularly and openly with families and stakeholders in the wider community; develops partnerships with families to support student learning at home; monitors engagement with families and community; represents the school effectively to parents and the community to manage enrollments and secure support and services.

8. *Operations and management.* Ensuring effective and efficient management of the school or district to promote student social and academic learning. Leadership functions to carry out this standard include: develops and demonstrates well-honed interpersonal skills; manages student behavior with a focus on learning; ensures effective leadership throughout the school or district; crafts and connects management operations, policies, and resources to the vision and values of the school; monitors and evaluates all aspects of school or district operations for effect and impact; ensures the implementation of data systems that provide actionable information; uses technology at the school or district to improve operations; manages organizational politics with an eye on school or district values and mission; enables others to understand and support relevant laws and policies; acts as a steward of public funds; develops and manages relationship with the feeder and connecting schools; develops and manages relationships with the district office or the school board; acts entrepreneurially in the service of the school or district; manages enrollment under conditions of competition.

9. *Ethical principles and professional norms. Adhering to ethical principles and professional norms.* Leadership functions to carry out this standard include: nurtures the development of schools that place children at the heart of education; acts in an open and transparent manner; maintains a sense of self-awareness and attends to his or her own learning; works to create productive relationships with students, staff, parents, and members of the extended school community; maintains a sense of visibility and is approachable to all stakeholders; acts as a moral compass for the school or district; and safeguards the values of democracy, individual liberty, equity, justice, community, and diversity.

10. *Equity and cultural responsiveness. Ensuring the development of an equitable and culturally responsive school.* Leadership functions to carry out this standard include: ensures equity of access to social capital and institutional support; fosters and monitors schools as affirming and inclusive places; advocates for children, families, and caregivers; attacks issues of student marginalization, deficit-based schooling, and limiting assumptions about gender, sexual orientation, race, class, and special status; promotes the ability of students to participate in multiple cultural environments; and promotes understanding, appreciation, and use of diverse cultural, linguistic, ecological, social, political, and intellectual resources.

11. *Continuous school improvement. Ensuring the development of a culture of continuous improvement.* Leadership functions to carry out this standard include: anticipates, assesses, analyzes, and discerns the value of emerging trends to shape school or district decision making; initiates and manages school and system-wide change; enables others to engage productively with change improvement processes; navigates improvement efforts in the midst of ambiguity and competing demands and interests inside and outside the school district; promotes a culture of evidence-based inquiry and continuous learning linked to processes of planning, decision-making, and implementation of improvements; maintains a systems perspective and promotes alignment across all dimension of the school or district; and promotes a culture of collective direction, shared engagement, and mutual accountability consistent with vision, mission, and values.

Because the ISLLC Standards' paramount goal is the success of each student, we begin this introduction to the principalship by looking at how principals can develop a student-centered learning environment in their schools. We continue by describing the processes and practices by which principals and other school leaders can nurture and sustain it.

• *Learning objectives.* Each chapter begins with learning objectives that identify the concepts educational leadership students and their professors will be able to analyze, assess, define, describe, discuss, evaluate, explain, list, relate, or summarize after reading the chapter. These objectives tend to be "big picture" issues. For example, after reading Chapter 1, the reader will be able to "describe the differences between the principal's responsibilities of providing 'access for all' and ensuring 'learning for all,'" and "summarize the social, political, and economic reasons why it is essential that all American children successfully learn to high levels."

• *Reflections and relevance.* Located immediately following major concepts in each chapter, these individual, paired, and small group exercises—questions, class discussions, analysis, role plays, and assignments—ask students to apply the new concepts to their own experiences and responsibilities. The activities give future principals personal meaning as well as opportunities to try out and receive feedback on their growing leadership behaviors. Connecting theory to practice in this way facilitates students' transfer of learning from the text and graduate classrooms to their current and future schools. Likewise, interacting with peers during socially mediated activities can help graduate students extend and cultivate their network of colleagues who know them, share and understand their professional leadership challenges, and can help them problem solve "back at school." Professors can adapt and revise activities as needed to accomplish their instructional goals.

- *Companion website.* This volume has a companion website that includes links to supplementary materials that can bring additional insights and perspectives to the chapter content. These include PowerPoint slides for each chapter, additional readings, and video clips with related teaching and learning activities.

## ORGANIZATION

The text is organized into 10 chapters.

**Chapter 1, Principal Leadership for a Student-Centered Learning Environment,** discusses how societal and technological shifts and a nationally driven school reform agenda have changed the principal's role. Now expected to be transformational leaders, principals have become change agents whose job is to increase every child's achievement by improving teaching and learning. For principals, educating all children to high standards begins with creating a student-centered learning environment. This includes instructional leadership, high teacher expectations for students, a safe and purposeful learning environment, academic press and academic/social scaffolding, and respectful, caring relationships that help students become proficient in the high-standards curricula. The chapter spells out what these mean and what they look like in practice. The chapter concludes by discussing how having mental models, role models, informed perspectives, and trying out, reflecting on, and refining their own growing leadership behaviors can help principals new to the profession grow into their role.

**Chapter 2, Leadership: A Brief Look at Theory and Practice,** explains how our understanding of leadership has evolved and reflects a particular culture's viewpoint. Understanding human motivation is an essential leadership task, and the chapter discusses how principals can use Abraham Maslow's hierarchy of needs, Victor Vroom's expectancy theory, Douglas MacGregor's Theories X and Y, William Ouchi's Theory Z, and Frederick Herzberg's motivation-hygiene theory to incentivize teachers, staff, and students to accomplish the school's goals. In addition, situational leadership theory, transformational leadership theory, and the instructional leadership model provide a variety of frameworks to help understand how principals can lead. The chapter continues by presenting the research on principal leadership and student achievement and concludes by discussing several approaches—colorblind, multicultural, and all-inclusive—to how principals can successfully lead a diverse faculty and staff.

**Chapter 3, Developing Your Philosophy of Education,** describes how having a philosophy of education and a philosophy of educational leadership can help principals decide where and how to lead their schools and to what ends. Educational philosophies are belief systems that shape how principals see the world and how they intend to prepare our children—intellectually, civically, socially, and economically—for the world they will live in. John Dewey, Elliot Eisner, and Paulo Freire, three leading educational thinkers from different eras, offer views about the purpose and process of education in a pluralistic society and its relationship to freedom, democracy, individuals, and the larger culture. The chapter continues by reviewing the University Council for Educational Administration (UCEA) and Interstate School Leaders Licensure Consortium (ISLLC) Standards as useful guides for developing a philosophy of educational leadership. Discussions about educational leadership and social justice—equity, equality, and fairness—conclude the chapter.

**Chapter 4, Understanding and Leveraging School Culture,** explains how school leadership *is* culture building. The chapter presents the open systems model as a conceptual framework to understand school dynamics, defines *school culture,* and illustrates how it appears in schools. The chapter also discusses change as organizational learning, clarifies how principals create the environment that improves school culture, introduces the research on school culture and climate as it affects school functioning and student outcomes, and gives principals suggestions on how to involve their teachers and staff in school culture reshaping.

**Chapter 5, Initiating and Sustaining Change,** looks at the relationship between culture and change. It identifies the school culture and climate factors that help teachers learn new attitudes and skills. Additionally, the chapter considers several conceptual models by which to understand and lead change in schools. Kurt Lewin's three-stage change theory model, Chris Argyris' and Donald Schön's single- and double-loop learning paradigm, Robert Chin's three strategic orientations to organizational change, Lee Bolman and Terrence Deal's "multiple frames" theory, and Michael Fullan's "change leadership" all receive attention.

**Chapter 6, Building Ethical Behaviors and Relational Trust,** views education as a "people profession" and expresses how ethical behaviors and trustworthiness lie at the heart of leadership. It describes how effective principals, as moral stewards, use ethical principles in building relationships and resolving ethical dilemmas in school. Varied perspectives—utilitarianism, categorical imperative, altruism, ethical pluralism, and multiple ethical paradigms (ethics of justice, critique, care, and profession)—for making ethical decisions are discussed. The chapter then reviews how school members develop and uphold relational trust, the benefits trust brings to school improvement and student learning, and principals' role in modeling, generating, sustaining—and when necessary—repairing it. Principals' role in building trusting relationships between educators and parents/guardians ends the chapter.

**Chapter 7, Communicating Effectively,** examines how verbal and non-verbal expression affect principals' leadership effectiveness. The communication process, one- and two-way communications, formal and informal communications, improving principals' communication skills, and communicating with parents and community all receive attention. This chapter also includes strategies that principals can use to strengthen their own sending, listening, and feedback skills with school staff and with diverse                                                                                        parents and community—and the barriers and challenges to overcome—to make coopera- tion around student learning and achievement more likely and miscommunications less likely.

Chapter 8, Building Teacher Capacity, describes how schools rely on leadership throughout the organization to shape instructional practices and generate successful student outcomes. This chapter analyzes why principals will want to develop teachers' professional capacity. It describes how teachers' unvoiced expectations and "psychological contracts" influence their willingness to grow professionally and contribute to school improvement. It explores how principals can help teachers develop, fulfill, and if neces- sary, repair their psychological contracts and examines the ways principals can motivate teachers to develop their instructional and leadership capacities. Professional learning communities' contributions to teachers' instructional growth, ways for principals to help teachers develop their leadership skills, and means for principals to prepare themselves to share school leadership (and to strengthen their own) conclude this chapter.

Chapter 9, Conflict Management, Decision Making, and Problem Solving, talks about the opportunities and pitfalls for schools inherent in each of these distinctly human behaviors. This chapter defines conflict and reviews its functional and dysfunctional outcomes for individuals and organizations. It explains how to find the right balance between too little or too much conflict and offers constructive actions for handling organizational conflict. This chapter also addresses the practical steps in making effect- ive decisions and the real-world constraints on making "perfect" decisions. Rational decision making; satisficing, optimizing, and simplifying; how to decide when to include teachers in decision making; and the groupthink phenomenon, its symptoms, defects, and how principals can prevent it from happening, enter the discussion. The chapter finishes with a look at the research on leadership and group decision making.

Chapter 10, Data-driven Decision Making, explores the student achievement and other data available in schools and their purposes, strengths, and limitations for improving teaching and learning, school accountability, and teacher and principal performance evaluations. It discusses which data—formative, interim, and summative assessments—are best used to improve teaching and learning and debates how much and what types of assessment data are—or are not—appropriate to use for "high stakes" purposes. Mathematical growth models (gain-based models) and value-added models and their contributions and limitations for understanding student learning or teacher and principal effectiveness receive attention. The chapter also presents, step-by-step, the school improvement's data gathering and analysis process to close student achievement gaps. The chapter concludes with an analysis about the types of data that can and cannot, ethically or psychometrically, be used for teachers' and principals' evaluations.

Before you begin . . . The contemporary principalship stands at the point where professional knowledge (the know-how of leadership, curriculum, instruction, assess- ment, organizational development, school finance and law, and other factors) meets human personality (individual values, temperament, philosophy, respect for others, flexibility, patience, energy, goal directedness, sense of human, and so on). At its most basic level, educational leadership is about relationships: people working together, sharing their influence, knowledge, and skills to effectively address a mutual concern. Successful principals create a positive, focused *human* environment—a school climate of mutual respect, high expectations, and warm regard in which others want to invest their hearts, minds, and energies. But although professional knowledge and skills are essential, they are not sufficient.

Throughout this book, you will see the human side of the principalship in action and there are opportunities within each chapter to create personal meaning and try out new ways of seeing and doing leadership in your own work setting. With each chapter, we encourage you to start thinking and acting like a school leader, learning the viewpoints, understanding the human motives and behaviors, trying out the skills, and building your own—and your classmates'—leadership capacities. They will help you become the effective principal you want to be.

# Acknowledgments

It has been our sincere pleasure to work with the Routledge team. Heather Jarrow, our editor, has been a first-rate companion on this publishing journey, always ready with encouragement, flexibility, and useful guidance. We have totally enjoyed our conversations, especially with a glass of wine and a good meal. Sam Huber and Karen Adler, our editorial assistants, have also been valued colleagues. In addition, we appreciate the rest of the Routledge group, including Sioned Jones, our production editor, and Rachel Norridge, our copy editor.

We owe a special thanks to our book reviewers. They engaged with our writing, understood our intent, and gave us a useful perspective to make this book more meaningful to readers. These reviewers include: Patricia Hoehner, Chris Jenkins, Perry Berkowitz, Barbara Rieckhoff, Eleni Elder, Steven David Brazer, Gloria Jean Thomas, and Michael Pregot. And my heartfelt Thank Yous go to Michael Fullan and Joseph Murphy who read the first proofs and graciously gave this book their endorsements.

## NOTE

1. Wilson, J. (2014,November). *The new ISLLC standards: Building a future of excellence in the profession*. Paper presented at the UCEA 2014 National Conference, Washington, DC. Updated draft standards available at: http://www.gapsc.com/Commission/Media/Downloads/2014_Conference/B7_Handout2.pdf

# ISLLC 2015 MATRIX OF LEADERSHIP STANDARDS AND FUNCTIONS BY CHAPTERS

| | Chapters | | | | | | | | | |
|---|---|---|---|---|---|---|---|---|---|---|
| | 1 | 2 | 3 | 4 | 5 | 6 | 7 | 8 | 9 | 10 |
| **Standard 1** Vision & Mission | X | X | X | X | X | | X | X | X | X |
| **Standard 2** Instructional Capacity | X | X | X | X | X | X | X | X | X | X |
| **Standard 3** Instruction | X | X | X | X | X | | X | X | | X |
| **Standard 4** Curriculum & Assessment | X | | X | X | X | X | | X | | X |
| **Standard 5** Community of Care for Students | X | X | X | X | X | X | X | X | X | X |
| **Standard 6** Professional Culture for Teachers and Staff | X | X | X | X | X | X | X | X | X | X |
| **Standard 7** Communities of Engagement for Families | | | X | X | X | X | X | X | X | X |
| **Standard 8** Operations & Management | X | X | X | X | X | X | X | X | X | X |
| **Standard 9** Ethical Principles and Professional Norms | X | X | X | X | X | X | X | X | X | X |
| **Standard 10** Equity and Cultural Responsiveness | X | X | X | | X | X | X | X | | X |
| **Standard 11** Continuous School Improvement | X | X | X | X | X | | X | X | X | X |

# CHAPTER 1

# Principal Leadership for a Student-Centered Learning Environment

Out of the public schools grows the greatness
of a generation.

—Mark Twain

## LEARNING OBJECTIVES

1.1 Describe the differences between the principals' responsibilities of providing "access for all" and ensuring "learning for all."

1.2 Summarize the social, political, and economic reasons why it is essential that all American children successfully learn to high levels.

1.3 Define what a student-centered learning environment means and identify its components.

1.4 Trace how principals' role, responsibilities, and focus have evolved with changes in society from colonial times until today.

1.5 Describe the process and focus of transformational instructional leadership and its relationship to teaching and learning.

1.6 Discuss the research underlying the view that teachers' expectations influence how they teach children and student achievement.

1.7 Define what a safe and orderly environment is and explain how it promotes academic success.

1.8 Analyze how academic press and academic/social supports promote academic success.

1.9 Summarize the studies that support the view that peer norms can strongly influence students' academic achievement.

1.10 Discuss why high-quality teacher–student relationships predict high academic achievement.

**2015 ISLLC STANDARDS: 1, 2, 3, 4, 5, 6, 8, 9, 10, 11**

## INTRODUCTION

Principals make the difference between schools that serve all their children well and schools that don't. Successful principals create the conditions for effective leading, teaching, and learning to happen. Yet education research shows that most school factors, taken separately, have only small effects on student learning. The real payoff comes when individual variables combine to reach a significant mass, forming a series of constructive interactions rippling throughout the school and community.

Without a doubt, the principalship is an important, intensive, and complex job. Schools need capable leaders who can rally faculty, staff, students, parents, and community members to invest their time and effort in educating all children. For many students, attending an effective school—adding to what their families provide—can make the difference between having adult opportunities for productive work and a satisfying quality of life or a life marked by frustration and need.

From *day one*, new principals need to demonstrate an array of competencies: a vision for every child's academic success; complex knowledge and skills related to organizational development, leading, teaching, and learning; the aptitude to build countless working relationships; and the capacities to successfully meet public accountability requirements. Given these realities, new principals can become overwhelmed, disappointed, and frustrated at the yawning gaps among the goals they set for themselves, the seemingly unlimited expectations that their constituents place on them, and the realities—both urgent and mundane—of running and leading a school.

There is no simple formula for preparing effective school leaders. Fully and accurately understanding what principals should understand, know, and be able to do—what successful school leadership looks and feels like in practice—is essential. Likewise, learning appropriate mental models, perspectives, and leadership behaviors, finding occasions to try out these professional skills in graduate courses and in field-based experiences, and then reflecting on and refining one's own leadership performance with competent colleagues and mentors can guide aspiring principals' growth. Additionally, fully participating in professional development and formative evaluations once on the job will generate essential feedback about how well the principal is conducting his/her responsibilities and how to continually mature in the role.

Although principal preparation programs may be able to inform aspiring principals about *what* they need to do as school leaders, the challenge remains for helping principal candidates to develop the mental models, perspectives, knowledge, experiences, and skill sets to master *what* to do and *how* to do it well if they are to "hit the ground running."

This book provides such a guide. And, it begins—and ends—with the students.

## EDUCATING EVERY CHILD TO HIGH LEVELS

Public schools were established as the great equalizers, placing all the community's children on the path to responsible citizenship, economic survival, and social mobility.

Historically, our schools have not served all children and their families well, however. This situation is changing.

Presently, the United States is experiencing one of the most profound demographic transformations our country has ever gone through, with serious implications for our nation's unity, democracy, and prosperity. Our ability as a nation to make this transition successfully depends, to a great extent, on how well we can educate every child to high levels. This, in turn, depends on the health and vitality of our public schools, their leaders, and their teachers.

We are becoming a minority-majority nation. The U.S. Census Bureau predicts that by 2050, minorities will account for 53 percent of the United States population. By 2043, Latinos, African Americans, Asian Americans, Native Americans, and Hawaiian and Pacific Islanders are predicted to collectively make up most of our nation's populace.[1] Non-Latino whites will represent the remaining 47 percent, down from their existing 63 percent share. By comparison, in 2000, whites were 69 percent of the population; in 1989, they comprised 80 percent.[2] Most noteworthy for educators, America's racial and ethnic minorities now compose about half of the under-five age group, a first for our nation—and estimates predict that in five years, minorities will make up more than half the children under age 18.[3]

In short, American classrooms will be increasingly filled by children from minority cultural backgrounds—the very student cohorts with whom our schools have been least successful. African American students are nearly three times as likely as white students to be retained in a grade, while Latino students are twice as likely to be held back—a valid and reliable predictor for dropping out of school.[4] Research also finds that only slightly more than half of students from historically disadvantaged minority groups are earning high school diplomas.[5]

Failing to successfully educate large numbers of minority children could have major consequences for the American workforce. The National Center for Public Policy and Higher Education predicts that by 2020, the white working-age population will have declined from 63 percent of the total U.S. population (down from 82 percent in 1980). Because large numbers of white Baby Boomers will be retiring, the workforce will swing from a majority of white workers to include more people of color.[6] And fewer workers will be supporting an increasing number of retirees. Consider this: the Social Security Administration data show that in 1950, 16.5 workers paid taxes to support each Social Security recipient. In 2011, the ratio was 2.9 workers for each recipient. In 2013, about 157 million U.S. workers supported approximately 55 million Social Security recipients while in 1950, 48 million workers supported 2 million recipients.[7]

These facts hold tremendous implications for America's schools. Unless this upcoming workforce has the high-quality education and skills to provide the necessary national, state, and local leadership and to earn robust and consistent wages, our entire society will feel the impact. This upcoming workforce will shape our society through its political, social, economic, and artistic influences. It will fuel our economy through their retail purchases and taxes as their salaries subsidize the Social Security and Medicare Trust Funds which support retirees, disabled citizens, and ailing elders. It will impact our ability to fund our national defense and our future education expenditures. The bottom line: if tomorrow's workers have lower capacities for providing the public vision and governance and earn lower personal incomes than do present and retiring workers, our body politic and social networks might not be able to meet our obligations.

Given this reality, the typical sorting-and-selecting of students into high- and low-challenge courses based on their presumed abilities and life goals becomes an even more questionable practice. Too frequently, these placements correlate closely with the learners' race, ethnicity, and socioeconomic status (SES). Race, ethnicity, and SES both predict and contribute to student outcomes. Lower-income and minority students typically fill lower-level classes while more affluent, white and Asian students tend to enroll in more advanced ones. Students in higher-level classes usually have more effective teachers, a more demanding and enriched curricula, and higher achievement levels than peers in lower-level classes.

Policy makers and educators forget that the human brain is surprisingly malleable. When motivated, individuals can nearly always outperform expectations set for them. Research affirms that virtually all students would benefit from the kinds of meaningful reasoning, problem-solving, and transfer-of-learning curriculum and instruction usually reserved for high-achieving learners.[8] Since low-level classes largely cater to students from groups that are soon to become the majority of our citizens, the social, political, and economic costs of *not* educating all students to high levels are far greater than we can afford.

Unless school leaders step up and make the changes needed in schools that can close education gaps between the affluent (largely white and Asian) and low-income students (largely children of color), the most highly educated generation in our history might be followed by a generation with far fewer diplomas, college degrees, knowledge and skill levels, and lower lifetime earnings. As a result, many people's wellbeing and lifestyles will falter. In countless ways, our nation will be the poorer. Clearly, it is in every principal's and teacher's best interest—as citizens, neighbors, and future retirees—to make certain that every child, including those traditionally underserved, receives the high quality education needed for 21st-Century competence. Establishing a student-centered learning culture and environment in every school is a productive way to successfully meet this concern.

## REFLECTIONS AND RELEVANCE 1.1

## Changing Student Demographics

**Unless we successfully educate large numbers of minority children, our national wellbeing could be in jeopardy.**

Working individually, draw a pie chart and indicate the percentages of your current school's student demographics by race and ethnicity (e.g. white, African American, Latino, Asian/Pacific Islander, other). Then identify how well each demographic group is currently performing in your school by noting Honor Roll, C-average, Below C-average, or Failing next to that segment. What does this tell you about how well each group is achieving at your school?

Working in pairs, take three minutes each to discuss your circle's student demographics, and describe how well you believe your school is currently enabling students from all socioeconomic and racial/ethnic backgrounds to achieve to high levels. What are your expectations for their success in school and afterwards?

After both have shared their information, discuss as a class how traditionally underserved students are faring—academically and behaviorally—in your school. What data do you have to support these views?

- Disaggregated student achievement test scores?
- Disaggregated enrollment and grades in high-challenge courses?
- Disaggregated daily attendance rates?
- Disaggregated school suspension rates?
- Disaggregated drop-out and graduation rates?
- All students have access to most effective and respected teachers?
- Anecdotal, "gut feeling" data?
- Other data?

If you do not have objective data to support these views, where can you find them?

Do your expectations (and those of your colleagues) need to change in order to enable each student to achieve to high levels? If "yes," in what ways?

## CREATING A STUDENT-CENTERED LEARNING ENVIRONMENT

To best prepare for the principalship, let's start with the end in mind: ultimately, principals are responsible for leading a school in which every child successfully meets high academic standards. Principals can *only* do this by working with teachers to create a student-centered learning environment. By starting here, it becomes easier to see how the other pieces of school leadership fit and contribute to this end.

A *student-centered learning environment* is the sum total interactions of the school culture, climate, people, and behaviors that protect every child's physical and emotional safety and personalize education in ways that allow each one to master a high-challenge, standards-based curriculum. Accomplishing this takes a variety of means. Beginning with instructional leadership, it includes high teacher expectations for students, a safe and purposeful learning environment, academic press and academic/social scaffolding, and respectful, caring relationships that help students become proficient in the high-standards curricula.

The student-centered learning culture gives young people the academic and interpersonal resources to grow and develop, intellectually, socially, and behaviorally. In countless daily exchanges among educators and students, the school environment affirms the following beliefs:[9]

- Students are children, people first, with an array of personal characteristics and life experiences that respond well to encouragement and learning.

- Young people do well if they can.
- Students are smart and can be motivated to learn.
- Teachers have (or can learn) the attitudes, skills, and accountability for helping each child learn to high levels.
- The school will provide the resources to help teachers and students reach this goal.
- Behind every defiant student behavior is an immature and needed skill.
- Problems should be solved proactively (rather than in the urgency of the moment or promptly afterward) and collaboratively with the student.

Since the 1980s, education reform has advanced the idea of uniform curriculum standards, common assessments, and rigorous accountability rules for schools, principals, teachers, and students. At present, 46 states have adopted the common core standards in English, Language Arts, and Mathematics. The reading expectations will also affect science, history, and social studies teachers. Teachers and others in each state will write the actual curriculum to meet these standards. Yet although the curriculum identifies *what* to teach, classroom teachers have choices about *how* they teach. They can tailor instruction to meet their students' interests, ambitions, and learning needs within the curriculum. If they are to help each student learn to high levels, educators must include varied approaches that respond to both the class as a whole and to individual differences within it. And while it is unrealistic to think that a single instructor can teach 20 to 35 different lessons to as many students in one class, a certain amount and type of individuation is necessary and beneficial. Instead of ignoring these individual differences, effective teachers develop the perspectives and resources that enable them to actively meet each student's learning needs within a standards-based academic program.

## WHAT A STUDENT-CENTERED LEARNING ENVIRONMENT LOOKS LIKE

In a school with a well-established, student-centered learning environment, everyone expects to learn and expects everyone else to learn—and they act on these beliefs. Forecasts for every student's academic learning are high, and the supports are available to make it happen. Teachers are ready to make the time to regroup and fill in the learning gaps for students who are not making satisfactory progress. Educators understand that constructing a solid cognitive foundation is more important than racing through the curriculum ("covering the content") and ignoring students' actual learning needs. Depending on how each student learns best, many opportunities exist to learn in multiple ways and at varied rates. At the same time, students accept more responsibility for what and how they learn and how they show what they know and can do. Classrooms and school hallways highlight samples of high-quality student work.

In student-centered learning environments, teachers focus on "they learned it" rather than on "I taught it." The cultural emphasis moves from teaching to learning. Teachers consciously integrate what the school offers and what each student needs.

Teachers come to understand their students—the way they learn best, at what pace, their interests and concerns, their personal and family assets—and use these insights to make the curriculum relevant and personally meaningful for each learner. Principals work with teachers to help them improve their instructional skills and work with those who don't improve to help them find more suitable employment.

Likewise, in student-centered learning environments, people respect each other and know that they matter. It feels good to be there. Each student has constructive relations with other students and with many teachers and other adults in the community. Successful learning and accomplishment are celebrated. People work together in small and large groups on projects that capture their interest. Across the campus, conversations whirr with thought-provoking and relevant discussions. People listen respectfully and carefully to one another, feel free to disagree politely, take risks, be wrong, learn from errors, and try something new. Ethical behaviors and interpersonal trust are widespread and visible in all exchanges. Newcomers are welcomed, and diversity is a resource to make the community stronger and deeper. Students feel known and valued, surrounded by others who care for them and "have their backs." Feeling good and being productive are the school's normal vibes. What is more, "This is the way we do things around here."

As you can see, a student-centered learning environment consists of many variables —instructional leadership that creates the focus and environment that facilitates students' learning, high expectations for all teachers' instruction, high expectations for all children's academic growth and achievement, a safe and orderly learning environment, academic press and academic/social supports, and caring, respectful relationships. The sum total of all these factors is a school where all children learn to high levels and all teachers continue developing their instructional and leadership effectiveness. We will consider each one in turn. Creating and sustaining this student-friendly milieu is the principal's central focus and daily reality. All other school leadership functions and responsibilities serve this end.

# INSTRUCTIONAL LEADERSHIP

To generate successful outcomes for each child, every school needs a great principal. Principals and other school leaders have the responsibility for creating a student-centered learning environment and the culture that sustains it. But principals have not always had a measurable impact on teaching and learning. In fact, school leaders' roles have evolved along with the changes in American society and the public schools.

## School Leadership: The Early Days

Throughout our country's history, schools have served as a powerful agency to socialize varied communities into the American mainstream. From our earliest days as a nation, public schools' mission was to create an American populace with the cognitive, economic, and civic skills needed to develop their shared allegiance to the United States, enable their financial survival, and meet their civic responsibilities. These were essential

## REFLECTIONS AND RELEVANCE 1.2

# Beliefs and Actions about Your Students

Teachers' beliefs about their students influence their actions to help them learn.

Working individually, complete the following table, noting your beliefs (e.g. agree, disagree, depends on the child, other) and actions (e.g. make instructional content relevant and meaningful to most students, give extra time for students needing more help, tutor students daily or weekly after class, give students choices of what and how they learn, other) and your work colleagues' beliefs and actions concerning your school's students' capacity to learn challenging content. Then compile the views for the entire class and discuss your findings.

| My School's Environment | My Beliefs/ Actions | Colleagues' Beliefs/ Actions |
|---|---|---|
| Everyone expects to learn and everyone expects everyone else to learn—and they act on these beliefs. | | |
| Almost everyone—teachers, students, and staff— agrees that it feels good to be here. | | |
| "They learned it" is more important than "I taught it." | | |
| Students are children, people first, with an array of personal characteristics and life experiences that respond well to encouragement and learning. | | |
| Young people do well if they can. | | |
| Students are smart, and I can motivate them to learn. | | |
| Teachers have (or can learn) the attitudes, skills, and accountability for helping each child learn to high levels. | | |
| The school will provide the resources to help teachers and students reach this goal. | | |
| Behind every defiant student behavior is an immature and needed skill. | | |
| Problems should be solved proactively (rather than in the urgency of the moment or promptly afterward) and collaboratively with the student. | | |

- To what extent do you think your colleagues' beliefs about "all students learning" match with their actual behaviors towards all students? What evidence or examples support your views?
- In terms of teachers' attitudes and actions, how ready is your present school for developing a student-centered learning environment?
- If it is not ready, what do you think needs to be done to get teachers ready?

elements in ensuring our nation's unity and viability. To a large extent, despite the rush of change, this mission remains valid today.

As shifts in society often prompt adjustments in institutions that serve it, American schools have undergone substantial changes since their inception. And as schools changed, school leadership changed, too.

In the colonial American public schools, most teachers in New England town schools were "schoolmasters," educated men who earned a living as a teacher while preparing for careers in the ministry or other profession. Some became teachers to repay debts owed from their ocean passage from Europe to North America. In the late 17th Century, a few towns did hire "school dames" (women) as teachers but only as adjuncts to the town schoolmaster.

But by 1870, women outnumbered men in the nation's classrooms, and men largely served as school administrators. For many generations, women teachers tended to stay in the classroom only for a few years; many married and left teaching to raise their families. As a result, female teacher turnover became an expected aspect of the school culture. In contrast, school administrators, usually men, were viewed as professionals who stayed with the school and provided continuity. Principals also supervised and trained women, who actually did the teaching.

Schools' traditional "egg crate" structure—in which teachers worked alone with their students behind closed doors—made it easy for principals to hire teacher replacements with little disruption to the rest of the organization and efficiently get the newcomers up to speed. At the time, schools typically held an unsophisticated view of teaching. If teachers knew their subjects better than their students; if they could keep their classrooms orderly, quiet, and on-task; if they could move their students quietly and quickly through the halls; and if students could perform sufficiently well on exams so administrators (and parents) could infer what the students learned, teachers could keep their jobs.

In 1900, only about 6 percent of students (as compared with about 80 percent today) received a high school diploma.[10] Almost all these earlier graduates went on to enroll in college. The rest left school before earning diplomas, going to labor on family farms, in factories, in apprenticeships, or as domestic workers or homemakers—jobs that did not require high-level knowledge or skills to be gainfully employed and earn a living.

At that time, the early-20th-Century ethos of scientific management—organizing business, industry, and schools for maximum efficiency and standardized quality outcomes—made principals into educational efficiency experts. They helped schools develop academic tracking practices to place students into separate programs of study (typically, college preparatory, general, or vocational) based on students' demonstrated or presumed intelligence, social backgrounds, and employment goals. For the most part, the low-information, low-skill economy of the time had opportunities for students who left school without substantial stores of knowledge or critical thinking skills as long as they came to work every day, showed effort, and carefully followed their supervisors' directions.

Given this milieu, between 1900 and 1930, school administrators began to see themselves as managers rather than as educators. They used scientific management ideas to help their schools accommodate large numbers of immigrant children at low cost. Children enrolled in school and moved through the grades with their age-mates, changing classes at scheduled intervals to ringing bells. Today, we know that children develop at different rates, and children who were born—or whose parents were born—in other countries often speak English as a second language. Thus, automatically advancing students in tandem with those of the same chronological age benefitted those with the necessary language skills, background knowledge, and work habits to learn faster. Since this system appeared to reward student merit, educators liked it. Students who learned well and quickly received recognition; students who did not learn as well or as quickly did not. Likewise, students saw themselves either as intelligent, superior, and worthy of a promising economic and social future or as unintelligent and unworthy. And so a self-fulfilling prophesy was set in motion.

But in the decades after World War II, teaching changed from an occupation requiring relatively little specialized training into a profession that needed increasing levels of preparation and competence. At the same time, the world became more complex. As the new century approached, an increasingly globalized, high-tech environment required more workers throughout the economy to be able to use high-level knowledge and critical thinking to identify and solve problems. And, American school children continued to reflect increasingly diverse backgrounds and varying levels of readiness for academic learning. The principal's role also needed to adjust.

### School Leadership: Today

As the world has become more complicated, so has the practice of leadership. Simply defined, *contemporary leadership* is a process. It involves an influence relationship purposefully directed toward achieving shared organizational goals. And it involves meaningful change.[11] These five elements—process, relational, purposeful, shared, and change—create a dynamic greater than the sum of their parts. In short, a leader influences others to effect a mutually desired adjustment. Whether in a family, business, nation, or school, the leader must organize, educate, team build, and facilitate transformation from one reality to another. Accordingly, the principal's role has evolved from a largely administrative, managerial responsibility—primarily attending to "buses, budgets, and buildings"—to a leadership position that focuses on enhancing leading, facilitating, teaching, and learning—with a different and expanded set of expectations. Because leadership today is so demanding, it requires a greater range of emotional, social, and intellectual skills than ever before—a reality that requires leaders to continue their learning.

As transformational leadership is the *process* of leadership, instructional leadership is its *focus*. *Instructional leadership* is a particular type of school leadership that makes improvement of teaching and learning the school's mission. In this role, principals help teachers become more effective at generating student learning, are involved in school problem finding and problem solving, and are able to share decision making and enact organizational change. Finding ways to improve every student's learning—and every teacher's capacity to facilitate student learning—have become the principal's central focus.

Instructional leadership carries two benchmarks. The first includes the leader's ability to stay focused consistently on the school's core purposes: teaching, learning, curriculum, and assessment. The second is to make all the other schooling dimensions—administration, organization, finance, and so on—work to enhance the core purposes. The results: improved teaching and increased student learning.

In fact, the Educational Leadership Policy Standards (1996, 2008, 2015) redefined school leadership. Developed by the Interstate School Leaders Licensure Consortium (ISLLC), these standards present a comprehensive vision of what today's educational leaders should look like and be able to accomplish. Their authors' intent was no less than to rebuild and re-culture schools' leadership infrastructure—moving the principal-ship beyond the management model as well as away from the practice of providing a high-quality education to only the top-achieving students.

Accordingly, today's principal is a transformational instructional leader whose efforts aim to promote the success and wellbeing of every student (see more about transformational leadership in Chapter 2). Unlike the school administrator's role, effective instructional leadership is a collaborative responsibility. It does not invest all leadership in one individual. Rather, instructional leadership develops teachers' capacity to provide leadership throughout the school as they continually refine and enhance their abilities to increase student learning and achievement. In this view, leadership is not about what an individual leader does but what leaders and collaborators do together, sharing a vision of a better future for their school and their students, and then making it happen.

Transformational leadership requires good "people skills" and the ability to develop mutually respectful, cooperative, trusting, and ethical relationships. It sharply reorients the perspective about who is a leader and what leaders do. Instead of top-down management, school leadership today becomes:[12]

- a relationship rather than an individual;
- a process entirely separate from management (although the same persons may be responsible for doing both jobs);
- a situation in which people other than official position holders can be leaders (leadership and leaders are not necessarily the same, and roles may vary with the purpose);

- a focus on the leaders' and collaborators' interactions rather than simply a focus on the leader's traits and behaviors;
- a relationship of shared purposes rather than the leader's wishes;
- a relationship that relies on influence and persuasion rather than authority or coercion to accomplish identified ends; collaborators and leaders can influence and persuade each other;
- a pursuit of purposes and goals that intend actual, substantive, and transforming change to the organization, its people, and its outcomes.

Still, the buses must run on time and supplies must be on hand for the first and each succeeding day of school. Thus, depending on their particular task, principals alternately may be the leaders of school improvement or the managers of building operations. And since principals' role includes developing leadership capacity among the faculty and other administrators, school leadership becomes widespread and flexible, even as the principal retains the final responsibility for ensuring the school's success.

## HIGH TEACHER EXPECTATIONS

Teachers tend to form impressions about which students are likely or unlikely to perform well in school. These expectations have a significant influence on how they teach the children in their classrooms. Research supports this theory.[13]

Four classic studies illustrate this point. The landmark Hawthorne study at Western Electric's plant in Cicero, Illinois (1927–1932) examined how a workplace's physical and psychological environment affected workers' output. No matter how the investigators manipulated the working conditions—using bright or dim lighting, instituting long or short work breaks, for example—workers' productivity improved. Like the workplace, the classroom is a powerful social network, and students' beliefs and feelings about their teachers and classmates—rather than their aptitudes alone— have important implications for how much time, thought, and effort they are willing to put into learning well.

Similarly, in *Pygmalion in the Classroom*,[14] a Harvard professor and an elementary school principal told elementary teachers that their students' standardized test scores indicated that certain children were academic "late bloomers" who would likely become "growth spurters" during the school year.[15] In reality, the tests never existed, and the children identified as "spurters" were chosen randomly. Nevertheless, findings showed that changes in teacher expectations can produce changes in student achievement. When the teachers expected their students to perform well, they usually did; when teachers expected students to fail, they usually did.

Finally, studies by Jeanne Oakes,[16] a University of California at Los Angeles education professor, and James Coleman,[17] a Johns Hopkins sociology professor and his colleagues, conducted studies that confirmed the teacher expectation-student achievement connection. Teachers' expectations about their students' capacity for learning strongly affected how teachers treated these students in self-fulfilling ways. In Oakes' study, students treated as high achievers acted in high-achieving ways. Students regarded as low achievers performed as low achievers. In Coleman's study, teacher survey data suggested that achievement gaps in the same school between African American and white students were higher when most of the teachers had expressed preference for teaching college-oriented children of white-collar professionals. These teachers expected less achievement from their minority and low-income students—and they got it.

Additional research has found several relationships between teachers' expectations and student achievement:

- Teachers develop expectations for student academic performance.[18]
- Teachers' behaviors reflecting these expectations are related to measures of student achievement.[19]
- Teachers' perceptions of current students' performance are mostly accurate.[20]
- Once formed, teachers' expectations change little.[21] In school, first impressions count, a lot.
- Student characteristics, such as physical attractiveness, socioeconomic status, race, use of Standard English, and history of grade retention are related to teachers' expectations for academic achievement.[22]
- Teachers who expect students to be low achievers attribute their improved achievement to luck, whereas teachers attribute the perceived high achievers' success to their ability.[23]
- Teachers overestimate high achievers' achievement, underestimate low-achievers' achievement, and predict low-achievers' responses the least accurately.[24]
- The better teachers know their students, the more accurate their expectations for students' academic success, especially in grades 1 and 2.[25]
- The more inviting and responsive instruction is to children's efforts to improve, the less accurately teachers' initial perceptions and expectations predict later student success.[26]
- The higher teachers' beliefs in their own and their colleagues' abilities to help all children make the academic advances that their school expects, the higher the correlation with student achievement levels and gains.[27]

From these data, one can reasonably conclude that the more effectively teachers teach, the higher all their students will achieve, and the less accurate teachers' initial predictions become about who will or will not learn to high levels. As teachers learn and use more effective instructional practices that help more students learn, teachers become increasingly optimistic about their students' success. Then, they treat all students as high achievers—providing them with similar praise and feedback and making similar demands for effort and quality outcomes. In turn, their students become more successful. In a virtuous cycle, each player's positive expectations influence the others.

To maintain high expectations for students, teachers and principals must first hold high expectations for themselves. In successful schools, teachers believe in both their students' ability to master the challenging curriculum and in their own individual and collective efficacy to make this a reality. At the same time, schools as cultural organizations transform from institutions designed for *instruction* into institutions desired to ensure *learning*.

Expectations can create reality. In a circular fashion, teachers' and students' expectations for their academic progress both reflect—and determine—their achievement outcomes. These expectations influence the strategies teachers and students use to meet their learning goals; the skills, energy, and other resources they use to apply learning strategies; and the rewards they expect from investing (or not investing) this effort. And, as research suggests, teachers' behaviors reflecting these expectations are related to measures of students' academic achievement. Clearly, developing teachers' instructional capacities (discussed in Chapter 8) pays off well.

When teachers hold high expectations for every student's academic success, it is possible to see them in the following school indicators:[28]

- The school develops a shared vision of a school with all students—regardless of family background—achieving highly in a rigorous curriculum.
- The school has standards and practices that avoid both grade retention and social promotion by keeping all students learning apace throughout the year.
- Teachers have confidence in their own—and their colleagues'—abilities to help all their students master the basic and higher-level knowledge and skills.
- Teachers continuously upgrade their pedagogical skills to make their instruction increasingly accessible for all students.
- Teachers help students use what they already know to comprehend new knowledge, expand their understanding, and develop new skills.
- Students and teachers work together during class and after/before school (as needed) to master the expected content and skills.
- The school has on-going, collegial professional development tied to classroom curriculum to help every teacher improve his or her instructional effectiveness.
- Teachers and students believe that effort is more important than ability in producing their final achievement—and they invest effort in learning.
- The school has very low suspension and dropout rates and very high promotion or graduation rates.
- Parents and students say that their schoolwork is challenging but doable.

## A SAFE AND ORDERLY LEARNING ENVIRONMENT

A student-centered learning environment has a safe, orderly, purposeful, cooperative and nurturing milieu free from threat of physical or emotional harm. More than the absence of undesirable behaviors, such as students fighting or bullying, safe and organized surroundings reflect the pervasive presence of desirable actions and attitudes that show respect for every individual, foster healthy relationships, and build appreciation of human diversity and democratic values.

**REFLECTIONS AND RELEVANCE 1.3**

## Teacher Expectations for Student Achievement

Teachers' expectations for students' achievement has a strong impact on student achievement.

Individually, write six words or phrases on the graphic organizer or "cluster web" below about teacher expectations and student achievement that have the most relevance and personal meaning for you. When you have completed this, work with a partner to share your products and explain why you find these phrases so meaningful.

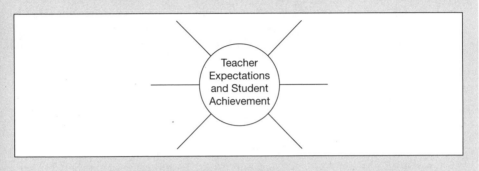

Then discuss the following questions as a class:

1. What examples from your own experiences as a student or as an educator can you share that support this evidence about teacher expectations and student achievement?
2. What criteria do you currently use to form your own expectations for any of your student's learning potential?
3. Why must teachers first hold high expectations for themselves if they are to hold high expectations for all students' academic advancement?

Many studies have identified a safe and orderly environment as essential to academic achievement:

- The more safe and orderly the school's learning climate, the higher the students' math and reading achievement levels.[29]
- A secure and organized learning setting is significantly related to less student fear, lower dropout rates, and higher student commitment to their learning.[30]
- Generally, the higher the school's academic quality and the more positive its emotional climate, the lower the level of school crime and violence.[31]

Teachers and students need to feel physically and emotionally secure and at ease if they are to produce the psychological energy needed for teaching and learning.

Worry about safety shifts the brain's attention. When students and teachers feel anxious about their personal wellbeing—whether out of concern for physical harm, humiliation in front of their friends, or simply feeling discounted—their focus swiftly turns to self-protection. At these times, the emotional parts of their brain become more fully aroused, and their cognitive areas grow less active. In such stressful environments, they cannot find extra energy to pay attention to teaching and learning. Achievement suffers. Without a minimum level of security and calm, a school has little chance of positively affecting student achievement.

In contrast, in a school with a well-structured and business-like environment, teachers and students feel no personal danger. Teachers and students sustain a safe, comfortable, and cared-for climate. Adults' and children's cognitive capacities can become more fully activated and engaged. Teachers can carry through on their commitment to build a strong, encouraging academic focus with high yet achievable goals for students. At the same time, students invest their energies in academic matters, are highly motivated to learn, and respect peers who achieve well. Teachers and students can work collaboratively to make academic success happen.

Several indicators can signal when a safe and orderly school environment is present:[32]

- The school looks clean and inviting. Custodians sweep and tidy up the halls and common areas after students use them during the day, promptly noticing and removing graffiti or disorder.
- Students, faculty, staff, and parents at the school say that they feel safe, cared for, and trusted.
- Students sit in mixed race, mixed gender groups in the cafeteria and classrooms.
- People in the building smile at each other freely and often.
- Teachers' visible and friendly presence in student areas—including student restrooms, hallways, unlikely corners, and occasionally riding the school bus—whenever students are using them are tangible reminders for students to act in mature and accountable ways.
- Rules and expectations are clearly, visibly, and frequently communicated to students and parents, and emphasize mutual respect and responsibility.
- Principals and assistant principals are mindful of the details and tensions at play in the school, have practices to identify potentially disruptive students, and use this information to prevent and solve problems.
- All adults in the school—including administrative personnel, custodians, and cafeteria workers—develop relationships with students to help them learn self-discipline and responsibility.
- Students who break rules receive fair and consistently administered consequences, including problem solving to help them make better decisions next time.
- Challenging students have adult mentors in the school with whom they meet regularly to discuss frustrations and resolve problems.
- Students willingly remain after school to work closely with teachers to make up missed or unsatisfactory work and to strengthen their understanding of the academic content.
- Teachers and students are actively involved in developing school rules.

**REFLECTIONS AND RELEVANCE 1.4**

## Safe and Orderly Learning Environment

Teachers and students need to feel safe—psychologically and physically—if effective teaching and learning are to occur.

Work in pairs for five minutes to discuss the following questions. Then discuss your findings as a class.

1.  On a scale of 1 ("Rarely felt safe") to 5 ("Always felt safe"), how would you rate your own experiences as a K-5, 6–8, 9–12, and college student as it relates to a safe and orderly environment?

    a.  In which school levels did you feel the safest (emotionally and physically)? In which levels did you feel the least safe?
    b.  What were the characteristics of the people, program, and facility that influenced you to assign this either positive or negative rating?
    c.  What was the effect on you and your learning from spending time in this environment?

2.  On a scale of 1 ("Rarely feel safe") to 5 ("Always feel safe"), how would you rate your present school setting as it relates to a safe and orderly environment?

    a.  What are the characteristics of the people, program, and facility that influence you to give it this rating?
    b.  What is the effect in you as an educator spending time in this environment?
    c.  Would your students rate this school the same way? Why or why not?
    d.  How do you perceive this environment is affecting your colleagues? Your students? Your parents or other community members? What examples can you offer to support this?

## ACADEMIC PRESS AND ACADEMIC/SOCIAL SUPPORTS

*Academic press* refers to the extent to which students, teachers, and administrators feel a strong emphasis on educational success and meeting specific achievement standards. *Academic supports* refer to the actions that teachers and students take to ensure that students succeed scholastically. *Social supports* are those personal relationships that students have with others, including teachers, parents, relatives, and peers, which may help them perform well in school. Research finds that both high levels of academic press and support are positively related to gains in students' achievement.[33] This is true regardless of student or school demographics. If either academic press or supports is weak, students learn less.

## Academic Press

Academic press stresses content rigor as well as student and teacher accountability for student learning and achievement. It affirms that students learn and achieve more when they clearly know what they are supposed to learn, when expectations for academic learning are high, and when both parties are held accountable for their performance. Academic press provides direction for student work and incentives for students and teachers to achieve at high levels.

Varied sources generate academic press. The school culture creates press when it sets expectations that every student can master a high-standards curriculum. Principals create academic press when they expect teachers to teach the standards-aligned curriculum and help each student reach the required mastery levels. Teachers create academic press by expecting each student to learn the class's objectives, by providing intellectually challenging and engaging work, by familiarizing students with the specific standards and criteria for work quality and quantity, and by the types and frequency of assignments and assessments students must complete as evidence of their mastery and accountability.

Improving learning requires students to engage deeply in rigorous academic work: more demanding content and complex skills, understanding and applying concepts, problem solving, and developing students' facility with critical thinking. At the same time, academic press typically includes more homework, extended instructional time, more projects in which students can apply and extend their new learning in products and performance, more complex assessments, and stricter requirements for grade promotion and graduation.

Teaching for intellectual rigor and depth of understanding is not just for high-achieving affluent suburban students. Too often, teachers assume that low-income or slower-learning students may be so lacking in basic competencies that they should teach for memorization and transmission of basic facts and skills rather than teach for concepts, generalizations, and connections. But this assumption is incorrect. Increasing the curriculum's personal meaning for students and dealing with ideas that matter and make sense to them—increasing its relevance—allow even low achievers to develop a deep understanding of the content and how to use it.

Research affirms that when teachers become familiar with children's interests and life experiences, they can use interactive instruction to build on students' prior knowledge to engage them in higher-level thinking and comprehension.[34] Students can learn to express their ideas orally, graphically, and in writing as they engage in authentic intellectual work—the original application of knowledge and skills (instead of routine use of facts and procedures as often occurs in slow-paced, low-level courses). They can create a product or performance that has meaning beyond school. This is the type of multifaceted intellectual work needed for success in life. At the same time, students taught this way not only produce more intellectually complex work but they also increase their scores on standardized tests—because information that makes sense and has personal meaning for the student can be understood, learned, remembered, and transferred to new situation's beyond the class period.[35]

Teaching all students to interact with a cognitively demanding curriculum that teachers deliberately make meaningful and relevant to them can meet both learning and accountability demands. And as indicated, research links strong press for academic success with greater student effort, more time spent on academic tasks, and higher student performance. Additionally, academic success can strengthen students' self-concept, a valued psycho-emotional school outcome. When levels of academic press and social and academic supports for students are high, students learn and achieve more. But when either academic press or supports is low, students learn less.

Academic press in school can be seen in the following ways:[36]

- The school establishes, expresses, and enforces high achievement standards for every student.
- Evidence of high-quality student work and accomplishments (such as "A+" work samples and college acceptances) are exhibited and celebrated publicly.
- Students in all courses are expected to learn and apply concepts and ideas central to their discipline in a variety of high-quality products or performances.
- Teachers know their students well and often use examples related to students' interests or life experiences to connect them with the curriculum.
- Teachers expect students to complete their homework every night.
- Teachers encourage students to ask questions and do extra work when they don't understand or master a topic or skill.
- The school provides teachers with on-going, high-quality professional development to improve instruction and push students towards more challenging work and higher-order thinking.
- Students are assessed often and teachers use results to inform instruction, appraise student progress, and hold teachers and students answerable for their actions and outcomes.

## Academic Supports

*Academic supports* are those practices teachers use to personalize learning by providing individualized opportunities for their students to strengthen and advance their knowledge and skills. Supports include instructional and assessment strategies that deliberately account for individual uniqueness, create more personal meaning for the content, and give students more occasions to give input into what and how they learn and how they express it. Academic supports also include giving struggling students more time and interactions with teachers to enlarge and reinforce their learning as well as opportunity to learn.

*Connecting students to the curriculum.* Increasing the curriculum's relevance and personal meaning for students increases their academic support. Teachers must know their students well enough as individuals and as learners in order to relate the content to each student's prior learning, experiences, and interests in ways that make sense and has meaning to the learners. Meaningful information is better remembered and available to use in new situations; it is learned.

*Assessing to promote learning.* Teachers' instructional interactions with students most benefit student learning when they are focused, direct, intentional, and characterized by feedback loops to student performance. Daily use of formative assessments help teachers ensure that students never stray too far from the expected learning outcomes. Students use the feedback promptly to refine and improve their work. Over time, they develop the habit of reflecting seriously on their efforts, assessing their work products or performances against standards of excellence, and mature their attitudes about learning outside the classroom. Finally, teachers can use the feedback to adjust their own instruction, to reteach essential information and skills, or provide extra time and guidance to those students who need it.

*Increasing students' choices.* Giving students a say in their learning—providing them options about classroom routines or assignments—can inspire strong cooperation, engagement, and investment in their own learning. Teachers can allow students to select topics (often from a teacher-approved list) they wish to pursue within the unit. More capable students may be able to design their own projects within approved criteria. Students can have opportunities to express their preferences about sequence (which activity to do first), location (where in the classroom they want to work on their assignment), social preferences (with partner, group, or working alone), or type of presentation to show their knowledge (oral, written, multimedia, or some combination).

*Using resources.* Technological tools and a common core curriculum make it easier to personalize and motivate learning. Online learning—often available anytime and anywhere a computer can be wi-fi'd to the Internet—can give students opportunities to practice and strengthen missed or weakly grasped knowledge or skills so they can catch up with classmates. For the highly motivated and accomplished students, technology resources can let students investigate special interests that can accelerate and deepen their learning. Websites offer a range of educational options including digital or adaptive lessons and exercises in various subjects; programs can help educators, students, and parents collaboratively build personal learning plans. Students who lack confidence writing and can barely budge the pen across the paper may soar in front of a laptop. Blogs and social bookmarks as a part of the learning culture can help students and teachers stay organized, focused, and moving forward. In addition, wanting access to these media may prompt students to develop their academic skills in order to gain access.

*Providing more time and opportunity to learn.* Struggling students often need more instructional time in order to understand the curriculum and master new skills. Often, they lack the background experiences or vocabulary to make sense of what the teacher is teaching. They need occasions to acquire the terms and ideas that underpin what they are learning before they can fully understand and apply it. When students appear to be not grasping the lessons, teachers can diagnose the weaknesses and make opportunities to remedy them. Summer learning opportunities, before and after school tutoring, hosting study rooms after school on Monday through Thursday for students who have not completed their homework and for those needing extra help to get through the course successfully can increase the number of students who successfully complete the course.

But ensuring sufficient learning time means more than offering extra study periods. Student achievement depends not only on students' abilities, but also on opportunity to learn. Did the students actually attend the class? Did the teacher teach the subject with enough content coverage, emphasis, and rigor as aligned with the standards and assessment? Did the teacher use high-quality instructional strategies appropriate to the students—for example, allowing sufficient wait time after a question to allow all students to process the information? Did the teacher provide enough explanation, practice, feedback, and help in a positive learning environment needed for students to learn it? Likewise, a student who is frequently absent or whose teacher does not follow the school district's curriculum or pacing guide—or whose classroom is frequently disrupted by student outbursts—does not have the same opportunities to learn as a classmate with perfect attendance, a teacher who teaches what the school district expects him or her to teach, and a calm, caring, focused, and orderly classroom environment.

*Opportunity to learn*—the equitable conditions or circumstances within the school that promotes learning for all students—is an issue of fairness. Principals need to make certain that *all* students from every group—low-income, middle class, and affluent, slower and faster learners—have equal chances of working with the most effective teachers and are enrolled in the most challenging courses. Lack of opportunity to learn will seriously undermine students' academic growth and achievement.

## Social Supports

*Social supports* for academic learning refer to the personal relationships that students have with people who may help them achieve well in school. Social supports motivate students to persist and achieve, building their confidence that they are capable of learning and attaining academic success. Social supports also help foster the psychological safety that allows students to value learning and achieving at school, take risks, admit errors, ask for help, and experience failure constructively as they progress towards high levels of understanding and proficiency. Support may come from parents encouraging their children to work hard and learn at school; teachers providing individual attention, care, and assistance; and peers pushing each other to study. Neighborhood members and community organizations may also aid, incentivize, and inspire students to continue investing in their learning.

*Support from teachers and other adults at school.* Strong and encouraging relationships with reliable teachers (as well as dependable and caring secretaries, custodians, cafeteria workers, or security officers) can create strong motivators for students to keep attending school and working at learning despite challenging academic expectations and occasionally frustrating school experiences. Adults' caring and mutual respect boosts students' self-assurance and fortifies their resilience and persistence. These relationships may serve as safety valves, giving young people outlets to express their concerns and gain emotional support, reassurance, information, and guidance about how to best handle difficult personal or academic decisions.

In contrast, varied studies find that students who leave high school before graduation often point to a lack of social and academic support—sometimes expressed as "school is boring," or "I wasn't motivated"—as one of the reasons they dropped out.[37] Feeling disconnected from teachers, not getting along with other students, and failing their coursework, these students did not like being at school, so they left.

*Support from friends and classmates.* Most young people of middle- and high-school ages want to feel a sense of belonging to a peer group. If their friends act in ways that help them achieve well in school, they are likely to do the same. On the other hand, if friends don't care about schoolwork and refuse to complete assignments or study for exams, students and their friends are likely to perform poorly at school. Given this reality, educators can use positive peer supports to help students achieve well and act appropriately in school. Several studies support this idea.

For instance, one of the ground-breaking Coleman Report's findings was that, after family characteristics, the students with whom young people attend school were almost as important as family background in predicting academic success. In this study, African American students achieved better when they attended schools that were predominantly middle class. Working in classrooms with other students who expected to achieve well in school and life influences peers to do the same.[38]

Likewise, John Ogbu, the late University of California anthropologist, developed *oppositional culture theory* to explain how peer cultural norms can discourage students from learning or acting well in school. He suggested that African American students responded to institutionalized racism by believing that doing well in school is "acting white."[39] In this view, many minority students believe that they must choose between their minority identity and not learn (keep their peers happy) or learn and achieve well (and keep their teachers and parents happy). As a result, these students cope with the conflicting expectations in a variety of ways—sometimes responding adaptively, other times in self-defeating ways—in efforts to please their friends or teachers.

Similarly, Stanford University's Professor Claude Steele's *stereotype threat* theory argues that people tend to underperform when they get into situations that might confirm negative stereotypes about their racial, ethnic, or gender group. In these situations, highly capable students become so nervous about performing poorly that they often make careless mistakes, they underachieve, or they stop caring about performing well. Instead of showing their real concern about failing, these students may act disinterested in schools or its rules, become class clowns, study in secret, or stay away from situations where high achievement is expected. Not caring about school outcomes may become the group's norm.

One notable study highlights the relationship between academic achievement and peer group norms and popularity among white, African American, and Latino students. At low grade point averages (GPAs), popularity within ethnic groups shows little difference. But when a student achieves at 2.5 GPA (an equal mix of Bs and Cs), measurable differences among ethnic groups begin to appear. As African Americans' GPA rise beyond Bs and Cs, they tend to have fewer and fewer friends. An African American student with a 4.0 GPA has about 1.5 fewer friends of the same minority group than a white student earning the same GPA. Meanwhile, a Latino student with 4.0 is the least popular of all Latino students. In contrast, the higher the white students' grades, the higher their popularity, especially in public schools.[40]

Even though schools cannot change peer norms, student-centered learning environments can overcome them. Adults in public, charter, and parochial schools can create and sustain school cultures for academically disadvantaged young people. In these schools, learning is valued, and students cheer each other on to work hard, achieve highly, and act appropriately. The Effective Schools Movement—whose model and research supports the idea that high-poverty schools can be high-performing schools—has over 40 years of research documenting that school cultures that commit to every student learning to high levels actually do generate high student achievement.[41] At the same time, the Education Trust, a Washington, DC research and advocacy organization, has many current case studies affirming that teachers and principals can create student-centered school learning environments in low-income, high-minority schools in which peer norms support increases learning and achievement.[42]

When classmates and friends value achieving and behaving appropriately in school, they reinforce a student-centered learning environment. High student achievement and a learning-focused climate reinforce "the way we do things around here." Students' own expectations and behaviors create powerful social control mechanisms that informally guide much of what students do every day in school, giving teachers space to concentrate on teaching rather than on scolding or punishing. This results in enhanced instructional effectiveness and more students learning to high levels.

Academic and social supports in school appear in the following ways:[43]

- All students are enrolled in high-challenge, high-status courses with high-quality curriculum and effective teachers.
- Schools establish curricular priorities, ensure appropriate teacher course assignments, and provide students with needed academic and social supports.
- Schools keep the expectations for student achievement high but vary the time and other resources needed to help every student reach the standards.
- Teachers make opportunities to really understand their students as people and as learners.
- Teachers use a variety of instructional strategies to meet students' learning needs.
- Teachers routinely relate their subjects to students' personal interests and life experiences, making them relevant in ways that facilitate student learning.
- Teachers involve all students in analyzing, synthesizing, generalizing, explaining, hypothesizing, and drawing conclusions to increase meaning and understanding.
- Teachers identify students' individual learning problems, lack of background knowledge, or misunderstandings early in the learning process and provide them with additional supports—time, one-on-one help, tutoring, interactive technology-based instructional resources aligned with the curriculum—as needed.
- Most teachers offer individual tutoring and after-or-before-school help to students needing additional resources to keep up with the class.
- Teachers receive the relevant materials, equipment, and ongoing professional development needed for their successful job performance.
- Students encourage each other to perform well in school.
- Teachers engage coaches, school staff, parents, and community members to help students with personal or academic problems.

## CARING AND RESPECTFUL RELATIONSHIPS

In the end, it is all about relationships. Children learn through relationships. If they like their teachers, they are willing to work hard to learn *for* them as well as *from* them. In contrast, when educators cannot establish caring and respectful relationships with

## REFLECTIONS AND RELEVANCE 1.5

# Academic Press, Academic and Social Supports

Having clear, high, and accountable expectations for learning, linked with strong and varied supports to advance it, creates an environment that can generate academic success.

Ask the class to separate into three groups. Each group will consider the academic press and academic and social supports available for one of the following student groups: low achievers, average achievers, high achievers. Each group will complete the graphic organizer "cluster web" for their chosen group: decide whether they are addressing an elementary, middle, or high school, and identify in writing (attached to the web spokes) the types of academic press, academic supports, and social supports available in their schools to help these students succeed. (If possible, draw these graphic organizers onto large newsprint to permit easier viewing by the entire class.)

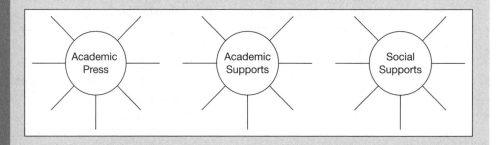

After completing the "mind maps," each group will display their "maps" and identify their findings. When all groups have finished, discuss as a whole class:

1. What similarities do you find among the academic press and academic and social supports for these three types of students?
2. What difference do you find among the academic press and academic and social supports for these three types of students?
3. What obstacles to all students learning to high levels might appear in schools that consciously think of students as high, average, and low achievers?
4. What ideas have you gained from conducting this activity that you can put into practice in your own classrooms?
5. Which academic and social supports do you think would be the easiest to establish in your school—and why? Which academic and social supports do you think would be the most difficult to set up in your school—and why?

the students they teach, they have a difficult time creating the positive learning environment in which children want to learn. And when children don't want to learn, they don't. In fact, high quality teacher–student relationships predict academic achievement.[44]

Effective teachers genuinely care about their students and show their interest in ways that students understand, see, and feel. These educators motivate students to do and be their best, affirming and encouraging them with respect, patience, honesty, listening, understanding, and assistance when needed, and knowing their students as individuals. Teachers establish rapport and credibility by being fair and showing esteem. When their students have difficulties, teachers work with them rather than scold or blame. They tell students what they need to do right and gather all the facts before addressing what students did wrong.

Effective teachers also show their interest in students outside the classroom. Cheering from the bleachers during football games and attending student drama and choral events to watch their students perform show young people in real time that their teachers truly value them. This out-of-the-classroom interest increases students' sense of belonging in their classrooms and their readiness to invest their attention and energies for their teacher—even when the academic work is challenging or barely holds their interest. Likewise, the personal bonds teachers build with students, getting to know their experiences and interests, allows teachers to tailor their instruction to best encourage and advance each student's learning and persistence. This human connection generated through private conversations, verbal and nonverbal encouragement, patience, and specific help learning the content and mastering the skills gradually persuades each student that school is not a cold, unfriendly place. Rather, school is where at least one person likes him or her, is looking after their best interests, and is actively trying to help build success.

Regardless of background, students have the capacity to enter into a mutually respectful, receptive, and helpful relationship with their teachers.[45] Studies on the quality of teacher–student relationships, especially with minority students, find that teachers who proactively anticipate and address problems before they happen as well as build a positive rapport and classroom climate can increase student achievement.[46] Academically successful African American students describe their teachers as accessible and approachable persons who recognize and build their capacities, and who hold high prospects for their achievement.[47] Interestingly, high-quality teacher–student relationships not only affect student engagement in the present; they also predict students engagement and achievement in later years.[48] What is more, high-quality teacher–student relationships are related to African American and Latino students' language skills and reading scores, increase their engagement in learning the academic content, and motivate these students to learn not simply *from* their teachers but *for* their teachers.[49]

Likewise, investigators agree that the classroom's instructional and emotional factors predict students' academic efforts, perseverance, and achievement gains in reading, writing, and math. Young people in supportive relationships with at least one adult who believes in and holds high expectations for them, models successful behaviors, and consistently remains in their lives can thrive in school—while peers in similar circumstances who lack this relational support do not. This is especially true for students most at risk for low achievement.[50] Providing students with a variety of affective and academic scaffolding helps them overcome obstacles that poverty, low expectations, family stability, or other life situations present. Additionally, researchers find that many boys are *relational learners* who need to feel their teachers' caring, interest, mastery, and encouragement before opening themselves to invest in learning.[51]

Positive teacher–student relationships also influence students' behavior in school. When a student acts disruptively, caring educators focus on the student's actual concerns that lie behind the offensive actions, work with the student to identify and solve the real problem, consider what the student needs in order to get back on track academically, help the student learn more appropriate ways to handle frustrations— and work to prevent misbehavior rather than punish students by separating them from the classroom. In turn, students who believe that their teachers like and understand them are more willing to behave appropriately. The results: a calmer school environment and more students behaving well.[52]

Moreover, students' positive relationships in school do not only have to be with teachers. Students can benefit from relationships with principals, school counselors, teacher aides, coaches, secretaries, and custodial staff. As these school personnel thoughtfully listen to young people's concerns and understand their views and values, adults can provide insight, encouragement, and new ways of understanding and responding to difficult situations. All adults in school can become advocates for students with other educators, parents, community agencies, and college admissions officers. To this end, a well-designed and run advisory program can deepen and expand relationships between students and adults at school—giving each student a small group with a consistent and caring adult who creates a safe place in which to share their views about events and issues important to them, review their academic progress, and give encouragement and wise advice. Similarly, successful peers can also serve as confidants and mentors to other students who need a thoughtful listener and wise role model.

Relationships such as these can help young people build their *resilience*—their capacity to have winning outcomes despite challenging circumstances. Stable and caring relationships can help young people develop the internal resources and external supports needed to overcome stormy family circumstances, frustrating school experiences, and negative peer group norms. Research finds that children who experience chronic adversity do better or recover more completely when they have a positive, stable, emotional relationship with a competent adult, are good learners and problem solvers, are likeable, and have areas of competence and perceived effectiveness in a range of situations by themselves and with others.[53]

Strong and caring relationships between students and adults in school can increase student achievement and build their resilience. This may appear in schools in the following ways:

• Every student has at least one strong and caring relationships with an adult in this school.
• Each adult in this school genuinely likes to be around the young people.

- Teachers greet each student daily by name and with a smile.
- When students and teachers see each other in the halls, they exchange lots of smiles and greetings.
- Teachers and staff actively mentor students who are struggling academically or personally.
- The school has a program to systematically identify students needing mentoring and provides them with a suitable adviser and frequent occasions to meet at school.
- The school has an active and well-organized advisory program with a regular time each week (or day) for educators and staff to interact with a few students in ways that young people find personally meaningful.
- Teachers and counselors regularly identify and use students' personal or family assets to help them prevent or solve problems and build resilience.
- Most teachers attend student concerts, plays, and sports events to watch their students perform and encourage their efforts.

**REFLECTIONS AND RELEVANCE 1.6**

## Relationships and Learning

Relationships between teachers and students affect both students' academic achievement and the way they see themselves as students.

Draw an illustration using stick figures, images, words, and/or free-form lines and shapes (using colors, if available) of your personal experience in a high-quality relationship with a teacher at any grade level who strongly influenced your academic achievement and view of yourself in a positive way.

Next, draw an illustration depicting the relationship qualities between teachers and students in your current school for high-, average-, and low-achieving students and how it affects their academic achievement and views of themselves as students.

Present your drawings to the class, and explain what you have depicted. After everyone has displayed and explained their illustrations, the class will identify and discuss the factors that characterize high- and low-quality teacher–student relationships.

## CONCLUSION

Principals are instructional leaders who care about every student's wellbeing and access to and success in a high-quality curriculum. Perhaps a principal's most important challenge is establishing a student-centered learning culture in each school: with high teacher expectations, a safe and orderly learning environment, academic press linked with academic and social supports, and strong, caring relationships between educators and students and among educators.

**REFLECTIONS AND RELEVANCE 1.7**

## Learning in a Student-Centered Environment

A student-centered learning environment can make "learning for all" a reality.

Working in pairs, take two minutes each to discuss your own experiences in a student-centered learning environment, K-12 and collegiate:

- Which aspects were largely present in each setting? Which aspects were largely absent in each setting?
- Which aspects do you think would have been most helpful to you had they been part of your K-12 learning?
- Which aspects of a student-centered learning environment are present in your current school work setting? Which aspects are missing?

After each pair has spent two minutes sharing their experiences with student-centered learning environments, discuss the findings as a whole class.

As influential instructional leaders, principals consistently express the "learning for all" mission to teachers, staff, students, parents, and the larger community. They understand the principles and practices of effective instruction and use that knowledge to guide, monitor, and improve teaching and learning. Largely, principals do this through their abilities to build their own—and their teachers'—instructional and leadership capacities as well as understand and shape their school with full awareness that education begins—and ends—with a focus on the students.

## NOTES

1. Yen, H. (2013, June 13). Census: White majority in U.S. gone by 2043. *Associated Press*. U.S. News on NBC News.com. Retrieved from: http://usnews.nbcnews.com/_news/2013/06/13/18934111-census-white-majority-in-us-gone-by-2043
2. Bass, F. (2013, June 13). White share of U.S. population drops to historic low. *Bloomberg*. Retrieved from: http://www.bloomberg.com/news/2013-06-13/white-share-of-u-s-population-drops-to-historic-low.html
3. Associated Press (2013, June 13). Whites losing majority in U.S. in under-5 group. Retrieved from: http://www.cbsnews.com/8301-201_162-57589109/
4. Robelin, E. W., Adams, C. J., & Shah, N. (2012, March 7). Data show retention disparities. *Education Week, 31* (23), 1, 18–19.
5. *Education Week* (2011, June 7). National graduation rate rebounds, 1.2 million students still fail to earn diplomas. Diplomas Count 2011. Washington, DC: *Education Week*. Retrieved from: http://www.edweek.org/media/diplomascount2011_pressrelease.pdf
6. Lewis, A. (2006, February). A new people. *Phi Delta Kappan, 87* (6), 419–420.
7. PolitiFact.com (2013). Va. senator says fewer workers supporting more Social Security retirees. Washington, DC: PolitiFact.com. Retrieved from: http://www.politifact.com/georgia/statements/2011/apr/12/mark-warner/va-senator-says-fewer-workers-supporting-more-soci/

8. National Research Council (1999). *How people learn: Brain, mind, school, and experience.* Washington, DC: National Academies Press.

9. Kaplan, L. S., & Owings, W. A. (2013). *Culture re-boot. Reinvigorating school culture to improve student outcomes* (p. 141). Thousand Oaks, CA: Corwin.

10. Murname, R. J., & Hoffman, S. (2013, Fall). Graduations on the rise. *EducationNext, 13* (4). Retrieved from: http://educationnext.org/graduations-on-the-rise/

11. Patterson, J. L. (1993). *Leadership for tomorrow's schools* (p. 3). Alexandria, VA: Association for Supervision and Curriculum Development.

12. Rost, J. C. (1997). Moving from individual to relationships: A postindustrial paradigm of leadership. *Journal of Leadership and Organizational Studies, 4* (4), 14.

13. See, for example, Brookover, W. B., & Lezotte, L. W. (1979). *Changes in school characteristics coincident with changes in student achievement.* East Lansing, MI: Michigan State University, Institute for Research on Teaching; Education Trust (2005, November). *Gaining traction, gaining ground. How some high schools accelerate learning for struggling students.* Washington, DC: Education Trust; Ferguson, R. R. (2003). Teachers' perceptions and expectations in the black-white test score gap. *Urban Education, 38* (4), 460–507; Lezotte, L., & Snyder, K. M. (2011). *What effective schools do: Re-envisioning the correlates.* Bloomington, IN: Solution Tree.

14. Rosenthal, R., & Jacobson, L. (1968). *Pygmalion in the classroom: Teachers' expectations and pupils' intellectual development.* New York, NY: Rineholt and Winston.

15. Pygmalion, a mythological Greek character who fell in love with one of his statues which then came to life, inspired the Broadway play, *My Fair Lady.*

16. Oakes, J. (1985). *Keeping track: How schools structure inequality.* New Haven, CT: Yale University Press.

17. Coleman, J. S., Campbell, E. Q., Hobson, C. J., McPartland, F., Mood, A. M., Weinfeld, F. D., et al. (1966). *Equality of educational opportunity.* Washington, DC: U.S. Government Printing Office.

18. Brophy, J., & Good, T. (1970). Teachers' communication of differential expectations for children's classroom performance: Some behavioral data. *Journal of Educational Psychology, 61,* 365–374; Dusek, J. B., & O'Connell, E. J. (1973). Teacher expectancy effects on the achievement test performance of elementary school children. *Journal of Educational Psychology, 65,* 371–377; O'Connell, E., Dusek, J., & Wheeler, R. (1974). A follow-up study of teacher expectancy effects. *Journal of Educational Psychology, 66,* 325–328; Rist, R. (1970). Students' social class and teacher expectations: The self-fulfilling prophesy in ghetto education. *Harvard Educational Review, 40,* 411–451.

19. Brophy & Good, 1970; Dusek, J. B. (1975). Do teachers bias children's learning? *Review of Educational Research, 45,* 661–684; Rosenthal, R. *On the social psychology of the self-fulfilling prophesy: Further evidence for Pygmalion effects and their mediating mechanisms.* New York: MSS Modular Publications; Rosenthal, R. (1976). *Experimenter effects in behavioral research* (2nd ed.). New York: Irvington.

20. Egan, O., & Archer, P. (1985). The accuracy of teachers' rating of ability: A regression model. *American Educational Research Journal, 22,* 25–34; Hoge, R., & Butcher, R. (1984). Analysis of teacher judgments of pupil achievement level. *Journal of Educational Psychology, 76,* 777–781; Mittman, A. (1985). Teachers' differential behavior toward higher and lower achieving students and its relation to selected teacher characteristics. *Journal of Educational Psychology, 77,* 149–161; Monk, M. (1983). Teacher expectations? Pupil responses to teacher mediated classroom climate. *British Educational Research Journal, 9,* 153–166; Pedulla, J., Airasian, P., & Madaus, G. (1980). Do teacher ratings and standardized test results of students yield the same information? *American Educational Research Journal, 17,* 303–307; Good, T. L. (1987). Two decades of research on teacher expectations: Findings and future direction. *Journal of Teacher Education, 4,* 32–47.

21. Ferguson, R. R. (2003). Teachers' perceptions and expectations in the black–white test score gap. *Urban Education, 38* (4), 460–507.

22. Cecil, N. L. (1988). Black dialect and academic success: A study of teacher expectations. *Reading Improvement, 25* (1), 34–38; Crowl, T. K. (1971). White teachers' evaluation of oral responses given by white and Negro ninth grade males (Doctoral dissertation, Columbia University, 1970). *Dissertation Abstracts International, 31,* 4540-A; Dusek, J. B., & Joseph, G. (1983). The bases of teacher expectancies: A meta-analysis. *Journal of Educational Psychology, 75* (3), 327–346; Gaines, M. L., & Davis, M. (1990, April). *Accuracy of teacher prediction of elementary student achievement.* Paper presented at the annual meeting of the American Educational Research Association, Boston, MA. (ERIC Document Reproduction Service No. ED 320 942); Kenealy, P., Neil, F., & Shaw, W. (1988). Influences of children's physical attractiveness on teacher expectations. *Journal of Social Psychology, 128* (3), 373–383; Williams, J. H., & Muehl, S. (1978). Relations among student and teacher perceptions of behavior. *Journal of Negro Education, 47,* 328–336.

23. Peterson, P. L., & Barger, S. A. (1984). Attribution theory and teacher expectancy. In J. B. Dusek (Ed.), *Teacher expectancies* (pp. 159–184). Hillsdale, NJ: Lawrence Erlbaum Associates.

24. Coladarci, T. (1986). Accuracy of teacher judgments of student response to standardized test items. *Journal of Educational Psychology, 78* (2), 141–146; Hoge, R. D., & Butcher, R. (1984). Analysis of teacher judgments of pupil achievement level. *Journal of Educational Psychology, 76* (5), 777–781; Patriarca, L. A., & Kragt, D. M. (1986, May/June). Teacher expectations and student achievement: The ghost of Christmas future. *American Review,* 48–50.

25. Raudenbush, S. W. (1984). Magnitude of teacher expectancy effects on pupil IQ as a function of the credibility of expectancy induction: A synthesis of findings from eighteen experiments. *Journal of Educational Psychology, 76* (1), 85–97.

26. Ferguson (2003). Op. cit.; Guskey, T. (1982, July–August). The effects of change in instructional effectiveness on the relationship of teacher expectations and student achievement. *Journal of Educational Research, 75* (6), 345–349.

27. Goddard, R. D., Logerfo, L., & Hoy, A. W. (2004). Collective efficacy beliefs. Theoretical developments, empirical evidence, and future directions. *Educational Researcher, 33* (3), 3–13.

28. Kaplan & Owings (2015). Op. cit. (pp. 510–511).

29. Chubb, J. E., & Moe, T. M. (1990). *Politics, markets, and America's schools.* Washington, DC: Brookings Institute; Mayer, D. P., Hoy, W. K., & Hannum, J. (1997). Middle school climate: An empirical assessment of organizational health and student achievement. *Educational Administration Quarterly, 33* (3), 290–311; Mullens, J. E., Moore, M. T., & Ralph, J. (2000). *Monitoring school quality: An indicators report.* Washington, DC: U.S. Department of Education, National Center for Education Statistics; Grogger, J. (1997). Local violence and educational attainment. *Journal of Human Resources, 32* (4), 659–692.

30. Hoy & Hannun (1997); Hoy, W. K., Hannum, J., & Tschannen-Moran, M. (1998, July). Organizational climate and student achievement: A parsimonious and longitudinal view. *Journal of School Leadership, 8* (4), 1–22; Hoy, W. K., & Sabo, D. (1998). *Quality middle schools: Open and healthy.* Thousand Oaks, CA: Corwin Press; Goddard, R. D., Sweetland, S. R., & Hoy, W. K. (2000). Academic emphasis of urban elementary schools and student achievement: A multi-level analysis. *Educational Administration Quarterly, 36* (5), 683–702.

31. Goddard, R. D., Sweetland, S. R., & Hoy, W. K. (2000). Academic emphasis of urban elementary schools and student achievement: A multilevel analysis. *Educational Administration Quarterly, 36* (5), 683–702; Lezotte, L., & Snyder, K. M. (2011). *What effective schools do: Re-envisioning the correlates.* Bloomington, IN: Solution Tree; Haahr, J. H., Nielsen, T. K., Hansen, M. E., & Jakobsen, S. T. (2005). *Explaining student performance. Evidence from the international PISA, TIMSS and PIRLS surveys.* Denmark: Danish Technological Institute.

32. Kaplan & Owings (2015). Op. cit. (pp. 508–509).

33. See, for example, Brookover, W. B., & Lezotte, L. W. (1979). *Changes in school characteristics coincident with changes in student achievement.* East Lansing: Michigan State

University, Institute for Research on Teaching; Cuban, L. (1984). Transforming the frog into a prince: Effective schools research, policy, and practice at the district level. *Harvard Educational Review, 54*, 129–151; Education Trust (2005, November). *Gaining traction, gaining ground. How some high schools accelerate learning for struggling students.* Washington, DC: Education Trust; Heck, R. H. (2005). Examining school achievement over time: A multilevel, multi-group approach. In W. K. Hoy & C. G. Miskal (Eds.), *Contemporary issues in educational policy and school outcomes* (pp. 1–28). Greenwich, CT: Information Age.

34. See, for example, Bransford, J. D., Brown, A. L., & Cockling, R. R. (Eds.) (2002). *How people learn: Brain, mind, and school* (p. 8). Washington, DC: National Academy Press; Abbott, M. L., & Fouts, J. T. (2003, February). *Constructivist teaching and student achievement: The results of a school-level classroom observation study in Washington.* Seattle, WA: Washington School Research Center, South Pacific University, Technical Report #5. Retrieved from: http://www.spu. edu/orgs/research/ObservationStudy-2–13–03.pdf; Newmann, F. M., Bryk, A. S., & Nagaoka, J. K. (2001, January). *Authentic intellectual work and standardized tests: Conflict or coexistence?* Chicago, IL: Improving Chicago's Schools. Retrieved from: http://ccsr.uchicago.edu/publications/p0a02.pdf; Goddard, R. D., Sweetland, S. R., & Hoy, W. K. (2000). Academic emphasis of urban elementary schools and student achievement: A multi-level analysis. *Educational Administration Quarterly, 36* (5): 683–702; Lee, V. E. , Smith, J. B., Perry, T. E., & Smylie, M. A. (1999, October). *Social support, academic press, and student achievement: A view from the middle grades in Chicago.* Chicago, IL: Improving Chicago Schools. Retrieved from: http://ccsr.uchicago.edu/ publications/p0e01.pdf

35. Newmann, Bryk, & Nagaoka (2001). Op. cit.

36. Kaplan, L. S., & Owings, W. A. (2013). *Culture re-boot* (p. 157). Thousand Oaks, CA: Corwin.

37. See, for example, Bridgeland, J. M., Dilulio, J. J., & Morrison, K. B. (2006, March). *The silent epidemic. Perspectives of high school dropouts.* Washington, DC: Civic Enterprises. Retrieved from: https://docs.gatesfoundation.org/Documents/TheSilentEpidemic3–06FINAL. pdf; Croninger, R. G., & Lee, V. E. (2001). Social capital and dropping out of high school: Benefits to at-risk students of teachers' support and guidance. *Teachers College Record, 103* (4), 548–582; Lee, V. E., & Burkam, D. T. (2003). Dropping out of high school: The role of school organization and structure. *American Educational Research Journal, 40* (2), 353–393. Retrieved from: http://civilrightsproject.ucla.edu/research/k-12-education/school-dropouts/dropping-out-of-high-school-the-role-of-school-organization-and-structure/lee-role-school-organization-2001.pdf

38. Coleman, J. S., et al., op. cit. (1966); Coleman, J. S. (1968). The concept of equality of educational opportunity. *Harvard Educational Review, 38*, 7–22.

39. Ogbu, J. U., & Simons, H. D. (1998). Cultural–ecological theory of student performance with some implications for education. *Anthropology and Education Quarterly, 29* (2), 155–188; Fordham, S., & Ogbu, J. (1986). Black students' school successes: Coping with the burden of "acting white." *Urban Review, XVIII*, 176–206; Ogbu, J. U. (1995). Cultural problems in minority education: Their interpretations and consequences—part one: Theoretical background. *Urban Review, 27* (3), 189–205.

40. Fryer, R. G. (2006, Winter). "Acting white." The social price paid by the best and brightest minority students. *EducationNext, 6* (1), 52–59. Retrieved from: http://educationnext.org/ actingwhite/

41. See, for example, Brookover, W. B., & Lezotte, L. W. (1979). *Changes in school characteristics coincident with changes in student achievement.* East Lansing: Michigan State University, Institute for Research on Teaching; Edmonds, R. R., & Fredericksen, J. R. (1978). *Search for effective schools: The identification and analysis of city schools that are instructionally effective for poor children.* Cambridge, MA: Harvard University, Center for Urban Studies; Heck, R. H. (2005). Examining school achievement over time: A multilevel, multi-group approach. In W. K. Hoy, & C. G. Miskal (Eds.), *Contemporary issues in*

*educational policy and school outcomes* (pp. 1–28). Greenwich, CT: Information Age; Lezotte, L., & Snyder, K. M. (2011). *What effective schools do: Re-envisioning the correlates.* Bloomington, IN: Solution Tree.

42. The Education Trust resources can be retrieved from: http://www.edtrust.org/dc/resources/publications

43. Kaplan & Owings (2013), op. cit. (pp. 165–166).

44. Hamre, B. K., & Pianta, R. C. (2001). Early teacher–child relationships and the trajectory of children's school outcomes through eighth grade. *Child Development, 72* (2), 625–638.

45. Boykin, A. W., & Noguera, P. (2011). *Creating the opportunity to learn. Moving from research to practice to close the achievement gap.* Alexandria, VA: ASCD.

46. See, for example, Baker, J. A. (1999). Teacher–student interaction in urban at-risk classrooms: Differential behavior, relationship, quality, and student satisfaction with school. *The Elementary School Journal, 100* (1), 57–70; Byrnes, J. P., & Miller, D. C. (2007). The relative importance of predictors of math and science achievement: An opportunity-propensity analysis. *Contemporary Educational Psychology, 32* (4), 599–629; Hamre, B. K., & Pianta, R. C. (2005). Can instructional and emotional support in the first-grade classroom make a difference for children at risk of school failure? *Child Development, 76* (5), 949–967.

47. Brand, B. R., Glasson, G. E., & Green, A. M. (2006). Sociocultural factors influencing students' learning in science and mathematics: An analysis of the perspectives of African American students. *School Science and Mathematics, 106* (5), 228–236; Stewart, E. (2006). Family- and individual-level predictors of academic success for African American students: A longitudinal path analysis utilizing national data. *Journal of Black Studies, 36* (4), 597–621.

48. See, for example, Hughes, J., & Kwok, O. (2007). Influence of student-teacher and parent-teacher relationships on lower achieving readers' engagement and achievement in the primary grades. *Journal of Educational Psychology, 99* (1), 39–51; Sutherland, K. S., & Oswald, D. P. (2005). The relationship between teacher and student behavior in classrooms for students with emotional and behavioral disorders: Transactional processes. *Journal of Child and Family Studies, 14* (1), 1–14; Hughes, J. N., Luo, W., Kwok, O., & Loyd, L. (2008). Teacher-student support, effortful engagement, and achievement: A 3-year longitudinal study. *Journal of Educational Psychology, 100* (1), 1–14.

49. See, for example, Burchinal, M. R., Peisner-Feinberg, E., Pianta, R., & Howes, C. (2002). Development of academic skills from preschool through second grade: Family and classroom predictors of developmental trajectories. *Journal of School Psychology, 40* (5), 415–436; Casteel, C. (1997). Attitudes of African American and Caucasian eighth grade students about praises, rewards and punishments. *Elementary School Guidance and Counseling, 31* (4), 262–272; Ware, F. (2006). Warm demander pedagogy: Culturally responsive teaching that supports a culture of achievement for African American students. *Urban Education, 41* (4), 427–456.

50. See, for example, Vargas, B., & Brizard, J.-C. (2010, November 3). Beating the odds in urban schools. Commentary. *Education Week, 29* (10), 22–23; Reichert, M. C. (2010, November 17). Hopeful news regarding the crisis in U.S. education. Exploring the human element in teaching boys. *Education Week, 30* (13), 27.

51. Reichert, M. D. (2010, November 17). Hopeful news on teaching boys. *Education Week, 30* (12), 27. Retrieved from: http://blogs.edweek.org/edweek/whyboysfail/2010/11/boys_as_relational_learners.html

52. See, for example, Shah, N. (2012, October 17). "Restorative practices" offer alternatives to suspension. *Education Week, 32* (8), 1, 14–15.

53. Masten, A. S., Best, K. M., & Garmezy, N. (1990). Resilience and development: Contributions from the study of children who overcome adversity. *Development and Psychopathology, 2* (4), 425–444.

# CHAPTER 2

# Leadership: A Brief Look at Theory and Practice

Be the chief but never the lord.
—Lao-Tzu, legendary ancient
Chinese philosopher

---

## LEARNING OBJECTIVES

2.1 Explain how our understanding of leadership has evolved from pre-history to today, and identify several factors that account for these changes.

2.2 Discuss how in schools, leadership and management may be separate processes but they need not involve separate people.

2.3 Describe how understanding Maslow's needs hierarchy can help principals better understand and motivate teachers, staff, and students in the school work setting.

2.4 Summarize how principals' understanding of expectancy theory can help the leader better understand and motivate teachers and staff.

2.5 Explain how principals can use insights from Theories X, Y, and Z to better motivate teachers and staff in schools.

2.6 Discuss how principals can use their understanding of motivation-hygiene theory to better motivate the teachers and staff in schools.

2.7 Analyze how principals' understanding of situational leadership theory and developmental levels can help them provide more effective supervision of teachers and staff.

2.8 Evaluate the relative effectiveness of principals using transactional and transformational leadership theory for motivating teachers and staff.

2.9 Explain the Wallace Foundation's five key instructional leadership practices that effective principals perform well.

2.10 Identify and discuss the research-based factors that support the principal's critical importance in student achievement.

2.11 Assess the three different approaches to creating an inclusive workforce environment in schools.

---

**2015 ISLLC STANDARDS: 1, 2, 3, 5, 6, 8, 9, 10, 11**

## INTRODUCTION

Leadership is a long-studied phenomenon, and our understanding of who leaders are and what they do continues to evolve. Principals are leaders of complex organizations called schools, and they are the second most important school-based factor in students' learning and achievement. When principals can lead well, their schools perform well.

One of a school leader's most important challenges is motivating teachers, staff, and students to work hard and accomplish the goals they set for themselves as well as meet the standards set by their school district and state. By developing a more sophisticated understanding of human nature, principals can learn how to inspire teachers and staff (and students) to higher levels of effort and commitment in ways that generate worthwhile outcomes. Learning how to help employees meet their needs within the school, recognizing how leaders can most effectively attend to task and relationship issues, and understanding how to create an inclusive workplace from a culturally diverse workforce are key avenues to improving school employee satisfaction and student achievement.

## LEADERSHIP DEFINED

Psychology, business, sociology, and education have all contributed perspectives and data to the extensive study of leadership. Google the word "leadership" and approximately 500 million results appear. Enter the same word in Google Scholar (scholarly articles) and more than 2.8 million results are available—rather sweeping, indeed. A bit of etymology (the study of word origins) is helpful here. The word "leader" is derived from the Old English word *laedan*, meaning "to show the way."[1] A *leadere* was someone who literally showed others the safe path on a journey—perhaps leadership's first operational definition. Leadership's study and definitions continue to evolve—from straightforward commanding subordinates and demanding loyalty to today's complexities of collaboration and facilitation—largely in the last century.

While our understanding is recent, leadership study is old. In pre-historic times, the leader was the strongest member of a clan—the best hunter or fiercest warrior—essential to protecting and providing for the clan's needs. As civilizations advanced in Egypt, Greece, and Rome, leadership as the greatest warrior or hunter retained respect, but brute strength or skill was no longer sufficient criteria to be the leader. Politics, strategy, and alliances became paramount. Society and its leaders had become more complex.

One of the earliest writings on leadership comes from an advisor to an Egyptian king (2300 BCE) in *Instruction of Ptahhotep*.[2] Confucius, Lao-Tzu (600 BCE), Plato (380 BCE), Cicero, Seneca, Plutarch (around 50 CE), and Machiavelli (1513) all wrote of the responsibilities and conduct required of leaders.[3] Many consider the pragmatic Renaissance politician Machiavelli's *The Prince* relevant today. He argued that the social benefits of stability and security can be achieved in spite of a leader's moral corruption and in political leadership the ends justify the means—clearly not in the best interests of social justice.

Modern leadership research, however, began in the early 1900s with Alfred Binet's concept of mental age and Louis Terman's adaptation of the Stanford-Binet Intelligence Scale, or the IQ test, for the American population. Along with other concepts, researchers studied *intelligence* as one of several leadership traits. World Wars I and II prompted additional attention, as military investigators focused on the relationship between intelligence and leadership behavior. Following World War II, Ralph Stogdill's work at Ohio State University initiated a paradigm shift in leadership studies—moving away from examining leaders' traits and towards studying the situational aspects of task and relationship behaviors. In turn, Stogdill's investigations led to research dealing with relational aspects of leadership in organizations. While current research in leadership is varied, it is interesting to note that examinations of leader personality characteristics—self-confidence, stress tolerance, emotional maturity, integrity, and extroversion—are coming back in vogue.[4]

Importantly, leadership studies are largely culture bound. A society defines leadership in ways that fit its cultural image of what a leader is. A review of social science leadership studies concluded that leadership literature is based largely on a limiting set of assumptions that reflect Western industrialized culture. Almost all the most popular leadership theories and about 98 percent of the empirical evidence display a distinctly American perspective.[5] For example, conventional Western leadership theory focuses on the image of a powerful leader, typically male, who stands atop of a hierarchal structure and controls all outcomes derived from this arrangement. The leader's power is based in knowledge, control, and the ability to win and impose his or her will through direct or indirect threats of violence—physical or economic. Given this slant, understanding *leadership* means appreciating that it shows a particular culture's viewpoint. What makes a "leader" varies with the cultural context.

Regardless of one's definition of leadership, everyone agrees that leadership does not occur in a vacuum. A leader must work with people in an organization to accomplish a task. Remembering the open systems model,[6] everything takes place within an environment. Environmental inputs include the people within the organization, their skills and motivation levels, state and local policies and politics, and the school's culture. In school organization, the principal's primary job is as the instructional leader. That requires building the capacity of those in the organization to share the school vision and accomplish the school goals. The instructional leader's role in that regard is vital in fostering student achievement.

## LEADERSHIP VS. MANAGEMENT

When people look at the wide range of principals' responsibilities—from vision setting to managing people, information, and processes—many are confused about whether principals are leaders or managers. Those who ask this question set up a false choice: which is more important, leadership or management? International management consultant and educator Peter Drucker best clarifies this in his quote, "Management is doing things right; leadership is doing the right things."[7] While some believe this means management is not important, imagine a school year starting out without a master schedule, without the books and supplies needed to start the year, or students not being assigned to classes. Good management is important to operating a school efficiently. Leadership is important to operating a school effectively.

In reality, however, in day-to-day practices in schools managers can be leaders and leaders can be managers. Managers, usually assistant principals and department heads, become leaders when they provide vision, direction, strategy, and inspiration to their organizational units. They become leaders when they act in ways that reinforce the school's vision and its values. At the same time, school leaders, usually principals and occasionally assistant principals and department heads, must perform management functions. So although leadership and management involve separate processes, they do not have to involve separate people. This is especially true in schools. Principals must be able to act as both leader and manager, depending on the situation.

## MOTIVATION THEORY

Education is a people business. A large part of the principal's role is to understand the people in the organization and help build their capacity to share the school's vision and to accomplish its goals. To deal with people effectively, principals must first understand human nature and how to provide the incentives that influence individuals to want to accomplish organizational goals.

Motives—as the conscious representations of desired conditions or as unconscious or implicit strivings—are the purposes which guide our behaviors.[8] Motives direct people to act in certain ways so they may fulfill their basic survival, social, and growth needs. When people are hungry, they look for something to eat. When they fear for their safety, they prepare to fight or flee. When they are lonely, they seek friends and companionship. Motivation prompts many actions and behaviors in people's personal and professional lives.

Appreciating employees' motivations helps educational leaders be more successful in working with others to achieve organizational goals. *Workforce motivation* may be seen as an individual's degree of willingness to exert and maintain an effort toward organizational goals.[9] Principals can begin to comprehend human and workforce motivation with the theories of Abraham Maslow, Victor Vroom, and Frederick Herzberg.

## MASLOW'S HIERARCHY

American psychologist Abraham Maslow conceived a unique perspective when he synthesized research related to human motivation in his book, *Motivation and Personality* (1954).[10] He posited a hierarchy of human needs on two groupings—those necessary to preserve life (physiological and safety) and those necessary to promote social connections and development (social, esteem, and self-actualization). Maslow argues that individuals must meet their basic-level needs before they can meet their higher-level needs. The needs hierarchy includes the deficiency needs (physiological and social, items 1–4) and the growth needs (self-actualization, item 5):

1. Physiological: survival: air, water, food, sleep.
2. Safety/security: out of danger (physical, psychological), financial security.

3.  Social: belonging and love, acceptance, affection, and affiliation with others.
4.  Esteem: approval, recognition, accomplishment.
5.  Self-actualization: cognitive understanding, aesthetic awareness, and fulfilling one's potential.

Maslow's ideas can help school leaders see teachers, staff, students, and parents as complex individuals with increasingly sophisticated sets of unmet needs that they seek to meet in their environments, including work. In addition to wanting a salary that allows them to support their families' basic survival and social needs, teachers and staff also want work settings that keep them safe, secure, and with opportunities to gain social respect and acceptance as part of a valued group working for a common goal. In addition, certain employees and students seek the high regard gained from becoming more knowledgeable, skilled, and proficient at their work; and many desire the challenge of intellectually demanding assignments and responsibilities. Part of a principal's role is to help identify and provide venues for employees to satisfy their needs and gain recognition and regard in ways that also support the organization's goals.

At the same time, principals can apply Maslow's theory at the student and faculty levels to understand why certain behaviors may or may not be occurring and what they say about teachers' and students' unmet needs. First, at the student level, principals can appreciate how students who are hungry, sleepy, are homeless, or who feel bullied and who are falling behind academically do not feel safe at school. Their basic survival needs are not being met. Likewise, when faculty members are going through difficult emotional or financial times, experiencing divorces or serious illness of a loved one, for instance, school leaders can realize that their motivation to achieve those higher level needs may be quite limited.

While Maslow helps astute school leaders understand some basic concepts about motivation based on a hierarchy of needs, other theories can also help principals frame their understanding of work-related behavior and motivation to achieve. Expectancy theory is one of those lenses that can help.

## REFLECTIONS AND RELEVANCE 2.1

### Understanding Maslow's Hierarchy with Students and Staff

Abraham Maslow posited that humans were motivated to meet survival needs (food, shelter) and growth needs (safety, belonging, esteem, and cognitive understanding).

Working in groups of four, conduct the following activities. Then discuss your findings as a class.

1.  Imagine you are the new principal of a school where 75 percent of the students qualify for free or reduced price lunch, but only 15 percent have completed the paperwork to use the program. Five percent of the students are thought to be homeless, and only 7 percent live in a two-parent household. State test scores are declining in your school. Use Maslow's

theory to explain what is happening with test scores and what steps the school might take to improve the situation.
2. Your faculty seems not to care that student test scores are declining. You have just been told that seven of your thirty-five teachers are going through a divorce, and two faculty members whose husbands are partners in a construction firm have filed for bankruptcy protection. A lead teacher's husband has just been diagnosed with stage 4 pancreatic cancer. Use Maslow's theory to explain what may be happening with the faculty. What could you do to help improve the situation?

## EXPECTANCY THEORY

"A fair day's work for a fair day's wage" has been a hallmark of labor and remains relevant today. The concept of giving a certain level of effort in trade for a certain level of pay or reward is a basic tenet of social or economic exchange theory.[11] Victor Vroom is generally credited with making expectancy theory relevant to organizational settings. Expectancy theory has four basic assumptions:[12]

- Individuals join organizations with certain expectations about their needs, motivations, and past experiences that influence how they relate to the organization.
- Individuals consciously choose their behaviors suggested by their own expectancy calculations.
- Individuals' wants from the organization vary and include salary, job security, advancement, and challenge.
- Individuals will choose from among alternatives so as to optimize outcomes for themselves.

Four key elements attached to these assumptions explain motivation: outcomes, expectancy, instrumentality, and valence. How those elements interact determines the level of worker motivation. When principals understand that each faculty and staff member holds certain expectations about what he/she wants to get from the school in return for their efforts, they can better motivate their staff's energies to work hard and well by finding ways to have their personal preferences coincide with the school's goals. Figure 2.1 shows a model of how these elements interact.

*Outcomes* are the end results of work behaviors. First-level outcomes refer to various performance aspects that arise from expending some level of workplace effort. For instance, principals expect teachers to generate a year's worth of academic growth in each student during the school year. Second-level outcomes are the end rewards that the individual expects from those first-level outcomes—such as helping each student in the class become proficient in the content taught—which will lead eventually to

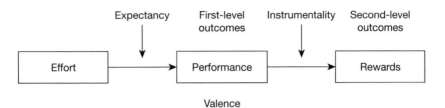

**FIGURE 2.1** Expectancy Model

Source: Lunenburg, F., & Ornstein, A. (2008). *Educational administration* (5th ed.). Belmont, CA: Cengage. Reprinted with permission.

rewards such as salary increases, promotions, recognitions from peers and supervisors, and an overall sense of accomplishment.

*Expectancy* is an individual's belief that effort related to the job will result in the expected performance level. Expectancy ranges from 0 to 1. If an employee sees no probability that effort will result in accomplishing the task at some desired performance level, the expectancy level is 0. If the employee is 100 percent certain the task will be completed at the expected performance level, the expectancy level is 1. Most often the level of expectancy falls between 0 and 1.

*Instrumentality* is the individual's subjective estimate that his or her performance (first-level outcomes) will lead to the end rewards (second-level outcomes). Instrumentality also ranges from 0 to 1. If an individual sees that good performance (first-level outcomes) consistently results in second-level outcomes (such as salary increases, promotions, or recognitions) the instrumentality is 1. If no perceived relationship exists, the instrumentality is 0.

Finally, *valence* is the individual's preference for a specific type of reward (such as salary increase, promotion, or recognition). Valence has a range of –1 to +1. For any employee, the valence of a work performance (first-level outcome) depends on the extent to which it ends in a desired reward (second-level outcome). A strong preference for an outcome has a valence of 1. For an employee with no preference or who feels indifferent to the outcome, the valence is 0. If one strongly dislikes the outcome, the valence is –1. An individual's valence for a particular outcome or reward indicates how motivated that person is to give the effort needed to accomplish the performance.

To sum up expectancy theory, the motivation someone has for the job depends on two factors: (1) the individual's expectancy that a certain level of performance will result from the level of effort spent; and (2) the individual's estimate of probability that his or her performance level will lead to the desired rewards.

What does expectancy theory look like in schools? In education, generally principals do not have the authority to increase outstanding teachers' salaries. For the most part, schools still use a unified salary schedule based on degrees and number of years in the district. Given that, principals need to establish a culture centered on student achievement that looks to other types of rewards or second-level outcomes for teachers. These may include providing a compelling vision of excellence for all students that teachers can value and relate to, opportunities for professional learning that enhances teachers' instructional skills and classroom effectiveness, opportunities for teachers to lead colleagues in learning, problem solving, and school improvement, and frequent occasions for recognition and celebration of their efforts and accomplishments.[13]

---

**REFLECTIONS AND RELEVANCE 2.2**

## Expectancy Theory in Schools

Expectancy theory offers a way for school leaders to understand faculty and staff and more meaningfully reward their successful performances.

In groups of four, identify how expectancy theory operates in your own experiences. What are your most important first- and second-level outcomes? What is the strength of your expectancies—how much effort (from 0 to 1) will it take from you to do the quality job you and your current principal expect? What is the probability that in your current school, your performance will result in the rewards you desire? What is the valence of strength of your preference for a particular reward or outcome (from –1 to +1)? Discuss your findings in your group. To what extent do you think your principal is using expectancy theory to help motivate your best efforts at work—and what data prompt you to say this?

After the small-group discussion, as a whole class examine the relevance of expectancy theory for principals and teachers and identify how principals can make better use of its concepts to motivate their faculty and staff.

---

# THEORIES X, Y, AND Z

While Maslow's needs hierarchy and Vroom's expectancy theory offer ideas about motivation, a principal's philosophy or beliefs about staff will also impact teachers' motivation levels in the classroom. Social psychologist and MIT management professor Douglas McGregor's seminal book, The Human Side of Enterprise, showed how particular management concepts were inadequate to motivate worker's behaviors.[14] McGregor believed that managers could view workers from two perspectives—Theory X or Theory Y. William Ouchi's Theory Z offers another perspective.

## Theory X

Theory X managers believe that the average worker is lazy, does not like work, and avoids exertion whenever possible. Therefore, Theory X managers tend to control and direct employees to perform to expected standards, and workers prefer being directed, avoid responsibility, and seek job security. Theory X reflects Maslow's lower-level needs (security) and might best be described as the "carrot and stick" management approach.

## Theory Y

Theory Y, in contrast, believes that employees enjoy work, and managers do not need to control or punish them to achieve the organization's goals. Theory Y managers believe that if employees find their work satisfying, they will commit their efforts to the organization's goals. Managers' job, therefore, is to arrange organizational conditions so employees can achieve their own goals by targeting their efforts towards achieving the organization's goals. Theory Y reflects Maslow's upper-level social and growth needs as employees work together to achieve the organizational goals.

How do Theory X and Y look in schools? In a school where the principal espouses Theory X, the leader retains tight control over almost every aspect of the school. Little is delegated, and everything is supervised closely. The principal is the solver of all problems. In a school where Theory Y is espoused, in comparison, shared leadership is evident. Teachers work with school leaders to solve problems. The principal is a facilitator, not a dictator. The school is a professional place to work where collaboration is its hallmark.

## Theory Z

In the late 1970s and early 1980s, William Ouchi, an internationally known American business management professor, produced a best-selling book extending McGregor's Theories X and Y.[15] Appropriately, Ouchi named his concept Theory Z. Until Ouchi's writings, most study of management involved Western societies. With the rise of Japan's industrial machine and culture in the 1960s through the 1980s, Ouchi's work focused on comparing North American and Japanese management and identifying how their differences impacted organizational effectiveness. By doing so, Ouchi took McGregor's Theory Y to a new level.

Theory Z focuses on the employee's work life quality. In this view, consensual decision making, quality circles (groups of workers and managers who exchange information for organizational improvement), and a team approach to management are necessary components for the organization to create a work culture in which employees share values, goals, beliefs, and open communications. In these work environments, employees build trust among employees and managers.[16] Ouchi believes that individuals who cross-train in various jobs can gain a "big picture" of the organization and, as a result, provide more insight and data needed to improve organizational efficiency while improving employee morale. The leaders' job is to foster the culture that develops employees' shared vision, shared values, beliefs, priorities, and experiences. Theory Z has been called "Theory Y on steroids." Today, such practices are commonplace in business and schools.

What does Theory Z look like in schools? It is most commonly seen in school improvement teams: groups of teachers, school counselors, and administrators examining student test data and developing a plan to improve teaching for learning. It is seen in the overall operation of a school when the principal works with the entire staff, students, and community to build a common vision for what the school can be at its best for students and where teacher leadership is *de rigueur*.

**REFLECTIONS AND RELEVANCE 2.3**

## Theory X, Y, and Z Leaders

School leaders' beliefs about their faculty and staff's willingness to work hard to improve organizational outcomes influences their choice of management and leadership behaviors.

In groups of three, discuss principals with whom you have worked. Describe their leadership characteristics in terms of Theory X, Theory Y, and Theory Z. Were the characteristics helpful or unhelpful to you as a teacher? In what ways? What effect did that principal have on the school's climate and culture? Finally, list what you would like to have changed about the principal to help people in the school perform more effectively. Explain why this change would make the school a better place for students and teachers to do their work.

Discuss your findings with the entire class and draw conclusions about what conditions might be helpful or harmful in working with Theory X, Theory Y, and Theory Z principals. Explain your answers.

## MOTIVATION-HYGIENE THEORY

Frederick Herzberg, late Case Western Reserve psychology professor, developed the motivation-hygiene theory.[17] Building on Maslow, Herzberg believed that people had two types of needs: survival needs and growth needs. Survival needs (biological drives and learned behaviors derived from those drives) are related to Maslow's lower-level needs of survival and safety. Growth needs (psychological) are related to Maslow's higher-level needs of affiliation, esteem, and self-actualization. Herzberg identified those distinct factors that prevent or cause job dissatisfaction from factors that prevent or cause job satisfaction.

Herzberg posited that work satisfaction and dissatisfaction are not opposite ends of a continuum. Rather, work satisfaction and dissatisfaction are separate and distinct human dimensions. Herzberg summarized that, "The opposite of job satisfaction is not job dissatisfaction but, rather, no job satisfaction; and similarly, the opposite of job dissatisfaction is not job satisfaction, but no job satisfaction."[18] Thomas Sergiovanni, late education professor at Trinity University, San Antonio, Texas, replicated Herzberg's work with teachers and drew the same conclusions.[19]

In his motivation-hygiene theory, Herzberg states that factors that cause worker satisfaction are called motivation factors while the factors that cause dissatisfaction are called hygiene factors. In this theory, growth or motivation factors are intrinsic to the job and include variables such as achievement, recognition, responsibility, and advancement. The hygiene factors are extrinsic to the job and include company policies, interpersonal relations with subordinates or peers, supervision, administration, working conditions, wages, and employment security variables.

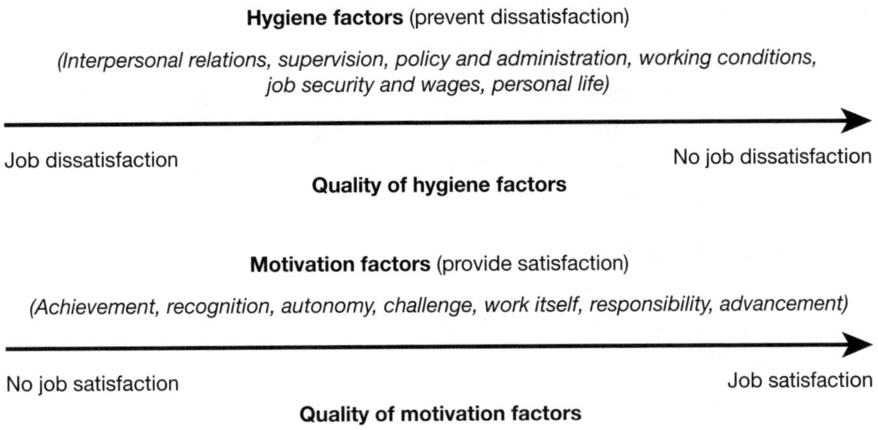

**Hygiene factors** (prevent dissatisfaction)

*(Interpersonal relations, supervision, policy and administration, working conditions, job security and wages, personal life)*

Job dissatisfaction                                                                      No job dissatisfaction
**Quality of hygiene factors**

**Motivation factors** (provide satisfaction)

*(Achievement, recognition, autonomy, challenge, work itself, responsibility, advancement)*

No job satisfaction                                                                          Job satisfaction
**Quality of motivation factors**

**FIGURE 2.2** Herzberg's Motivation-Hygiene Theory
Source: Kaplan, L. S., & Owings, W. A., 2014.

As you can see in Figure 2.2, the absence of hygiene factors produces job dissatisfaction while the increase of motivators causes job satisfaction. As the hygiene factors decrease in quality, dissatisfaction increases. When the hygiene factors increase in quality a "no dissatisfaction" level is approached. On another continuum, as motivation factors increase in quality, employees move from "no satisfaction" levels to "job satisfaction" levels.

What does this look like in schools? Focusing on building a culture of professionalism where individuals treat each other with dignity and respect (hygiene factor—interpersonal relations) helps to prevent job dissatisfaction. Likewise, examining and ending outdated school policies that de-professionalize teachers—such as punching a time clock for attendance (hygiene factor—policy and administration)—can also prevent dissatisfaction. On the other hand, granting teachers more authority in their job activities (motivation factor—autonomy) increases job satisfaction. Similarly, when principals implement recognition programs for teachers, teams, grade levels, to reward student success (motivation factor—recognition) job satisfaction increases. Successful principals seek to decrease the negative hygiene factors in the school to prevent job dissatisfaction and increase the positive motivation factors to provide job satisfaction.

Understanding the theory that job satisfaction is not the opposite of job dissatisfaction helps administrators better frame a bigger picture of how leadership can improve school culture and practices.

## LEADERSHIP THEORY AND BEHAVIORS

Motivating employees is an essential leadership task, and the sections above discuss several theories that school leaders can use to incentivize their teachers and staff to commit their talents and efforts for the school's goals. Considering several key leadership theories can also provide principals with models of how to enact their role effectively.

## Situational Leadership Theory

Future principals might logically ask, "How does one lead?" Under what circumstances might a specific leadership approach best be used? Is there one best leadership theory? Are different theories of leadership available for use in dissimilar situations? All these are important questions and the topic of much scholarly research. A bit of history will offer some context.

### Shartle, Stogdill, and Hemphill

As noted above, modern leadership studies began in the early 1900s and gained popularity during World Wars I and II. After World War II, Carroll Shartle, Ralph Stogdill, and John Hemphill at Ohio State University became the first group to examine leadership from a multidisciplinary approach that included education, sociology, psychology, and economics. These studies generated two important leadership factors—*initiating structure* and *consideration*. *Initiating structure* is defined as task-oriented behavior: concern for getting the job done (such as organization, scheduling, and following procedures). *Consideration* is defined as the relationship-oriented behavior at work: concern for the people with whom one works (such as respect, trust, and regard for coworkers).[20] As illustrated in Figure 2.3, these two factors provided a dual axis framework—and a new schema—for considering leadership behaviors: the degree to which the leader exhibits task-oriented behavior or relationship-oriented behavior.

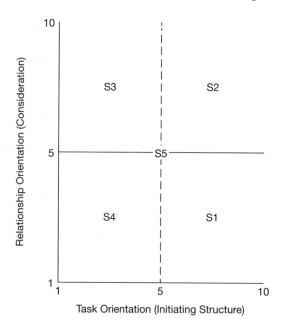

**FIGURE 2.3** Dual Axis Model with Task-Orientation and Relationship-Orientation Behaviors

Source: Based on the work of Hemphill, J. K. (1949). *Situational factors in leadership*. Columbus: The Ohio State University, Bureau of Educational Research, Monograph No. 32; Stogdill, R. M. (1959). *Individual behavior and group achievement*. New York: Oxford University Press; Hersey, P., & Blanchard, K. (1977). *The management of organizational behavior* (3rd ed). Englewood Cliffs, NJ: Prentice Hall; Blake, R. R., & Mouton, J. S. (1985). *The managerial grid III*. Houston, TX: Gulf.

Conceptualizing this dual axis, it is possible to exhibit the following mix of leadership behaviors:

- High task orientation and low relationship orientation (S1: Style 1).
- High task orientation and high relationship orientation (S2: Style 2).
- Low task orientation and high relationship orientation (S3: Style 3).
- Low task orientation and low relationship orientation (S4: Style 4).

It is important to remember that a low level of a certain behavior does not mean there is no level of that behavior existing. Low relationship or low task does not mean there would be no concern or respect for others or that there would be no concern for accomplishing the task.

### Blake and Mouton

Psychologists Robert Blake and Jane Mouton further refined this idea.[21] They called S1 *control-compliance,* S2 *people and results,* S3 *people over results,* and S4 *weak management.* They also added a fifth way of conceptualizing leader behavior, plotted at 5, 5 (S5) on our 10-point grid: *moderate management* or middle-of-the-road leadership. Figure 2.3 shows it as S5. This style balances production and relationship concerns; neither production nor relationship needs are fully met. Average performance is usually expected and achieved.

### Hersey and Blanchard

Behavioral scientist Paul Hersey and educational leadership professor Ken Blanchard further developed the situational leadership theory.[22] They called S1 *telling,* S2 *selling,* S3 *participating,* and S4 *delegating,* and each has an appropriate use with the appropriate group or individual. Situational leadership theory answers the question, "Does one 'best' style of leadership exist?" The answer is, "No—because leadership style depends on the situation."

## How Situational Leadership Theory Works

According to situational leadership theory, the leader needs to know the developmental level (also known as maturity level) of the individual or group with whom he/she is working. The developmental level (maturity) is operationally defined using two constructs—*competence* (capacity) to accomplish the task and *commitment* (willingness) to accomplish the task. There are four developmental levels—D1 through D4—that complement the four leadership behaviors. The key to understanding and applying this theory is to match the leadership behavior with the appropriate developmental level of the individual or group.

Table 2.1 illustrates how these developmental levels are defined. In the situational leadership model, as competence and commitment increase, so does the developmental (or maturity) level of the individual or group. D1 and D4 are easily defined—either low on both or high on both the competence and commitment level. D2 and D3 are a bit trickier. To determine these two levels, competence is more valuable to the organization

**TABLE 2.1** Determining Developmental (Maturity) Levels

| D1 | D2 | D3 | D4 |
|---|---|---|---|
| Low competence/ Low commitment | Some competence/ Lower commitment | Moderately high competence/ Moderate commitment | High competence/ High commitment |
| A newer teacher with lower skill levels and unsure about whether or not to remain in education. | A teacher increasing in skill level but still uncertain as to whether or not to remain in education. | A teacher who does well in the classroom showing good skill level and fairly certain he or she will remain in education. | A master teacher committed to education and mentoring others. |

Source: Based on Owings, W. A., & Kaplan, L. S. (2012). *Leadership and organizational behavior in education.* Boston, MA: Allyn and Bacon.

than willingness. Therefore, some competence and a lower level of commitment defines D2 while moderately high competence and a moderate level of commitment define D3. The information following Table 2.1 also provides examples for how this works in schools to determine a teacher's or the faculty's developmental level.

Table 2.2 depicts and summarizes how to match the leader behavior with the group's or individual's developmental level. Matching the leadership style with the developmental level is straightforward. For a D1 group or individual the appropriate leader behavior is S1; for D2 S2; D3 S3; and D4 S4. Once one understands the premise for this pairing, the rationale appears logical.

### Situational Leadership in Schools

What does situational leadership look like in schools? Imagine a first-year teacher who may not have completed an outstanding teacher preparation program, and who is not really sure if he wants to stay in education (low competence and low commitment, or D1). This teacher needs a high level of direction and lower level of relationship from the principal or assistant principal. Here the theory calls for a high-task, low-relationship behavior from the administrator—S1.

Now visualize a teacher who has reached her third or fourth year of teaching. As a teacher, her competence level has increased, she is more effective in generating student learning than she was several years earlier, and she is leaning more towards remaining in education (some competence and somewhat increasing commitment—D2). The appropriate leadership behavior here would still require a high level of direction and a higher level of relationship behavior that may increase the level of commitment to the profession. Here the theory calls for the administrator to provide a high-task, high-relationship behavior—S2. This behavior would manifest itself with frequent monitoring of classroom practices with constructive feedback and increased friendly interest in the person.

**TABLE 2.2** Applying Situational Leadership's Leader Behaviors and Developmental Levels

| Development Level | Characteristics of Individual or Group | Appropriate Leader Behavior or Style | Rationale |
|---|---|---|---|
| D1 | Low competence and low commitment levels | S1 | Workers have low competence and low commitment and need high levels of direction. |
| D2 | Some competence but lower commitment level | S2 | Workers' competence is increasing and commitment remains low. They still need high levels of direction, with increased interpersonal support. |
| D3 | Moderately high competence and somewhat moderate commitment levels | S3 | Workers are competent and commitment is increasing, but they still need a high level of support to enhance commitment. |
| D4 | High competence and high commitment levels | S4 | Workers' levels of competence and commitment are high. High levels of direction and support tend to be distracting. Lower levels of direction and support are needed. |

Source: Based on Hersey, P., & Blanchard, P. (1988). *Management and organizational behavior.* Englewood Cliffs, NJ: Prentice Hall, in Owings, W., and Kaplan, L. (2012). *Leadership and organizational behavior in education* (p. 157). Boston, MA: Prentice Hall.

Next imagine a teacher who has taught for eight years. His competence level is proficient and his level of commitment has increased, too. He could well be described as D3. Given this, the principal does not need to tell the teacher what needs to be done nearly as much as would be needed with an inexperienced teacher. Therefore, the principal can pull back on the task-oriented behavior but maintain a high level of relationship-oriented behavior—S3.

Last, picture a skillful teacher who has become a department or grade-level chair or a master teacher. This experienced teacher is mentoring new teachers and considering becoming a school administrator. Both the competence and commitment levels are high—D4. The principal no longer needs to tell the teacher what needs to be done. And, since the teacher is now busy mentoring others or chairing a department or grade level, and starting a Master's degree program in educational leadership, she may no longer have the time or energy to spend as much relationship-oriented behavior time with the principal. The principal can now pull back on task- and relationship-oriented behaviors —S4. Intuitively, this theory makes a great deal of sense and its purposeful application involves the artfulness of leadership.

**REFLECTIONS AND RELEVANCE 2.4**

## Identifying Your Present Developmental Level and Maturity Needs

School leaders develop their skills in working with tasks and people over time with a variety of learning experiences and reflection.

Using Table 2.2, identify your present developmental level as a school leader. Then identify the type of leadership behavior or style you need from your current (or next) principal and professor to help you move to the next developmental level. Then, list the types of learning experiences (instruction, mentoring, coaching, opportunities to practice new skills and receive feedback, other) that you want to help you increase your maturity as a school leader and how your principal or professor can help you achieve it.

After you have completed this task, discuss as a whole class what you need to increase developmental levels (maturity) in school leadership.

### Transformational Leadership Theory

Transformational leadership is a contemporary leadership model in which leaders and followers help each other advance to a higher level of morale, motivation, and improved outcomes. In his 1978 book, *Leadership*,[23] historian and political scientist James McGregor Burns introduced the concept of transformational leadership.

Burns contrasted transformational leadership with more traditional leadership that he called *transactional*—or quid pro quo (Latin meaning "this for that"). In transactional leadership, for example, money is exchanged for labor, recognition for loyalty, and other rewards for the desired behaviors—in other words, "this reward for that behavior." In transactional leadership, the emphasis is on using power—of punishments and rewards—to achieve a goal. Transactional leadership rewards followers' compliance and inflicts negative consequences for its absence. For instance, principals use transactional leadership when they give teachers opportunities to attend a desirable professional conference in another state (with the school paying for registration, airfare, hotel, transit, and meals) if they agree to serve on certain school committees or head up the principal's "special projects." Teachers employ transactional leadership when they give student higher grades for actively participating in class. Much of everyday life is built around transactional relationships. If we think back to Maslow, transactional leadership appeals to individuals' lower-level motivations—food, shelter, belonging, and security.

By comparison, transformational and transactional leadership are very different concepts and elicit very different relationships between the leader and the "led." Transformational leadership empowers employees by meeting their higher-level motivation needs—esteem, competence, and self-actualization. Leaders accomplish this by using empowering strategies to change employees' core attitudes and beliefs about the organization, about the nature of their work, and developing a shared vision for what needs to be accomplished. According to Burns, transformational process raises both leadership and followers to higher levels of motivation to accomplish the shared vision. Transformational leaders provide the medium for this culture growth by emphasizing competence, equality, liberty, justice, and morality.

Additionally, transformational leadership includes three concepts that affect how leaders lead. First, the leader becomes the moral embodiment of the organization's mission, personally exemplifying the organization's vision and goals. Without saying a word, the leader's physical presence alone signals to employees their organization's desirable values and goals. For instance, in schools, whenever teachers or students see the transformational principal, they see him or her as the embodiment of the school's "Every Student Achieving" motto, reminding them of their purpose and their own role in making this happen. Second, the transformational leader expresses and builds awareness of this vision for a better future while, at the same time, showing concern for the employees' needs, interests, and motives. In schools, the transformational principal shows genuine consideration and acts to help successfully address the faculty and staff's human issues as well as focus on the school's improvement plan. Third, the leader helps followers by building the team's capacity to enhance both ethical and technical behaviors.[24] In schools, transformational principals consistently model ethical and trustworthy behaviors, provide relevant and job-embedded professional development to help teachers improve their classroom practices, and give teachers frequent opportunities to become instructional and school leaders. These three components clearly define the differences between transactional and transformational leaders. As assessed by the influence transformational leaders have on their followers, this impact rises above and beyond a simple exchange (transactional) level.

## REFLECTIONS AND RELEVANCE 2.5

## Theories X/Y/Z and Transactional/Transformational Leadership

Different leadership theories share common factors. Consider the commonalities among Theories X, Y, and Z and transactional and transformational leadership.

Working individually, create a list of what Theory X and transactional leadership have in common. Then construct a list of what Theory Y, Theory Z, and transformational leadership have in common.

Identify and list the commonalties among transactional and transformational leadership and situational leadership theory. For example, identify times in situational leadership theory—if any—where a transactional approach may be most appropriate. Identify times in situational leadership— if any—in which transformational leadership may be more appropriate.

Regroup and discuss your findings and conclusions with the class.

## Instructional Leadership

Despite the organization, successful leadership shares certain commonalities. Their differences, however, tend to reflect the nature of the work to be accomplished. In schools, effective principals are instructional leaders. In this role, principals focus all members of the organization on teaching and learning. This is a huge challenge. Future principals can understandably feel overwhelmed by the scope of the work, the innumerable responsibilities, and the life-affecting outcomes that affect hundreds of teachers and students over the years. Gaining a clearer idea on what instructional leaders actually do can help future principals begin to plan for learning the necessary attitudes, knowledge, and skill sets to help them be effective in this role.

The Wallace Foundation, a national philanthropic organization that funds projects to test innovative ideas for solving important social problems, has issued more than 70 research reports on school leadership. Its findings highlight five practices that effective principals perform well. They include:[25]

- shaping a vision of academic success for all;
- creating a climate hospitable to education;
- cultivating leadership in others;
- improving instruction;
- managing people, data, and process to foster school improvement.[26]

Shaping a vision of academic success for all involves working with the faculty to develop shared understandings about what the school should become and the values, beliefs, goals, and actions that set the organization's direction. Developing these basic organizational underpinnings requires an understanding of motivational psychology: people tend to be incentivized by having personally compelling purposes that are challenging yet attainable and help them find a meaningful professional identity in their work.[27] This shared vision includes realizing that in a globally competitive economy, all students in their school must learn and achieve to high levels. Failure to close achievement gaps could result in denying students' access to the economic and social opportunities as adults that will give them a satisfying quality of life and make them responsible citizens and neighbors.

Creating a climate hospitable to education involves crafting a climate of caring, ethical behaviors, and relational trust with students and adults. This will be discussed more fully in Chapter 6. With these environmental conditions in place and growing, everyone feels safe and respected. Teachers and students, alike, can take the necessary risks involved in learning to high levels. Professional learning communities composed of mutually respectful, ethical, and trusting colleagues help teachers grow and work more effectively with their students. In short, learning is central to the school's mission, and students, faculty, staff, parents, and the community know it.

For schools to succeed, cultivating leadership in others is essential. The principal, alone, cannot do the work of educating all students well: the task is too big and too complex. Educating a community's young people must be accomplished with and through others. To develop that shared vision and the professional skills needed to make

**TABLE 2.3** Key Findings of the 2010 Wallace Foundation Report

| Key Findings |
| --- |
| Collective leadership has a stronger influence on student achievement than individual leadership. |
| Almost all people associated with high-performing schools have greater influence on school decisions than is the case with people in low-achieving schools. |
| Higher-performing schools award greater influence to teacher teams, parents, and students in particular. |
| Principals and district leaders have the most influence on decisions in all schools; however, they do not lose influence as others gain influence. |
| Schools leaders have an impact on student achievement primarily through their influence on teachers' motivation and working conditions; their influence on teachers' knowledge and skills produces less impact on student achievement.[28] |

Source: Seashore Louis, K., Leithwood, K., Wahlstrom, K. L., & Anderson, S. E., et al. (2010, July). *Learning from leadership: investigating the links to improved student learning: Final report of research to the Wallace Foundation.* St. Paul, MN: Center for Applied Research and Educational Improvement, University of Minnesota and Toronto, CA: Ontario Institute for Studies in Education, University of Ontario.

higher levels of learning happen across the school, leadership needs to be developed across the organization.[29] Principals do this by developing teachers' ability to see the whole picture, to collaborate with others, to make informed decisions that reinforce school values, and to learn and apply the knowledge and skills that make them better able to generate every student's learning. In short, principals help faculty and staff learn how to think and act as classroom and school leaders as a means to increase the leadership's positive impact throughout the school. In other words, leadership builds capacity.

As Table 2.3 indicates, almost all the 2010 Wallace Foundation's conclusions deal directly with principals cultivating leadership in others. By building capacity and empowering teachers, work motivation increases and improves the working conditions in the classroom for teachers and students.

Next, instructional improvement occurs when principals focus teachers' attention and efforts to teaching's "technical core"—that is, improving the quality of teachers' classroom instruction and student learning. Educational leadership professors Wayne Hoy and Cecil Miskel define teaching's "technical core" as "the teaching–learning process"—knowledge about learning and student development, instruction, curriculum, assessment, and classroom management—with all other administrative decisions or activities "secondary to the basic mission of teaching and learning."[30] Here, in the classroom, the actual "product" of education—student learning—is produced. An instructional leader, the principal must have the ability to observe a class and provide suggestions for improvement when needed.

Finally, the principal must manage the people, data, and processes in the school in ways that keep the emphasis on improving teaching and learning. Principals must hire competent teachers and staff who care for every child and are willing to put in the effort, time, and professional knowledge to help each student succeed. Principals must identify teacher leaders in every department and at every grade level who can help guide teaching, learning, and professional development in their areas—and who can help the school administrators solve school-based problems and make better informed decisions. Similarly, principals need to design and implement a master schedule that makes the best use of available people, time, space, and materials. They must direct the school's budget to best support teacher and student learning priorities. Principals must design ways to involve parents and the community as respected partners in their children's education and communicate with them regularly in ways that parents appreciate and understand. And, principals must design and manage the school's climate and culture in ways that respect all persons, nurtures ethical behavior and relational trust, establishes student-centered learning, supports distributive leadership, creates strong parent–community ties, develops teacher capacity, and brings improved approaches to increasing students' academic outcomes.

## REFLECTIONS AND RELEVANCE 2.6

### Your Personal Readiness for Instructional Leadership

Effective principals have mastered a professional knowledge and skills base that helps them perform their roles well.

As an aspiring principal, on a scale of 1 to 5 below, how prepared do you feel to perform the following?

- Work with faculty and staff to shape a vision of academic success for all.
- Create a climate hospitable to education.
- Cultivate leadership in others.
- Improve instruction.
- Manage people, data, and process to foster school improvement.

| 1 | 2 | 3 | 4 | 5 |
|---|---|---|---|---|
| No knowledge, No experience, No confidence. | Little knowledge, Little experience, Little confidence. | Some knowledge, Some experience, Some confidence. | Good knowledge, Good experience, Good confidence. | Deep knowledge, Deep experience, Deep confidence. |

Based on your self-assessment, what experiences and knowledge do you need the most? Where and when do you plan to get them? What evidence will you use to assess how well you are performing these responsibilities?

# RESEARCH ON PRINCIPAL LEADERSHIP AND STUDENT ACHIEVEMENT

As effective instructional leaders, principals can make a measurable difference in student achievement. In the last 20 years, much educational research has been devoted to studying principals' leadership role in student achievement.

Robert Marzano's book, *What Works in Schools: Translating Research into Action*, a meta-analysis of instructional best practices, affords much attention to the teacher's role in student achievement.[31] Marzano estimates effect sizes (a percentage of one standard deviation) of certain school practices on student learning outcomes. Teachers' effects on student learning can be thought of as direct influences—they instruct the students daily. In contrast, principals rarely engage students in instructional activities over extended periods of time; their influence on student learning is indirect. But that indirect influence is significant. In fact, a 2004 Wallace Foundation report concludes, "Leadership is second only to classroom instruction among all school-related factors that contribute to what students learn at school."[32] Marzano (2003) observes that "leadership could be considered the single most important aspect of school reform" (p. 172).

In Marzano's meta-analysis (2003, p. 10), many of the school-based factors that influence student achievement are anchored in instructional leadership. They are, in the order of their impact on student achievement:

1. Guaranteed and viable curriculum.
2. Challenging goals and feedback.
3. Parent and community involvement.
4. Safe and orderly environment.
5. Collegiality and professionalism.

Many of these factors are not new. Leadership's instructional role in generating strong learning outcomes has been documented since Ron Edmonds and Larry Lezotte began their effective schools research in the early 1970s.[33] Edmonds, doubtful of the Coleman Report[34] findings—that family backgrounds rather than schools were responsible for student achievement—researched what are called "outlier schools" (where high achievement was found in high poverty and high minority populations). Over time, the effective schools correlates grew to include:[35]

- strong instructional leadership;
- clear and focused mission;
- safe and orderly environment;
- climate of high expectations;
- frequent monitoring of student progress;
- positive home–school relations;
- opportunity to learn.

In 1979, Edmonds' colleagues studied a set of eight Michigan schools enrolling large numbers of low-income and minority children characterized by consistently improving academic performance. After visiting the schools and interviewing the leadership and staff, researchers identified the following factors that consistently separated schools in which students achieved well from those where they didn't:[36]

- *Clear instructional focus.* Improving schools stressed the importance of reading and math objectives. Schools with declining academic performance did not.
- *High teacher expectations.* Staffs of improving schools tended to believe that *all* their students could master the basic academic objectives and would eventually complete high school and college. Teachers at declining schools did not hold these high expectations.
- *Commitment to and responsibility for student achievement.* In improving schools, teachers and principals were more likely to accept responsibility for teaching students the academic skills they needed to succeed. Principals and teachers at declining schools did not.
- *High time on-task.* Teachers in improving schools spent more time on achieving reading and math objectives. Teachers in declining schools spent less time in direct reading instruction.
- *Principal as instructional leader.* In improving schools, principals were more assertive as leaders, held higher expectations for students' behavior, and more regularly evaluated student achievement of basic academic objectives (and their schools' effectiveness in generating basic academic objectives). In declining schools, principals did not and were not.
- *Accountability.* Improving schools showed greater acceptance of accountability and used measures of students' learning as one key indicator of their effectiveness. Declining schools did not.
- *Dissatisfaction with current achievement.* Teachers in improving schools tended to be less satisfied than teachers in declining schools with their students' achievement.

The effective schools studies' findings challenged Coleman's *Equality of Educational Opportunity* conclusions; what happens in schools matters to student learning—and "schools can and do make a difference."[37] What is more, all the correlates, and many of Marzano's factors, support principals' leadership role in student learning.

Contemporary studies have also determined that principals rank as the second most important school-based factor—after teachers and far ahead of other factors such as student body composition—in their impact on student achievement.[38] More than 30 years of research concludes that successful schools have dynamic, knowledgeable, and focused principals who affect school climate and student achievement.[39] In fact, a five-year study of school reform found that "the most distinguishing feature of improving [as compared to stable or declining] schools was [that] they were led continuously by strong principals who had a vision of improvement for their school."[40]

Another national analysis of 15 years of research on school leadership finds that an outstanding principal exercises a "measurable though indirect effect" on school effectiveness and student achievement.[41] An important 2004 study approximates that direct and indirect leadership effects account for about one-quarter of the total school effects on student learning.[42] Similarly, a 2005 meta-analysis of 30 years of research on the effects of principals' practices on student achievement finds a significant, positive correlation of .25 between effective school leadership and student achievement. This means that for an average school, having an effective leader can mean the difference between scoring at the 50th percentile or the 60th percentile on a given achievement test.[43] And, a 2012 study estimates that highly effective principals raise a typical student's achievement in their school by between two and seven months of learning in a single academic year whereas ineffective principals lower their students' achievement by that same amount.[44]

Indirect though it may be, the principal's impact on student achievement is critical and measurable. The principal controls the most important factors affecting a school's teaching and instructional quality. These include:[45]

- attracting, choosing, developing, and keeping outstanding teachers;
- working with the school community to form and express a common mission, instructional vision, and goals;
- creating a school culture firmly grounded in collaboration and high expectations for students and teachers;
- facilitating ongoing instructional improvement;
- finding fair, effective ways to improve or remove low-performing teachers;
- effectively allocating resources to support teaching and learning;
- developing organizational structures to support teaching and learning;
- producing high measured student academic outcomes aligned with state standards for all student groups.

Additionally, principals continue to have increased responsibilities for traditional areas such as security, public relations, finances, personnel, technology, and dealing with interest groups.

It is clear that principals have a profound influence and play an essential role in shaping their schools' environments and instructional climate. This, in turn, influences the quality of teaching and learning within them. Since instructional leadership includes building teachers' capacity for improved classroom instruction and school leadership —and the teacher is the school's most important factor in generating student achievement—helping teachers develop high expectations for every student's academic success is an essential step in creating a student-centered learning environment.

Teachers, students, and parents can see principals' actions as effective instructional leaders when the principals:[46]

- set high, clear, and public standards and appropriately challenging goals for every student and teacher;
- create a safe, learning-centered school culture that clearly stresses improving teaching and learning;
- develop a climate of caring, respect, and trust among teachers, students, and parents;
- make "learning for all" and problem solving the norms;
- frequently and informally observe classroom instruction and provide teachers with timely and specific feedback for their instructional improvement;

- systematically and routinely engage staff in discussions about current research, theory, and practice that helps advance teacher and student learning;
- involve teachers in the design and implementation of important decisions and policies affecting them and their students;
- provide sufficient and timely resources for effective instruction, including professional development and time and opportunities for collaborative planning and learning;
- provide an effective, continuous system for evaluating the school's progress toward its goals and communicating this with teachers, students, parents, and the community;
- publicly celebrate student academic achievement and teacher effectiveness;
- proactively, promptly, and effectively resolve student concerns to prevent problems and keep students in school and learning.

---

**REFLECTIONS AND RELEVANCE 2.7**

## Instructional Leadership

Today's principals act as instructional leaders with a focus on improving teaching and learning.

Working in groups of three, take 10 minutes to discuss the following questions. Then discuss your observations and conclusions as a class.

1. In what ways is today's principalship a process and a relationship?
2. In what ways are today's principal's roles and responsibilities similar from those of principals from past generations? In what ways are they different?
3. In your view, in what ways are principals' roles and responsibilities more complex and demanding—intellectually, socially, and emotionally—today than in earlier times?
4. What are the implications of these increased professional responsibilities and personal demands for principal preparation programs—and your own professional learning needs?

---

## LEADING A DIVERSE FACULTY AND STAFF

As leaders of their organizations, principals are responsible for leading and motivating all employees. This becomes especially challenging with an increasingly diverse teacher and staff workforce. *Workforce diversity* usually refers to workforce composition, including race, gender, disability, ethnicity, and age cohorts.[47] The U.S. is expected to become a minority-majority nation in 2043. All in all, minorities, now 37 percent of the U.S. population, are projected to comprise 57 percent of the population in 2060.[48]

Public schools' workforce reflects a range of differences. Among both males and females, in 2011–2012, about 82 percent of all public school teachers were white, 7 percent were African American, and 8 percent were Latino. Overall, public schools had a larger percentage of female teachers (76 percent) to male teachers (24 percent), especially at the primary level. On average, public school teachers had 14 years of teaching experience, and 48 percent of teachers held a master's degree.[49] For principals, creating a workplace environment that respects and appreciates employees' wide variations in family, social, and educational backgrounds, cultural styles, and work expectations creates unique leadership demands.

The existing literature on workplace diversity's impact on organizational functioning and employee motivation has mixed findings. Some studies note that diversity increases employees' creativity, productivity, and quality[50] while other investigations find workplace diversity harms organizational outcomes, increases conflict, decreases social integration, and harms decision making.[51] Nonetheless, organizational leaders can draw upon members' differences as resources for building on employees' strengths and cultivating a climate of respect, compassion, openness, and opportunities for learning—as well as generate a competitive advantage by nurturing feelings of inclusion among all employees.

At present, three popular approaches are used to manage workplace diversity. Colorblind and multicultural strategies are the most widespread.[52] The colorblind approach—"treating all people the same"—speaks to America's cultural ideals of individuality, meritocracy, equality, and the "melting pot" assimilation of varied cultures into the American "stew." Colorblind practices include ignoring cultural group identities or replacing them with an overarching identity, such as being an American or an employee of a certain company.[53] Emphasizing individual accomplishment and qualifications over other factors, the colorblind approach discourages diverse employees from fully using their distinct experiences and viewpoints within the organization. It also reduces their motivation to do their best at work. In fact, evidence suggests that minorities often interpret the colorblind strategy as exclusionary.[54] When they suspect their organization is ignoring or devaluing their racial or ethnic differences, they feel frustrated and dissatisfied. Conflict occasionally results.[55] Although the colorblind approach may appeal to white employees, it may not only alienate and demotivate minority employees; it may also allow a culture of racism to develop.[56]

In contrast, the multicultural approach to workplace diversity stresses the benefits of a diverse workforce and openly acknowledges employee differences as an asset and source of organizational strength. Multicultural strategies include networking and mentoring programs, "diversity days" that celebrate employees' backgrounds, and diversity training workshops designed to lesson bias and increase cultural awareness among non-minority employees. But although minorities are attracted to organizations that use multicultural approaches because they recognize their value,[57] multicultural initiatives often fail to produce an inclusive or accepting climate. Non-minority employees frequently dislike them; they resist, resent, or don't comply with the "diversity" practices.[58] And, instead of advancing workplace inclusion, multicultural activities may produce skepticism, stereotyping, and discriminatory culture and behaviors.[59]

Despite the best of intentions, the colorblind approach does not motivate minority employees, and the multicultural approach does not motivate non-minority employees. Nevertheless, a third strategy to managing workforce diversity—using an all-inclusive approach—does successfully motivate all employees. More a viewpoint with related behaviors than a collection of activities, all-inclusive multiculturalism (AIM) recognizes and values everyone's individual differences and contributions. AIM explicitly supports the view that the racial and ethnic groups to which people belong have important meaning for individuals, addressing minority concerns. It clearly expresses the importance that everyone plays in the workplace, addressing non-minority concerns about exclusion and disadvantage.[60] This all-inclusive perspective fits comfortably within the American values of equality and egalitarianism. In this way, all subgroups can keep their unique identities in addition to keeping the larger group identity. The empirical evidence studying this approach supports this all-inclusive strategy as having the potential to strengthen rather than harm positive intergroup relations as well as motivate individuals and organizational performance.[61]

To create truly inclusive work environments, principals must move beyond the superficial "celebrations" of diversity. Instead, they must inspire teachers and staff to integrate diversity into their work lives by forming high-quality, positive relationships with others in their schools who, on the surface, seem unlike themselves. Principals can express their expectations to employees and the larger public that every person in the school is an individual as well as part of a larger community. By knowing each other as individuals and professionals and by recognizing each other's strengths, assets, and differences, they can create a school in which all teachers and students can succeed. To further this goal, school leaders can use inclusive language—such as calling for "traditional family recipes" rather than "ethnic recipes" when compiling a PTA cookbook. Every employee should be expected to develop and refine their intercultural competence.

Additionally, to be all-inclusive, the school leadership should visibly reflect both genders, younger and older teachers, and minority and majority members. Having diversity on a school's leadership team can help the team see and understand various perspectives with which they may not be familiar or sensitive. For example, if the school leadership team has no religious diversity on the team and schedules a Parent Teacher meeting on Yom Kippur, the Jewish High Holy Day, they disenfranchise Jewish faculty from the event. Diversity helps the faculty see issues in a more holistic fashion so they can make more effective solutions. Moreover, including diversity in the decision-making process may help frame the school's mission and goals to be accepted by a greater number of its constituents.

By nurturing an environment where individual differences are not ignored (as with the colorblind approach) and where feelings of inclusion are common (unlike excluding non-minorities in the multicultural approach), principals can encourage all employees to participate in open, honest, and respectful conversations about their individual differences and common purposes. In this culture, individuals can build genuine and trusting relationships without the prejudice and stereotyping usually associated with "diversity" programs.

**REFLECTIONS AND RELEVANCE 2.8**

## Leading an Inclusive Workplace

Creating an inclusive workplace is an important leadership challenge.

Individually research and answer the following questions:

1. How have the student demographics of your school changed in the last ten years?
2. How have the teacher demographics changed in your school over the last ten years?

Now reflect on the following questions and answer them thoughtfully:

3. As a teacher, what have been your experiences and perceptions about gender differences in your school's faculty?
4. As a teacher, what have been your experiences and perceptions about racial and ethnic differences in your school's faculty?
5. How does your school address workplace diversity: colorblind, multicultural, or other?
6. How does school leadership tend to manage workplace diversity and how successful is it in creating an inclusive workplace?
7. What would you change should you be the principal? Why?

## CONCLUSION

Leadership is about working with others to accomplish a task. Understanding human nature and learning how to motivate and sustain the desired behaviors to attain a desired end are essential leadership challenges. Principals' job is to help teachers and staffs build their abilities so they can share the school's vision and meet its goals. Principals do this by effectively addressing both the tasks of educating students and the relationships that occur in schools.

Accordingly, principals and their schools benefit when leaders understand how people meet their physical, social, and intellectual needs; how they set expectancies for their efforts and accompanying rewards; how different views of human nature lead to different leadership and organizational practices; what employees find that either satisfy or dissatisfy them in the workplaces, and how to create inclusive schools with a diverse workforce. Understanding how to assess situations and select the appropriate leadership approach can also make principals more effective. And, since research confirms that excellent principals have an indirect but measurable impact on students' learning and achievement, the more principals can develop and exercise their leadership skills, the higher the return for students and teachers.

## NOTES

1 Hoad, T. F. (Ed.) (1988). *The concise Oxford dictionary of English etymology.* Oxford, United Kingdom: Oxford University Press.

2. For an interesting read on Ptahhotep see: http://www.fordham.edu/halsall/ancient/ptahhotep. asp

3. Bass, B. M. (2008). *Handbook of leadership: Theory, research, and managerial applications* (4th ed.). New York: Simon and Schuster.

4. Yukl, G. (2002). *Leadership in organizations* (5th ed.). Upper Saddle River, NJ: Prentice Hall.

5. House, R., & Aditya, R. (1997). The social science study of leadership: Quo Vadis? *Journal of Management, 23* (3), 409–473.

6. Open systems model is introduced in the Preface and discussed more fully in Chapter 4.

7. Drucker, P. (2001). *The essential Drucker: Management, the individual, and society.* Oxford: Butterworth-Heinemann Ltd.

8. Owings & Kaplan (2012), op. cit. (p. 201).

9. Franco, L. M., Bennett, S., & Kanfer, R. (2002). Health sector reform and public sector health worker motivation: A conceptual framework. *Social Science and Medicine, 54* (8), 1255–1266.

10. Maslow, A. (1954). *Motivation and personality.* New York, NY: Harper.

11. See Emerson, R. M. (1976). Social exchange theory. *Annual Review of Sociology, 2,* 335–362, for an explanation of how this theory was derived, its strengths, and its weaknesses.

12. Vroom, V. H. (1994). *Work and motivation.* San Francisco, CA: Jossey-Bass.

13. Chapter 4 will discuss how to develop a school climate and culture that rewards teachers' efforts and increases the students'—and their own—learning.

14. McGregor, D. M. (1960). *The human side of enterprise.* New York, NY: McGraw Hill.

15. Ouchi, W. G. (1981). Theory Z: How American business can meet the Japanese challenge. New York, NY: Avon.

16. Ouchi, W. G., & Jaeger, A. M. (1978). Type Z organization: Stability in the midst of mobility. *Academy of Management Review, 3* (2), 305–314.

17. Herzberg, F. (1959). *The motivation to work.* New York: John Wiley and Sons. Note: Herzberg studied accountants and engineers in the experiment.

18. Herzberg, F. (1987). One more time: How do you motivate employees? *Harvard Business Review, 65* (5), 109–120.

19. Sergiovanni, T. J. (1967). Factors which affect satisfaction and dissatisfaction of teachers. *Journal of Educational Administration, 5* (1), 66–82.

20. Hemphill, J., & Coons, A. (1950). *Leader behavior description questionnaire.* Columbus, OH: Personnel Research Board, Ohio State University.

21. Blake, R., and Mouton, J. (1964). *The managerial grid.* Houston, TX: Gulf Publishing.

22. Hersey, P., and Blanchard, K. (1969). Life cycle theory of leadership. *Training and Development Journal, 23,* 26–34. Also see Hersey, P., & Blanchard, K. (1969). *Management of organizational behavior: Utilizing human resources.* Englewood Cliffs, NJ: Prentice Hall. Hersey and Blanchard's model was based on Bill Reddin's 3-D theory. See Reddin, W. (1967, April). The 3-D management style theory. *Training and Development Journal, 21* (4), pp. 8–17.

23. McGregor, J. M. (1978). *Leadership.* New York, NY: Harper and Row.

24. Owings & Kaplan (2012), op. cit. (p. 162).

25. Seashore Louis, K., Leithwood, K., Wahlstrom, K. L., & Anderson, S. E., et al. (2010, July). *Learning from leadership: Investigating the links to improved student learning: Final report of research to the Wallace Foundation.* St. Paul, MN: Center for Applied Research and Educational Improvement, University of Minnesota and Toronto, CA: Ontario Institute for Studies in Education, University of Ontario.

26. The Wallace Foundation (2013). *The school principal as leader: Guiding schools to better teaching and learning.* New York, NY: The Wallace Foundation.

27. Bandura, A. (1986). *Social foundations of thought and action*. Englewood Cliffs, NJ: Prentice-Hall; Locke, E. A., Latham, G. P., & Eraz, M. (1988). The determinants of goal commitment. *Academy of Management Review, 13*, 23–29.
28. Yukl, G. (2009). *Leadership in organizations*. Saddle River, NJ: Prentice Hall.
29. Ibid (p. 19).
30. Hoy, W., & Miskel, C. (2013). *Educational administration: Theory, research, and practice* (p. 30). New York, NY: McGraw Hill.
31. Marzano, R. (2003). What works in schools: Translating research into action. Alexandria, VA: ASCD.
32. Leithwood, K., Seashore Lewis, K., Anderson, S., & Wahlstrom, K. (2004). *Review of research: How leadership influences student learning* (p. 5). New York, NY: Wallace Foundation.
33. For a review of the Effective Schools literature see: Lezotte, L. W., & Snyder, K. M. (2010). *What effective schools do: Re-envisioning the correlates*. Bloomington, IN: Solution Tree; Kaplan, L., & Owings, W. (2009). *Effective schools movement: History, analysis, and application*. Pocatello, ID: Intermountain Center for Education Effectiveness. The entire monograph can be found at: http://issuu.com/odujes/docs/journal_for_effective_schools/1?e=0
34. Coleman, J., Campbell, E. Q., Hobson, C. J., & McPartland, J. (1966). *Equality of educational opportunity*. Washington, DC: U.S. Government Printing Office.
35. Edmonds, R. (1982). Programs of school improvement: An overview. *Educational Leadership, 40* (3), 4–11; Lezotte, L. W., & Snyder, K. M. (2011). *What effective schools do: Re-envisioning the correlates*. Bloomington, IN: Solution Tree.
36. Brookover, W. B., & Lezotte, L. W. (1977). *Changes in school characteristics coincident with changes in student achievement*. East Lansing, MI: Michigan State University, College of Urban Development.
37. Good, T. L., & Brophy, J. E. (1986). School effects. In M. C. Wittrock (Ed.), *Handbook of research on teaching* (3rd ed.) (pp. 570–602). New York, NY: McMillan.
38. Leithwood, K., Louis, K. S., Anderson, S., & Wahlstrom, K. (2004). *How leadership influences student learning*. New York, NY: Wallace Foundation. Retrieved from: http://www.wallacefoundation.org/knowledge-center/school-leadership/key-research/Documents/How-Leadership-Influences-Student-Learning.pdf
39. See, for example, Hallinger, P., & Heck, R. (2000, October). Exploring the principal's contribution to school effectiveness, 1980–1995. In *Leadership for student learning: Reinventing school leadership for the 21st century*. Washington, DC: The Institute for Educational Leadership; Heck, R. H., Larsen, T. J., & Marcoulides, G. A. (1990). Instructional leadership and school achievement: Validation of a casual model. *Educational Administration Quarterly, 26* (2), 94–125; Leithwood et al. (2004), op. cit.; Marzano, R. J., Waters, T., & McNulty, B. A. (2005). *School leadership that works. From research to results*. Alexandria, VA: Association for Supervision and Curriculum Development; Sammons, P., Hillman, J., & Mortimore, P. (1995). *Key characteristics of effective schools: A review of school effectiveness research*. London: OFSTED.
40. Schnur, J. (2002, June 18). An outstanding principal in every school: Using the new Title II to promote effective leadership (p. 2). Washington, DC: National Council on Teacher Quality.
41. Hallinger, P., & Heck, R. (2000, October), op. cit.
42. Leithwood et al. (2004), op. cit.
43. Marzano, R. J., Waters, T., & McNulty, B.A. (2005), op. cit.
44. Branch, G. F., Hanushek, E. A., & Rivkin, S. G. (2013, Winter). School leaders matter. *EducationNext, 13* (1), 62–69. Retrieved from: http://educationnext.org/school-leaders-matter/
45. Kaplan, L. S., & Owings, W. A. (2015). *Educational foundations* (2nd ed.). Stamford, CT: Cengage.

46. Kaplan & Owings (2015), op. cit. (pp. 504–505).
47. Jehn, K. A., Northcraft, G. B., & Neale, M. A. (1999). Why differences make a difference: A field study of diversity, conflict, and performance in workgroups. *Administrative Science Quarterly, 44* (4), 741–763.
48. United States Census Bureau (2012, December 12). U.S. Census Bureau projections show a slower growing, older, more diverse nation a half century from now. Washington, DC: United States Census Bureau. Retrieved from: https://www.census.gov/newsroom/releases/archives/population/cb12–243.html
49. Goldring, R., Gray, L., Bitterman, A., & Broghman, S. (2013, August). *Characteristic of public and private elementary and secondary school teachers in the United States. Results from the 2011–12 schools and staffing survey. First look.* (NCES 2013–314), (p. 3). Washington, DC: National Center for Education Statistics, U.S. Department of Education. Retrieved from: http://nces.ed.gov/pubs2013/2013314.pdf
50. See, for example, Earley, P. C., & Mosakowski, E.(2000). Creating hybrid team cultures: An empirical test of transnational team functioning. *Academy of Management Journal, 43* (1), 26–49; Ely, R. J., & Thomas, D. A. (2001). Cultural diversity at work: The effects of diversity perspectives on work group processes and outcomes. *Administrative Science Quarterly, 46* (2), 229–273; Polzer, J. T., Milton, L. P., & Swann, W. B, Jr. (2002). Capitalizing on diversity: Interpersonal congruence in small work groups. *Administrative Science Quarterly, 47* (2), 296–324; Swann, W. B., Jr., Kwan, V.S.Y., Polzer, J. T., & Milton, L. P. (2003). Fostering group identification and creativity in diverse groups: The role of individuation and self-verification. *Personality and Social Psychology Bulletin, 29* (11), 1396–1406.
51. See, for example, Chatman, J. A., Polzer, J. T., Barsade, S. G., & Neale, M. A. (2006). Being different yet feeling similar: The influence of demographic composition of organizational culture on work processes and outcomes. *Administrative Science Quarterly, 43* (4), 749–780; Jehn et al. (1999), op. cit.; Morrison, E. W., & Milliken, R. J. (2000). Organizational silence: A barrier to change and development in a pluralistic world. *Academy of Management Review, 25* (4), 706–725; Westphal, J. D., & Milton, L. P. (2000). How experience and network ties affect the influence of demographic minorities on corporate boards. *Administrative Science Quarterly, 45* (2), 366–398.
52. Owings & Kaplan (2012), op. cit., pp. 230–232.
53. Markus, H. R., Steele, C. M., & Steele, D. M. (2000). Colorblindness as a barrier to inclusion: Assimilation and non-immigrant minorities. *Daedalus, 129,* 233–259; Plaut, V. C. (2002). Cultural models of diversity: The psychology of difference and inclusion. In R. Shweder, M. Minow, & H. R. Markus (Eds.), *Engaging cultural differences: The multicultural challenge in a liberal democracy* (pp. 365–395). New York: Russell Sage.
54. Markus et al. (2000), op. cit.
55. Chrobot-Mason, D., & Thomas, K. M. (2002). Minority employees in majority organizations: The intersection of individual and organizational racial identity in the workplace. *Human Resource Development Review, 1* (3), 323–344; Markus et al. (2000), op. cit.
56. Bonilla-Silva, E. (2003). *Racism without racists: Color-blind racism and the persistence of racial inequality in the United States.* Lanham, MD: Rowman & Littlefield.
57. Plaut, V. C., & Markus, H. R. (2007). *Basically we're all the same? Models of diversity and the dilemma of difference.* Unpublished manuscript, University of Georgia; Verkuyten, M. (2005). Ethnic group identification and group evaluation among minority and majority groups: Testing the multiculturalism hypothesis. *Journal of Personality and Social Psychology, 88* (1), 121–138.
58. Brief, A. P., Umphress, E. E., Dietz, J., Burrows, J. W., Butz, R. M., & Scholten, L. (2005). Community matters: Realistic group conflict theory and the impact of diversity. *Academy of Management Journal, 48* (5), 830–844; Kalev, A., Dobbin, F., & Kelly, E. (2006). Best practices or best guesses? Assessing the efficacy of corporate affirmative action and diversity

policies. *American Sociological Review, 71* (4), 589–617; Mannix, E. A., & Neale, M. A. (2006). What differences make a difference? The promise and reality of diverse teams in organizations. *Psychological Science in the Public Interest, 6* (2), 32–55; Thomas, K. M. (2008). *Diversity resistance in organizations: Manifestations and solutions.* Mahway, NJ: Lawrence Erlbaum.

59. Linnehan, F., & Konrad, A. M. (1999). Diluting diversity: Implications for intergroup in organizations. *Journal of Management Inquiry, 8* (4), 399–413; Thomas, K. M., & Plaut, V. C. (2008). The many faces of diversity in the workplace. In K. M. Thomas (Ed.), *Diversity resistance in organizations: Manifestations and solutions* (pp. 1–22). Mahwah, NJ: Lawrence Erlbaum.

60. Stevens, F. G., Plaut, V. C., & Sanchez-Burks, J. (2008). Unlocking the benefits of diversity: All-inclusive multiculturalism and positive organizational change. *Journal of Applied Behavioral Science, 44* (1), 116–133.

61. Plaut, V. C., Sanchez-Burks, J., Buiffardi, L., & Stevens, F. G. (2007). What about me? Understanding non-minority aversion to diversity initiatives in the workplace. Unpublished manuscript, University of Georgia; Stevens et al. (2008), op. cit.; Markus et al. (2000), op. cit.

# CHAPTER 3

# Developing Your Philosophy of Education

If you don't know where you are going, any
road will take you there.

—Lewis Carroll

## LEARNING OBJECTIVES

3.1 Define *philosophy* and explain the benefits to a principal of having a philosophy of education.

3.2 Discuss how John Dewey's ideas about education and democracy and effective teaching contribute to developing a philosophy of education.

3.3 Describe how Elliot Eisner's ideas about education fully developing children's minds and preparing them to live in a complex world by engaging them in humanities, math, sciences, and the arts contribute to developing a philosophy of education.

3.4 Explain how Paulo Freire's ideas about education as a basic human right and learning as an act of culture and human freedom contribute to developing a philosophy of education.

3.5 Compare and contrast Dewey, Eisner, and Freire on their goals for education, their ideas on the process of education, and how they view the effective teacher's role.

3.6 Identify components of UCEA and ISLLC Standards that can help future principals develop their philosophy of educational leadership.

3.7 Define *social justice* and explain its relevance for contemporary school leadership.

3.8 Analyze John Rawls' "justice as fairness" concept as an effective way for school leaders to understand social justice issues in their own schools.

3.9 Discuss several aspects of education in which social justice issues may become a principal's concern.

**2015 ISLLC STANDARDS: 1, 2, 3, 4, 5, 6, 7, 8, 9, 10, 11**

## INTRODUCTION

For a principal, nothing is more important than deciding where to lead a school and to what purposes. Deciding which school outcomes are most important rests on values and viewpoints as well as facts. Individuals' and communities' beliefs about education— their philosophies of education—shape how they see the world and how they think we should prepare our children—intellectually, civically, socially, and economically—for the world they will live in as adults, neighbors, and citizens. Different philosophies and visions for education lead in different directions.

This chapter describes what a *philosophy of education* entails and explains how that differs from a *philosophy of leadership*. Each philosophy presented includes a brief history of its development in education with insights from notable individuals such as John Dewey, Elliott Eisner, and Paulo Freire. All three are leading thinkers in the field of education for democracy. All three see education as a means to develop the human capacity for a meaningful life that can flexibly adapt to—and occasionally improve—their society. The chapter also examines how an educational philosophy addresses social justice, equality, and equity issues. Through this exploration, readers can begin to construct and articulate their personal philosophies of education and leadership.

## A PHILOSOPHY OF EDUCATION

As illustrated in Chapter 2, motives direct individuals to act in certain ways. When we are hungry, we look for something to eat. Deciding what to eat is a more complex matter—a Twinkie or yogurt, junk food or healthy food? Decisions that guide our behaviors may reflect our momentary whims or our enduring principles.

Everyone has standards even if they are not well informed, carefully thought out, or clearly articulated. Some individuals may not be aware of the important relationships between personal health and what they eat. Through modeling and training, parents and others in children's lives tend to shape their eating habits. Learning that cholesterol, triglycerides, and blood sugar levels are actual biological conditions that, when out of balance can jeopardize one's health and life (for example, lead to heart disease and diabetes), influences a person's viewpoint about nutrition and health. It also changes what people consider and do when they open the refrigerator door at 2 a.m., hunting for a snack.

The move from having personal preferences or opinions about eating to having a philosophy of nutrition is the shift from subjective impulse to information-based decision. *Philosophy* is an orderly attempt to make sense of our experiences and shape our behaviors. When principals have a philosophy of education, it helps them make sense of their experiences, helps them prioritize what receives their time and attention, and helps them plan and act purposefully to accomplish their desired outcomes.

## PHILOSOPHY DEFINED

What is *philosophy*? The word literally means the love of wisdom—from the Greek *philos*, meaning love, and *sophy*, meaning wisdom. A *philosophy* is a systematic attempt to make sense out of our individual and collective human experience.[1] In everyday usage, philosophy refers to the general beliefs, concepts, and attitudes that an individual or group possesses. It is an inquiry into the nature of things based on logical reasoning rather than empirical methods. More than an opinion, philosophy requires intellectual and rational questioning, a systematic critical thinking without reference to scientific experiments or religious faith. Having a philosophy of critically analyzed viewpoints gives individuals a frame of reference by which they can make sense of their life experiences and plan for their future. Philosophy directs one's beliefs and actions based on their reasoning about reality.[2]

A *philosophy of education* attempts to interpret, find meaning, and direct the work of education by answering questions such as:[3]

- What are the goals of education?
- What is school?
- What is an educated person?
- What curricula are worth learning?
- What is the teacher's role?
- What is the student's role?
- What is the role of research on educational practice?

Answers to these questions depend on one's experiences, beliefs, and perspectives. In America's pluralistic society, different individuals' and groups' ideas about how schools should educate children may vary widely. Influences including the historical era, the geographic location, the local and larger cultures, the ease of communication and travel between these cultures and others, and the specific persons involved all affect the leading educational philosophies. Of course, educational philosophies change over time as events and persons appear and alter thinking and living.

Socrates' dictum, "know thyself" is good advice. A philosophy of education asserts your beliefs about education, the principles that will guide your professional decisions and actions. When educational leaders have a well-developed and articulated philosophy of education and educational leadership, they have a consistent and well-reasoned basis of action that faculty, staff, and community will see and understand. Otherwise, your behaviors will appear as inconsistent and arbitrary, confusing your communities about where you want to take the school and how you plan to get there. When educational leaders know themselves—and what they believe about education and leadership—they can act in a manner consistent with those beliefs.

Jayson Richardson, an educational leadership professor at the University of Kentucky, states the case for having a reasoned philosophy of education.[4] He writes:

I can think of no career where having a well-developed personal philosophy is more important than in education. Particularly with the increased politicization of education, the ability to understand why you believe what you do and how it fits within a larger societal context is essential. This is best seen in the current ed[ucation] reform debates where the discussions typically lack any depth of understanding and fall back to political soundbites [sic].

Educators should have a well-reasoned point of view as to why they are engaged in the profession of teaching. Furthermore, even the process of learning is based to a certain extent in philosophy (What is the nature of knowledge? How is knowledge elicited? What is the role of the learned within society?) The practical realities of the classroom often keep us from reflecting on such topics, though. It's also easy to fool ourselves into believing that whatever I once believed is necessarily true still. Things can change without our realization. The process of reflection and continual analysis allows us to place our current thinking in context. I may have originally become a teacher because I loved the language that I taught and thought. Now I view that as a small component to my philosophy and instead emphasize the social justice aspect of education.

## REFLECTIONS AND RELEVANCE 3.1

## Defining a Philosophy of Education

Working in four separate groups as listed below, each group will take 10 minutes to address one of the following issues raised in Jayson Richardson's comments:

*Group 1*: What does Richardson mean by "the increased polarization of education"? How do charter schools, teacher performance ("merit") pay, and Common Core State Standards, for example, reflect this politicization? Can you think of other politicized education issues?

*Group 2*: What are some of the "political sound bites" you have heard politicians use? Why are they not adequate to describe the issues? Provide examples. How has education become politicized—and how is this either helpful or harmful to educators and children?

*Group 3*: What do you think Richardson means by: "The practical realities of the classroom often keep us from reflecting on such topics . . ."? Give an example of a time when you were so focused on the "immediate" that you did not make time to consider or act on the "important."

*Group 4*: Can our ideas about what we once believed to be true change? Give an example from your own experience as a teacher of how events and reflection have altered the way you view or understand something.

After all four groups have finished, each group will report their findings to the rest of the class. Discuss how developing a philosophy of education may help teachers and principals deal with the issues that Richardson raises.

Educational leaders must consider their values and philosophy of education and leadership if they are to make appropriate, reliable decisions in the best interest of all students. Just as deciding whether to eat a Twinkie or yogurt reflects one's values and nutritional habits, thoughtful educational leaders make decisions from a professionally informed and well-articulated philosophy. Absent that, decisions about school improvement are likely to be ad hoc, inconsistent, occasionally contradictory, easily swayed by others' opinions, and not likely to accomplish the student outcomes sought.

## THREE PERSPECTIVES ON A PHILOSOPHY OF EDUCATION

As future principals develop an informed and well-articulated philosophy of education, they will benefit from considering several insightful educators whose thinking advanced our field. While educational philosophy boasts many great thinkers, and educational leaders' readings and experiences during their career will prompt them to continuously rethink their views on education, examining the ideas of John Dewey, Elliott Eisner, and Paulo Freire is a good place to begin. Each has something to say that can deepen our understanding of what we believe about the purposes, processes, and outcomes of education. Admittedly, it is challenging to do justice to these "big thinkers" in approximately four paragraphs apiece, but we focus on their fundamental contributions to educational theory and encourage interested readers to pursue them more deeply in other sources.

### John Dewey

John Dewey (1859–1952), a philosopher and educator, asks us to consider education's civic role in sustaining a diverse and democratic society and the need to teach effectively in ways that children can learn. A Columbia University professor of philosophy from 1905 to 1952, Dewey influenced education during turbulent and changing times when varied parts of society clamored for education reform. Labor unions and businesses wanted schools to prepare children for factory work in a rapidly industrializing economy. Social workers advocated for public schools to provide America's large numbers of recently arrived immigrant children with basic instruction in hygiene, childcare, and speaking English. Rural communities desired schools to train children to appreciate farming, remain in their home communities, and slow the migration to cities for jobs. Social and political elites intended schools to teach children to develop a shared new heritage and become law-abiding, patriotic Americans. By default, American public schools inherited expanded educational and socializing roles from other social institutions; by the mid-to-late nineteenth century, the world had already become too large and complex for the family, church, workshop, and community to continue doing these roles.[5]

Dewey saw such sweeping social and economic changes as potential threats to our democratic form of government. He knew that a representative democracy, such as we have in the United States, is not inevitably inherited; it must be consciously and continuously constructed and reconstructed. He concluded, "Democracy must be born anew in every generation and education is its midwife."[6] Moreover, as Dewey saw it, "A democracy is more than a form of government: it is primarily a mode of associated living, of conjoint communicated experience."[7] Schools' mission, therefore, was to advance democratic principles. Teachers would help children learn the knowledge, habits of mind, and behaviors that would allow them to use their intellects well, interact respectfully with others who may be unlike themselves, and live responsibly in a democratic society. Accordingly, Dewey pressed for common schools that would bring children of all classes, religious beliefs, and ethnic backgrounds together. Schools would form democratic communities where students learned to understand and respect their individual differences and similarities, and where vocational and academic studies could coexist as valued and egalitarian areas of study.

In addition, Dewey believed that effective teachers facilitate students' learning. He saw each student as unique—with cognitive, social, emotional, and physical differences. As a result, each student responds differently to the learning situation. Accordingly, effective teachers should address three factors. First, teachers must know each child—his or her interests, problems, and developmental levels. Next, teachers needed to present academic content and skills to children in relevant ways that make sense to and have personal meaning for the students. Finally, the classrooms' practices should reflect democratic values including tolerance, cooperation, critical awareness, and political consciousness.[8]

For Dewey, education's goals should enable all children to become valued, equal, reasoning, self-directed, and responsible citizens. Through education, children could become more mature, knowledgeable, and reliable persons who could live life fully. They could continually add to the meaning of their experience, use personal initiative and adaptability to control (or influence) their surroundings rather than passively adjust to them, and continue learning throughout their lives.[9]

## Elliott Eisner

Today, with our insistent focus on organizing teaching and learning around increasing students' test scores, Elliott Eisner (1933–2014), the late Stanford University professor of art and education, encourages us to consider education more broadly: as an experience to help students to live personally satisfying and socially productive lives by fully developing their minds. For Eisner, education's goal is not to enable children to do well in school; it is to enable children to do well in life.[10]

Eisner believes that "Mind is a form of cultural achievement."[11] Humans are born with *brains*, but their minds are *made*.[12] The culture into which they are born shapes how they think. For children, school is the primary culture for their cognitive development. Schools' decisions about its priorities, therefore, are basic choices about the types of minds our children will have the opportunities to develop. Both the curriculum schools teach and the time allotted for different subjects lets children know what adults believe is important for them to know; and these factors influence the kinds of mental skills a child will develop. And, although reading and math are essential skills, they are not all an educated person needs to know, especially in the 21st Century.

For Eisner, a valuable education employs a rigorous curriculum that incorporates multiple ways of thinking about and knowing the world—including humanities, math, sciences, and the arts. These disciplines develop students' thought processes, including the rational (logical, sequential, inductive, and deductive reasoning) and the affective (how this experience affects one's senses, emotions, and intuition), the planned and the unexpected. In contrast to the traditional core curriculum of language, math, science, and social studies, the arts (instrumental music, visual arts, drama, and dance) celebrate imagination, a range of perspectives, and the importance of personal expression and interpretation. Giving students assorted cognitive and affective learning experiences allows them to mature their perceptions and skills in ways that will let them ably adapt to complex and changing conditions outside the school. To nurture their students' full mental development, insightful educators need to understand that not all problems have one correct answer. Unlike school, solutions to real-world problems take many forms. Real problems, Eisner reminds us, are more like those in the arts. Clearly, both cognitive and affective ways of knowing are necessary because life is rarely ever like a multiple-choice test.[13]

For Eisner, effective teachers make schools *intellectual* rather than merely *academic* places. They create learning experiences for students that increase their opportunities to experience the world fully and meaningfully. Lastly, Eisner states, "What's at stake is not only the quality of life our children might enjoy but also the quality of the culture they will inhabit."[14] He asks us to ponder a broader question—how do educators give children the types of learning experiences that will make them more knowing, aware, competent individuals who can make their way in a very complex, rapidly changing world?

## Paulo Freire

Paulo Freire (1921–1997), an internationally respected Brazilian educator and philosopher, persuades us to think about education as a basic human right, and learning as an act of culture and human freedom. As a result of the world economic crisis during the Great Depression, young Freire lived among poor rural families and laborers; he knew hunger and poverty. He saw first-hand the relationship between socioeconomic class and knowledge. Although trained as a lawyer, Freire married an elementary school teacher and taught Portuguese in secondary schools. He gained recognition in Brazil for his work in remediating massive adult illiteracy, educating those no longer in school so they could meet the literacy requirements and become eligible to vote in presidential elections. Following a military coup in 1964, Freire was imprisoned briefly for treason and later exiled.

Freire believed that a society's prevailing social, economic, and political elite influence how and what we teach as a means to perpetuate the status quo. This elite want poor and minority students to be passive, uninquiring, and accepting of an unchanging reality that keeps the privileged on top and the others—the "oppressed"— far below. In contrast, a good education teaches children (especially poor and working-class children) how to question, reason, and challenge those views and practices that reinforce unfairness and injustice in their society. Through knowledge, questioning, and action gained through education, ordinary people can overcome the limitations that those in their society with more power and influence have placed upon them. In his view, knowledge transformed into action can help people change the world.[15]

In his culture-shaking book, *Pedagogy of the Oppressed* (1968, 2007),[16] Freire presents a theory of education in the context of a revolutionary struggle.[17] Highly conscious of the disparate levels of power and influence in his own society (and others), he critiques schooling as implementing the "Banking Theory" of education. In this view, the society sees knowledge as a "gift" that it gives, through well-informed teachers, to "ignorant" students. These students' minds are like empty containers that teachers "fill" with information—like depositing money into a bank account. In turn, students compliantly and mechanically record, memorize, and recite back the information without truly understanding what it means. They acknowledge their ignorance and learn to accept their wider society as it is. But, Freire argues, unless students learn to become active participants in their learning, persistently questioning their teachers about the nature of their historical and social situation—"to read their world" as well as their word[18]—they cannot truly know anything, be creative, or act competently in the outside world in ways that transform it to be more fair.

Rejecting the banking notion, Freire advances a concept of education as the practice of freedom. To him, people are conscious beings who are interested in the problems of humans and their relations with the world. He prefers "problem-posing" education in which teachers develop students as critical thinkers to uncover reality, to question why conditions are as they are, and how they can change their world for the better. To do this, teachers must first go into the students' (be they children or adults) communities, understand the social realities under which they live, ask questions, and amass lists of words and themes that students use in their daily lives. Teachers then use these relevant words and ideas to lead class discussions, engaging students in genuine dialog mediated by the real world. This process develops students' cognitive awareness of the society around them—their critical consciousness—and allows them to act intentionally to make their world a better place. Through their dialog process, both teachers and students teach each other and grow.

Problem-posing theory and practice undermine the fatalism that poor and minority individuals often have about succeeding in their society. They replace resignation with a deep critical understanding of what is happening to them, how and why it is happening, and how to change the situation for the better. Problem-posing education helps people look ahead and move forward, transforming them instead of teaching them to accept their society as it is. As Freire concludes, "In sum, banking theory and practice, as immobilizing and fixating forces, fails to acknowledge men and women as historical beings; problem-posing theory and practice take the people's historicity as their starting point. Problem-posing education affirms men and women as being in the process of becoming—as unfinished, uncompleted beings in and with a likewise unfinished reality."[19]

Dewey, Eisner, and Freire bring us several ideas about education's goals, its process, and the role of effective teachers, which underpin a philosophy of education. Table 3.1 compares them on these three dimensions.

**TABLE 3.1** Comparing Three Educators' Philosophies

| Goals of Education | Process of Education | Role of Effective Teachers |
|---|---|---|
| **John Dewey** | | |
| Schools' mission is to advance democratic principles. Schools' mission is also to enable all children to learn the knowledge, skills, habits of mind, and behaviors that allow them to use their intellects well; to interact respectfully with others; and become valued, equal, reasoning, and responsible citizens who can live their lives in a satisfying and productive way in a democratic republic. | Schools teach democracy by practicing the democratic values of appreciation and respect for individual differences and similarities, cooperation, and critical and political awareness. Learning is life-long as individuals adapt to—and influence—their environments. | Teachers should know and respect each child as a unique learner. Effective teaching matters. Teachers should know each child's interests, problems, and developmental levels, and present academic content in a way that makes sense and has personal meaning to each child. |
| **Elliott Eisner** | | |
| Schools' mission is to help students develop their minds and learn the knowledge and skills necessary to live personally satisfying and socially productive lives. By fully developing their minds, young people will be able to live aware, flexibly, and competently in a rapidly changing world. The goal of education is to help students do well in life! | Schools' curriculum and time allotted for different subjects influences the types of minds and mental skills children develop. Children need the humanities, math, sciences, and the arts to fully develop their intellects, cognitively and affectively so students can become competent to solve problems and live productively in the "real world." | Effective teachers make schools intellectual—not merely academic—places. They give students varied learning experiences in which students can expand their knowledge, perceptions, imaginations, and skills, ready to solve problems in many forms. |
| **Paulo Freire** | | |
| Education is a basic human right. Learning is the practice of freedom and culture. Schools' mission is to free people from tyranny and injustice by helping them develop their minds, to be fully informed about their world, and to think critically about the conditions in which they live so they can act thoughtfully to improve them. | Society's dominant elites decide what and how schools teach. Using the "banking concept" of instruction, teachers gain students' passive consent to accept the social, political, and economic structures that benefit the "haves" and undermine opportunities for the "have nots." Teachers should challenge this approach. | Teachers should get to know their students and their communities well, learn the vocabulary and themes that affect the children's daily lives, and help students learn how to critically question events and conditions around them and take constructive actions to improve them. |

Source: Kaplan, L. S. & Owings, W. A. (2014).

Dewey, Eisner, and Freire agree on three key issues that play a role in developing an educational philosophy. First, they all believe that societies educate their children for the nation they want. Education reflects the culture of the society surrounding it—and, in turn, the larger society reflects its education. Those with power and influence in the society decide what to teach children and how to teach it. By fully educating a society's children, education can influence its surrounding culture in ways that can either reinforce society as it is or agitate for it to change. Democratic nations that value individuals from diverse backgrounds need well-educated, knowledgeable, reasoning individuals who act responsibly if they are to continue living in a free society. And, in reverse, more oligarchic societies (where power rests with a small number of prominent people) try to limit (other people's) children's capacities to think and challenge their subordinate place in the social order. Accordingly, curricula for a free society should include subjects that matter and make sense to students and that develop their rational and affective capacities in ways that permit them to be competent, responsible, and flexible persons in a complex, rapidly changing world. Democratic societies depend on having a critical thinking, educated citizenry for their survival, while undemocratic societies need a critical thinking, educated citizenry if they are to become more equitable and just.

Second, Dewey, Eisner, and Freire believe that education's goals are civic, economic, and personal. A good education can lead to civic responsibility, personal fulfillment, and a more fair culture. As children develop their knowledge, skills, habits of mind, and behaviors, they can develop a fuller awareness of their environments—economic, social, political, and aesthetic. They can adapt when necessary and, in turn, challenge—and change—the larger society when necessary.

Third, they all agree that effective teaching matters. Children are not empty vessels into which teachers pour knowledge. Teachers need to instruct students in ways that help them fully develop their intellectual and affective capacities: to become thinking, reasoning individuals, aware of their society, and able to act purposefully and wisely to improve their lives and their world. To do this, teachers need to deeply understand their students as individuals and the communities from which they come and use this knowledge to help prompt student engagement and learning. Likewise, teachers should encourage students' questioning of what they are learning inside and outside the classroom. Through these endeavors, teachers make schools into intellectual—not merely academic—places.

**REFLECTIONS AND RELEVANCE 3.2**

## Three Perspectives on Philosophy of Education

A "wordle" is a tool for generating a "word cloud" from written text by giving greater prominence to words that appear more frequently in the text. Words can be used to communicate meaning at the same time as it creates an image that relates to the topic at hand. You can Google "wordle" for examples.

Working in groups of three or four, each group will create a "Wordle" for Dewey, Eisner, or Freire. Be sure that each philosopher is the focus of at least one group. Working as a group, identify at least 10 words that can represent that thinker's views on education, agree on the most important word that represents his thinking, and use the other words in various sizes, shapes, and colors to complete the wordle. After all groups have completed their wordle, the group members will explain their product to the rest of the class and briefly summarize that thinker's contribution to a philosophy of education. Then, as a class, discuss the following:

1. Dewey believed that education had a duty to promote democracy. Can schools still afford to do this with the current emphasis on test results? Explain why or why not.
2. Eisner believed that the arts are important to understanding complexities that will make students successful in life in a global economy. What, in your experience, would lead you to accept or reject this argument? Provide specific examples.
3. Freire believed that education tended to promote the status quo in order to maintain a country's power structure. In what specific instances do you see that happening—or the opposite happening—in our public education system?
4. With which points do you agree or disagree with Dewey, Eisner, or Friere? List each and explain why you agree or disagree.

## A PHILOSOPHY OF EDUCATIONAL LEADERSHIP

Principals need to have not only a well-developed philosophy of education, but also a philosophy of educational leadership—describing the key factors of content and process they will use to guide how they will lead schools.

Two models offer guidance for developing a philosophy of educational leadership. One comes from the University Council for Educational Administration (UCEA), a consortium of higher education institutions committed to advancing the preparation and practice of educational leaders to the benefit of schools and children. UCEA posts a sample statement of leadership philosophy on its website.[20] It contains five belief statements and an explanation for each. Educational leadership professors are their primary audience. The other model, from the Council for Chief State School Officers, is the Educational Leadership Policy Standards: ISLLC 2015 (Interstate School Leaders Licensure Consortium).[21] ISLLC Standards provide direction on how school leaders can ensure academic press and a productive school culture—the key essentials of a successful school—along with other necessary components. Both sets of belief statements offer examples for developing a philosophy of educational leadership.

Briefly, the UCEA standards affirm:

1.  *Educational leadership is collaborative.* Although an individual can be the catalyst in transforming an organization, no one individual can do it all. They must collaboratively develop and implement a shared vision—and share leadership—with other colleagues, parents, and community members. Educational leaders must have strong "people skills," be able to promote the work of meaningful change, and engage with others to create working and learning environments that spur individual motivation and success.

2.  *Educational leadership focuses on achieving effective educational and social outcomes for children.* Educational leaders should develop an instructional program that focuses on the individual children's learning and meeting their psychological, social, and emotional needs. Likewise, leaders develop assessment and accountability systems to monitor and evaluate student progress and revise plans. As learning communities, schools must foster high expectations for all students along with an ethic of care that recognizes that students differ and values these differences. The educational leader should be able to create effective curricula and learning environments and successfully include families and communities in their children's education.

3.  *Educational leadership should be based on principles of inclusion and facilitation.* Schooling's primary emphasis should be to facilitate students to reach their full potential. Educational leaders' professional, ethical, and legal duty obliges them to be able to facilitate the inclusion and success of all students, without regard to sex, color, social class, disability, sexual orientation, national origin, or other factor.

4.  *Educational leaders respond to changing expectations while also supporting schools' many daily successes.* Educational leaders understand and manage the subtle balance between responding to legitimate political and community expectations and advocating for current successful practices. Educational leaders should understand the political, economic, and cultural contexts surrounding education and be proficient communicators with—as well as educators of—their legislators and communities.

5.  *Educational leadership is an art informed by research and practice.* Effective educational leadership is both an art and a science. The science of school leadership rests in the growing research-generated knowledge base that provides the foundation from which leaders' creativity can emerge. All educational leaders can benefit from familiarity to current theories, research findings, practices, and models of effective leadership and successfully integrate relevant information into their leadership practices.

Similarly, the ISLLC Standards look at the work of people in formal leadership positions from the building and district levels, defining principles and leadership functions to enact them. They apply at every leadership phase, from preparation for a job, to professional learning as leaders, to evaluation throughout their leadership careers. In brief, the ISLLC Standards include:

1.  *Vision and mission.* An educational leader promotes the success and wellbeing of every student by ensuring the development, articulation, implementation, and stewardship of a child-centered vision of quality schooling that is shared by all members of the school community. (Key leadership functions: collaboratively

develops, implements, promotes, and assesses a shared vision and mission for quality teaching and learning; revises plans; acts consistently within the school's and district's vision, mission, and values.)

2. *Instructional capacity.* An educational leader promotes the success and wellbeing of every student by enhancing instructional capacity. (Key leadership functions: recruits, hires, and develops effective teachers and professional staff; employs research-anchored and valid systems of performance management; buffers learning and teaching from disruption; provides emotional support to teachers and staff.)

3. *Instruction.* An educational leader promotes the success and wellbeing of every student by promoting instruction that maximizes student learning. (Key leadership functions: maintains culture of high expectations; focuses on authentic, relevant instruction based on best understandings of child development; uses effective, culturally congruent pedagogy that respects students as individuals; provides teachers with on-going, salient, actionable feedback.)

4. *Curriculum and assessment.* An educational leader promotes the success and wellbeing of every student by promoting robust and meaningful curricula and assessment programs. (Key leadership functions: ensures rigorous, authentic, and culturally relevant curricula and assessments; maximizes opportunities to learn and enjoy learning; and measurement congruent with understandings of children's development and standards of measurement.)

5. *Community of care for students.* An educational leader promotes the success and wellbeing of every student by promoting the development of an inclusive school climate characterized by supportive relationships and a personalized culture of care. (Key leadership functions: ensures formation of culture defined by trust; knowing, valuing and respecting each student; a safe, secure, emotionally protective, healthy, and academically and socially supportive environment.)

6. *Professional culture for teachers and other professional staff.* An educational leader promotes the success and wellbeing of every student by promoting professionally normed communities for teachers and other professional staff. (Key leadership functions: develops productive trusting relationships, commitment to shared goals and shared ownership; collaborative leadership skills, and a climate of collective efficacy and shared accountability.)

7. *Communities of engagement for families.* An educational leader promotes the success and wellbeing of every student by promoting communities of engagement for families and other stakeholders. (Key leadership functions: promotes understanding, appreciation, and use of the community's diverse cultural, social, and intellectual resources; nurtures approachability, positive relations, and open communications with families and caregivers; builds and sustains productive relationships with community partners; understands community needs, priorities and resources and advocates for them.)

8. *Operations and management.* An educational leader promotes the success and wellbeing of every student by ensuring effective and efficient management of the school or district to promote student social and academic learning. (Key leadership functions: develops and uses strong interpersonal skills; manages student behavior with focus on learning; crafts and connects management operations, policies, and

resources to the school's vision and values; monitors and evaluates all aspects of school operations for effect and impact; implements data systems that provide actionable information to improve operations; acts as steward of public funds; develops and manages relationships with the district office and/or school board.)

9.  *Ethical principles and professional norms.* An educational leader promotes the success and wellbeing of every student by adhering to ethical principles and professional norms. (Key leadership functions: creates culture that places children at education's heart; acts in open, transparent, and self-aware manner; attends to own learning; works to create productive relationships with students, staff, parents, and community members; acts as school's moral compass; safeguards values of democracy, equity, justice, community, and diversity.)

10. *Equity and cultural responsiveness.* An educational leader promotes the success and wellbeing of every student by ensuring the development of an equitable and culturally responsive school. (Key leadership functions: ensures equity of access to social capital and institutional support; fosters schools as affirming, inclusive places; advocates for children, families, and caregivers; attacks issues of student marginalization and deficit-based schooling; promotes understanding, appreciation, and use of diverse cultural, ecological, social, political, and intellectual resources.)

11. *Continuous school improvement.* An educational leader promotes the success and wellbeing of every student by ensuring the development of a culture of continuous school improvement. (Key leadership functions: assesses, analyzes, and anticipates emerging trends to shape school or district decision making; initiates and manages system-wide change, despite ambiguity and competing demands and interests, and enables others to engage with it productively; keeps a systems perspective and promotes coherence across all school and district dimensions; promotes a culture of data-based inquiry, continuous learning, and mutual accountability.)

Developing a philosophy of educational leadership can provide busy principals with theoretical and practical direction about how to understand and enact their responsibilities. Educational leadership is an applied science derived from research in human learning, school leadership, and student achievement. Practicing school leadership involves making many complex judgments, often rapidly. At the same time, principals must be open to new evidence and be able to respond flexibly and appropriately to the unexpected, relying on tacit knowledge from prior experience. Being a "born leader" may give one a heightened intuition. But instinct does not necessarily give one the articulate and relevant knowledge that can guide one's actions or be expressed to others in ways that motivate their efforts and point them towards effective solutions. Coming to the principalship with a strong and growing professional knowledge base, a philosophy of professional practice, as well as the insights gleaned from first-hand school-based experiences working with children, teachers, and parents provides opportunities for integrated learning and effective behaviors.

Standards for educational leaders include a clear focus on social justice, inclusion, equity, and equality. In a diverse nation, a philosophy of educational leadership naturally considers how principals enact social justice. A closer look at social justice in education comes next.

## REFLECTIONS AND RELEVANCE 3.3

### Developing a Philosophy of Educational Leadership

A philosophy of educational leadership can help guide principals in the ethics, values, and practices of how to lead schools.

Working in three large groups, each group will consider one of the following: five UCEA Standards, ISLLC Standards 1–5, or ISLLC Standards 6–11.

1.  Thinking about your own experiences in schools as a student and as an educator, describe what each standard would look and sound like if operating effectively in a school. Give examples of what the principal who upheld each standard for educational leadership might say and do.
2.  Which standards relate directly to social justice—educating every student for academic and social success?
3.  Which standards do you believe would be the easiest for a principal to enact—and why? Which standards do you think would be the most challenging for a principal to enact—and why?
4.  In your own words, why do you think having a philosophy of educational leadership would benefit you as a principal?
5.  Do you see a standard that might be missing from these lists? If so, what is it?
6.  Identify the top five standards from this section that you think you might want to adopt as part of your own philosophy of educational leadership?

After each group has completed their discussions, the groups will report their findings, identifying the standard and describing how this might look in actual practice. Discuss the extent to which you see any of these standards enacted regularly in your present work setting.

## SOCIAL JUSTICE AND PHILOSOPHIES OF EDUCATION AND LEADERSHIP

In remarks to soon-to-be teachers at the University of Virginia in 2009, U.S. Secretary of Education Arne Duncan boldly asserted that every child in our country is entitled to a high-quality public education—but not every child is getting one. He asserted, "I believe that education is the civil rights issue of our generation. And if you care about promoting opportunity and reducing inequality, the classroom is the place to start. Great teaching is about so much more than education; it is a daily fight for social justice."[22] To many of our children, the dream of equal educational opportunity still seems beyond reach.

## WHAT IS SOCIAL JUSTICE?

*Social justice* is the philosophy that promotes a fair society by challenging injustice and valuing diversity. It affirms that all people share a common humanity and have the right to equitable treatment, support for their rights as human beings, and a fair share of community resources. When a society supports social justice, individuals do not experience oppression or have their wellbeing restricted or prejudiced based on their age, gender, sexuality, religion, political affiliations, beliefs, social class, education, disability, home location, or any other background, personal characteristics, or group membership.[23] In short, social justice is about ensuring that even the least advantaged among us has the protection of equal access to liberties, rights, and opportunities for healthy and fulfilling lives.

According to Marilyn Cochran-Smith, Cawthorne Professor of Teacher Education at Boston College, *social justice* is a framework that actively addresses the dynamics of oppression, privilege, and -isms (such as racism, sexism, or classism). It recognizes that society is the product of historically rooted, institutionally sanctioned stratification along socially constructed group lines that include race, class, gender, sexual orientation, and ability (among others). Cochran-Smith explains that working for social justice means guiding others and being guided in critical self-reflection about our own socialization about unequal relationships and its implications, identifying and analyzing the means by which we unfairly use our social, political, or economic power to dominate others, and developing the abilities to challenge these unequal power relationships.[24]

Taking action to end unfair practices is the work of social justice. And enacting social justice is what ISLLC Standards expect every school leader to do. Each ISLLC Standard begins with, "An educational leader promotes the success of every student by . . ."[25] The key word, "every," requires each principal, assistant principal, and all teachers in a formal leadership position to actively consider social justice concerns in their decisions and actions. For example, if "every" student deserves fair and equitable treatment, school leaders must consider whether certain students or groups of students receive suspensions for discipline infractions more frequently, are routinely assigned to less rigorous classes led by less effective teachers, or whether the school is placing other obvious or subtle barriers to equality of educational opportunity.

## SOCIAL JUSTICE IN AMERICAN EDUCATION: A BRIEF HISTORY

Expanding social justice is not a new concept in American public education. In 1641, the Massachusetts Bay Colony codified slavery.[26] The following year, the Massachusetts Law of 1642 required parents and masters to attend to the education of sons and servants—the first education law in the American colonies. By including servants, the law made education more inclusive—even if it applied only to males.

Two centuries later, public schools experienced another major push for inclusion. Horace Mann, Secretary of the Massachusetts Board of Education (1837–1848) argued for the creation of the common school: a free, universal, and non-sectarian expansion of the public schools open to all students regardless of social class—schooling with a common political and social purpose for all.[27] Common schools expanded school inclusion to children of low-income parents, who, even if they wanted their child to receive a basic education, could not afford tuition at the available church-run or proprietary schools. Yet in these years, universal was not "universal." African American children still faced segregation from public schools.[28]

In the late 1800s and early 1900s, boatloads of impoverished immigrant families arrived in the United States. Affluent U.S. citizens realized that their nation's best interests lay in educating these "lower classes" to the American tradition and the basic knowledge and skills needed to be employable in factories and responsible as citizens. As a result, between 1842 and 1918, all states passed compulsory attendance laws. Although social justice may not have been the intent, to a large extent, it was the outcome. Millions of children from foreign-born parents attended public schools to learn the attitudes, knowledge, and skills they needed to become loyal and productive American citizens.

## JUSTICE AS FAIRNESS

Winston Churchill, the United Kingdom's Prime Minister during World War II and after, is alleged to have said, "history is written by the victors." If so, the "vanquished" have little voice with which to present their side of the story. The winners build social structures and institutions to reinforce their view of the world, facilitate their political and economic arrangements, and express their prides and prejudices. At the same time, they marginalize the losers, relegating them to subservient, less powerful, and often-invisible, "second-class" roles.

For example, for nearly 400 years, Native Americans negotiated with an encroaching foreign culture that killed them with European weapons and diseases, diminishing their numbers, territory, resources, cultures, and freedom. The early American pioneers and settlers (the "victors") claimed their "manifest destiny" to possess Native American homelands. The Native Americans (the "vanquished") were disregarded legally, socially, and economically, pushed from buffalo-rich prairie lands onto barren reservations in a substratum of life. From today's perspective, was their treatment morally right? Was it fair? Knowing what we know now, would we repeat the same actions?

Consider, too, those who were kidnapped from their homes on a far continent, chained in ships bound for foreign countries, sold as slaves, and forced to work, amassing wealth for their owners while living in deplorable conditions. Debates ensued as to whether these individuals were even human or had a soul. Legislators passed laws that openly discriminated against them. They, too, were marginalized legally, socially, and economically, pushed into a substratum of life. Was their treatment morally right? Was it fair? Knowing what we know now, would we repeat the same actions?

To better understand the concept of "fairness," John Rawls offers a reasonable perspective to frame these social justice questions.

## John Rawls

John Rawls, late Harvard professor of philosophy, developed a concept called "justice as fairness." Presenting a thought experiment, he asks us to imagine that we have been given the responsibility for setting up a new and unbiased social contract for society. Since each of us holds certain partialities or prejudices, this task would be virtually impossible.

Next, imagine that as a fair-minded social contract writer, all of your biases and prejudices have magically vanished. You know nothing about the social constructs of gender, nationality, race, specific cultures, ableness, or stereotypes. Rawls calls this societal naiveté the "veil of ignorance." In his thought experiment, individuals with this "veil" do not hold their society's knowledge, views, or judgments about particular abilities, preferences, or status positions within the prevailing social order. Rather, individuals see themselves and others as rational, free, and morally equal. Nonetheless, in setting up this new social contract, you begin to notice certain behaviors and trends. Certain individuals and groups receive different treatment than others or have more power and influence over others. Laws and policies in place appear to treat selected individuals and groups more generously—or more harshly—than others.

Aware of these differential treatments, your role in setting up the new social contract requires you to make certain decisions. What rationale will you use for making these choices? Rawls posits that fairness—justice—would be the rational choice because your "veil of ignorance" would prevent you from knowing whether you will be a "victor" or a "vanquished" member in the new order. For that reason, the logical person would want rules that are fair to everyone—including the least among us. And on what basis do we make fair decisions? Rawls suggests that two rules apply. First, every individual has an equal right to the most extensive basic liberties that everyone shares. Second, social and economic inequalities should be structured so they advantage everyone and open opportunities to all.[29] With this view, we do not risk placing ourselves at a disadvantage in this new society.

### Rawls' application to educational leadership

Rawls' "justice as fairness" has relevance for the philosophies of education and leadership when considering if a certain process, practice, or outcome is consistent with ideals of social justice. Consider the following scenario: you are the new principal of a high school located 3,000 miles from where you grew up, went to college, began your teaching career, and became an assistant principal. The region and its traditions are new to you. The 2,000-strong student body is 42 percent white, 36 percent African American, 19 percent Hispanic, and 3 percent Asian. About 80 percent of the students graduate and 45 percent of the graduates enroll in college.

Since you are new to the area, you might have a limited "veil of ignorance" as you observe how the school operates. As you examine demographic data and talk with the school counselors, you determine that teachers and counselors don't encourage children from low-income homes and minorities to take the more academically rigorous courses that may lead to college admission and scholarships. They simply pick up the students' educational program where the middle school teachers left off. As a result, educators advise these students (who lack algebra and geometry on their middle school tran-scripts) to take vocational classes and "general level" classes. If low-income or minority students or their parents ask to enroll in the more rigorous academic courses, the educators report, sadly, that the student has missed taking the "prerequisite" courses and therefore lacks the background knowledge and skills needed to succeed in the advanced course. Moreover, the Handbook says that the course requires "permission of the instructor," but no instructor will sign the students' permission forms (because students have not completed the prerequisites).

In contrast, the children of professionals—physicians, lawyers, professors, engineers, and teachers—are encouraged (with extensive parental conferences) into the high-challenge Honors, Advanced Placement, and International Baccalaureate courses (again, because they have algebra and geometry on their middle school records). Additionally, you notice that four school counselors are assigned to work with 40 percent of students planning for college while only two school counselors are assigned to the other 60 percent of students.

Immediately, the neutral observer might ask, "Are these academic placement practices fair?" The answer is, "No." On what basis do you draw that conclusion? First, not all students have an equal opportunity to take the high-status, high-challenge college preparatory courses that other "selected" students can take. Second, these institutional practices and structures between school levels appear to advantage only students with parental influence who know how to get their children into the "right" courses early on if they plan to attend a competitive college. Once an academic door has closed, the organization will not reopen it (nor will it provide a window to permit access through an alternate approach). As a result, one might conclude that this situation contains socially unjust processes and practices.[30]

## REFLECTIONS AND RELEVANCE 3.4

### Understanding Social Justice

In groups of three or four complete a graphic organizer for the "social justice" concept, adding words or phrases to the graphic that illustrate what social justice is or looks like in schools.

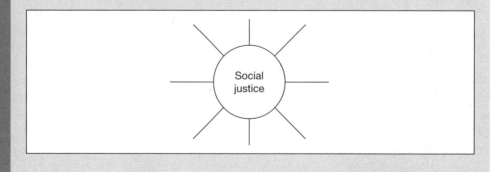

After each group has completed its social justice graphic, display and explain it to the rest of the class. After each group has presented its product, the class will discuss the following questions:

1.  How are Winston Churchill's comments about history being written by the victors similar to Paulo Freire's concept of the banking theory of education?
2.  In your own words, what does "social justice" mean to you? Why should this topic be explored as we develop our philosophy of education or of educational leadership?
3.  Describe the conditions you might find upon entering a school with a new set of eyes with a "veil of ignorance"? Give specific examples.
4.  In your own words, explain what the concept of "justice as fairness" entails.
5.  Identify additional social justice issues that you might find in schools. How would you go about addressing those issues with the faculty, the parents in the school, and the community at large?

## EQUITY, EQUALITY, AND FAIRNESS IN EDUCATION

Many educational leadership students initially conflate the terms *equality* and *equity*. These two different concepts overlap. *Equity* is defined as the state, ideal, or quality of being just, impartial, and fair.[31] As used in an educational context, *equity* involves giving people what they need. *Equality*, in contrast, involves treating people the same way. Most people believe that everyone should be treated equally. In education, this is not the best approach, however, since every student begins school with different family backgrounds and sets of experiences, knowledge, and skills. To treat everyone the same when many arrive at school *not* the same is to disadvantage countless students. Rather, everyone in school should be treated equitably. Let's explore that issue further.

Children come to school from a variety of circumstances. Some arrive in kindergarten knowing their colors, letters, and numbers. Others come much less well-prepared. Holding each five-year-old child to the same standard despite the wide variance in readiness would be devastating—to the children and to schools' reputation in the community. Instead, teachers treat children equitably by building upon what they know and giving them what they need. To say that we treat all children equally and hold that all children should know their colors, recognize all the alphabet letters, and count to 25 by their fifth birthday would require schools to send many children home as unprepared.

Here's a medical analogy. If you visit your physician with an earache and the doctor looks in your ear and tells you that your appendix should be removed, you might understandably ask, "Why?" If the physician says, "I treat all my patients equally— I do appendectomies on everyone," you would quickly excuse yourself and find a more sensible physician. We want our physicians to treat us *equitably*—giving us what we need according to our condition—in this case treating our earache. In schooling, we do the same with our students. In the same kindergarten classroom, teachers work with the five year olds who are already reading and with their classmates who do not yet recognize basic shapes, letters, numbers, or colors. We build on what students know and provide them with the instruction they need to grow from there.

## Equity in Staffing

The relationships among equity, equality, and fairness can be understood by looking at school staffing. Imagine a school system with two high schools. One school, Alpha High, serves the more affluent north side of town and the other, Omega High, serves the less wealthy south neighborhoods. Both schools enroll approximately the same number of students, and the student population demographics are almost identical, as illustrated in Table 3.2. The average years of experience for the teachers, administrators, and school counselors appear after the number in each school.

Since the two schools are in the same school system with approximately the same number of students, one would expect them to be staffed almost equally. But as Table 3.2 reveals, this is not the case. Alpha has 18 more teachers, 2 more administrators, and 2 more school counselors than Omega. Alpha employs the more experienced staff. Because teacher salaries follow years of experience, the per-pupil expenditure at Alpha is almost $4,700 more than at Omega. Clearly, this situation is not equitable. And the result of this inequity may be very different educational and learning experiences for the Alpha students as compared with the Omega students: the Omega students may not be receiving the quality of education they need. Can the school district say that they are treating all children fairly?

Additionally, the equity may be viewed from another perspective: treating children who are unequal, unequally. For example, we know that it costs more to educate children from economically and educationally impoverished backgrounds than it does to educate students who come to us from high-advantage backgrounds. For example, young children who begin kindergarten without knowing their alphabet, colors, or shapes might need more teacher attention and smaller class sizes (so they can get more teacher or aide attention) than their peers who are already reading simple books! What might a situation in schools look like that does not recognize and respond to differences in student needs? Let's picture two K through grade 5 elementary schools—coincidentally, also named Alpha and Omega (see Table 3.3).

Table 3.3 shows the student and faculty demographics. Alpha serves the wealthier "white-collar" neighborhoods while Omega serves the economically depressed "blue-collar" neighborhoods. Alpha has 1 percent of its students qualifying for free or reduced-price lunch; Omega has 85 percent of its students who qualify for free or reduced-price lunch. Each school has 600 students: 100 students per grade level with four teachers per grade level. Alpha has three additional teachers for the 25 gifted and talented students for a total of 27 faculty. Omega has no students identified for gifted and talented services, but it does have two special education teachers. Alpha has 92 percent of its students passing the state exams; Omega has only 32 percent passing.

On the surface, the different staffing levels at Alpha and Omega elementary schools may appear justified—Omega has no students identified for the talented and gifted

**TABLE 3.2** Comparison of Alpha and Omega High Schools[32]

| School | Alpha High | Omega High |
|---|---|---|
| Students | 1,000 | 1,007 |
| Teachers/Years of Experience | 109/23 | 91/7 |
| Administrators/Years of Experience | 5/29 | 3/11 |
| School Counselors/Years of Experience | 5/24 | 3/9 |
| Student to Staff Ratio | 8.4/1 | 10.4/1 |
| Per Pupil Spending | $14,569 | $9,872 |

## REFLECTIONS AND RELEVANCE 3.5

# Equity, Equality, and Fairness in Education Staffing #1

School districts treat children equitably by giving them what they need. To treat unequal children equally is to treat them unfairly.

In groups of three or four, discuss the equity practices at Alpha and Omega High Schools. When the small groups are finished, the whole class will consider its findings. Address the following:

1.  Given the difference between the two schools in the number of teachers per student and the teachers' years of experience, how might the Omega students be at an instructional disadvantage as compared with the Alpha students?
2.  Given the difference between the two schools in the number of administrators per student and the administrators' years of experience, how might this place the Omega students in a less favorable circumstance?
3.  Given the difference between the two schools in the number of counselors per student and the counselors' years of experience, how might this place the Omega students in a less favorable situation?
4.  If the school system has a transfer policy for educators to work in another school after 5 or 10 years of experience, is it fair to the students to allow experienced teachers to transfer from Omega to Alpha? Explain your reasoning.
5.  If all the student demographics remained the same and the student population at Omega were 60 percent minority, do you think a stronger case could be made for a more equitable funding? Explain your answer.

**TABLE 3.3** Comparison of Alpha and Omega Elementary Schools

| School | Alpha High | Omega High |
| --- | --- | --- |
| Students | 600 | 600 |
| Teachers/Years of Experience | 27/26 | 26/7 |
| Administrators/Years of Experience | 2/23 | 2/9 |
| School Counselors/Years of Experience | 3/14 | 2/6 |
| Student to Staff Ratio | 18.75/1 | 20/1 |
| Per Pupil Spending | $9,541 | $6,008 |

## REFLECTIONS AND RELEVANCE 3.6

## Equity, Equality, and Fairness in Education Staffing #2

School districts treat children equitably by giving them what they need. To treat unequal children equally is to treat them unfairly.

In groups of three or four, discuss the concepts of equity at Alpha and Omega Elementary Schools. Then discuss your findings as a class. Address the following:

1. Alpha and Omega Elementary Schools have the same number of students and approximately the same teacher/student ratios. Why is the staffing a social justice issue?
2. What types of additional services might the Omega Elementary School need in place to increase the students' learning and achievement? Explain your reasoning.
3. Cite the evidence of why educating students from poverty to high standards costs more than educating more affluent students.
4. Justify the position that increased high quality staffing (resulting in increased spending) is necessary at Omega to educate the children. What types of programs might benefit the children at Omega?

program but does have two special education positions. As we examine the situation more closely, the fact that 85 percent of Omega's population (510 students) qualifies for free or reduced-price lunch may require more teachers per student to give children the extra help they need to catch up and keep up academically with their peers at Alpha. Treating unequal populations equally (the same classroom teacher/student ratio) regardless of the children's learning needs violates the equity concept.

## Social Justice and Philosophies of Education

Educators tend to accept their schools as fair to students. Teachers did not create the institutions in which they work; most try to fit themselves into the school's existing patterns and norms. They typically see their schools as meritocracies in which students who work hard and learn fast sprint ahead while those who work less diligently and learn more slowly plod forward—or leave. Teachers may not be aware of the private biases that frame their perceptions and interactions with others who are unlike them. They may have little cross-cultural experience and knowledge of the students they teach. Socialized as Americans and as transmitters of our cultural heritage, many teachers simply do not see, understand, or value that other ways of knowing and understanding exist.[33]

Principals, however, cannot say the same, because part of their leadership role is to create the climate and structures that support high-quality teaching and learning for all students. Guided in part by the ISLLC Standards, most school leadership programs will engage aspiring principals to broaden their outlook and consider the diversity of their student body, the varied communities they serve, and the cultural assets diverse students bring that can aid their learning. Over time, principals will want to infuse other school leaders and teachers with more open and flexible perspectives and practices that shift the school's culture and climate from one that may (overtly or inadvertently) disadvantage certain students to one that gives every student the opportunities for full academic and social growth.

Although people have a universal desire to be treated as full and equal citizens, they do not have equal needs or equal opportunities within an unjust society. Because most whites have not had to struggle against prejudice and discrimination in this culture, they tend not to recognize equity concerns. Rather, to recognize and admit such discrimination could create *cognitive dissonance*[34] and its accompanying discomfort. Nonetheless, it is important for educators to consider the ways that school, as an American institution, may appear to those who do not share our mainstream norms or whom our practices harm. Unless we can see our schools' limitations and acknowledge when our unifying beliefs, structures, and practices are unfair to certain student groups, we will likely interpret student failure or resistance as "their" responsibility—not ours— to remedy. As multicultural scholars Colleen Larson and Carlos J. Ovando observe, "Although we have expanded our geographic borders in many of our school systems, we have failed to expand our psychic circles of community."[35]

Becoming a school leader in a pluralistic society involves examining more deeply the complexities of contemporary education. A variety of perspectives exist surrounding educational goals, educational process, and need to ensure that every student receives a high-quality education. At the same time, school leaders need to understand that teacher resistance to school improvement initiatives may reflect their silent (or not so silent) struggle to reconcile the new approach with its set of unfamiliar assumptions and expectations with those older, firmly held beliefs and practices. Teachers (and certain parents) may need multiple occasions to engage with new ways of understanding education's goals, mull them over, understand their impact on all children, tally up the gains, and eventually, make these views their own (or not). What they cannot do is swallow their principals' philosophies of education and leadership in one gulp.

In a highly diverse society, social justice is an important aspect of education and an educational philosophy. It reflects what we want education to accomplish with students. Perhaps, as James A. Banks, Diversity Studies Chair at the University of Washington, Seattle, observes, the goal of education in a globalized world is "to help all students acquire the knowledge, attitudes, and skills needed to participate in cross-cultural interactions and in personal, social, and civic action that will help make our nation more democratic and just."[36]

## REFLECTIONS AND RELEVANCE 3.7

### Social Justice and Philosophies of Education

Unless we can see our schools' limitations and acknowledge when our unifying beliefs, structures, and practices are unfair to certain student groups, we will likely interpret student failure or resistance as "their" responsibility—not ours—to remedy.

Working individually, compose your current philosophies of education and of educational leadership (approximately 250 words each). Then, in groups of three to four, work to express the appropriate wording and rationale of what you have written using the guidelines below:

1.   List the aspects or qualities you believe the philosophy statements should contain.
2.   By these criteria, what more does each person need to add to his or her statement?
3.   Are the writings clear and understandable? Are details vague or contradictory? How would you suggest these be fixed?

Share the key aspects or qualities your group believes should be part of a philosophy of education or philosophy of educational leadership. Compile the class's ideas on the board.

Date the two philosophy statements and reflect on them when you need to make instructional or leadership decisions in your present position. Revise them as needed as you continue in this course and throughout your principal preparation program. Remember that as you read, learn, and grow, your philosophies of education and educational leadership will evolve.

## CONCLUSION

For a principal, nothing is more important than deciding where to lead a school and to what purposes. The direction for leadership comes from well-grounded and articulated philosophies of education and educational leadership. As aspiring principals read and grow professionally, their philosophy will evolve and they will be able to articulate ideas into words and actions. Increasingly they will be able to promote the success of all students by establishing a culture of teaching for learning that is accepted and endorsed by faculty, staff, students, and the community.

Philosophies of education and leadership will include enacting social justice. This perspective offers a means of assuring that all students—including low-income, minority, disabled, and others with cultural, economic, learning, or physical differences—have equal and equitable opportunities to enroll and succeed in rigorous courses, work with highly effective teachers, have sufficient and varied supports to scaffold their success, and opportunities to learn and grow.

## NOTES

1   De George, R. T. (1999). *Business ethics* (5th ed.). Upper Saddle River, NJ: Prentice Hall.
2.  Kaplan, L. S., & Owings, W. A. (2015). *Educational foundations* (2nd ed.) (p. 66). Stamford, CT: Cengage Learning.
3.  Kaplan & Owings (2015), op. cit. (p. 67).
4.  Richardson, J. (2013, September 26). Practical educational philosophy. *BigThink* Retrieved from: http://bigthink.com/education-recoded/practical-educational-philosophy
5.  Cremin, L. (1961). *The transformation of the school: Progressivism in American education 1876–1957* (p. 117). New York: Vintage.
6.  Dewey, J. (1916). The need of an industrial education in an industrial age. In J. Boydston (Ed.), *The middle works of John Dewey, 1899–1924* (p. 139). Carbondale: Southern Illinois University Press.
7.  Dewey, J. (1916). *Democracy and education* (p. 87). New York: The Free Press.
8.  Cremin, L. (1961), op. cit. (p. 118).
9.  Cremin, L. (1961), op. cit. (p. 123).
10. Eisner, E. W. (1999, May). The use and limits of performance assessment. *Phi Delta Kappan, 80* (9), 658–660.
11. Eisner, E. W. (1992, April). The misunderstood role of the arts in human development. *Phi Delta Kappan, 73* (8), 592; Eisner, E. W. (2001, January). What does it mean to say a school is doing well? *Phi Delta Kappan, 82* (3), 367–372.
12. Kaplan & Owings (2015), op. cit. (p. 184).
13. Eisner (1992, April), op. cit. (p. 595).
14. Eisner (1999), op. cit. (p. 660).
15. McLaren, P. (2001). Che Guevara, Paulo Freire, and the politics of hope: Reclaiming critical pedagogy. *Cultural Studies—Critical Methodologies, 1* (1), 108–131. Retrieved from: http://pages.gseis.ucla.edu/faculty/mclaren/mclaren%20and%20che.pdf
16. Freire, P. (2007). *Pedagogy of the oppressed.* New York, NY: Continuum. Originally published in Portuguese in 1968.
17. *The New Observer* (2012, June 7). *Review of Paulo Freire's Pedagogy of the oppressed.* UK: *The New Observer.* Retrieved from: http://thenewobserver.co.uk/review-of-paulo-freires-pedagogy-of-the-oppressed/
18. Bentley, L. (1999). *A brief biography of Paulo Freire.* Omaha, NE: Pedagogy & Theater of the Oppressed, Inc. Retrieved from: http://ptoweb.org/aboutpto/a-brief-biography-of-paulo-freire/
19. Ibid. (p. 84).
20. Adapted from McLeod, S. (2001). Statement of leadership philosophy. *UCEA Online Handbook.* Charlottesville, VA: UCEA. Retrieved from: http://ucea.org/storage/pdf1/

UCEA%20Online%20Handbook%20-%20Sample%20Statement%20of%20Leadership %20Philosophy.pdf; Council of Chief State School Officers (2008). *Educational leadership policy standards: ISLLC 2015*. Washington, DC: Council of Chief State School Officers.

21. *Educational leadership policy standards 2015*. As adopted by the National Policy Board for Educational Administration. Washington, DC: Council of Chief State School Officers. Retrieved from: http://www.ccsso.org/Resources/Programs/Developing_and_Supporting_ School-Ready_Leaders.html. As of this writing, the updated draft version of the standards are available from: Wilson, J. (November, 2014). The new ISLLC Standards: Building a future of excellence in the profession. Paper presented at the UCEA 2014 National Conference, Retrieved January 19, 2015 from: http://www.gapsc.com/Commission/Media/ Downloads/2014_Conference/B7_Handout2.pdf

22. Duncan, A. (2009, October 9). *A call to teaching: Secretary Arne Duncan's remarks at the Rotunda at the University of Virginia*. Washington, DC: U.S. Department of Education. Retrieved from: http://www2.ed.gov/news/speeches/2009/10/10092009.html

23. Robinson, M. (2014). *What is social justice?* Boone, NC: Appalachian State University, Department of Government and Justice Studies. Retrieved from: http://gjs.appstate.edu/social-justice-and-human-rights/what-social-justice

24. Cochran-Smith, M. (2004). *Walking the road: Race, diversity, and social justice in teacher education*. New York: Teachers College Press.

25. Council of Chief State School Officers (2014). *Educational leadership policy standards: ISLLC 2014*. Washington, DC: Council of Chief State School Officers.

26. Wood, B. (1997). *The origins of American slavery* (p. 103). New York: Hill and Wang.

27. Cremin, L. A. (1957). *The republic and the school: Horace Mann on the education of free men* (p. 12). New York: Teachers College Press.

28. From your school law class see *Roberts v. City of Boston*, 59 Mass. (5 Cush.) 198. 1849.

29. Rawls, J. (1999). *A theory of justice* (revised ed.). Cambridge, MA: Harvard University Press.

30. For more reading on this topic see: http://gjs.appstate.edu/social-justice-and-human-rights/what-social-justice; Jacobs, J. (2013). Book review: What every principal needs to know to create equitable and excellent schools, in *Educational Administration Quarterly 49* (4), 685–692; DeMatthews, D., & Mawhinney, H. (2014, February 6). Social justice leadership and inclusion: Exploring challenges in an urban district struggling to address inequities. *Educational Administration Quarterly*. Retrieved from *Educational Administration Quarterly* 0013161X13514440, first published on January 7, 2014 as doi:10.1177/ 0013161X13514440; Santamaria, L. J. (2013, October 11). Critical change for the greater good: Multicultural perceptions in educational leadership toward social justice and equity. *Educational Administration Quarterly*, 0: 0013161X13505287v1–13161X13505287.

31. Morris, W. (Ed.) (1970). *The American heritage dictionary of the English language*. New York, NY: American Heritage Publishing Co.

32. This is a hypothetical case. For an actual case, see Owings, W., & Kaplan, L. (2010). The Alpha and Omega syndrome: Is intra-district funding disparity the next "ripeness" factor? *Journal of Education Finance, 36* (2), 162–185.

33. Kaplan & Owings (2015), op. cit. (pp. 239–241).

34. *Cognitive dissonance* can be defined as a theoretical construct used to explain how people respond to information that does not fit with their current beliefs or understandings—usually with psychological tension or dissonance. See Festinger, L. A. (1957). *A theory of cognitive dissonance*. Evanston, IL: Peterson.

35. Larson, C. L., & Ovando, C. J. (2000). *The color of bureaucracy: The politics of equity in multicultural school communities*. Belmont, CA: Wadsworth Cengage Learning.

36. Banks, J. A. (2006). Democracy, diversity, and social justice: Educating citizens for the public interest in a global age. In Ladson-Billings, G., & Tate, W. F. (Eds.), *Education research in the public interest: Social justice, action, and policy* (p. 145). New York, NY: Teachers College Press.

# CHAPTER 4

# Understanding and Leveraging School Culture

A school's culture has more influence on life and
learning in the schoolhouse than the president of the
country, the state department of education, the
superintendent, the school board, or even the
principal, teachers, and parents can ever have.
                    —Roland Barth, *The Culture Builder*

---

## LEARNING OBJECTIVES

4.1  Define *school culture* and explain how it influences educators' attitudes
     and actions in the school.

4.2  Explain why sustainable school improvement requires changing the
     school's culture.

4.3  Summarize the open systems theory's concept and components and
     analyze the model's relationship to school culture.

4.4  Identify the various ways that school culture infuses a school with certain
     assumptions, expectations, and practices.

4.5  Analyze the ways that school culture can either promote or inhibit all
     children's academic success in school.

4.6  Relate the differences between the needs and culture of industrial age
     schools and 21st-Century economy schools and the implications for
     today's schools.

4.7  Describe the variety of cultural elements that explicitly or implicitly appear
     and operate in schools and explain how they influence teachers and
     students.

4.8  Discuss why school leadership's main job is culture creation and describe
     the components principals can use to accomplish it.

4.9  Explain the components of a learning organization and describe how
     principals can use these to improve their teachers' performance and
     student outcomes.

4.10 Summarize the research findings connecting school culture and climate
     to school functioning and outcomes.

**2015 ISLLC STANDARDS: 1, 2, 3, 4, 5, 6, 7, 8, 9, 11**

## INTRODUCTION

Despite more than 40 years of school reform and as many years of research generating deeper understanding of teaching and learning, little progress in advancing all students' achievement is evident. Enthusiastic principals and school district superintendents arrive at new positions bursting with ideas of how they are going to "make their mark" on the academic programs and boost student test scores. Although these leaders may find compliant teachers and agreeable school boards willing to go along with their fresh approaches, their improvement strategies seldom stick beyond the leader's tenure. The reason: enduring, sustainable changes cannot be imposed from outside—or from outsiders joining—the organization. Rather, the process of generating lasting and meaningful school change to improve teaching and learning only occurs when principals, teachers, and others share the experiences of reshaping their school's culture to better align with their goals.[1] Sustainable change requires school culture change.

This chapter explains how school leadership *is* culture building. Principals and superintendents who want to lead viable school improvement must first understand and appreciate their school (or district's) culture's capacity to derail even the best-conceived plans. The chapter presents the open systems model as a conceptual framework to understand school dynamics, defines *school culture* and illustrates how it appears in schools, discusses change as organizational learning, explains how principals create the environment that improves school culture, introduces the research on school culture and climate as it affects school functioning and outcomes, and gives principals suggestions on how to involve their teachers and staff in school culture change.

## OPEN SYSTEMS THEORY

Schools are complex organizations. As a key agency for socializing young people into the American community, public schools have traditionally been seen as the "great equalizers" where students from every background who work hard can learn the necessary knowledge and skills to reach any station in life. This ideal image of schools leveling the playing field for children from diverse circumstances starkly contradicts schools' traditional "sorting and selecting" practices which separate youngsters by socioeconomic backgrounds, ethnic mores, languages, ways of knowing the world, and unique funds of knowledge and experience into different academic and vocational paths. On top of this, the bureaucracy supplies another layer of values, beliefs, assumptions, communication styles, and prescribed ways for making decisions, prioritizing issues, and allocating resources. Lastly, educational governance's political nature interacts with all the other variables, coloring the intellectual, material, fiscal, and morale-enhancing resources available to students in any particular school at any certain time.

When dealing with complex environments, such as schools, it helps to have a mental model to orient principals to the many competing tensions, interests, and relationships that affect their schools and any plans for improvement. The open systems perspective can help new principals better understand their circumstances and the many factors at play which must be considered in leading a successful school.

As Figure 4.1 illustrates, the open systems model[2] depicts human enterprises, organizations such as schools, as social systems that interact with their larger environment. In this model, organizations take inputs from their environment, transform them, and generate outcomes. In schools, inputs may include technical capital (such as money and resources the schools need to improve teaching and learning); human capital (including the educators' knowledge, skills, perspectives, and instructional capacity); and social capital (namely, the relationships, social networks, trust, and shared commitment).[3] The transformation process includes principal and teacher leaders working together to define a shared vision, establish effective professional learning communities to support teachers' growth, and provide appropriate and timely professional development tied directly to teachers' classroom needs. Transformation process also includes assessing how well the principal is targeting the available resources and using them wisely to meet key goals.

In the open systems model, outcomes involve educating students with increasingly mature knowledge, skills, and capacities (and inclination) for life-long learning and, eventually, producing graduates with the abilities needed to act as responsible citizens, informed voters, and self-supporting wage earners and tax payers. Outcomes also include increasing teachers' and principals' professional skills to affect the desired learning from each student. Feedback comes in a variety of formats and frequencies, qualitative and quantitative, including regular formative assessments and assorted measures of student progress and formal assessments aligned to high standards. Teachers receive feedback in multiple measures of their students' achievement and in the growth and increasing effectiveness of their own professional knowledge and skills. Feedback for principals' effectiveness takes a variety of measures as well.

Within the school's orbit, its environment also exerts a powerful influence on what happens inside. Like a stone thrown into a lake creates rippling waters extending far beyond its entry point, even a principal's seemly small decision can impact more than the immediate target group. Accordingly, the environment may be as near as the hallway or faculty lounge or as large as the world.

Here's a simple example of how the open systems viewpoint applies to schools. Seventh-grade teachers in two separate medium-size suburban middle schools ask their

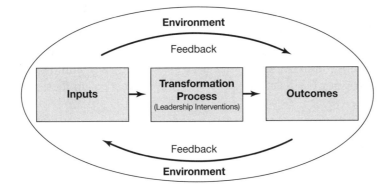

**FIGURE 4.1** Open Systems Model
Source: Owings, W. A., & Kaplan, L. S., 2014.

principals to approve adding two more minutes of instructional time each day before lunch. Since the whole grade is teamed, teachers control their students' instruction, time, and movements between classes and lunch. Principal A—who does not think in open systems terms—listens, hears an easy request, and promptly says OK.

In contrast, Principal B—who has an open systems mindset—listens, and asks before deciding: Who else will be affected by this decision and how? Will students from other grades be in the halls at the same time as the delayed seventh graders? Will the students in the halls have enough supervision to keep them safe and purposeful? Will this change increase the possibility of disruptive interactions between children? Will the seventh graders have enough time to eat their lunch and socialize briefly with their friends before the next group arrives for lunch? If seventh grade lunch time runs into another grade's lunch time, will shortening the seventh graders' lunch or delaying the next group's lunch frustrate the children and annoy their parents? And by what time must the cafeteria workers legally finish the day's service and leave the building? With an open systems mindset, any input—or request for change—potentially affects other people and interests in the larger environment. To be effective, therefore, principals must thoughtfully consider the decision within the larger environments before deciding even "simple" requests.

But in schools, open systems environments extend well beyond the schoolhouse. Regional, state, and national politics, economics, societal and legal trends, advancements in technology, and even international events can shift viewpoints and behaviors in ways that affect public schools. How will this year's state budget for public schools impact the local district's funding? Will the district have the funds to support teachers having team planning periods? Will new educational programs move forward or will the district cut staff and increase class sizes? Looking at an international scale, for example, Russia's Sputnik satellite's launch into Earth orbit in 1957 prompted the United States, suddenly afraid of losing the "space race" to its Cold War enemy, to invest significant dollars into teaching more rigorous math, science, and modern foreign languages at all education levels to strengthen our national security. Likewise, consider how the 21st Century's digital technology has made virtual education possible and how smart phones and tablet computers have modified instructional practices in the classroom.

Through all these interactions, the school and its environments influence each other. A successful principal, therefore, must be mindful to balance—and satisfy—both the internal and external expectations coming from their environments. Teachers, students, parents, and interest groups must be considered in decisions. Therefore, new principals are wise to consult individuals familiar with the school, its operations, and its many stakeholders when making decisions that may impact more than those folks sitting at the table.

## SCHOOL CULTURE

School culture is "the way we do things around here." It is the feeling one gets walking through the halls and watching teachers, staff, and students at work. It is the school's unique persona. Often operating beneath conscious awareness, school culture is a stable,

**REFLECTIONS AND RELEVANCE 4.1**

## Assess Your Own School with the Open Systems Model

The open systems model can help principals understand the context and influences within which they make decisions.

Individually assess your current school using the open systems model on a scale of 1–5 (1 lowest, 5 highest) in the table below. After everyone has completed their individual school assessment, discuss common findings as a class.

| Open Systems Components | Factors | Feedback (Evidence, Data) | Rating 1–5 |
|---|---|---|---|
| | | Basis For Assessing | |
| Inputs | • Technical capital: money, resources<br>• Human capital: educators' knowledge, skills attitudes (instructional and leadership)<br>• Social capital: relationships, networks, trust, shared commitment to school's goals | | |
| Transformation Process | • Teachers and principal develop shared vision<br>• Teachers collaborate for improved professional practice, more student learning<br>• Timely professional development tied to classroom needs | | |
| Outcomes | • Educating all students for life-long learning<br>• Students' maturing attitudes, knowledge, skills<br>• Teachers and principals increasing knowledge and skills for instruction, leadership | | |
| Environments | • School's influential internal environments<br>• School's influential external environments | | |

historically transmitted set of unwritten rules, beliefs and practices about what the organization's members think is important and how they should act. It affects expectations, behaviors, and relationships among teachers, administrators, staff, students, parents, and the community. It gives meaning to what people say and shapes how they interpret even small daily events. Influencing almost everything that happens in schools, the culture impacts which children the teachers predict are able to learn the high-challenge curriculum, who should be involved in making school decisions, what professional attire are appropriate for the classroom, and the topics typically mulled over in the parking lot. Deeply rooted over the years, these patterns of meaning generally resist change.

*School culture* is a form of *organizational culture*—a set of norms, dominant values, philosophy, shared behavioral routines, rules, and feelings that a group holds and that determine how it perceives, thinks about, and reacts to its various environments.[4] Conceived by Edgar H. Schein, Professor of Management Emeritus at MIT's Sloan School of Management and an expert on organizational development, organizational culture as a concept integrated social psychology, sociology, and anthropology in a holistic way to better understand group and institutional phenomena. By focusing on organizational culture, Schein was able to identify the psychological factors that either advance or limit organizational change and explain why people in organizations act as they do.[5] As organizations, schools follow these rules.

Schein (1985) calls culture "a pattern of basic assumptions—invented, discovered, or developed by a given group as it learns to cope with programs, that has worked well enough to be considered valid and, therefore, to be taught to new members as the correct way to perceive, think, and feel in relation to those problems."[6]

According to Schein, cultural norms knit a community together. Organizational (school) cultures develop over years and even centuries through three related concepts:[7]

- A body of solutions to internal and external problems—invented, discovered, or developed—that has consistently worked well enough so that it is taught to new group members as the correct way to understand, think about, and feel in relation to those problems.
- These attitudes and actions eventually become assumptions about the nature of reality, truth, time, space, human nature, human activity, and relationships.
- Over the years, these assumptions come to be accepted as true, unchallenged, and finally drop from conscious awareness. Culture's power lies in the fact it works below everyday attention as a set of unexamined assumptions that are taken for granted.

Once a group has learned to hold common assumptions, its behaviors become automatic. The group members tend to perceive, think, feel, and act in similar ways that provide meaning, stability, and comfort. The shared learning—knowing that all members see, interpret, and act in certain situations in the same ways—reduces members' worries that they might not be able to understand or predict events occurring around them. In an inverse manner, as their anxieties lessen, their culture grows even stronger.

The terms *school culture* and *school climate* are often used interchangeably, although they express slightly different phenomena. *Culture* refers to the enduring patterns of meaning and practices affecting faculty attitudes and actions while *climate* tends to refer to the current physical, intellectual, psychological, and social environment, the school's "feel," that either encourages or discourages students' efforts at learning. School culture responds only to deliberately identifying unvoiced and unwritten rules that shape attitudes and behaviors and challenging their "good fit" with the school's evolving needs and goals. Without direct intervention, culture tends to outlast individual principals and teachers. In contrast, climate more readily reflects the emotional tone set by the present principal and teachers. School climate may change with principal turnover, and a new principal brings new sets of expectations and practices—and a new climate.

## SCHOOL CULTURE INFUSES A SCHOOL

Three important assumptions shape a school's culture: ideas about students (which children can or cannot learn to high standards?), ideas about academics (are we here to "educate" or "school" our students?),[8] and ideas about relationships (how should teachers treat their leaders, colleagues, students, and parents?).[9] These play out in many aspects of school life:[10]

- *Social climate.* The psycho-social environment in which persons either feel safe, cared for, accepted, and respected as individuals capable of learning and maturing— or an environment that feels threatening, risky, isolating, and which respects and nurtures only certain individuals, children or adults. Collegiality and collaboration may be prized or devalued.
- *Intellectual climate.* The expectations in every classroom about which children have the capacity to do their best and grow cognitively in the rigorous, relevant, and engaging curriculum with high-quality pedagogy and supports. Similarly, the people, time, and material resources to make high-level learning happen are available for all—or only for certain—children.
- *Relational and behavioral norms.* The expectations and actions that create the school's professional and ethical culture of mutual trust and respect—or their absence and the presence of practices which undermine these.
- *Rules and policies.* The guidelines and procedures hold that all—or only certain— school members, adults and young people, are accountable to high standards of learning and behavior.
- *Structures.* The policies and procedures that give teachers, staff, and students a voice and shared responsibility for making decisions and solving problems that affect the school environment and their lives in it—or those which deny teachers or students input into decisions that directly affect them.
- *Traditions and routines.* The practices established from shared values that honor and strengthen the school's academic, ethical, and social standards or traditions— or practices that discourage teacher and student excellence in effort, ethical behaviors, trust-based relationships, or achievement.

- *Partnerships*. The ways the school members effectively join with parents, businesses, and outside organizations to support students' learning and character development —or the lack of such relationships to support students' growth.

As these dimensions interplay and shape the school as an organization, they create a psycho-social milieu that deeply affects teachers, administrators, staff, and students. By strengthening shared meaning among school community members, culture provides the group with an identity, generates a sense of commitment, sets and enforces behavioral standards, and provides a means of social control. When the school's cultural norms and behaviors support professional collegiality and ensure every child's academic success, the principals and faculties agree about "our school" and what it stands for. They gain a clear sense of who they are and their uniqueness as a group. As part of an organization charged with society's mission to educate all children to become informed, responsible citizens and self-sustaining adults, school members feel a dedication to something larger and more important than their individual self-interests. Through the school's norms and unwritten rules, the culture guides its members on how to interpret and handle particular situations, enforcing a consistency of expectations and actions. Members see how their work fits in and contributes to the whole. Such a positive school culture is not always the case, however.

The downside of school culture occurs when members are socialized by their colleagues to follow the school's informal rules and institutionalized norms in an un-thinking, self-perpetuating cycle that increases the social system's stability but does not support the principal's, teachers', and parents' expressed goals. In such schools, individuals whose attitudes and actions go against the grain—for example, in desiring to improve teaching and learning so all children can experience academic success rather than reserve academic excellence to quick-learning high achievers—may be considered as "rule breakers." These iconoclasts tend to receive their colleagues' disapproval.

From an open systems perspective, school culture is part of the professional, psychological, and social environment that envelops the school and influences the attitudes and actions of those within it. And as a system, schools consist of interacting parts, each part depending on the others to function effectively. For this reason, principals who want to improve their schools must consider—and perhaps overtly challenge—their school's members' underlying belief structures and behaviors—their shared culture—and the environment it creates, as an essential step in planning for change.

## SCHOOL CULTURES: STRONG/WEAK, HEALTHY/TOXIC

School cultures may be strong or weak. Strong cultures build community while weak cultures do not. In schools with strong cultures, the organization's mission and philosophy are clear, and members widely share the organization's core values. Teachers, staff, students, and parents agree on what the school stands for. The stronger their commitment to these core values, the more vigorous the culture. These common ideals and the intensity with which members hold them create a unity of purpose, group

**REFLECTIONS AND RELEVANCE 4.2**

## Identifying Your School's Cultural Norms

A school's culture defines for its members what they value, who they value, and how they will conduct their business.

Answer the following questions individually and consider the evidence you are using to inform your opinion. After each has completed the assignment, discuss answers as a class. How difficult is it to accurately complete this assignment? If you know the answers, what informs your view? If you do not know the answers, how might you find out? What differences do these answers mean for teachers, students, and parents?

What are the common assumptions and practices regarding each of the following in the school where you currently work?

1. Which students belong in AP or Honors courses (or their elementary or middle school equivalents)?
2. To what degree do teachers accept responsibility for educating all their students to high academic standards?
3. Who should be involved in making decisions that impact teaching and learning?
4. What is the appropriate way to view parents' and guardians' role in educating their children?
5. How does the school define "disruptive student behavior" and what are the appropriate consequences?
6. What is the school's responsibility for improving the relationships among students' disruptive behaviors, their learning needs, and their lack of academic success?
7. To what degree do teachers respect and trust each other?
8. To what degree do teachers respect and trust their building administrators?
9. To what degree do teachers respect their colleagues' capacities to educate all students to high academic standards?
10. Other.

Before the next meeting of this class, bring these questions to your current workplace and ask these questions to at least two colleagues—teachers or administrators. Compare their views with yours. What would you say is the "cultural norm" at your school?

Note: Professors may want to have students complete these questions with colleagues from their current schools the week before the class discusses this chapter so they can develop a fuller understanding of school cultural norms.

cohesiveness, loyalty, and an internal climate that directs behaviors towards these desired outcomes.

Likewise, school cultures may be healthy or toxic. As depicted in Table 4.1, healthy school cultures treat people well. Members share a consistent sense of purpose and value as they enact the norms of continuous learning. They feel good and productive about working together; teacher turnover is low. Everyone appreciates professional development, staff reflection, and sharing the best of their professional practice. Members collaborate around their craft to improve teaching, leading, and learning. In contrast, toxic cultures generate the opposite responses: intellectual drift, closed classroom doors, general disrespect for colleagues and leaders, competing subgroups working at cross purposes, discouraging hard work and excellence from any members, widespread belief that "teachers' job is to teach, students' job is to learn"—and professional indifference to any goals beyond "putting in one's time."

You can tell a school with a healthy culture from one with a toxic culture by how it responds to teachers' extra efforts at helping struggling students learn. A school with a healthy culture celebrates teachers' initiative and movement towards their shared goals of academic success for all children. In contrast, schools with a toxic culture make it difficult for any teacher or administrator to step out and defy the inertia of "same old, same old." In fact, challenging school culture elements and practices can be profoundly disturbing to those who have long followed the unwritten rules. They may perceive the current questions about their assumptions, beliefs, and practices as an assault on who they are, what they believe, and how they do their jobs. Accordingly, reshaping school culture must consider not only people's actions but also the ideas and values behind the actions and people's feelings about these ideas, values, and actions.

Strong and weak cultures exist on their own continuum (from most to least), and healthy and toxic cultures exist on a different continuum (from most to least). This means it is possible to have, for example, healthy (but) weak cultures in which only a few key teachers and administrators share values, views, and practices that help all children feel included, respected, and competent learners. They may want every teacher to make their content personally relevant to students to facilitate learning. Until these key educators' views are widely accepted, the school's impact on student learning will be modest, at best. In contrast, it is also possible to have strong (but) toxic cultures in which many teachers and administrators share values, views, and practices that undermine community in the school. For instance, they may insist that "teachers teach and students learn," refusing to provide the necessary supports to help every student successfully master the content. Obviously, the ideal culture would be healthy *and* strong where all—or almost all—the faculty and leadership share the beliefs, customs, and habits that build community and that generally are accepted as "the way we do things around here."

Leaders facilitating school improvement by looking at culture need to be people-sensitive and to listen and watch team members carefully so they can fully understand what each member means and respond respectfully to their views—whether expressed in words or with gestures and whether the principal agrees or not. Such emotional considerations make school counselors and their professional listening and group facilitation skills important allies in leading school change.

**TABLE 4.1** Features of Healthy and Toxic School Cultures

| Healthy School Culture | Toxic School Culture |
| --- | --- |
| Faculty, staff, and students feel valued and respected by the principal, students, parents, and central office administrators. | Faculty and staff feel as if they are treated poorly, disrespected, as if they were "cogs" in the machine. |
| Faculty and staff share a sense of meaningful purpose, caring, and concern; agree on what is important; continuous improvement norm; and genuine commitment to help all students learn. | Faculty and staff lack a shared sense of meaningful purpose or caring; norms reinforce inertia. Employees want to do their job and leave. Slower learning and lower achieving students are left to struggle and fail. |
| Collegiality, collaboration, continuous learning, openness to new ideas, problem solving, improvement, and hard work are well-respected norms. | Complaisant administrators and faculty avoid or resist change. Oppositional and prickly interpersonal relations. Collaboration is discouraged. |
| Every (or almost every) faculty and staff member feels responsible for every student's learning to high levels. | Faculty and staff blame students and parents for students' lack of progress and achievement. |
| Everyone (or almost everyone) values professional development, reflection, sharing professional practice so all can improve their skills in teaching and leading. | Professional development and staff reflection seen as wasting time: "If it ain't broke, don't fix it" and "This too shall pass" are the ethos. |
| Data, problem solving, and decision making are shared with faculty, staff, students, and parents. | Principals see all data and make all decisions. |
| Faculty and staff feel motivated, productive, mutually supportive, confident in their own and colleagues' skills, and successful. | Faculty and staff feel exhausted, unproductive, frustrated, unhappy, unsupportive of colleagues; occasional hostility among staff. |
| Rituals and traditions celebrate student accomplishment, teacher innovation, and parental commitment. | Individual and group innovations and achievements go unnoticed (or become focus of ridicule). |
| Informal network of storytellers, heroes, and heroines provide a social web of ideals, information, support, and history. | No school traditions or heroes exemplify the school's purpose or values. |

Source: Adapted from Kaplan, L. S., & Owings, W. A. (2013). *Culture re-boot*, pp. 14–15. Thousand Oaks, CA: Corwin. Reprinted by permission of Sage Publications.

**REFLECTIONS AND RELEVANCE 4.3**

## Assessing Your School's Culture for Strength and Health

School cultures can be strong or weak, healthy or toxic. These differences affect how the school treats its members and conducts its business.

Using Tables 4.1 and 4.2, assess your current school's culture for strength and health. Assign one point for each item for which you find your school to be strong and healthy. Add up your points (maximum points = 16, one per item on both tables, inclusive). Have someone draw a horizontal line across the board or chart to form a continuum. Place number 1 on the far left and continue numbering to 16 on the far right end. Without naming schools, have each student place an X on the line where their school rated on strength and health. See where the schools array along the continuum.

As a class discuss the following questions:

1. Where do most schools fall in terms of having a strong and healthy culture?

2. At which number on the school culture strength/health continuum do you think you would find it most enjoyable to work as a principal or teacher? Explain why.

3. At which number on the school culture strength/health continuum do you think you would find it the most unpleasant to work as a principal or teacher? Explain why.

4. At which number on the school culture strength/health continuum do you think you would find it most challenging to work as a principal or teacher? Explain what you mean by "challenging" and give reasons for your decision.

5. At which number on the school culture strength/health continuum do you think you would be most productive regarding student achievement? Explain why.

6. What are you presently doing in your current school to make working there more pleasant and productive?

7. What else could you do this year to make your school more pleasant and productive for teachers and yourself?

8. What might you do next year to make your school more pleasant and productive for teachers and yourself?

## WHY YESTERDAY'S SCHOOL CULTURE DOESN'T WORK TODAY

In an open system, public schools are influenced by their surrounding environments —political, economic, social, and technological. As illustrated in Figure 4.2, 19th and early 20th-Century high schools were designed to meet industrial age needs. In 1900, only 9 percent of 17 year olds in the U.S. graduated from high school.[11] The booming manufacturing economy welcomed low-skill, low-information workers and a few college educated professionals. Preparing future employees for factory jobs, schools were designed to run like mini-factories, sorting, selecting, and preparing labor for assembly lines using bell schedules to structure learning time and academic and vocational departments to guide instruction. Principals were efficient managers of people, time, space, and money. With schools' traditional top-down culture, teachers worked alone with their students behind closed classroom doors. The economic, political, and social realities did not require every child to learn to high levels.

In contrast, today's successful schools operate in a very different environment: information-rich, hyper-connected, technologically-based, and global in scope. The labor market requires every high school graduate—regardless of family background— to have high levels of knowledge, problem-finding and problem-solving skills; excellent communication competences; critical thinking; and the ability to work in teams, often

**FIGURE 4.2** Yesterday's Factory Model of the American High School
Source: Jem Sullivan. Reprinted with permission of the artist.

with others unlike themselves and perhaps located in another country. Over the past 40 years, entry-level job requirements have increased as the economy has shifted from a manufacturing to a knowledge-based economy. From 1983 to 2010, the salary premium earned by workers with a BA or higher—over that earned by their peers with a high school diploma—rose from 40 percent to 74 percent. Likewise, by 2020, it is estimated that 65 percent of job openings will require at least some postsecondary education and training.[12]

In response, many school realities are also changing. Principals are now expected to enact leadership and well as managerial roles. Classroom doors are opening as more teachers grow professionally through collaborative study with their colleagues and participate in school decisions that affect them. In short, American public schools' 19th-Century cultural assumptions are no longer relevant, and principal leadership is necessary to reshape them.

## FINDING CULTURAL ELEMENTS IN SCHOOLS

Despite its broad dimensions, school culture is more than an abstraction. People can see, hear, touch, and sense it in the school building, in its art and technology, and in its employees' beliefs and behaviors.

Edgar H. Schein, the MIT professor who first coined the idea of organizational culture, suggested that it exists on three levels. These appear arrayed vertically in Figure 4.3 along a continuum from concrete to abstract. Applying this concept to schools, at the top, artifacts such as the iconic schoolhouse itself, motivational banners and slogans, school colors, sports team mascots, awards and trophies, and displays of students' best work can be seen and touched; they represent the school's public identity at the most tangible level. Although these are cultural symbols, their deeper meanings tend to lie below conscious awareness. Next, less visible, lie the school's cultural values as they appear in a written mission statement (such as "Meeting every child's full development: intellectual, social, emotional, and physical"), philosophy (e.g. "We educate *all* children"), or motto (for example, "A great place to learn"). While not easily visible or touchable, such documents or slogans help express the school's basic assumptions and goals. Lastly, the assumptions lying outside consciousness and taken for granted—the culture's heart—deal with individual relationships to other people and to the environment. These beliefs form inherent, unconscious ideas that members accept uncritically—unless a public questioning process brings them into full awareness and challenges their continued benefit to the school's current goals.

Learning a school's culture is a cognitive, behavioral, and emotional process. Through a formal or informal induction route, members new to the school learn the "correct way" to perceive, think, and act in relation to organizational members, clients, and problems. Once they have learned the common assumptions and actions, their responses become almost automatic. They know how to predict recurring events and how to respond to them appropriately. These shared ways of navigating organizational concerns provides meaning, stability, and comfort to its members. The communal

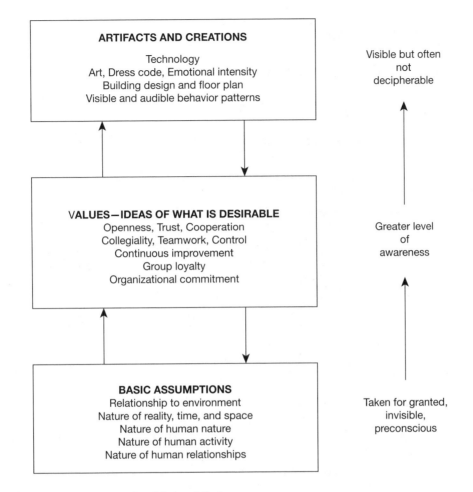

**FIGURE 4.3** Three Levels of School Culture

Sources: Adapted from Schein, E. H. (1985). *Organizational culture and leadership* (p.14, Figure 1). San Francisco, CA: Jossey-Bass; and Schein, E. H. (1990). Organizational culture. *American Psychologist, 45* (2), 109–119 (p. 114, Table 2); Hoy W. K., & Miskel, C. G. (2008). *Educational administration. Theory, research, and practice* (8th ed.), (p. 178, Figure 5.1). Boston, MA: McGraw Hill. Reprinted with permissions.

learning helps reduce the members' anxiety about not knowing what's coming, what's happening, or how to respond. As stress is lowered, the culture is strengthened.

While school culture tends to be stable, it is not static. Interactions among principals, teachers, students, and the larger community continually reshape and reassemble culture as members reflect publicly on how their school's traditional norms and practices fit with contemporary realities, current needs, and educational purposes. Since school culture is organic to its community, if the culture changes, the community changes.[13] And as an open system, changes in one place cause a cascade of reactions elsewhere. Improving schools requires considering the effects of change on the entire system, and the principal has the responsibility for making it happen.

## REFLECTIONS AND RELEVANCE 4.4

# Identifying Cultural Elements in Your School

A school's culture exists on three levels: its artifacts, its values, and its basic assumptions. Only the first two levels are immediately visible to onlookers.

Take a leisurely 20-minute walk around your school from the main entrance to the various centers of student activity (halls, classrooms, gym, library, cafeteria, and a restroom). You can invite a colleague to join you in this activity. Identify all the cultural artifacts and creations, written materials describing the school's deepest values, and the school's basic, taken-for-granted assumptions about the environment, reality, human nature, human activity, and relationships that you notice during your walk. Then complete the table below and consider the questions that follow. (Your professor may want you to bring a sample of each culture level to class to display and discuss.)

| Levels of School Culture | Examples Found (or known from experiences interacting with others in the school) | Those Likely to See or Be Aware of These Cultural Elements (teachers, students, parents, visitors) |
|---|---|---|
| *Artifacts and visual creations* | | |
| School colors, slogans, logos, mascots, slogans, letterheads, etc. | | |
| *Written materials expressing deepest values and goals* | | |
| Mission statement | | |
| Student Handbook | | |
| Parent Handbook | | |
| School improvement plan | | |
| *Basic assumptions about:* | | |
| Relation to environment | | |
| Nature of reality | | |
| Human nature, activity | | |
| *Relationships | | |

\* For example: When, if ever, does a teacher intervene in a student conversation?; Identify some of the daily topics of conversation in the teachers' lounge; Describe the tone of voice and amount of interaction between administrators and teachers at monthly faculty meetings.

**Questions to discuss as a class:**

1. What types of school culture artifacts and visual creations are easily found in your school?
2. What do the artifacts say about your school cultural values and goals? What do the written materials say about your school cultural values and goals? What do the basic assumptions say about your school cultural values and goals?
3. What positive assumptions, norms, or behaviors are some of your teachers and administrators using that might not be apparent to those people who spend less time in your school?
4. What do you think your principal and teachers can do to make the positive aspects of your school culture's values more visible or audible to students, parents, and casual visitors?

## LEADERSHIP AS CULTURE CREATION

For Schein, leadership and culture are two sides of the same coin: a leader's core responsibility—in fact, the heart of leadership—is to create and manage the dynamic process of culture creation. As Schein saw it, the "ability to perceive the limitations of one's own culture and to evolve the culture adaptively are the essence and ultimate challenge of leadership."[14] And more importantly, if leaders do not become conscious and manage the cultures in which they find themselves, these cultures will manage them.[15]

The principal's job, therefore, is to create the conditions that bring together the varied factors that positively impact student learning. Leaders create culture by seeing the big picture and making it coherent to others. From their vantage point scanning the entire organization and its environments, they can see the values and beliefs, the desired outcomes, the resources, and the people and influences that connect them. Principals are positioned to create the rationality and logic to help teachers make sense of their work and how it fits into the larger endeavor.

As the school's culture leader, principals work with others to define, strengthen, and express the school's enduring values, beliefs, and cultural themes that give the school its special identity. As culture leaders, principals articulate the school's purposes and mission, tell stories to continue or strengthen the positive traditions and beliefs underpinning "the way we do things around here," and induct new organizational members into the school's norms and practices. Principals work with others to create and reinforce meaningful cultural symbols—school colors, mascots, touchstones, mottos, and heroes (of any gender)—that can infuse value into all school activities and that visibly express significance deeper than words. Rituals, traditions, and ceremonies reinforce school members' excitement by generating an identity, strengthening ties to the school, and building a cohesive community. Cultural leadership connects students, teachers, and others as believers in the school's work, helping them experience a more profound purpose and feelings of belonging to an exceptional enterprise.

Research suggests that the cultural elements identified below support hard work and high achievement in organizations.[16] Each rests on a continuum from more to ess. Principals engage in culture creation when they invest time, energy, and faculty involvement in developing and enacting the following ten elements:

- *An inspiring vision.* The principal influences how well the school shapes and expresses a goal of academic success for all students by guiding the faculty to express their values and steering principles for the school. A clear and motivating purpose focused on student learning, reinforced by a well-defined, limited, and rousing mission can help principals lead a school to better outcomes.

- *Leadership.* Principals can purposefully guide the school's formal and informal leaders toward collaboration and meaningful changes aimed at achieving shared goals around teaching and learning, and continually making these values and outcomes a daily reality.

- *High expectations.* Principals can persistently model and emphasize the need for students' and teachers' working and learning to high standards. Ongoing conversations about everyone's work quality and inspiring school members with the energy, optimism, and behaviors that lead to improved outcomes can result in more effective teachers and more students learning to high levels.

- *Innovation and risk taking.* The degree to which the principal encourages faculty, staff, and students to be inventive, experiment, and take thoughtful risks to improve teaching and learning for all students. This includes securing flexibility, encouragement, and resources from the school district.

- *Trust and confidence.* Knowing that relationships matter in solving problems and working towards shared goals, principals set the tone, model, and informally coach others to behave with integrity, honesty, dependability, reliability, and trustworthiness. Over time, as these qualities become integral to all interactions, school members can build a caring community in which everyone feels safe to learn and grow.

- *Referring to the knowledge base.* The "instructional core"—the intersection between students, teachers, and content[17]—including curriculum, instructional practices, assessments, and learning opportunities—are clearly tied to the school's vision and mission and tailored to students' needs and interests. Similarly, managing accurate quantitative and qualitative data and skillfully questioning what they mean for the school's improvement can help educators continually enhance their processes, performances, and outcomes.

- *Involvement in decision making.* Leaders in all organizations depend on others to help accomplish the group's goals. Principals deliberately cultivate leadership in others—teachers, staff, students, parents, and community members—by providing them with relevant and timely information, occasions to discuss its meaning for the school values and goals, and opportunities to participate in making decisions that affect the school.

- *Honest, open communication.* Principals create an inviting climate when they provide many chances for school members to share information in clear, unambiguous, and respectful ways. Creating a culture that supports teacher collaboration for all students' academic success, discussing essential values, accepting responsibility for effectively teaching and supporting each student's learning, and coming together as a community to celebrate individual and group successes fosters such communication.
- *Tangible support.* Principals ensure that the faculty and staff receive sufficient encouragement, resources (including curricular materials and time for collaboration, professional development, and teamwork) and opportunities to effectively meet their professional responsibilities and contribute to their school's—and their own—wellbeing.
- *Appreciation and recognition.* Principals create occasions for the school community to show its gratitude and respect for those members who are making meaningful contributions to the organization or to its members. A school's customs, traditions, and general ways of doing things pinpoint the vigor of this quality in action.

Taken together, these ten elements can be assessed and used to construct a school's cultural profile. Does the principal share leadership with teachers who have the skills and perspectives to improve decision making? Does the school respect all people? Does the school encourage collaboration and teamwork? Does it reward thoughtful innovation in service of improved student learning and achievement? Does it value continuous improvement? Does the school welcome persons from differing ages, backgrounds, genders, races, ethnicities, languages, or abilities? In turn, this profile can become the basis for the members' shared understanding of the school, how it accomplishes its purposes, how members are expected to act, and helps identify areas needing further attention.

As is evident from this list, school culture is invested in relationships. In fact, schools where staffs have developed good working interactions, share a rapport and trust each other, and have a common understanding of what they are doing and why have more opportunities to exchange expertise and information and are more likely to be effective with their students.[18] In a virtuous circle, improved working relationships make it possible to strengthen these 10 elements in a school as well as being one of its most important outcomes.

What is more, recognizing and responding to cultural clues can leverage the principal's investment of time. Simple acts such as greeting students by name as they get off the school buses or out of cars can build relationships with them, provide them with a sense of order and safety, and offer occasions to interact with parents, young people, and community members. Being "out there" also gives leaders a sharper sense of "situational awareness"—one of the top leadership behaviors with the highest correlation to student achievement.[19]

Payoffs from principals' focus on building or reshaping their school's culture appear in varied ways. First, a school with a strong and healthy culture that shares a sense of important mission is more likely to activate improvement efforts.[20] Second, the culture's collegiality norms are related to teachers' collaborative planning and effective

**REFLECTIONS AND RELEVANCE 4.5**

## Assessing Yourself as a Culture Leader

Leadership is culture building, which is accomplished by providing direction and exercising influence.

How ready are you to be a school's culture leader? Read the culture leader's behaviors below and assess your present functioning from "Frequently" to "Infrequently" on each. Give an example to support your self-assessment, considering something that you have already done or are planning to do in the next few weeks. After everyone has completed the table, discuss as a class where you might be able to increase your experiences and expertise in each of the areas identified in the table.

| Culture Leader Behaviors | Self-rating: "Frequently" or "Infrequently" | Example of Use |
|---|---|---|
| See the "big picture" about our school's vision and goals. | | |
| Make the "big picture" coherent and logical to others. | | |
| Able to perceive limitations in own school's culture. | | |
| Can identify the values, beliefs, desired outcomes, resources, people, and influences that connect them (open systems thinking). | | |
| Can tell stories to highlight key school cultural values to strengthen positive traditions and rituals. | | |
| Work with teachers and others to create meaningful school culture symbols. | | |
| Help teachers new to the school to learn positive attitudes and behaviors of our school culture. | | |
| Design and participate in school rituals, traditions, and ceremonies that reinforce the school's positive identity and community. | | |
| Help inspire teachers, students, and parents to feel pride and belonging to a special enterprise (our school). | | |

## REFLECTIONS AND RELEVANCE 4.6

# Profiling Your School's Culture

A healthy and strong school culture has certain identifiable elements.

The following school culture elements support a hard-working, high-achieving organization. Rate the extent that each dimension is present and active in your current school, from 1 (lowest) to 5 (highest), and give examples that support your judgment. After each person has completed the list, have the class compile examples of how each cultural dimension might appear in a hard-working, high-achieving school and how each cultural dimension might appear in a complaisant, low-achieving school.

| Cultural Element | Rating: Extent Dimension is Present and Active in Your School 1–5 | Examples to Support Your Assessment |
|---|---|---|
| An inspiring vision | | |
| Leadership | | |
| High expectations | | |
| Innovation and risk taking | | |
| Trust and confidence | | |
| Referring to the knowledge base | | |
| Involvement in decision making | | |
| Honest, open communication | | |
| Tangible support | | |
| Appreciation and recognition | | |

decision making.[21] Third, cultures actively focused on improvement are more likely to put into place new instructional strategies that make measurable differences in student learning.[22] Finally, schools improve the most when their members recognize and celebrate small wins through ceremonies that highlight both individual and group contributions.[23]

Leadership can be described as enacting two essential functions: providing direction and exercising influence.[24] Creating culture in schools requires both. As the school's culture leader, the principal is the one who can head efforts to re-boot a school culture that is no longer serving its students' best interests. Principals who understand change dynamics and recognize how energizing faculty, staff, and parents to reflect on their deepest values for education—and what their children need to thrive in the present and future—can leverage their schools from brick-and-mortar buildings into places where teachers want to commit to investing their time, talent, and energy for improved student outcomes. Clearly, school leadership is culture building.

## PRINCIPAL AND FACULTY LEARNING CHANGES SCHOOLS

Effective principals build or reshape their schools' culture—but not singlehandedly. Schools cannot improve unless everyone in them learns how to improve their performance. Reinvigorating a school's culture requires enough faculty and staff to master the perspectives, knowledge, and skills needed to help every student succeed academically. They learn new or expanded ways of seeing and doing education. Any change in their behavior implies that learning has occurred. In fact, learning requires *change*—adjustments that individuals make in their thinking or doing by using feedback gained from interacting with their environment. Principals build culture, therefore, only when they create the conditions that encourage teachers and other employees to see their own learning as ongoing parts of their professional work responsibilities. Ironically, increasing adult capacity happens most readily when principals can help their schools truly become *learning*—rather than *schooling*—organizations.

According to Peter Senge, an MIT management expert, a *learning organization* is one in which its members glean important lessons from its past and present experiences, find meaning to help clarify their purpose, energize themselves for renewed and informed commitment to their work, and continually expand their capacity to create their desired results.[25] Organizations only learn (improve) when its members learn. *Organizational learning*, then, refers to its members' continually acquiring new perspectives and practices in the quest for improved outcomes. In today's world, successful organizations improve less by the traditional control and top-down directives and more by learning as members continually create and share new knowledge. Schools can only improve when their faculty and staff learn. And although individual learning does not ensure organizational learning, organizational learning cannot happen without it.

In his book, *The Fifth Discipline* (1990), Senge identifies five factors that together strengthen an organization's—in this case, a school's—ability to learn and make constructive changes that benefit its students. By understanding and adapting these factors for their own settings principals help faculty and staff learn what they need to know and do to reshape their culture. Briefly, these include the following:

- *Personal mastery.* The lifelong process of clarifying and heightening individuals' objective understanding of their actual situation, identifying the values they hold most dear, developing patience, integrating reason with intuition, and working with—rather than against—changes to improve outcomes for students. Continually developing their personal and professional skills motivates individuals to keep monitoring how their actions impact their students'—and their colleagues'— learning and achievement.
- *Mental models.* The deeply ingrained assumptions, generalizations, or images (often unconscious and outdated) that influence how we understand and act in our lives and organizations, telling us what we can or can't, should or shouldn't do— or which children can or can't learn to high standards. Expanding our thinking to more accurate representations of the world, rigorous inquiry, and challenge helps us identify limitations and flaws in our current ways of knowing the world and become open to change.
- *Building a shared vision.* The essential leadership role that motivates people in organizations to a common vision of a desirable future, nurtures a shared identity and purpose, and triggers the collective desire to learn and excel because teachers and administrators genuinely want to advance their agenda of academic success for all students.
- *Team learning.* The team focus, openness, and interactions (based on earned trust and mutual respect) that enable the group to learn together, make the group's intelligence greater than any individual's intelligence, and develop the team's capacity for coordinated inquiry, reflection, and action. As members of the school's leadership team, members query their school's culture, note where it does and does not align with present realities, and construct a shared vision better matched to contemporary needs. Team learning also occurs in academic departments, at grade-level meetings, and in professional learning communities when teacher leaders involve colleagues in defining and owning the shared vision and accepting the need for continual professional growth so all children may benefit.
- *Systems thinking.* The holistic conceptual framework in which understanding the whole depends on recognizing the contributions of its individual parts. As in the open systems model, all aspects of the school organization—inside and outside the building—are connected to all other parts; and all must be considered in planning any organizational change. By this view, the physical education, art, and social studies departments—as well as the secretaries, custodians, and cafeteria workers— are as essential, in their own ways, to children's holistic growth, overall wellness, and academic learning as the English, math, and science departments. Systems thinking is the dynamic that helps integrate the other factors into a coherent whole that helps all children succeed in school.

Becoming a learning organization does not simply mean acquiring more information. Rather, when a school becomes a learning organization, group members' abilities

**REFLECTIONS AND RELEVANCE 4.7**

## Assessing Your School as a Learning Organization

A *learning organization* is one in which its members can learn, find purpose and meaning, renew their commitment to their work, and expand their abilities to achieve their desired goals.

Is your school a learning organization? Are your educators continually learning in ways that generate the results they want from themselves and their students? Reread the definitions of the learning organization components given in the text and rate yourself and your current school using the table below on each dimension, on a scale from 1 (lowest) to 5 (highest). Then discuss the following questions in pairs, providing examples for your conclusions, and then discuss as a class.

| Learning Organization Dimensions | Self-rating on Learning Dimension 1–5 | School Rating on Learning Dimensions 1–5 | Examples |
|---|---|---|---|
| Personal mastery: developing own skills, monitoring effectiveness. | | | |
| Mental models: expanding thinking and assumptions so all students can succeed academically in school. | | | |
| Building a shared vision: motivating faculty to a shared desirable future for students (and themselves and their school). | | | |
| Team learning: trust, focus, and regular interaction time to help faculty grow as individuals and colleagues. | | | |
| Systems thinking: seeing the whole and its parts, their interactions, and their role in school improvement outcomes. | | | |

1. What is your current school's role in teachers' and administrators' learning?
2. What is the social-emotional and trust environment in your school, and how does it influence teachers' and administrators' learning? What examples can you offer?

3.  As a future school leader, on which learning dimensions do you feel strongest? What experience or evidence suggests this?
4.  As a future school leader, on which learning dimensions do you feel you need more experiences and occasions to practice and get expert feedback? What experiences or evidence suggests this?
5.  Which aspects of yourself as a future school leader can you develop more fully this year—and by what means?
6.  Which aspects of your school as a learning organization can you help develop this year—and by what means?

expand to produce the professional results they truly want. The principal's task is to design the learning process in which school members can deal productively with the critical issues they face and develop their mastery in the core technology. To do this, principals become role models, dedicating themselves to increasing their own personal mastery, openly discussing the values and overriding purpose that direct the school's mission and daily activities, and providing a climate in which all school members can do the same.

First, however, principals must ensure a safe and respectful environment for teachers to reflect upon and express their previously unvoiced assumptions, values, and vision. In this climate, colleagues listen thoughtfully to each other and try to under-stand the speaker's viewpoints without prejudgment, war stories, or one-upsmanship. Inquiry and genuine reality-testing become expected parts of any discussion. Challenging "the way we do things around here" becomes predictable and encouraged. In this organizational climate, members learn through experience that the organization appreciates their personal and professional growth, and it provides frequent on-the-job occasions to learn, individually and as teams. Only when these things happen as part of the school's routine do they become part of its culture. And only as its members learn and act upon this learning in ways that promote the success of every teacher and every student can schools excel. Because organizations can only change when its members learn.

## RESEARCH ON ORGANIZATIONAL CULTURE AND CLIMATE

Over the years, interest in organizational culture and climate has led investigators to study the concept and its impact on organizational behavior and outcomes. In their book, *Shaping School Culture* (2010), Terrence Deal and Kent Peterson, two noted educational leadership professors, observe that research on school culture and climate supports its impact on school functioning and outcomes in the following ways:[26]

*   *Culture boosts school effectiveness and productivity, including student achieve-ment.*[27] Teachers improve student learning in a culture focused on productivity

(rather than status quo or undemanding work); performance (effort, commitment, and perseverance); and improvement (always refining teaching practices). A culture which emphasizes clear purpose, collegiality, and provides rewards (or sanctions) related to improving teaching quality motivates teachers to persist in their challenging work.

- *Culture directs attention to what is valued and essential.*[28] Unwritten rules, informal expectations, and traditions and ceremonies may have more influence on teacher behaviors than job descriptions, rules, and policies. Centering work on the bottom-line issues of quality instruction, continuous refinement of teaching, and faster learning motivates teachers towards positive action and sustained progress.

- *Culture enhances collegiality, teamwork, communication, and problem-solving practices.*[29] Schools that value teachers working together to improve their professional practice and increase student learning provide opportunities for social and professional exchange of ideas, improved pedagogy, and extensive professional problem identification and problem solving.

- *Culture advances innovation and school improvement through shared leadership.*[30] Schools that encourage change and informed risk-taking nurture people who seek innovative practices and experiment with new approaches rather than seek comfort in mediocrity, inertia, and apathy.

- *Culture builds commitment and stimulates motivation.*[31] People feel inspired and dedicated to an endeavor that is meaningful and valuable for a larger purpose. Rituals, traditions, and ceremonies fortify incentives to participate by cultivating identity, strengthening connection to the school, and building community.

- *Culture intensifies the school staff's, students', and community's drive and vigor.*[32] Social climate and culture shape a school's emotional and psychological environment, especially when schools are positive, thoughtful, helpful and lively. All school members are likely to adopt this outlook. In contrast, schools with negative milieus can discourage even upbeat individuals.

- *School climate influences students' learning and achievement.*[33] A positive, supportive school climate that helps individual students feel safe, respects individuals' background differences, and increases opportunities for students to develop affirming relationships can significantly and directly shape students' mental and physical health as well as students' degree of academic achievement in elementary, middle, and high schools. The positive effects seem to persist for years. A positive school climate also prevents maladaptive behaviors—especially in high-risk urban environments. School climate is also an important factor in successful school improvement.

In sum, studies consistently shows school culture's key role in school success.

Where schools' cultural patterns did not support and encourage reform, changes did not occur. In contrast, in schools where norms, values, and beliefs reinforced a strong educational mission, a sense of community, social trust among staff, and shared commitment to school improvement, positive outcomes resulted for teachers and students. The schools' culture supported teacher leadership, and collegiality in professional development focused on increasing student learning and involvement in problem solving. Over time, teachers in these schools developed a sense of group efficacy that generated the energy to improve. And, the greater the school's academic quality for all students and the more positive its emotional climate, the higher the student achievement and the lower the level of school crime and violence.

---

### REFLECTIONS AND RELEVANCE 4.8

## Leveraging School Culture for School Improvement

Research supports the conclusion that educators can deliberately use—or reshape—their school's culture as a means to improve student outcomes.

Working in pairs, use the research conclusions about school culture and climate—and any other information from this chapter—to develop a two- to five-minute talk to persuade your principal and school leadership team to focus on learning more about school culture—and how they can use it to advance their goals for improved student learning and achievement. You may create a graphic to help "sell" your idea. Then present your talk to the rest of the class and ask for their feedback about how to strengthen your argument. After the presentations, have the class identify the best points from all the talks.

---

### REFLECTIONS AND RELEVANCE 4.9

## Considering School Culture as Key to School Improvement

This chapter focuses on helping future school leaders understand how they can leverage school culture to improve student achievement. Here's an opportunity to be a leader in your current school.

Working with a partner, prepare and deliver a two- to five-minute persuasive talk on why your principal and school leadership team can be more effective if they consciously study their own school's culture, and, if needed, reshape their culture to better align with and support their vision and goals. Be sure to include reasons why focusing on culture can help your school better meet its goals for helping all children succeed academically. You may create a graphic to accompany your talk. When you are finished, present your talk to the class.

After all the presentations are over, the class as a whole will identify the strongest points from all the presentations—and identify what activities from this book you might use to help your own school leadership team begin to learn about their own school's culture. Volunteers may want to give their revised talk to their own school leadership team some time during this semester then receive objective feedback and reflect on its effectiveness.

## CONCLUSION

Positive school cultures begin with principals. Principals' central responsibility is to create a school culture that supports leading, teaching, and learning. Principals do this when they create a psychologically safe environment for teachers and students: safe to make mistakes and learn from them without worrying about looking incompetent; safe to express values, beliefs, and concerns about teaching and learning without fear of disrespect; safe to collaborate with colleagues without fretting about appearing either prideful or inept; and safe to work hard and invest time and energy in developing their own capacities without worrying about looking foolish.

In schools with strong and healthy cultures, principals provide many opportunities for professional growth and practice aimed at improving student learning. They coach and reward members for making efforts in the desired direction. And they ensure it is OK to make errors and learn from them. Principals who create a strong and healthy school culture ensure that everyone feels a sense of belonging, and that all are esteemed for their initiative, successes, dedication, and efforts. Only when the principal can guarantee a school environment open to new ideas and the freedom to challenge current assumptions, beliefs, and behaviors can teachers and staff learn what they need to build their capacities to help every student succeed academically.

## NOTES

1. Kaplan, L. S., & Owings, W. A. (2013). *Culture re-boot: Reinvigorating school culture to improve student outcomes*. Thousand Oaks, CA: Corwin.
2. Parsons, R. (1960). *Structure and process in modern societies*. Glencoe, IL: Free Press.
3. Hatch, T. (2013, November). Innovation at the core. *Phi Delta Kappan, 95* (3), 34–38.
4. Schein, E. H. (2004). *Organizational culture and leadership* (3rd ed.) (pp. 12–13). New York, NY: John Wiley.
5. Coutu, D. L. (2002). Edgar H. Schein. The anxiety of learning: The darker side of organizational learning. *Harvard Business Review, 80* (3), 100–106.
6. Schein, E. H. (1985). *Organizational culture and leadership* (1st ed.) (p. 9). San Francisco, CA: Jossey-Bass.
7. Schein, E. H. (1985). How culture forms, develops, and changes. In R. H. Kilmann, M. J. Saxton, & R. Serpa (Eds.), *Gaining control of the corporate culture* (pp. 19–21). San Francisco, CA: Jossey-Bass; Schein, E. H. (1985). *Organizational culture and leadership* (1st ed.) (p. 9). San Francisco, CA: Jossey-Bass.
8. *Schooling* is the program of formal instruction or training that happens inside a classroom during the school day, throughout the school calendar year, as legally defined in state law. *Educating* is learning that occurs all the time, often beyond the school walls, and includes a wider array of knowledge and skills than appears in the formal curriculum.
9. Firestone, W., & Louis, K. (1999). Schools as cultures. In J. Murphy, & K. Louis (Eds.), *Handbook of research on educational administration* (2nd ed.) (pp. 297–322). San Francisco: Jossey-Bass.
10. Kaplan, L. S., & Owings, W. A. (2013). *Culture re-boot: Reinvigorating school culture to improve student outcomes* (pp. 6–7). Thousand Oaks, CA: Corwin.
11. Snyder, T. D. (Ed.) (1993, January). *120 years of American education: A statistical portrait* (Figure 11, p. 31). Washington, DC: National Center for Education Statistics, U.S. Department of Education. Retrieved from http://nces.ed.gov/pubs93/93442.pdf

12. Carnevale, A. P., Hanson, A. R., & Gulish, A. (2013, September). *Failure to launch. Structural shift and the new lost generation* (p. 12). Washington, DC: Center on Education and the Workforce, Georgetown University. Retrieved from: http://www9.georgetown.edu/grad/gppi/hpi/cew/pdfs/FTL_FullReport.pdf

13. Donahoe, T. (1993). Finding the way: Structure, time, and culture in school improvement. *Phi Delta Kappan, 75* (4), 298–305 (p. 302).

14. Schein, E. H. (2004). *Organizational culture and leadership* (3rd ed.) (p. 2). New York, NY: John Wiley.

15. Schein (2004), ibid.

16. O'Reilly, C. A. III, Chatman, J., & Caldwell, D. R. (1991). People and organizational culture: A profile comparison approach to assessing person-organization fit. *Academy of Management Journal*, September, 49 (3), 487–516; Chatman, J. A., & Jehn, K. A. (1994). Assessing the relationship between industry characteristics and organizational culture: How different can you be? *Academy of Management Journal*, June, 37 (3), 522–553.

17. Elmore, R. (2000). *Building a new structure for school leadership*. Washington, DC: Albert Shanker Institute.

18. Bryk, A., & Schneider, B. (2002). *Trust in schools: A core resource for improvement*. New York, NY: Russell Sage Foundation; Leana, C. R. (2011, Fall). The missing link in school reform. *Stanford Social Innovation Review*. Retrieved from: http://www.ssireview.org/articles/entry/the_missing_link_in_school_reform/; Putnam, R. (2000). *Bowling alone: The collapse and revival of American community*. New York, NY: Simon & Schuster.

19. Marzano, R., Waters, T., & McNulty, B. (2005). *School leadership that works*. Alexandria, VA: Association for Supervision and Curriculum Development and Aurora, CO: McRel.

20. See, for example, Deal, T. E., & Peterson, K. D. (2009). *Shaping school culture. Pitfalls, paradoxes and promises* (2nd ed.). San Francisco, CA: Jossey-Bass; Rutter, M., Maughan, B., Mortimore, P., Ouston, J., & Smith, A. (1979). *Fifteen thousand hours*. Cambridge, MA: Harvard University Press; Levine, D. U., & Lezotte, L. W. (1990). *Unusually effective schools: A review and analysis of research and practice*. Madison, WI: National Center for Effective Schools Research and Development.

21. See, for example, DuFour, R., & Marzano, R. (2011). *Leaders of learning: How district, school, and classroom leaders improve student achievement*. Bloomington, IN: Solution Tree; Seashore Louis, K., Leithwood, K., Wahlstrom, K. L., & Anderson, S. E. (2010, July). *Learning from leadership: Investigating the links to improved student learning*. Final Report of Research to The Wallace Foundation, University of Minnesota and University of Toronto. Retrieved from: http://www.wallacefoundation.org/knowledge-center/school-leadership/key-research/Documents/Investigating-the-Links-to-Improved-Student-Learning.pdf

22. Abplanalp, S. (2008). *Breaking the low-achieving mindset: A S.M.A.R.T. journey of purposeful change*. Madison, WI: QLD Learning (Quality Leadership by Design); DuFour & Marzano (2011), op. cit.

23. See, for example, Deal & Peterson (2009), op. cit.; Waters, J. T., Marzano, R. J., & McNulty, B. (2004). Leadership that sparks learning. *Educational Leadership, 61* (7), 48–51.

24. Seashore, Leithwood, Wahlstrom, & Anderson (2010, July), op. cit.

25. Senge, P. M. (1990). The fifth discipline. The art and practice of the learning organization. New York, NY: Doubleday.

26. Deal, T. E., & Peterson, K. D. (2010). *Shaping school culture: Pitfalls, paradoxes, and promises* (2nd ed.) New York, NY: Wiley.

27. See, for example, Bryk, A. S., Sebring, P. B., Allensworth, E., Luppescu, S., & Easton, J. Q. (2010). *Organizing for school improvement. Lessons from Chicago*. Chicago, IL: University of Chicago Press; Leithwood, K., Louis, K. S., Anderson, S., & Wahlstrom, K. (2004). *Review of research. How leadership influences student learning*. Minneapolis, MN: University of Minnesota Center for Research and Educational Improvement; Levine, D. U., & Lezotte, L. W. (1990). *Unusually effective schools: A review and analysis of research and practice*. Madison, WI: National Center for Effective Schools Research and Development; Waters,

Marzano, & McNulty (2004), op. cit.; Vescio, V., Ross, D., & Adams, A. (2008). A review of research on the impact of professional learning communities on teaching practice and student learning. *Teaching and Teacher Education, 24* (1), 80–91.

28. See, for example, Deal, T. E., & Kennedy, A. A. (1982). *Corporate cultures: The rites and rituals of corporate life*. Reading, MA: Addison-Wesley; Schein, E. H. (1985). *Organizational culture and leadership* (1st ed.). San Francisco, CA: Jossey-Bass; Schein, E. H. (2004). *Organizational culture and leadership* (3rd ed.). San Francisco, CA: Jossey-Bass.

29. See, for example, DuFour, R. (2007). Professional learning communities: A bandwagon, an idea worth considering, or our best hope for high levels of learning? *Middle School Journal, 39* (1), 4–8; DuFour, R., & Marzano, R. J. (2013). *Leaders of learning. How district, school, and classroom leaders improve student achievement*. Bloomington, IN: Solution Tree Press; Kruse, S. D., & Louis, K. S. (1997). Teacher teaming in middle schools: Dilemmas for a school-wide community. *Educational Administration Quarterly, 33* (3), 261–289.

30. See, for example, Deal, T. E., & Peterson, K. D. (1990). *The principal's role in shaping school culture*. Washington, DC: U.S. Department of Education; Louis, K. S., & Miles, M. B. (1990). *Improving the urban high school: What works and why*. New York, NY: Teachers College Press; Kruse & Louis (1997), op. cit.; Spillane, J., Halverson, R., & Diamond, J. (2003). Toward a theory of leadership practice: A distributed perspective. *Journal of Curriculum Studies, 36* (1), 3–34; Waters, Marzano, & McNulty (2004), op. cit.

31. See, for example, Schein, E. H. (1985). *Organizational culture and leadership* (1st ed.). San Francisco, CA: Jossey-Bass; Schein, E. H. (2004). *Organizational culture and leadership* (3rd ed.). San Francisco, CA: Jossey-Bass.

32. Goddard, R. D., Hoy, W. K., & Hoy, A. W. (2004). Collective efficacy beliefs: Theoretical developments, empirical evidence, and future directions. *Educational Researcher, 33* (3), 3–13.

33. See, for example, Haynes, N. M. (1998). Creating safe and caring school communities: Comer School Development Program schools. *Journal of Negro Education, 65,* 308–314; Hoy, W. K., & Hannum, J. W. (1997). Middle school climate: An empirical assessment of organizational healthy and student achievement. *Educational Administration Quarterly, 33* (3), 290–311; McEvoy, A., & Welker, R. (2000). Antisocial behavior, academic failure, and school climate: A critical review. *Journal of Emotional and Behavioral Disorders, 8*(3), 130–140; Thapa, A., Cohen, J., Higgins-D'Allesandro, A., & Guffey, S. (2012). School climate research Summary: August 2012. *School Climate Brief No. 3*. New York, NY: National School Climate Center. Retrieved from: http://www.schoolclimate.org/climate/documents/policy/sc-brief-v3.pdf

# CHAPTER 5

# Initiating and Sustaining Change

> It must be remembered that there is nothing more difficult to plan, more doubtful of success, nor more dangerous to manage than a new system. For the initiator has the enmity of all who would profit by the preservation of the old institution and merely lukewarm defenders in those who gain by the new ones.
>
> —Niccolò Machiavelli, *The Prince*[1]

## LEARNING OBJECTIVES

5.1  Explain the meaning of Seymour Sarason's observation as it relates to leading school improvement: "Knowledge is external. Knowing is internal. Information remains external until it can be connected to personal experience and personal meaning."

5.2  Describe how various elements of a school's culture can either facilitate or resist change.

5.3  Discuss the factors that influence adult learning and relate how principals can use these to motivate teachers to improve their professional practices.

5.4  Analyze Kurt Lewin's three-stage change model and discuss its implications for leading school improvement.

5.5  Explain how Chris Argyris and Donald Schön's single- and double-loop learning paradigm can help school leaders more effectively initiate and sustain change in their organizations.

5.6  Assess Robert Chin's three strategic orientations to leading organizational change and evaluate each one's potential effectiveness for leading school improvement.

5.7  Describe how school leaders can use Lee Bolman and Terrence Deal's multiple frames perspective to lead effective school improvement.

5.8  Summarize Michael Fullan's suggestions about leading school change and discuss their usefulness to future and practicing principals.

**2015 ISLLC STANDARDS: 1, 2, 3, 4, 5, 6, 7, 8, 9, 10, 11**

## INTRODUCTION

High-achieving schools have excellent leaders. Research has repeatedly highlighted principals as key players—second only to teachers—of school-based factors in improving student's academic outcomes.[2] By shaping a vision of academic success for all students, creating a climate that supports teaching and learning, cultivating leadership in others so they may also assume roles in realizing the school's goals, improving instruction, and managing people, data and processes, principals focus their schools in ways that generate improvement.[3]

Improving schools mean initiating change. As culture builders, effective principals must create a climate and then a culture that supports teachers as they make the adjustments needed to help all students learn to high levels. They must work with faculty to determine what is and is not working well in their schools as it affects student learning and achievement. Then principals and teachers collaborate to design, implement, and assess structures and practices that increase teachers' capacity to improve student outcomes. Change occurs with each step.

Since change is a given in leadership, principals benefit when they understand its nature and learn how to manage it in their schools. They also gain when they understand the relationship between school culture and change, because teachers will resist any proposed change that runs against their unvoiced assumptions, guiding ideas, and current practices.[4] The basis for successful school improvement, therefore, is for principals to help teachers perceive the proposed change as something they genuinely want rather than as sometime "done to" them.

As Seymour Sarason (1996), the late Yale psychology professor and expert in community psychology observed, "Knowledge is external. Knowing is internal. Information remains external until it can be connected to personal experience and personal meaning."[5] The effective principal's objective, then, is to motivate teachers to make the learning needed to improve their internal performance, based on their shared experiences and values—to make them "knowing" rather than merely "knowledgeable."

This chapter will look at the relationship between culture and change and consider several conceptual models by which to understand and lead change in schools. Kurt Lewin's change model, Chris Argyris and Donald Schön's single- and double-loop learning paradigm, Robert Chin's types of organizational change, Lee Bolman and Terrence Deal's "four frames" theory, and Michael Fullan's "change leadership" all receive attention. Each one presents insightful cognitive maps to help leaders more clearly understand how to navigate their organizations through change.

## THE CULTURE OF CHANGE

School change begins in principal–teacher leader collaboration, looking closely at the assumptions that underlie and shape the school's attitudes and practices. *School culture*—those unvoiced, taken-for-granted assumptions accepted as true—affect school improvement's success or failure. These include norms that educators hold for students, about leadership and decision making, about the best practices for educating students, and about the value of change itself. For instance, in a school culture asserting that only certain children have the capacity to master a high-challenge academic curriculum, teachers will recoil if the principal proposes an "open access" policy for AP classes (coupled with academic and moral support for struggling students). Similarly, a school culture that operates via top-down authoritarian mandates and does not promote democratic involvement and shared decision making will have a difficult time implementing a curriculum that prepares students for active engagement in their classrooms or for full citizenship participation beyond the campus.

If the school culture reinforces the belief that nothing positive ever resulted from earlier change initiatives, change will be avoided. In contrast, if the school members' overall attitude about change is that it can be beneficial, challenging, and exciting, then school improvement and its attendant changes are more likely to be initiated and sustained.

## ELEMENTS THAT HELP CHANGE SCHOOL CULTURE

More specifically, certain elements of school culture actually make teachers more open to change.[6] Many of these factors may look familiar, because they also support hard work and high achievement in organizations (as discussed in Chapter 4).[7] Where these variables exist, they can be nurtured and encouraged, and where they do not yet exist, they can be developed. They are:

1. *Collegiality.* Teachers respect, cooperate, and look out for each other's wellbeing.
2. *Honest, open, communication.* Educators can speak to each other directly, are able to disagree, discuss, listen, and resolve issues without fear of losing respect, harming relationships, or facing penalties.
3. *Experimentation.* Teachers see teaching as intellectually exciting, feel encouraged to try out new ideas and approaches that will benefit students, and are not punished for trying.
4. *High expectations.* Teachers and administrators expect each other to keep growing professionally and hold each other accountable for high performance through regular evaluations and feedback.
5. *Trust and confidence.* Administrators and teachers trust each other to act in students' best interests, and parents trust teachers' professional judgment and commitment to improve.
6. *Involvement in decision making.* Both principals and teachers participate in discussions about important issues and make decisions affecting the school, their students, and themselves.
7. *Tangible support.* Time, people, and resources are available to help teachers improve their performance, and on-going professional growth is valued and upheld.
8. *Using the knowledge base.* The funds of information about teaching and learning continue to expand, and educators keep learning the necessary knowledge and skills to generate student learning and achievement.

9. *Appreciation and recognition.* Good teaching is recognized and honored in the school and community.
10. *Caring, celebration, and humor.* Opportunities for staff and administrators to show appreciation for each other and to enjoy their time and work together occur regularly.
11. *Protection of what's important.* Administrators do not interrupt instruction, planning time, or professional development, and they keep meetings and paper-work to a minimum.
12. *Traditions.* The school always has an important, exciting, or challenging academic or ceremonial event to look forward to celebrating.

Change is implicit to school improvement, and school culture can either actively facilitate or inhibit it. If principals are to improve—that is, change—their schools, the assumptions underlying both the change and the school's culture must agree.[8] Change cannot be forced on teachers by edict without their participation or consent. Rather, effective principals must work with teachers to create the climate, viewpoints, and incentives that lead them to want, design, pursue, and enact the changes as a way to reach mutually desired ends. Meaningful change that teachers desire and support will have to come from the inside out. "Stock taking" and "soul searching" will become routine parts of the process. Schools must be "recultured"—not simply reformed or restructured.[9] To be effective and sustainable, changes in schools must be cultural as well as structural.

## RESPECTING HOW ADULTS LEARN

Principals who inspire teachers to rethink how they are educating their students and invest their emotions and energies into improving their professional performance create the conditions that best advance that growth. Clearly demonstrating respect for teachers as competent professionals—even if they still have learning to do—is especially critical when the new principal is youthful relative to mature and experienced classroom educators. Some veteran teachers tend to believe they know what they are doing, have been doing it effectively for years, and see no need to change. In many cases, teachers have many more years of classroom experience than their nominal leaders. For these reasons, principals who wish to foster a culture of change need to understand and respect their teachers and the ways adults learn, and use practices that motivate and support teachers' continuous personal and professional growth.

Until the mid-20th Century, data on adult learning were limited. In fact, many investigators questioned whether or not adults *could* learn. Today we know that adults score better on certain aspects of intelligence testing as they get older and worse on others. The result is a fairly stable composite measure of intelligence until very old age.[10]

In addition, research and experience affirm that adults in our culture typically learn differently than children across several important dimensions as listed below.[11] Although

## REFLECTIONS AND RELEVANCE 5.1

# Self-Assessing on Cultural Dimensions of Change

A school's culture influences the success or failure of its school improvement initiatives. Are you ready to help foster a culture of change in ways that benefit teachers and students?

The following elements of school culture facilitate school improvement. Assess yourself (from 1: needing to grow, to 5: highly effective now) on the extent to which you presently initiate or elicit these dimensions in your current work setting. For a reality check, invite a colleague (someone who you do not evaluate) to assess you on the same dimensions. Then compare the two ratings and see where you might want to grow. When you have finished the self-assessment, discuss your findings with a partner. The class should survey its members for the areas in which you believe the class, as a whole, needs the most learning experiences and those areas in which they are already proficient. Where, when, and how might class members more fully develop the skills they need to create a supportive school culture?

| Cultural Element | Self-assessment 1 (need to grow)– 5 (highly effective) | Colleague Assessment 1 (need to grow)– 5 (highly effective) |
|---|---|---|
| Exhibits collegiality | | |
| Honest, open communication | | |
| Experimental | | |
| High expectations | | |
| Trust and confidence in colleagues, parents | | |
| Involves others in decision making | | |
| Provides tangible support | | |
| Uses the knowledge base | | |
| Shows appreciation and recognition | | |
| Shows caring, celebration, and humor | | |

these factors lie on a continuum from teacher-directed to student-directed—and both are appropriate with adults as well as children, depending on the individuals and the situation. Adults tend to favor the learner-directed pattern.

1. *Self-concept.* As a person matures, the self-concept evolves from being other-directed and dependent towards being increasingly independent and self-directed. Adults want to guide their own learning. Principals need to give teachers personal experiences in which they can discover for themselves the logical and verifiable reasons why they need to continue their learning and offer choices about how, what, and when they will learn.

2. *Experience.* As a person matures, the individual accumulates a growing reservoir of life events, creating larger sets of prior knowledge and resources for learning. Teachers need opportunities to see how their beliefs, values, experiences, and goals fit in with the school leaders' vision and goals and how these shared ideas can be used to facilitate their new learning.

3. *Readiness to learn.* A maturing person wants to learn what he or she needs to know. One's receptivity to learning becomes geared toward mastering the developmental tasks that one's social, economic, and political roles require. Teachers must come to understand how their new learning will contribute to their success as educators with all children. It helps, too, when they see the wider implications of improved student outcomes for their community and nation.

4. *Orientation to learn.* As an individual matures, the incentive to learn becomes increasingly internal and self-directed. These incentives are often problem-centered and focused on knowledge and skills appropriate for immediate use: teachers want to know the what, why, how, and when this new learning will be useful to them.

Although each of these statements and claims of differences between adult and childhood learning are debatable,[12] they do provide a reasonable basis for designing, implementing, and evaluating educational experiences with adults.

Accordingly, principals who want their teachers to accept change—and learn the new instructional strategies and skills—will want to provide a learning climate and settings in which teachers feel accepted, respected, safe, supported, and trusted. To do this, leaders and adult learners will want to share a spirit of joint inquiry as they all learn together. Principals do not play "experts" to teachers' "pupils." The ambiance will be informal and adult. The physical environment will be comfortable: appropriate room temperature, chairs that one doesn't mind sitting in for several hours, adequate lighting, good acoustics, refreshments, and a physical format that encourages inter-action. People will be encouraged to speak sincerely about their views, values, and practices without penalty or ridicule and encouraged to listen carefully so they may understand others. Hypothesis testing, prompt, honest and specific feedback, and accepting mistakes as a path to learning will be accepted behaviors. In short, principals who want teachers to be open to change will have to treat them as mature, know-ledgeable, and experienced individuals who are capable of helping to plan and direct their own learning.

## CONCEPTUAL MODELS OF CHANGE

If the culture of learning provides part of the environment for nurturing school improvement, conceptual models of change provide some of its inputs.

Different societies view change in their own ways. Until the mid-20th Century, U.S. culture viewed organizational life as relatively stable and bureaucratic. Hierarchical authority, clear-cut divisions of labor, and inflexible rules and procedures typified organizational life. After World War II, a rush of national and international events —the Iron Curtain dividing communist from capitalist societies, Russia's 1957 Sputnik satellite in orbit, civil rights' agitations and advances, political assassinations of beloved American political and moral leaders, for example—deeply shook our nation's sense of security. Naturally, these disturbing events influenced ideas about organizational functioning and the nature of change. One result: U.S. and Western European organizational models have increasingly considered not only how to deal with continuous change but also how to create it.[13]

In the mid- to late-20th Century, theorists began to study the more complex dynamics of modern organizations and the interactions of people within them. Scholars including Kurt Lewin, Chris Argyris, Robert Chin, Lee Bolman and Terrance Deal, and Michael Fullan provided insights to better help organizational leaders— including principals—understand the multifaceted nature of change, its impact on people at work, and how leaders could use these insights to improve their groups' productivity.

## KURT LEWIN: CHANGE THEORY

Kurt Lewin, a German-born psychologist, fled Nazism in 1933, became a U.S. citizen in 1940, and worked as a professor at universities from Cornell to Iowa to MIT. Recognized as the founder of modern social psychology, he played a central role in conceptualizing organizational development. Lewin saw humans as interdependent beings. His personal experiences as a Nazi refugee prompted him to find an effective, humanistic, ethical, and democratic approach to resolving social conflict. He viewed change as a complex learning process where stability was always fluid and outcomes could not be predicted but emerged as trial and error. Lewin surmised that only by changing group behavior—by creating an organization's members' own "felt need" and willingness to learn and participate in the change—could society's members act as buffers against the racism and totalitarianism that so dominated events during his life.[14]

As illustrated in Figure 5.1, Lewin perceived change as composed of three stages: Unfreeze, Movement, and Refreeze. He saw this model as one part of an integrated approach to analyzing, understanding, and eliciting planned change at the group, organizational, and societal levels. In his view, analyzing the driving and restraining forces around the proposed changes could help an organization's leaders shift the balance in the direction of planned adjustments.[15]

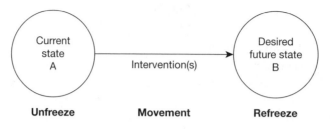

**FIGURE 5.1** Kurt Lewin's Three-stage Change Model

Source: Marshak, R. J. (1993) Lewin meets Confucius: A review of the organizational development model of change. *Journal of Applied Behavioral Science, 29* (4), p. 397, copyright © 1993 by Sage Publications. Reprinted by permission of Sage Publications.

## Stage 1—Unfreezing: Motivate People to Change

Lewin saw human behavior as based on a quasi-equilibrium supported by a complex field of forces. In his view, people tend to prefer a situation in which they feel relatively safe, stable, and in control; they will resist change even if the proposals appear to be beneficial. So before someone will discard (unlearn) old behaviors and successfully adopt (learn) new behaviors, the equilibrium must be destabilized (unfrozen). Unfreezing may require significant effort. Lewin's specific insight was that it was easier to change (unfreeze or destabilize) current behaviors if restraining forces such as personal defenses, group norms, or organizational culture also shift in ways that make individuals more open to a new approach.[16]

Thus, principals can create teachers' "felt need" and undo teachers' sense of safety and comfort by giving them information or providing situations that makes them dissatisfied with their current state. For example, Hilton High School traditionally boasts the best student achievement test scores in the school district, and teachers express pride in their students' high local standing. The teachers believe that they are doing a great job educating their community's children. Unfortunately, their students' average achievement is well below the state's and the nation's average—and far below that of other developed nations.

During a daylong retreat after the current school year ends, the principal meets with department heads and other school leaders to review the year's progress and set goals for the next academic year. The principal distributes their school's, district's, state's and national achievements test results (disaggregated) for review and discussion. Next, the principal distributes three current articles from well-respected national publications about globalization's effects on employment, compares American students' achievement with those of advanced and emerging economies, and describes how American students will be competing with workers in other nations for white- and blue-collar jobs—and the implications for the U.S. standard of living and the health of our social safety nets. Then the principal separates the teachers into four groups and gives each group one hour to read and discuss the articles and respond to the test data with what they think and how they feel. After that, the group meets as a whole to ask and answer: What do these data tell us? What do they mean for our students, our curriculum, and instruction?

How should we as a faculty respond—cognitively and emotionally? How do we share these data and this perspective with our faculty and parents? Where and when do we begin?

Most likely, considering their students' achievement within a larger context and longer time frame makes many teachers very uncomfortable, creates cognitive dissonance,[17] and unfreezes their complacency about their teaching effectiveness. Such a jarring and credible experience can motivate teachers to ask and begin to answer difficult questions about how well they are really doing in generating student achievement and how they can improve their professional practice.

## Stage 2—Movement: Change What Needs to Be Changed

Although unfreezing creates the incentive to learn, it does not predict the direction the learning or change will take. The favorable and resisting forces that support the status quo need to shift in size, direction, or number. At this point, teachers have become unhappy with their present situation and are ready to make positive adjustments. Now they need to know exactly what must change. They need a clear and concise view of where they are headed so they can see the gap between the present conditions and the proposed ones.

For instance, the Hilton High School principal and school leaders pore over their disaggregated test data. They notice that the even their highest-achieving English classes are scoring well below those of comparable peers across the state and nation. After further analysis, teachers in various subjects conclude that their students are not learning how to read complex discursive writings such as appear on the tests or in college texts or how to support their ideas with evidence from their readings. Nor do most students know how to effectively analyze, synthesize, or evaluate what they are learning in meaningful ways so it is deeply learned and available for future recall and use.

Given these findings, the leadership group decides on a plan to improve their students' achievement: all teachers will participate in two semesters of job-embedded professional development to learn how to help their students at every achievement level learn to read for evidence and ideas and increase critical thinking and problem solving using their regular—and some advanced—classroom reading materials. Teachers will work collaboratively to learn the techniques, design learning activities using them, and observe and offer constructive feedback to each other as they try out these intellectually rigorous approaches in their classrooms. In addition, every six weeks, teachers will use collaboratively developed assessments aligned with the standardized assessment to monitor how well their students are learning and make necessary instructional adjustments.

## Stage 3—Refreeze: Make the Change Permanent

Refreezing attempts to solidify and keep the group at a new equilibrium, trying to prevent the members' new attitudes and behaviors from reverting to the old ways. Instead of backsliding, teachers practice and receive high-quality feedback on their recently acquired attitudes and behaviors, and successful practices become habits (refreeze). As a result, the teachers develop expanded views of themselves, enhanced skills, and more helpful interpersonal relationships with colleagues who help them learn—and student learning increases.

For instance, as teachers collaboratively learn how to design and conduct lessons that deepen students' abilities to think critically, they help each other plan, implement, and evaluate their progress mastering these new approaches. They encourage and assist each other to enhance their teaching skills. And, as the formative and summative results return, teachers congratulate each other's increasing expertise and their students' growing cognitive and communication skills.

To some extent, the new attitudes and behaviors must be congruent with the teacher's other behavior, personality, and environment or it will simply lead to a new cycle of unfreezing, movement, and refreezing.[18] For this reason, Lewin saw the need for successful change to be a group activity. Unless organizational culture, group norms, policies, and practices are also transformed, individual behavior changes cannot be sustained. In schools, since teachers want to help each student succeed academically, conducting change as a group activity creates a positive peer pressure and shared norms that keep the changes going. Similarly, educating parents in groups about the reasons for the change and the likely benefits to their children can earn wider support.

## REFLECTIONS AND RELEVANCE 5.2

### Considering Lewin's Change Model

The changes that actually improve a situation are the ones that arise from a "felt need," have a clear direction for improvement, and are internally driven.

To what extent has this been true in your personal and professional lives?

1.  Working with a partner, describe a time in your personal or professional life when you developed a "felt need" that left you uncomfortable, dissatisfied, and open to change. If the change occurred in your professional life, did the leaders try to develop a "felt need"? If yes, how? And how successful were they? If the change occurred in your personal life, generally describe how the "felt need" developed.
2.  What did you (in your personal life)—or your leaders (in your professional life)—think, say, or do to provide direction for the change? If a professional situation, what role did teachers (or employees) play in providing the direction and nature of the change? How effective do you think you—or your leaders—were in this effort, and why?
3.  What did you—or your leaders—do to make the changes permanent? How effective do you think you—or your leaders—were in this effort, and why?
4.  Understanding Kurt Lewin's three-step change model, where do you think you—or your leadership—did well or mishandled the change process?
5.  As a class, discuss to what extent Lewin's change model can be useful for school improvement planning.

Additionally, Lewin suggested that although leaders might logically suppose that increasing the driving forces could pressure individuals to change, in many cases this approach could backfire. Instead of producing the desired changes, the undue pressure could arouse an equal and opposite increase in resisting forces. The end result: no change and more tension than before.[19] In short, principals cannot "require" teachers to change their ideas and practices without generating deep resistance and perhaps outright defiance. Teachers must knowingly and fully participate in the change process if they are to welcome it, adopt it, and keep improving their practices in the desired directions.

Although Lewin's model has attracted much interest and some criticism, a substantial body of evidence in the social and physical sciences support his three-step perspective on change.[20] His change model continues to be a generic recipe for organizational development.[21]

## CHRIS ARGYRIS: SINGLE- AND DOUBLE-LOOP LEARNING

Chris Argyris, the late Harvard Graduate School of Business professor and an organizational psychologist, studied how formal organizational structures, control systems, and management affect individuals—and how individuals respond and adapt to them. He also investigated how organizations can increase their learning capacity and how human reasoning—not simply behavior—can become the basis for diagnosis and action. Along the way, Argyris observed how people in organizations usually seek improvement by addressing symptoms rather than root causes—and he created a model to demonstrate how to find, treat, and resolve actual problems. His insights help practitioners, including principals, make informed decisions in rapidly shifting and uncertain environments and learn how to overcome barriers to organizational change.

Argyris believed that learning involves finding and correcting errors. When something goes wrong or works ineffectively, people look for a strategy to fix or improve it. How they define the problem and its possible solutions have implications for both the immediate dilemma and for the entire organization and those in it. Working with his colleague Donald Schön, Argyris developed the single- and double-loop learning paradigm (Figure 5.2). This exemplar illustrates how people in organizations can generate better outcomes if they address the underlying origins—often the cultural assumptions and traditional practices—rather than treat their visible expressions.[22]

In designing this model, Argyris and Schön identified three elements that affected problem solving:

- *Governing variables*—the dynamics that keep the organization's underlying values, assumptions, rules, and policies in play and upholding the status quo. In schools, governing variables are the school culture and its expression in the school's and school board's policies and procedures.
- *Action strategies*—the moves and plans that people use to keep their governing variables within acceptable limits—that is, plans that avoid discussing or generating solutions that may challenge (and perhaps overturn) the organization's underlying norms and assumptions. In schools, action strategies might include school improvement strategies and their implementation.

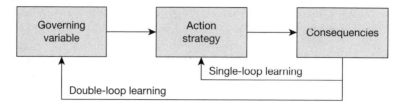

**FIGURE 5.2** Single and Double-loop Learning

Source: Anderson, L. (1997) Argyris and Schön's theory on congruence and learning. The Encyclopedia of informal education. Retrieved from: http://www.aral.com.au/resources/argyris.html. Reprinted with permission.

- *Consequences*—what happens as a result of the action. These can be intended and unintended and may affect the organization and individuals. In schools, consequences may include varied student, teacher, and parent outcomes, including achievement test results and enhanced instructional effectiveness.

Figure 5.2 explains why solutions that address an organization's governing variables—its underlying assumptions, values, and culture—can actually change the organization in ways that bring sustained improvement whereas simply adding new programs and practices (without challenging and reshaping the underlying assumptions) cannot. In single-loop learning, people typically look for a solution to a problem that fits within their organization's beliefs and norms. They tweak or add on to the current practices. They tinker around the margins. They do not directly ask whether the underlying rules upon which the actions rest are correct for the actual conditions at hand. Nor do they generate solutions for a more appropriate set of beliefs and rules. As in Figure 5.2, single-loop learning's feedback from the consequences returns to the action strategies and not to the governing variables. As a result, the original problem likely will continue or reappear in another form. The culture, therefore, remains the same, untouched, ready to undermine any future solutions.

In contrast, double-loop learning involves actively questioning the organization's assumptions, norms, and values that support the ineffective practices. With double-loop learning, principals and teachers critically scrutinize the underlying controlling variables and rules and adjust or reframe them if necessary to better fit contemporary realities. Then, they plan a solution (action strategies) to fit the revised assumptions and norms. As Figure 5.2 depicts, the outcome's feedback goes to the governing variables, which then influence the action strategies and affect the consequences. In the best of all worlds, with double-loop learning, when constructive change occurs, the organization's culture —now reshaped with more appropriate assumptions, norms, values, and behaviors— helps sustain it, and students and teachers benefit.

Here's how this might look in schools. Teachers assume that since children come to school from different starting points—from vastly different family circumstances and with varied funds of knowledge, skills, experiences, vocabularies, and opportunities to learn—they will finish school with different educational outcomes. The assumption: schools cannot alter this reality. In fact, research confirms that what students already know about the content—their background knowledge—is one of the strongest indicators of how well they will achieve in school.[23] Given this, schools, historically, have addressed the problem of high variations in students' knowledge, skill levels, and learning pace with single-loop learning solutions: select and sort children into different academic tracks (such as regular, college prep, advanced placement/international baccalaureate, or vocational) to keep children with similar knowledge and skill sets together (to make the classroom more manageable for teachers). The result: disproportionately high failure and dropout rates among low-income and minority students who lacked the extensive vocabulary and experiences—useful information that their middle class or affluent peers pick up in the normal course of family life—to help them do well in school.

In contrast, with double-loop learning, schools can challenge the governing variable that children's different starting points *always* mean different educational outcomes (and schools *cannot* alter that reality). Instead, these educators believe that what students learn depends on several factors: the teacher's skill, the student's interest, the content's complexity, and the student's existing knowledge about the subject. Contesting the school's governing variables, the educators act upon these new assumptions: they design and put into practice ways to help students with varying degrees of "readiness to learn" succeed academically. In these schools, administrators address teachers' skill deficits with effective classroom evaluation, feedback, and appropriate and extensive opportunities to learn a wider range of effective instructional approaches. Teachers address students' interests in class by directly relating their interests and experiences to the topic under study and provide motivating and relevant experiences—virtual, reading, and other—that build students' interests in the topic. Knowledge complexity can be addressed by separating the content into manageable and understandable segments, making these highly relevant to the students, and giving frequent opportunities for practice, feedback, and mastery before moving ahead. And teachers build students' vocabulary through direct instruction and by encouraging students' free reading. The results: more students learning successfully and advancing academically.

Critics of Argyris' work have noted that his model has minimized the influence of political forces that sway decision making in organizations.[24] Some would argue that organizations are inherently political, but Argyris overlooks the competing interests that impact organizational problem solving. Others note that decision making is usually more complicated than Argyris' linear approach would have it appear. Nonetheless, Argyris provides a graphic and useful way to conceptualize pragmatic problem solving—looking for solutions beyond the surface—that lead to better and more sustainable solutions.

## REFLECTIONS AND RELEVANCE 5.3

### Single- and double-loop learning

Argyris believes that learning involves finding and correcting errors. Understanding single- and double-loop learning can help leaders find more complex but effective and sustainable solutions to organizational problems.

1.  With a partner, identify a school or organizational improvement process that you observed or experienced.

2.  Decide whether the plan reflected single- or double-loop learning—and give reasons for concluding this.
3.  In your view, how effectively did the solution resolve the problem—and give reasons for your view.
4.  Apply Argyris' and Schön's model for problem solving (in an "ideal world," what do you think might have been a more effective and sustainable solution?).
5.  After partners have each shared their experiences and observations with organizational problem solving, the class as a whole will discuss why they think group members look for single- rather than double-loop learning. What do they see as the pros and cons of each approach? How do they think they may use this model when they are in organizational leadership positions?

## ROBERT CHIN: STRATEGIC ORIENTATION

Robert Chin, the late Chinese American psychologist and Boston University professor, was an expert in organizational theory. As a social psychologist interested in applying ideas about intergroup behavior, he joined the U.S. Army in 1943. He served in counterintelligence with the Office of Strategic Services (precursor to the CIA) in Washington, DC and China, gathering and analyzing information to protect the United States against espionage. He later studied minority students' intelligence, generating data that contributed to the psychological underpinnings of the *Brown v. Board of Education* ruling that desegregated America's public schools.[25]

Chin adds to our understanding of how to lead organizational change. Although Lewin's model identifies the major components of organizational development, he does not directly speak about ways to advance organizational change.[26] Chin does. He suggested three strategic orientations to leading organizational change: empirical-rational, power-coercive, and normative-re-educative strategies.[27]

### Empirical-Rational Strategies

This orientation assumes that people are reasonable beings who will pursue their own self-interest—once they know what it is. When sensible people receive new information about an idea, a technique, or a product, they tend to accept that item if they believe that they will benefit from doing so. Thus, successful change depends on communicating relevant information, offering the right incentives, and logically persuading employees to go along with it. This rational-empirical strategy fits comfortably within Western society's scientific-technological cultural traditions. For this approach to work effectively, however, the upside of change must greatly outweigh the downside—or at least be attractive enough to nullify any risks in making the change.[28] Empirical-rational strategies can be especially useful when leaders can sway the organization's more influential members to accept the change and help persuade their colleagues to join in.

For example, in the 1980s when the middle school movement gained popularity, junior high school principals wanting to convert their organizations into middle schools explained the concept to their teachers. Principals stressed teachers' work in collaborative interdisciplinary teams with colleagues who shared the same 100 students, teaching four periods on most days, having two daily planning periods (one with the team and one alone), and gaining three colleagues to assist during parent conferences. On the other hand, if teachers remained a junior high school faculty, they would instruct six out of seven periods a day, have only one daily planning period, and have to round up an administrator or counselor if they wanted adult support during a parent conference. Given these convincing reasons, many junior high teachers deemed the upside of becoming a middle school far outweighed the downside of remaining a junior high school.

## Power-Coercive Strategies

In a different way of leading organizational change, power-coercive strategies assume that people are essentially accommodating and will do as they are told. This strategy emphasizes using legitimate authority and threat of penalties (transactional leadership practices) to influence behaviors—whether by wielding an "iron hand in a velvet glove" or warning "my way or the highway."[29] Sanctions may be political, economic, or moral. For this orientation, rationality, reason, and human relations are placed second to the ability to make change happen by exerting dominance. Political-coercive clout can come from executive directives, legislation, and court rulings that assign penalties for not complying with the decision. Penalties may be very personal, including risks of humiliation, transfer, demotion, salary cut, or dismissal from employment. At times of high threat from the outside environment when everyone feels vulnerable but no one knows how to respond, employees may welcome their leader having a clear direction and change of behaviors in mind.

Principals have the authority to require a change in teacher behavior, and traditionally, this is how they implement change in schools. For instance, a middle school principal attends a national professional conference and learns about an innovative approach to improve student achievement. When she returns home, she announces at a faculty meeting that starting Monday, all teachers will write daily "Learning Targets" (detailing exactly what students will learn that day in class) and "Do-Nows" (learning activities for students to begin immediately upon entering the classroom) on the board before the students arrive. This structured and direct approach, notes the principal, will help quickly settle students into an academic mindset with the teacher in charge as they walk in the door and promptly get to work. This approach has been successful in many schools with students just like theirs. A 20-minute video showing teachers the practice in action comprises their staff development. Most likely, teachers will go along with the practice because they know their evaluations will reflect their compliance. Plus, it is a good idea. Excellent teachers know they need to start every class with order and a plan. But no matter how good the proposed intervention, unless the principal can connect this requirement to specific data showing why their students are not achieving well, have teachers reflect on these realities and generate a need for such an intervention—that is, make the strategy meaningful and relevant (a "felt need") for themselves and their students—teachers may obey. But they may do so without the essential understanding, enthusiasm, or follow-through to make the strategy really work well. And when the principal transfers or retires, the practice may fade, too.

## Normative-Re-educative Strategies

The empirical-rational strategy and the power-coercive strategy both assume that organizations must be made to change, either by using logical persuasion about the benefits to be gained by making the change or by threats of punishment for not making the change. In contrast, normative-re-educative strategies presume that organizations can change from within if the organizational culture stresses continuous renewal. In this view, dynamic leaders use organizational values to appeal to the listeners' emotions and ideas to leverage organizational change. This approach also views intelligence as socially mediated and not strictly rational. Principals as culture builders rely on normative-re-educative strategies.

In schools using normative-re-educative strategies, administrators and faculty anchor successful change in collaboratively redefining and reinterpreting existing norms and values, and building a commitment to new, more appropriate ones. More than relying on information alone, school leaders believe that people in organizations need to develop the incentive to change from their own inner values and aspirations. Change cannot successfully be imposed from the outside. The teachers must come to realize that the current system is not working well. Instead, the proposed changes are the best approach for correcting current inadequacies. Since culture does not change quickly, using the normative-re-educative strategy means taking the long view; results will not happen overnight, especially if they are to become sustainable.

For example, the middle school principal returning from a professional conference, rather than telling her teachers, "You will" begin using "Learning Targets" and "Do-Nows" employs a normative re-educative strategy. The principal would provide time, opportunity, and relevant data to help her teachers work in small groups to consider their students' low achievement, discuss what practices might improve students' focus and efforts at learning, and consider the "Learning Targets/Do-Nows" approach as a possible solution. The principal might want to send several influential teachers to visit other schools with students similar to their own where this approach is working—and return to the school with both evidence and personal anecdotes to support its use. When the principal can help the teachers work together to define their problem and generate possible solutions, the teachers make the need for action and its direction their own. They identify a felt need. They buy-in. The proposed change is no longer imposed from outside. The normative-re-educative approach to leading change views culture change alongside innovative, effective approaches to increasing student learning and achievement.

Critics note that Chin did not propose a right or wrong strategy. They contend, correctly, that any given initiative usually improves by using a mix of approaches depending on the conditions (i.e. power-coercive: "The bad news is that we are closing this business and firing every employee"; empirical-rational: "The good news is that we are starting a new business and need to hire new employees but on very different terms than the former businesses used"). Also, critics observe that more than three strategies for leading change may exist.[30] Unchallenged, however, is Chin's belief that regardless of the change's source or sources, planned change is most effective when it is based in knowledge, incorporates strategies resulting from this knowledge, and makes people integral to the process.

## REFLECTIONS AND RELEVANCE 5.4

## Using Robert Chin's Change Strategies

Robert Chin's critics remind us that he did not propose a right or wrong orientation strategy and that any given initiative usually improves by using a mix of approaches, depending on the situation. Let's see how this might work in schools.

1. Working in groups of four, identify a school-based issue needing an intervention strategy. Then, thinking as principals, identify when, where, or how you might effectively use each of Chin's change orientation strategies: empirical-rational, power-coercive, and normative-re-educative—and provide your rationale for using each. Make a graphic chart or image to illustrate the situation, Chin's strategy, and your rationale for using it there.
2. After all groups have finished work, each group will present its scenarios with their proposed strategic orientations and rationales, using the graphic to assist their explanation.
3. After each presentation, the class will give feedback about whether they think the group chose an appropriate strategy and rationale for each intervention—and suggest what other choices and rationales they might have used in their scenario.
4. When all presentations and feedback are over, the class will discuss the conditions under which leaders might best use each change orientation strategy.

## LEE BOLMAN AND TERRANCE DEAL: MULTIPLE FRAMES

In *Reframing Organizations* (2013), Lee G. Bolman and Terrence E. Deal, educational leadership and organizational behavior professors, observe that "cluelessness is a fact of life, even for very smart people."[31] They believe that leadership is contextual; different situations require different types of thinking. Unfortunately, they argue, leaders often lock themselves into ineffective ways of making sense of their situations: the information they receive is unclear, wrong, hard to get, ignored, or misinterpreted. To remedy this, Bolman and Deal propose that *framing* and *reframing*—consciously sizing up a situation from multiple perspectives and then deciding on a new approach to address these—helps clarify, anticipate, and comprehensively resolve organizational problems. Applying *structural, human resources, political,* and *symbolic* frames allows leaders to construct a more comprehensive understanding of their situation. This depth of insight is especially critical in times of crisis or overload because having more than one choice provides reasonable alternate paths to workable solutions.

Specifically, Bolman and Deal's four *frames* that help leaders understand holistically what is happening in organizations and how to respond most effectively include:

- *Structural frame.* This lens stresses clear organizational standards and goals, putting people in the right roles and relationships, valuing rationality over personal agendas, efficiently coordinating energy and resources, planning and control systems, and effective policies as ways to make schools work better. Using the structural frame allows leaders to work within a formal hierarchy, use data and analysis for decisions, budget accurately, set clear direction and measurable standards, hold people accountable for results, and try to improve organizational behaviors with new policies, rules, and practices. Example: "Is it legal? Is the proposed solution acceptable within the school district's policy handbook and guidelines? Does it fit within the scope of the teachers' contracts? If not, let's rethink this."
- *Human resources frame.* This lens stresses the interaction between individual needs (including emotions, relationships, needs, preferences, and abilities) and organizational needs (including people's skills, energies, commitment, and effective outcomes). People want the intrinsic and extrinsic rewards—such as for safety, belonging, respect, achievement, advancement, and meaning—while organizations require that the best work be done efficiently and effectively. Employing the human resources frame allows leaders to show concern for others, work towards win-win situations, and provide occasions for participation and shared decision making to motivate employees' involvement and loyalty. Example: "Is this ethical? Do all teachers affected by this decision or their representatives have a say in designing and enacting it? If not, let's get them involved."
- *Political frame.* This lens focuses on conflict or tensions among different groups and agendas competing for scarce resources. It highlights the limits of authority. Using the political frame allows leaders to be advocates and negotiators who invest much of their efforts in networking, building coalitions and a power base, encouraging autonomy and participation, bargaining and settling disputes among competing stakeholders over resource allocations, and finding common ground.

Example: "Who else inside or outside the school will be affected by this decision? How are they likely to view this? How can we get their views on solutions that might work for all? How can we educate them about the problem and our proposed solution to gain their support?"

- *Symbolic frame.* This viewpoint emphasizes a subjective world in which facts are interpreted rather than neutral, group consensus determines meaning and predictability, and members share tacit understandings and agreements. Every school and classroom invents its own "golden arches" and "geckos"—shapes, colors, mascots, slogans, and banners—to encourage students' belonging, commitment, and loyalty. Using the symbolic frame permits leaders to influence adults in ways that build deep purpose and dedication through shared values, heroes and heroines, rituals and ceremonies, stories, and other emblematic modes. Example: "What mascot, slogan, or colors might better represent what our school values? Might creating a new school mascot or changing our school colors upset our graduates, veteran teachers, parents, or our community? If it might, how do we address this during our planning and enacting?"

Since organizations contain many realities, each frame offers new possibilities for reaching successful ends. The structural frame produces clear organizational standards and goals, often leading to higher productivity. The human resource frame involves eliciting individuals' needs and motives and nurturing a sense of loyalty to the organization. The political frame focuses on conflict and compromise that can become a continual source of tension or renewal. And the symbolic frame highlights organizational culture, beliefs, and rituals which generate common values and significance. Since all these frames operate in organizations, any proposed changes must consider them if they are to be effective and sustainable.

Additionally, Bolman and Deal use their four-frame paradigm to facilitate organizational change. Table 5.1 presents actions that principals can use when they apply the four frames to their school improvement process.

Research supports Bolman and Deal's four cognitive frames' relationships to leadership and managerial effectiveness.[32] Studies have shown that more experienced leaders acquire greater cognitive complexity and are able to use multiple frames in their managerial and leadership experiences. In contrast, new leaders are more likely to use frames emphasizing managerial—not leadership—effectiveness. In addition, U.S. principals' effectiveness as managers was perceived to be most highly related to their use of structural and symbolic frames whereas their effectiveness as leaders were perceived highest on use of symbolic and political frames;[33] and male and female principals were found to be more alike than different on their use of these frames.[34]

Bolman and Deal's critics correctly note that it is difficult to choose the correct level of analysis, since the same problem might logically be considered from several different frames. Agreeing, the authors recommend the frames be used in an integrated fashion. Other complaints point to their unclear theoretical roots and their lack of attention to gender differences as the research's primary focus.[35] Neither of these complaints, however, undermines the frames' usefulness in broadening leaders' perspectives on organizational factors that deserve attention before more holistic and appropriate solutions can be identified.

**TABLE 5.1** Overcoming Barriers to School Change

| Frame | Psychological Barriers to Change | Essential Leadership Strategies |
| --- | --- | --- |
| Structural | Loss of direction, clarity, stability; confusion, chaos | Communicate, realign, and renegotiate formal patterns and policies; develop new information; add new structural units |
| Human resource | Anxiety, uncertainty, people feel incompetent, insecure, needing reassurance | Educate faculty to learn new viewpoints and skills; enlist teachers' participation and involvement in decisions affecting them; foster new relationships; provide encouragement and support; educate staff with workshops, retreats |
| Political | Disempowerment; conflict between competing interests, winners and losers of scarce resources | Bargain, negotiate, advocate, develop areas to renegotiate issues and form new coalitions with other key players |
| Symbolic | Loss of meaning and purpose; discuss symbolic importance of different practices; holding on to the past; resistance to change | Create or revitalize rituals and ceremonies; mourn the past, celebrate the future; work with teachers, students, and parents to develop or restate the organization's vision; create new symbols, including self as symbol |

Source: Adapted from Bolman, L. G., & Deal, T. E. (2013). *Reframing organizations* (p. 378) (Exhibit 18.1). San Francisco, CA: Jossey-Bass; Bolman, L. G., & Deal, T. E. (1991). Leading and management effectiveness: A multi-frame, multi-sector analysis. *Human Resource Management, 30* (4), Table 1, p. 515. Copyright © 1991 Wiley Periodicals, Inc., A Wiley Company. Reprinted with permission.

## MICHAEL FULLAN: CHANGE LEADERSHIP

Michael Fullan, professor emeritus at the Ontario Institute for Studies in Education and special advisor on education to the premier of Ontario, Canada, is a recognized international authority on educational reform. As a theorist, a practitioner, and a prolific writer, Fullan sees change as a journey, not a blueprint. To him change is a nonlinear, complex dynamic, full of uncertainty, messiness, and excitement (joy and terror).[36] He emphasizes two essential themes to improve student outcomes. First, Fullan focuses on building individuals' and schools' capacity for more effective professional practice. Second, he advocates ensuring the sustainability of educational change by modifying the school's culture and structure so they will encourage and assimilate innovation.

In *Change Forces with a Vengeance* (2003),[37] Fullan offers eight insightful, common-sense suggestions that only someone personally experienced in the theory and practice of leading change in schools can offer to help new and experienced principals better understand and manage this major responsibility:

**REFLECTIONS AND RELEVANCE 5.5**

## Using Bolman and Deal's Four Frames

Bolman and Deal offer four frames or perspectives by which to more fully understand an organization and generate positive outcomes. For this activity, all class members are leadership consultants who will develop an implementation plan for the school district.

In four groups, each group working on one of the four frames—structural, human resource, political, or symbolic—consider the following scenario and identify all the issues, the people or professional roles who need to be involved, the rationale for including this group in planning, and the order in which these individuals (or roles) should be involved. (In a large class, several groups may each be working separately with the same frame.)

> *Scenario*: For decades, a school district has educated children with disabilities in self-contained and resourced classrooms. Now, the superintendent wants each school to develop a plan that will offer children with special needs places in inclusion classes wherever possible. What would the consultants' recommendations be for who should be involved and why in developing the educational inclusion plan?

After the groups finish their work, each group will present its recommendations to the school board (the rest of the class and the professor). The school board members are free to ask questions that the consultants will answer. When all groups have completed their presentations and discussions with the board, the entire class will discuss the advantages and disadvantages of using the four frames for leading appropriate and sustainable change in school.

1.  *Give up the idea that the pace of change will slow down.* It won't—and thinking that it will only leads to frustration and burnout. The ability to deal with complexity is the ability to deal with reality. To lead change that will be sustainable takes time. Fullan advises principals who want to be productive to develop a more relaxed attitude toward uncertainty and work on the more subtle and powerful change forces: creating a shared vision for school improvement, distributing leadership, building teachers' capacity, and developing trusting and ethical relationships throughout the school community. These changes can bring greater results over time.

2.  *Coherence making is a never-ending proposition and is everyone's responsibility.* School improvement initiatives perceived as fragmented put teachers and school leaders into overload. One of a principal's most important jobs is helping teachers make sense of what is happening in their environments—inside and outside the school—and to help them see their own roles in fostering the educational enterprise.

Teachers benefit when they can see the forest *and* the trees. Principals create coherence for others by clarifying, prioritizing, focusing, aligning, and connecting the many school improvement facets into a sensible, recognizable whole. Accordingly, wise principals create many occasions for teachers, as individuals and as small groups, to talk through the related initiatives and goals, and coherently fit themselves into the bigger picture. When teachers see changes as meaningful, they can more easily commit their efforts to making them happen, and they can confidently explain the changes to others.

3. *Changing context is the focus.* Context refers to the set of conditions, i.e. the environment, the school culture, under which schools operate that strongly influence teachers' and principals' behaviors. But although difficult to change, context can be altered and reshaped—and teachers' behaviors will change accordingly. When principals publicly announce what they value, establish avenues to enact them, positively reinforce those who enact it (and show low tolerance for those who do not), and when more effective behaviors begin, principals can reinforce the desired actions, monitor their use, and keep the school moving forward.

4. *Premature clarity is a dangerous thing.* Unless it's a crisis, don't rush important decisions. Off-the-shelf or top-down solutions won't work for the long term. Quickly selecting an answer may feel good because it provides closure and direction. But choosing before considering a variety of relevant alternatives likely won't solve the problem. Rather than accept single-loop or single-frame remedies, principals need to help teachers look for and find the double-loop learning and multi-frame answers. Educators need to engage their hearts and minds, be skeptical about imposed ideas, and develop shared understandings with colleagues in order to find workable strategies for important goals in which they want to invest. These complex processes cannot be rushed. Only by taking the extra time needed to deeply engage, interact with peers, and problem solve, can teachers understand the school's purpose and their place in it. And only in these ways can students benefit and positive change be sustained.

5. *The public's thirst for transparency is irreversible (and on balance, this is a good thing).* The public deserves credible evidence of student learning. Parents insist on independent, objective, and measurable information about their children's academic progress and status. Principals are expected to help schools meet their needs for internal improvement and public accountability. And, while working within the legal and ethical limits respecting other children's and teachers' privacy, principals need to be transparent with the data that today's technology is making available. Principals need to help policy makers and the public understand the data and become informed users. In this way, schools and their communities build trust and use available data to make schools more effective.

6. *You can't get large-scale reform through bottom-up strategies—but beware of the trap.* Typically, schools are part of a school district or system of schools. This reality comes with a paradox: neither top-down nor bottom-up school improvement strategies work by themselves. True, principals need to build teacher ownership for school improvement, but without a larger infrastructure's support (such as the

school district), the individual school may show minimal improvement in outcomes, may move in the wrong direction, or may initiate effective changes that do not last. Effective and sustainable school solutions must be systemic. Securing buy-in and creativity from the district superintendent on down the organization ladder makes for more effective and long-term improvements. When the district's goals, resources, and politics align with the school's, fiscal, moral, and public relations support will likely follow.

7. *Mobilize the social attractors: moral purpose, quality relationships, and valuable knowledge.* Improving schools is hard because changing is uncomfortable and stimulates resistance. Change challenges teachers' habits, beliefs, and values. It asks them to experience a loss, feel uncertain and incompetent, question their own identity, and disown their prior behaviors. Since this is a lot to ask of anyone, principals can use several powerful incentives to get teachers on board: moral purpose, quality relationships gained through collaboration, and quality ideas. In schools, *moral purpose* means acting with the intention of making a positive difference in students' lives—regardless of their background—to help produce citizens who can live and work productively in increasingly dynamic and complex societies.[38] *Quality relationships* come from teachers having frequent opportunities to work collaboratively with colleagues and parents who may see the world and the work from varying perspectives; being cautious about easy consensus that sweetly masks serious disagreement; and skeptical enough to ask valid questions about the proposed changes. *Quality relationships* also stem from teachers working closely with students to individualize their learning while nurturing mutual respect and trust. *Valuable knowledge* comes from colleagues sharing and constantly turning information into purposeful knowing through a social process that builds strong relationships. In these ways, principals can successfully motivate teachers to learn how to improve their professional practice.

8. *Charismatic leadership is negatively associated with stability.* Many future principals aspire to become transformational leaders who make their schools collaborative and productive places where teachers enjoy their work and students learn to high levels. But principals usually begin their leadership careers with more modest professional gifts. The good news is that being a charismatic leader is no shortcut to sustainable school improvement. In fact, accumulating evidence suggests that charismatic or "savior-type" leaders may achieve short-term increases in student achievement outcomes but may be dangerous to an organization's long-term wellbeing.[39] Instead, the most effective leaders are individuals who mix personal humility with intense professional determination; are able to accept criticism; develop intelligence, purpose, and leadership capacity in themselves and others; appreciate the importance of sharing key information with teachers and parents; and share decision making across the organization. This is a real-world skill set which every future principal can master.

Unique among educational change scholars, Fullan's engagement in theory and practice connect him to big-picture concepts and to daily leadership behaviors.

Addressing principals as people, he recommends accepting responsibility for one's limitations and accepting disappointments, anxiety, and conflict as natural byproducts of complex situations. He advises school leaders to have the courage and emotional maturity to learn from both success and failure and reminds educators to keep learning. He counsels principals to grow other leaders in their schools, to think politically, and establish relationships with everyone—especially those with whom one disagrees—to develop empathy and learn from them. And Fullan reminds us that, although principals may understand the complexities of change, they cannot be controlled. In the long run, he concludes, principals' effectiveness depends on developing teachers' internal commitments to make their schools better environments for teaching and learning.

Fullan's critics seem to take him to task more for his commercial success than for any flaws in his thinking; and his support for improving public schools rankles those who prefer market-based educational reform—such as vouchers and charter schools. Some detractors assert that Fullan's attention to capacity building ("the easy stuff") diverts his attention away from accountability and testing ("the harder stuff"), and surmise that his school reforms' positive evaluations reflect his undue influence over his evaluators.[40] Fullan has also been censured for his work's lack of relevance for urban and rural schools, ignoring the health, housing, and employment challenges that poor children and their families face—and the constraints on their schools—that limit children's ability to benefit.[41] Nonetheless, Fullan's 30 years of continuously evolving theory and success in the practice of educational reform still speak to his ideas' validity and relevance.

## REFLECTIONS AND RELEVANCE 5.6

### Michael Fullan's Change Leadership

Michael Fullan offers eight insightful suggestions for principals leading school change.

Individually, review the suggestions, think about which three you find most reassuring and encouraging (and why), and which three you believe you might have the most difficulty mastering (and why). Then meet with a partner and share your responses to Fullan's ideas (the three most reassuring, the three most challenging for you). Also discuss what you might do—starting now—to become more familiar and confident using these suggestions.

When the pairs have finished their review and discussion, the whole class will discuss which suggestions they find to be the most reassuring and encouraging, which they suspect will be the most difficult for them to master, and where (when, how) they might learn how to become more skilled in school change leadership.

## CONCLUSION

Change is complex and uncertain. Environmental factors inside the school (such as school culture and its sway over faculty norms and actions) and outside the school (including local and national political, economic, and social influences) impact school change. Principals play a major role in shaping the culture that supports change that enables every teacher's and student's growth. Principals also develop the incentives and structures that will help teachers understand change as well as build the commitment and collaboration skills essential to sustainable school improvement.

No single correct way exists to lead school change. But when the existing norms of the school encourage introspection, improvement, and involvement, they facilitate change.[42] Encouraging the development of these norms is an important aspect of leadership for change.

## NOTES

1  Machiavelli, N. (1961). *The prince* (p. 27). New York, NY: Penguin Books. (Originally published in 1514.)
2. Leithwood, K., Louis, K. S., Anderson, S., & Wahlstron, K. (2004). *How leadership influences student learning.* New York, NY: Wallace Foundation. Retrieved from: http://www.wallacefoundation.org/knowledge-center/school-leadership/key-research/Documents/How-Leadership-Influences-Student-Learning.pdf
3. Wallace Foundation (2013, January). *The school principal as leader: Guiding schools to better teaching and learning* (expanded ed.). New York, NY: Wallace Foundation. Retrieved from: http://www.wallacefoundation.org/knowledge-center/school-leadership/effective-principal-leadership/Documents/The-School-Principal-as-Leader-Guiding-Schools-to-Better-Teaching-and-Learning-2nd-Ed.pdf
4. Sarason, S. (1996). *Revisiting "the culture of the school and the problem of change"* (pp. 136–137). New York: Teachers College Press.
5. Sarason (1996), ibid. (p. 320).
6. Saphier, J., & King, M. (1985). Good seeds grow in strong cultures. *Educational Leadership, 42* (6), 67–74.
7. O'Reilly, C. A. III, Chatman, J., & Caldwell, D. R. (1991). People and organizational culture: A profile comparison approach to assessing person-organization fit. *Academy of Management Journal,* September, *49* (3), 487–516; Chatman, J. A., & Jehn, K. A. (1994). Assessing the relationship between industry characteristics and organizational culture: How different can you be? *Academy of Management Journal,* June, *37* (3), 522–553.
8. Sarason (1996), op. cit.
9. Hargreaves, A. (1997). Cultures of teaching and educational change. *International Handbook of Teachers and Teaching, 3,* 1297–1319.
10. Shaie, K. W., & Willis, S. L. (1986). *Adult development and aging* (2nd ed.). Boston, MA: Little, Brown.
11. Knowles, M. et al. (1984). *Andragogy in action. Applying modern principles of adult education.* San Francisco: Jossey-Bass; Knowles, M. S. (1990). *The adult learner. A neglected species* (4th ed.). Houston: Gulf Publishing; Merriam, S. B. (2001). Andragogy and self-directed learning: Pillars of adult learning theory. *New Directions for Adult and Continuing Education, 89* (1), 3–13.
12. First, the concepts of dependence and independence are culturally bound. Second, certain critics say that these adult learning assumptions are not unique to mature learners. Some

adults are highly dependent on teachers for structure while some children are independent learners. Adults may be motivated to learn by external forces, such as keeping their jobs while children may want to learn because they are curious and internally driven. Likewise, certain life experiences may hinder learning while certain children may have a range of life experiences that are deeper and wider than those of many adults.

13. Marshak, R. J. (1993). Lewin meets Confucius: A review of the organizational development model of change. *Journal of Applied Behavioral Science, 29* (4), 393–415.

14. Bargal, D., Gold, M., & Lewin, M. (1992). The heritage of Kurt Lewin – Introduction. *Journal of Social Issues, 48* (2), 3–13; Burnes, B. (2004). Kurt Lewin and the planned approach to change: A reappraisal. *Journal of Management Studies, 41* (6), 977–1002; Dickens, L., & Watkins, K. (1999). Action research: Rethinking Lewin. *Management Learning, 30* (2), 127–140.

15. Lewin, K. (1947). Frontiers in group dynamics. In D. Cartwright (Ed.), *Field theory in social science*. London: Social Science Paperbacks.

16. Weick, K. E., & Quinn, R. E. (1990). Organizational change and development. *Annual Review of Psychology, 50* (1), 361–386.

17. *Cognitive dissonance* is a theoretical construct used to explain how people respond to information that does not fit with their current understandings or beliefs. This lack of fit creates an internal tension that motivates the individuals to reduce it.

18. Schein, E. H. (1996). Kurt Lewin's change theory in the field and in the classroom: Notes toward a model of managed learning. *Systemic Practice and Action Research, 9* (1), 27–47.

19. Zand, D. E., & Sorensen, R. E. (1975). Theory of change and the effective use of management science. *Administrative Science Quarterly, 20* (4), 532–545.

20. Elrod, P. D., & Tippett, D. D. (2002). The "Death Valley" of change. *Journal of Organizational Change Management, 15* (3), 272–291.

21. Weick, K. E., & Quinn, R. E. (1999). Organizational change and development. *Annual Review of Psychology, 50* (1), 361–386.

22. See for example, Argyris, C. (1974). *Behind the front page*. San Francisco: Jossey-Bass; Argyris, C. (1994). Initiating change that perseveres. *Journal of Public Administration Research and Theory, 4* (3), 343–365; Argyris, C. (1982). The executive mind and double-loop learning. *Organizational Dynamics, 11* (2), 5–22; Argyris, C. (1982). *Reasoning, learning, and action: Individual and organizational*. San Francisco: Jossey-Bass; Argyris, C. (1990). *Overcoming organizational defenses. Facilitating organizational learning*. Boston: Allyn and Bacon; Argyris, C., & Schön, D. (1978), *Organizational learning: A theory of action perspective*. Reading, MA: Addison Wesley.

23. See, for example, Dochy, F., Segers, M., & Buehl, M. M. (1999). The relationship between assessment practices and outcome of studies: The case of research on prior knowledge. *Review of Educational Research, 69* (2), 145–186; Marzano, R. J. (2004). *Building background knowledge for academic achievement*. Alexandria, VA: Association for Supervision and Curriculum Development; Tobias. S. (1994). Interest, prior knowledge, and learning. *Review of Educational Research, 64* (1), 37–54.

24. Easterby-Smith, M., & Araujo, L. (1999). Current debates and opportunities. In M. Easterby-Smith, L. Araujo, & J. Burgoyne (Eds.), *Organizational learning and the learning organization*. London: Sage.

25. Saxe, L., & Kubansky, P. E. (1991). Robert Chin (Chin Yuli) (1918–1990). Obituary. *American Psychologist, 46* (12), 1343.

26. King, N., & Anderson, N. (2002). *Managing innovation and change. A critical guide for organizations*. Belmont, CA: Cengage Learning.

27. Chin, R. E., & Benne, K. D. (1984). General strategies for effective change in human systems. In W. B. Bennis, K. D. Benne, & R. Chin (Eds.), *The planning of change*. (4th ed). New York, NY: Holt, Rinehart, & Winston.

28. Chin, R., & Benne, K. D. (1969). General strategies of change in human systems. In W. G. Bennis, K. D. Benne, & R. Chin (Eds.), *The planning of change* (2nd ed.). New York: Hold, Rinehart & Winston. As cited in Nickols, F. (2010, November 5). Four change management strategies. Distance Consulting LLC. Retrieved from: http://www.nickols.us/four_strategies.pdf

29. Nickols, F. (2010), ibid. Retrieved from: http://www.nickols.us/four_strategies.pdf

30. Nickols, F. (2012). *Change management 101: A primer.* Distance Consulting. Retrieved from: http://www.nickols.us/change.htm

31. Bolman, L. G., & Deal, T. E (2013). *Reframing organizations. Artistry, choice and leadership* (5th ed.) (p. 5). San Francisco: Jossey-Bass.

32. See, for example, Bolman, L. G., & Deal, T. E. (1991). Leadership and management effectiveness: A multi-frame, multi-sector analysis. *Human Resource Management, 30* (4), 509–534; Thompson, M. D. (2000). Gender, leadership orientation, and effectiveness: Testing the theoretical models of Bolman and Deal. *Sex Roles, 42 (*11–12), 969–992.

33. Bolman and Deal speculate that the human resources frame was not a significant predictor of school principals' effectiveness even though the human resources frame is their most dominant mode of interpreting issues in their schools (see p. 529). Since this frame is a "given" for principals, it is not considered a unique characteristic of their effectiveness.

34. Bolman & Deal (1991), ibid.

35. Bolman, L. G., & Deal, T. E. (1984). *Modern approaches to understanding and managing organizations* (p. 237). San Francisco, CA: Jossey-Bass; Mabey, C. (2003). Reframing human resource development. *Human Resource Development Review, 2* (4), 430–452.

36. Fullan, M. (1993). *Change forces. Probing the depths of educational reform* (p. 21). New York, NY: The Falmer Press.

37. Fullan, M. (2003). *Change forces with a vengeance* (pp. 23–38). London, UK: RoutledgeFalmer.

38. Fullan, M. (2007). *Leading in a culture of change.* San Francisco, CA: Jossey-Bass.

39. Collins, J. (2001). *Good to great.* New York, NY: HarperCollins Publishers; Khurana, R. (2002). *Searching for a corporate savior: The irrational quest for charismatic CEOs.* Boston, MA: Harvard Business School Press.

40. Bennett, P. W. (2011, February 13). The "school change" wizards: What drives Michael Fullan and his disciples? *Educhatter's Blog.* Retrieved from: http://educhatter.wordpress.com/2011/02/13/the-%E2%80%9Cschool-change%E2%80%9D-wizards-what-drives-michael-fullan-and-his-disciples/

41. Noguera, P. A. (2006). A critical response to Michael Fullan's "The future of educational change: systems thinking." *Journal of Educational Change,* 7, 129–132.

42. Schein, E. H. (1985). *Organizational culture and leadership.* San Francisco: Jossey-Bass.

# CHAPTER 6

# Building Ethical Behaviors and Relational Trust

> The best way to find out if you can trust somebody is to trust them.
>
> —Ernest Hemingway

## LEARNING OBJECTIVES

6.1 Define "ethics" and explain how "ethics is at the heart of leadership."

6.2 Identify how principals, as their schools' moral stewards, influence how they perceive and resolve ethical dilemmas and impact the schools' level of relational trust.

6.3 Assess and evaluate the relative merits and disadvantages of the general ethical perspectives and the multiple ethical paradigms for principals' day-to-day decision making.

6.4 Discuss the ways in which relational trust benefits schools.

6.5 Describe how educators develop relational trust in schools.

6.6 Summarize the personal qualities that allow individuals to develop relational trust in others and the qualities that make an individual trustworthy in others' eyes.

6.7 Explain the personal qualities that help individuals sustain relational trust in schools.

6.8 Identify the principals' behaviors that help teachers, staff, students, and parents see their school leaders as trustworthy.

6.9 Describe how individuals can harm relational trust, explain why it is important to quickly repair it, and identify the steps needed to do so.

6.10 Identify the challenges in developing relational trust with parents/guardians and ways to overcome them.

**2015 ISLLC STANDARDS: 2, 4, 5, 6, 7, 8, 9, 10**

## INTRODUCTION

Schools run on relationships. Good relationships depend on ethics and trust. *Ethics* describes how we act in our relationships with others. Integrity, honesty, fairness, and dependability are ethical behaviors. *Trust* is an individual's or group's willingness to be vulnerable to another person and put something they care about under that person's protection or control, based on the confidence that the person is caring, honest, reliable, and competent. Trustworthiness itself is an ethical behavior. For relationships to grow and thrive, they must be anchored in ethical interpersonal exchanges. We trust that ethical educators will always choose to do what is in our children's "best interests"— even when it is difficult to do so or unclear what their "best interests" are. When trust is absent, it is difficult to collaboratively develop a shared vision.

In fact, relational trust has been called "the social glue" necessary for school improvement.[1] For schools to succeed at ensuring every student's academic and social success, principals, teachers, students, and parents each have their job to do. And each relies on the others to achieve the desired outcomes and feel good about their efforts. At some level, each understands their mutual obligations and expectations, and these beliefs create the basis for judging relationships and role effectiveness. When relational trust is present, teacher and parent commitment increases, motivating their efforts to engage in the difficult tasks of school improvement. At the same time, relational trust lowers the risks associated with change. The processes of upgrading schools and building relational trust occur together over time, each fueling the other in a virtuous cycle: the higher the relational trust, the greater the effort in school improvement initiatives, and the better the outcomes for students. And, the more "small wins" in school improvement, the higher the trust.

Successfully meeting these mutual expectations ethically, in an honorable, principled manner, builds relational trust. Not doing so destroys it. When that happens, students and school outcomes suffer. Importantly, the principal is the school's key mover in modeling, generating, sustaining—and, if necessary, repairing—relational trust.

This chapter will explain how ethical behaviors and relational trust appear in schools and how principals' use of these in decision making and in relationship building can cultivate the school climate, culture, and practices that help schools succeed.

## SCHOOLING AS AN ETHICAL ENTERPRISE

According to many, "ethics is at the heart of leadership."[2] *Ethics* involves norms, values, beliefs, habits, and attitudes that we choose to follow, that we as a society impose on ourselves.[3] *Professional ethics* can be described as the rules or widely accepted standards of practice that govern members' professional conduct. As Pulitzer-Prize-winning author Thomas Friedman observes, "Laws regulate behavior from the outside in. Ethics regulate behavior from the inside out."[4] Ethics are voluntary.

Ethics is about relationships—"what we ought to do."[5] Ethics requires making a judgment about a situation. In complex circumstances, people must often choose among competing sets of principles, values, beliefs, or ideas. Ethical dilemmas result as competing sets of principles pull individuals in different directions. Making the situation even more complicated, the options are not always clear-cut, right or wrong. Rather, they can involve "right versus right" or "wrong versus wrong."[6] Even deciding what is "right" or "wrong" is difficult, varying with the locale, culture, and era.

Substantial agreement exists that certain types of actions are unconditionally better than others, not only for a particular individual or in relation to a certain set of cultural norms.[7] They are superior without qualification because they are morally good acts based on universal laws, including essential social values such as truth, goodness, beauty, courage, and justice. Prized in all cultures, dissimilar societies may apply these common values in differing ways, however.[8]

Typically, schools enact five ethical principles grounded in respect for individuals:[9]

- Do no harm to others.
- Respect individuals' autonomy.
- Benefit others.
- Treat others fairly.
- Be trustworthy.

Recognizing and reciting these five ethical principles is easy. Translating them into everyday behaviors is more difficult. Ideally, everyone in the school should act in an ethical manner, but principals need to provide the living example in word and deed. An ethical school leader is one whose actions rise above self-interest, who consistently tells the truth, even when shading or concealing it might bring a personal or professional advantage. An ethical principal respects every individual for who that person is and deals with people fairly and objectively. In these ways, over countless everyday experiences—that teachers, students, and parents see and hear—principals' ethical behaviors help generate trust in that person.

Ethical behavior and trust are related. *Trust* is the conscious awareness that one depends on another, and expects that other to act ethically to protect one's interests. In school, interpersonal trust formed upon ethical actions, is the foundation for schools where learning is on-going for both teachers and students.

## PRINCIPALS ARE MORAL STEWARDS

Educators are the *stewards*—caretakers—of schools and their educational promises to the community and nation.[10] As moral stewards, principals and teachers ensure that their school is dedicated to every student's advancement by using the highest-quality curricula, teaching, and learning in each classroom. As moral stewards, principals promote and protect the welfare and safety of students and staff. Educators accomplish these moral stewardship responsibilities by always behaving ethically.

As moral stewards, principals perform important work that benefits children, their families, and the larger society. Principals take direction from a powerful set of beliefs and values tied to issues of justice, civic good, and success for all children and youth. They must be able to perceive the moral implications of countless daily decisions and

## REFLECTIONS AND RELEVANCE 6.1

### Five Ethical Principles

Five ethical principles for schools include: do no harm to others, respect individual autonomy, benefit others, treat others fairly, and be trustworthy.

Separate the class into five groups, one group for each ethical principle. Each group will work with the "word web" graphic for their principle, identifying four examples that they have observed from their own work experiences in which their ethical principle was followed (+) and four examples when the ethical principle was not followed (−).

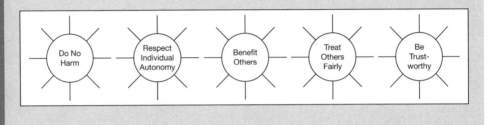

When all groups are finished, each group will report on what their principle looks like when followed and when violated. Discuss the impact on the teachers from either observing—or being party to—ethical or unethical behaviors.

act appropriately on each. Conscious of this larger responsibility, principals come to see their work more as a vocation than a job. The future economic and political health of individual children—as well as their region and nation—depend on principals (and their influence on teachers) enacting their roles effectively. Principals create the culture and the ethical coherence that connects all school employees to continuous improvement, and shape their thoughts and actions towards providing meaningful learning opportunities for all students.

As moral stewards, principals build individual relationships into larger, like-minded publics. Through networks of authentic interpersonal connections—working *with* people rather than *through* them—ethical principals use their professional expertise rather than positional authority to influence others. They make seemingly separate endeavors appear coherent and regularly point out the moral priorities of their work together. Leadership in schools depends on modeling and clarifying values and ideas— creating significant incentives for teachers to act in ways that advance their students' best interests—rather than telling other educators what to think or how to act. And, as community builders, principals encourage others to be leaders in their own right.

Leadership is about influence, and leaders consciously decide how they want to influence others. They can rely on logical persuasion, emotional appeals, and rewards for compliance. They can provide relevant information that creates a "felt need" and internal incentives to change in the desired direction. Or they can use their official power to require certain behavior changes with the unspoken threat of punishment for not obeying. Having this wide range of available options—reflecting varying degrees of respect for others—makes ethical considerations an essential part of leadership. Therefore, deliberately thinking about the ethical issues implicit in everyday decisions helps educators make more effective choices.

---

**REFLECTIONS AND RELEVANCE 6.2**

## Principals as Moral Stewards

As moral stewards, principals perform important work that benefits students, their families, and the larger society.

Reflect on and then write about the following questions. Then as a class, discuss the most salient points of your reflections.

1.   What is "moral stewardship" and what does it mean in a school context for principals?
2.   Do you agree or disagree with the view of principals as schools' moral stewards—and why or why not?
3.   Discuss why principals acting as their schools' moral stewards matters.

---

## ETHICAL DILEMMAS IN SCHOOL

When making complex decisions in the best interest of students, faculty, and community, principals often confront *ethical dilemmas*—complex situations in which one must choose between two moral rules, both of which could be considered "ethical," but doing one would violate the other, and neither would clearly resolve the situation in an ethically acceptable manner. For example, the expression, "Robbing Peter to pay Paul" illustrates an ethical dilemma. Should Peter's "best interests" or Paul's "best interests" be the basis for meeting one's obligation to repay a debt? Is hurting Peter to help Paul an exercise in fair and ethical play?

Ethical dilemmas may be related to students, staff, finance and resources, and external relations. Many ethical dilemmas involve reconciling the differing values between school and students' home. Addressing student misbehaviors, for instance, may require weighing the offense, the student's age and discipline history, the specific situation, and the available options for calling home, assigning time-out, and asking for restitution or remediation as compared with suspending the student from school and increasing the likelihood of the child's academic failure. Likewise, supervising staff performance—and assessing their willingness and capacity to improve—may require deciding whether to develop or dismiss an underperforming teacher, secretary, or custodian. Similarly, allocating resources means choosing whether to divide funds among competing areas. Ethical dilemmas also arise from resolving conflicts between central office directives, teachers, and community needs and interests.

Looking to increase democracy, equity, and diversity and to educate every child to high standards creates additional ethical dilemmas. Should the most experienced and respected teachers be assigned to work with the highest achieving students (usually more affluent) or to students with the greatest learning needs (usually low-income, minority students, or students with disabilities included in regular classes)? For example, a high school principal is building a master schedule. Three first-rate math teachers, each licensed to teach Algebra I through A.P. Calculus and each capable of generating at least one year's academic learning in a school year, are on faculty. Thirty students want to take Algebra I and 30 students want to take A.P. Calculus. Should the principal create two sections of A.P. Calculus with a student-to-teacher ratio of 15-to-1 and a single, 30-student section of Algebra I—or should the principal create two sections of Algebra I with 15 students per section using two of the math teachers and only one, 30-student section of A.P. Calculus? Which decision is in the "students' best interests"? Which students? Many factors come into play, and depending on the reasoning framework and priorities used, different principals could reach different "ethical" conclusions.

Ethical dilemmas also arise from competing views on education. Should the curriculum be focused primarily on those "tested" subjects so the school can meet public accountability standards—or should the arts, physical education, and opportunities for creative thinking and expression be included as part of a holistic academic education? Should the curriculum focus on traditional academic disciplines and classics of Western civilization—or should the school infuse a multicultural curriculum that stresses mastering rigorous academic skills while using authentic voices from diverse communities? What should be the balance on the school improvement team of community stakeholders who represent social, political, and financial resources and those without such assets but who hold important influence over large groups of students in underserved neighborhoods? All these situations generate dilemmas as well as offer opportunities for making ethical decisions.

Despite the complexity of identifying the situational details and criteria for making ethical decisions, principals try to uphold ethical standards when they consistently ask, "What is the right thing to do and what is the right way to do it?" In contrast, when they do not consistently think and act ethically, principals create an atmosphere of ethical cynicism.[11] The principals talk one way but act another. In these situations, teachers and other administrators may begin to distrust the principals, become resentful, and lose confidence in the leaders' judgment about what is in their children's—or in their own—"best interests." They may suspect that the principal's "fancy talk" about improving every student's learning outcomes is "all bun and no beef." Given this, a growing sense of resentment and futility may undermine teachers' motivation to improve.

The array of possible ethical dilemmas facing principals is virtually endless. When making complex decisions, should principals rely on their personal values, on their professional ethics, or on community desires? Should the deciding factor be what is best for the individual or what is best for the group? What criteria can help decide between what appear to be equally poor or equally positive options? Defining and choosing between alternatives that are in the students' best interests may not be clear-cut or unequivocal. As a result, ethical dilemmas may present some of the most challenging experiences that principals will face.

---

**REFLECTIONS AND RELEVANCE 6.3**

## Ethical Dilemmas in School

Ethical dilemmas are complex situations in which one must choose between two moral rules, both could be considered "ethical" but doing one would violate the other.

- In groups of four, identify a recorder and a reporter.
- Have the group identify a moral dilemma that you may have observed or experienced in your own workplace—or construct one that might reasonably appear in your work setting.
- Identify the two competing moral values in it, and identify possible criteria for deciding between them.
- After this, discuss why resolving moral dilemmas is so difficult to do. After all the groups have finished, discuss the examples and your conclusions as a class.

---

## PERSPECTIVES FOR MAKING ETHICAL DECISIONS

Learning about well-established ethical systems can help principals become familiar with varied ways of understanding ethical behavior. Although every situation that principals face is unique, being able to think in these terms will help leaders find fairer, more respectful solutions.

### General Ethical Perspectives

Although many systems of ethical thought exist, and they share similarities, no one perspective works best for all decisions. Each approach has its strengths and weaknesses. A brief look at several of our culture's most popular ethical systems include:[12]

- *Utilitarianism: "The greatest good for the greatest number."* This approach assumes that one should judge ethical choices by their consequences. Weighing the possible costs and benefits of taking a particular action, leaders seek an option that does the greatest good for the most people. This model is easy to apply to a variety of situations. The downsides: identifying and evaluating possible outcomes and positing which one will do the greatest good for the most people is difficult, especially for principals who represent a variety of stakeholders. What is considered "good"? Which "people" will—or will not—benefit? Outcomes can be unpredictable, unintended, and may neglect minority rights. As a result, leaders who use utilitarian ethics to address the same dilemma sometimes reach dissimilar conclusions.

- *Categorical imperative: "Do right no matter the cost."* This view, which assumes that certain behaviors are either right or wrong regardless of the circumstances, represents an ideal. For example, lying, cheating, and murder are always wrong. Leaders should follow universal truths imprinted on their consciences and treat everyone fairly, truthfully, respectfully, and kindly. Guilt is a sign that we have broken these universal moral rules. The downsides: almost every "universal law" has exceptions, and guilt is not a sure sign of inappropriate behavior. Plus, this model is difficult to use in a crisis demanding an immediate response.
- *Altruism: "Love your neighbor."* This view asserts that the ultimate ethical standard is helping others, whatever the personal cost. According to Western thought, as influenced by Judaism and Christianity, since all persons are made in God's image, and God is love, individuals have the duty to love and show concern for others. The downsides: altruism is difficult to practice. Cultural and personal differences mean that people disagree about what "loving behavior" is or looks like.
- *Ethical pluralism: "There are many right paths."* This view accepts that people do not have to choose to use one ethical system and discard the others. Rather, it sees areas of overlap among different ethical systems and contends that no one ethical perspective is right for all ethical decisions. A pluralistic view would have individuals apply more than one ethical perspective to a dilemma and select "what works best in this situation" from each viewpoint. The downsides: two well-intentioned leaders can use the same ethical theory and reach differing conclusions. Also, considering an array of workable options takes time.

These general approaches to making ethical decisions rely on applying universal rules in specific situations. Critics advise, however, that utilitarian and categorical imperative ethical guidelines apply to extraordinary situations, not the types of decisions normal folks typically make.[13] Educators are more likely to have to decide whether or not to tell a coworker that they do not appreciate the person's sexist and racist remarks than to have to steal in order to save a life. In addition, time pressures and ambiguity often complicate educational decision making. In a crisis, little time exists for weighing pros and cons to determine which abstract principle to follow. In short, these general ethical approaches sound good in abstract discussions of appropriate leadership behaviors, but they are hard to apply in real-world settings.

## MULTIPLE ETHICAL PARADIGMS

In contrast to the general ethical theories, principals might find an integrated approach to dealing with daily ethical dilemmas more useful. Multiple ethical paradigms is a

**FIGURE 6.1** Multiple Ethical Paradigms Model

Source: Shapiro, J. P., & Gross, S. J. (2008). *Ethical educational leadership in turbulent times. (Re)Solving moral dilemmas* (p. 7). Mahwah, NJ: Lawrence Erlbaum. Reprinted with permission of Taylor & Francis Group

contemporary theoretical model of problem solving that considers the ethics of justice, critique, care, and profession.[14] As illustrated in Figure 6.1, when working together each ethic complements and supports the others in helping school leaders make policy and practical choices. Although no one perfect ethical choice exists for any situation, the four perspectives help educators move toward the "best" choice under the circumstances or to select an option that will likely be later balanced by other choices.

## The Ethic of Justice

As part of a liberal democratic tradition, the ethic of justice focuses on rights, laws, and policies. It endorses the concepts of fairness, equality, individual freedom, making changes in small doses, a rational legal system, and hope for the progress of all peoples.[15] In this view, human reason, as expressed in rules and respect for people's equal rights, can create evenhandedness and equality in what otherwise would be a society of rampant self-interest. Although society hosts competing claims between the common good and individual rights that are impossible to totally resolve, reason can be an instrument of morality: it can calculate one's personal advantages and obligations to social justice and protect individuals' dignity. At the same time, ethical dilemmas are opportunities to interpret the rule of law, apply abstract concepts of fairness, liberty, and responsibility, and weigh the individual's rights versus the community's greater good.

In schools, an ethic of justice means respecting the individual teachers' and students' rights as well as serving the common welfare. The issue appears in discussions about student discipline policies, faculty and student due process procedures, multicultural education, standardized testing and grading practices, and agreements about faculty time commitments. Each of these areas raises moral questions about individual justice in public life.

The weakness of the ethic of justice lies in its inability to determine the "right-ness" of conflicting claims.[16] What is fair to one person might not be considered fair by another. This view narrowly confines justice to its written words rather than to its spirit.

Relevant questions for the school leader to ask when using the ethic of justice include: Is there a policy, law, or right that would be appropriate for resolving a particular ethical dilemma? Why is this law, policy, or right the correct one for this particular case? How should the law, policy, or right be implemented? Why or why not? If no law, policy, or right exists, should there be one—and whose views should it contain?

## The Ethic of Critique

Skeptical about the ethic of justice's analytic and rational approach, the ethic of critique reflects a critical theory perspective (Paulo Freire). It considers social relationships, social customs, social institutions, and laws as grounded in structured power relationships or in language reflecting a society's dominant members. In this view, no social arrangement is neutral, and tensions exist between laws and concepts such as democracy and social justice.[17] Critical analysis is needed to uncover which group has the advantage, determine how language and situations are structured to keep the present social power arrangements legitimate, and expose inherent injustice or dehumanization that result from these practices.

According to this viewpoint, schools socialize children from all social and economic groups to accept the dominant social group's beliefs, values, and practices as right and natural. In this way, schooling confirms, legitimizes, and reproduces the status quo by gaining the students' passive consent. Practices such as rigid curriculum tracking, for instance, ensures that working-class and low-income children are denied access to the resources available to more affluent children. This, in turn, leads students to differential access to high-quality curriculum, disparate opportunities to think complexly and use language expressively, and varying outcomes for their economic wellbeing and social mobility. The ethic of critique argues that school authorities and their communities deliberately design these practices to keep "less desirables" out of the cultural mainstream.

In schools, the ethic of critique challenges school leaders to work for social justice and create an ethical environment in which high-quality education can occur for every student. According to the ethic of critique, the Eurocentric curriculum (that does not respect the contributions of all races to American culture); the rigid curriculum tracking; the inflexible and zero-tolerance discipline policies; and the labelling of children for special services (children with disabilities and gifted) all contain unjustifiable assumptions and impose an unfair advantage to some at the expense of others (*Pedagogy of the Oppressed*). Instead, the ethic of critique calls educational leaders to confront the status quo by dealing with the inconsistencies between a school's vision of equal opportunities and its daily practices that disadvantage certain children. Accordingly, school leaders should ask hard questions about fairness and seek practices that would enable all children—regardless of social class, race, ethnicity, gender, or ability—to have real opportunities to grow, learn, and achieve. In these ways, ethical educators can change the world for the better.

A caveat in the ethic of critique is that it challenges the status quo. For this reason, many school communities may not receive it enthusiastically as a stand-alone rationale for implementing school change—because in a contest for scarce resources, affluent children risk losing certain benefits.

When using the ethic of critique, relevant questions for school leaders to ask include: Who makes the laws, rules, and policies that affect this school? Who benefits from these? Who holds the power, and whose voices are silent? Who deserves greater voice? And what could make a difference so that all may benefit from high-quality schooling?

## The Ethic of Care

Both the ethic of care and the ethic of justice consider human relationships and how people are treated within organizations. But while the ethic of justice considers treating people fairly and respectfully as equals from a contractual or legalistic perspective (the outcomes are fair), the ethic of care values the quality of personal relationships (the processes are fair). In the ethic of care, humans are persons in a relationship, and each person is due unconditional regard, dignity, and worth. Individuals have the right to be who they are and should allow others also to be authentic individuals. Therefore, the school, as an organization, should respect the wellbeing of persons within it, not simply use teachers as efficient means to generate higher student achievement scores. And, similar to the ethic of critique, caring in education is a means of enacting social justice.

School leadership based on an ethic of care attends to the uniquely human issues of self-esteem, personal confidence, and respect for each person's dignity and worth in all interactions. Leaders continuously monitor the school's cultural tone, engage in informal one-to-one interactions, and personalize caring in familiar language rather than speaking in distance-creating "bureaucratese" or "edu-jargon." Principals work to preventing miscommunications by not allowing negative stereotypes or defensive actions to taint their conversations. Instead, school leaders guarantee that teachers experience their relationships with them as one of high regard, mutual respect, and honest contact between two persons who care for each other and share common purposes. Making it a practice to greet each person by name, giving handwritten notes of congratulations for completing projects successfully, regularly displaying student work, and publicly highlighting photos of students engaged in school activities showcase a school that appreciates people for who they are.

Using the ethic of care to make moral decisions is more difficult than following rules in a policy and procedures manual. But when today's leaders are working in diverse communities with many voices and relationships to consider in decision making, the policy manual's rules may be inadequate to enact moral and ethical practices and outcomes.

A weakness in the ethic of care is accommodating the reality that principals are responsible for managing both tasks and people. Treating everyone in the school with courtesy and respect does not mean removing clear and enforceable criteria for evaluating employee performance and taking the necessary actions to either improve or dismiss incompetent individuals. Finding the balance between authentic caring and meeting one's responsibilities for supervision and accountability is an important and complex assignment.

Relevant questions for school leaders using the ethic of care include: Who will benefit from what I decide? Who will the actions hurt? What are the long-term effects of decisions I make today? If someone helps me now, what are my obligations to them or to society in the future?

## The Ethic of Profession

In what is arguably the original code of ethics, Hippocrates wrote, "First, do no harm." This concept serves members of all professions well.

Professions unite their members by common training, shared values, and mutual purposes. Professional expertise grants a degree of authority and influence upon its holders, but professional autonomy always has societal limits. Since every profession affects the wellbeing of those who depend on their skills and services, professional behaviors have both technical and moral dimensions. Technical skills determine what members have the capacity to do, while moral dimensions determine when, how well, and under what conditions members should do it. Society holds practitioners accountable for both aspects through a *professional code of ethics*—or rules that guide professional decisions and actions. These codes clarify for the general public and the professionals the rules and norms that inform members' actions. For practitioners, these codes of ethics are foundational guides for thought and deed in morally ambiguous situations. Because the professional entity is more stable, long lasting, and visible than any one practitioner and the profession as a whole, the professional group has a collective moral responsibility to ensure that its members uphold the highest standards of practice.[18]

Principals can find ethical guidance from an array of professional standards. The National Association of Elementary School Principals (NAESP), the National Association of Secondary School Principals (NASSP), and the American Association of School Administrators (AASA) all start with the premise that the school leader shall "make the wellbeing of students the fundamental value in all decision making and actions." Likewise, the teaching profession's "commitment to the student" is one of the National Education Association's (NEA) two ethical foundations. These organizations verify how the education professions' view their moral responsibility.[19]

In addition, principal preparation programs align their ethical standards and curriculum with the Interstate School Leaders Licensure Consortium (2015). These standards place the student in the center of the decision-making process where the school leader is responsible to act in accordance with ethical principles and professional norms by doing the following:[20]

- Place children's success and wellbeing at the heart of education.
- Ensure a system of instruction, academic and social support, and accountability for every student's academic and social success.
- Model principles of openness, transparency, self-awareness, reflective practice, and ethical behavior.
- Safeguard the values of democracy, equity, justice, community, and diversity.
- Ensure equity of access to social capital and institutional support.
- Act as the school's or district's moral compass.

The ethics of profession obliges principals to act within a wider ethical sphere—and think about their own personal ethics along with the ethics of justice, critique, care, and profession. These tenets expect principals to place students at the center of their decision making while also considering community standards. What is more, the ethics of profession expect principals to establish fair and honorable school environments in which high expectations for all students' education can occur.

When making decisions within the ethics of profession, school leaders should ask: What is in the students' best interests? What factors should I consider as I assess best interests of students whose backgrounds and needs may differ from the typical student? What do diverse communities expect this school to accomplish? Are the various codes of ethics that influence me congruent with how this situation should be addressed—and if areas of conflict exist, how should I select which to follow?[21]

## INTEGRATING THE MULTIPLE PARADIGMS

As a principal, defining a theory of ethical leadership and determining "right" from "wrong" is complicated. "Right" and "wrong" are not absolute; context affects meaning. It depends on whom one asks and which standards one decides to use—especially in an increasingly diverse and global community. Acting ethically requires consciously thinking about various ethical models and integrating the ethics of justice, critique, care, and profession into a rational basis for decision making.

Conflicts between varying ethical approaches are inevitable.[22] First, disagreements exist between an individual's personal and professional codes of ethics. For instance, principals who believe in creating a student-centered learning culture and a high-quality curriculum for all students (along with additional academic and social supports) may find themselves as parents arguing against opening their own child's enriched gifted classroom to "lower achieving" students who make the teacher "water-down the curriculum" so they won't be left behind. Second, conflicts within the professional codes themselves may exist—such as when an educator switches roles from school counselor to assistant principal. What counselors consider to be "confidential" the AP deems is important to tell parents. Third, conflict may exist between two different principals, even within the same school. Professionals of good will may define the same ethical dilemma differently. Fourth, a leader's personal and professional codes of ethics may be at odds with those set by the local community. What one community views as unethical (such as principals sending their own children to private school while leading a public school) may be seen as "personal preference" in another. These varying perspectives on what is or is not ethical suggest including community members in school decisions so their viewpoints can be identified and considered.

Principals can best address these possible ethical clashes by tying their decisions to the public school's mission: preparing every child to take on a citizen's role and responsibilities in a democratic society. In an increasingly diverse nation, advocating for each student's best interests fits the ethics of justice, care, critique, and profession. These are all grounded in the essential nature of human beings and their societies, and each complements the others. The ethic of justice assumes a rational ability to perceive injustice and at least a minimal level of caring about relationships in the society. The ethic of critique focuses on social justice, human rights, and how communities should govern themselves. The ethic of care considers the importance of individual dignity and respect as the basis for all social relationships. The ethic of profession offers sets of standards about how practitioners should appropriately enact their knowledge and skills for the community's wellbeing. These four ethical frameworks give school leaders more lenses by which to understand the world and make informed ethical choices. And even though people of good will may disagree about what is actually in the children's "best interests"—this question remains unanswered—they are less likely to argue with motives placing all their children in the center of educators' concerns.

---

## REFLECTIONS AND RELEVANCE 6.4

### Multiple Ethical Paradigms

Multiple ethical paradigms is a contemporary theoretical model of problem solving that considers the ethics of justice, critique, care, and profession together when making ethical decisions.

- In groups of four, identify a recorder and a reporter.
- Identify or construct an ethical dilemma that K-12 principals may have to resolve (identify what level school your principal is leading).
- Identify the various ethical considerations from the justice, critique, care, and profession perspectives, and explain how the principal might use each paradigm to help resolve the dilemma.
- When all groups have completed this task, each will describe to the class their school level, their ethical dilemma, and how each ethical perspective adds to the principal's problem solving.

---

## BUILDING TRUSTING RELATIONSHIPS

If schools run on relationships, relationships run on trust. Trust may be understood as an individual's or group's willingness to be vulnerable to another person and place something they care about—such as their money, their good reputations, or their children's education and welfare—under that person's protection or control, based on the confidence that the person is caring, reliable, competent, honest, and open.[23]

As a normative ethic, trust is related to the ideal of a good and moral society in which individuals work not only for personal advantage but also consider others' valid rights and interests. When we trust, we make ourselves vulnerable to another person who we expect to voluntarily accept the implied moral duty (or ethically justifiable behavior) to recognize and protect our rights and interests so we can better work together for a common purpose. If we depend on others to look out for our wellbeing, trust is necessary.[24] But if people trust unwisely in someone who does not deserve this confidence, they risk disappointment, or worse.

## TRUST IS IMPLICIT TO SCHOOL EFFECTIVENESS

Increasingly, trust is recognized as an essential part of well-functioning schools. The concept of *in loco parentis*—in place of parents—that American society has granted to its schools is anchored in trust. Parents trust principals and teachers to keep their children safe and learning. Principals trust teachers to act in every child's best interests. Teachers trust their administrators to provide a conducive learning climate, time, and instructional materials that allow them to teach all students well. They trust that when principals expect them to learn and use new approaches to increase all students' learning, teachers will be supported—and not judged unfairly—before they have had opportunities to practice and refine their new techniques. Faculty also trusts each other to uphold the high and consistent expectations for student behavior and achievement, and they trust parents to guarantee their children's daily attendance (unless they are ill) and study at home.

In fact, relational trust acts as a lubricant, easing the way for effective communication, collaboration, and reshaping school norms in ways that better serve all children's learning. Relational trust also serves as a moral resource for sustaining the hard work of school improvement.[25] Teachers invest their time and energies to improve their professional practice because they believe that they share the goal of increased student learning with their colleagues and leaders. They care about keeping their coworkers' respect, don't want to lose it by doing less than their best, and want to be part of doing something meaningful for children and their communities.

Notably, trust is not a given. It must be earned. In every relationship, parties must earn trust through repeated interactions in which individuals always keep their word, follow through on their commitments, act with honesty and integrity, and protect the other's interests.

School brings a unique social quality to relationships and trust. Relationships in schools tend to be more continuous and familiar than those found in most other modern institutions. Many teachers work in the same schools for years, developing and maintaining collegial ties over their careers. Likewise, families with several children may be part of a school community for a decade. Powerful personal ties can form when teachers, students, and parents genuinely believe that others really care about them and are acting in their best interests. Activities such as working with students after class, helping colleagues master new instructional techniques, participating with peers in parent conferences, and being dependable and reliable partners in educating children can build confidence in the others' trustworthiness.

Additionally, schools' social contexts influence how trust develops. Professionals may be inclined to trust other professionals with similar educational preparation and who hold state licenses to do their jobs—unless or until a reason appears not to. Friendship networks may form among teachers who teach the same grade levels or subjects. Relational trust may develop around shared instructional philosophies, locations in the school, teachers' ages or experiences, views about the principal, timing of their lunch or planning, race, ethnicity, gender, or many other variables. Group norms may reinforce ties within each group because having mutual friends increases the prospect of establishing trusting relationships ("the friend of my friend is my friend"). Alternately, group norms may weaken trust for those viewed as "outsiders"—even if these "others" work across the hall.

Without relational trust, educators will not take the risk to enact new norms and behaviors needed to create a student-centered learning environment. Traditional norms that prize teacher autonomy, privacy in the classroom, and indifference to professional development, collegiality, and improved practice must give way to more collaborative ways of teaching so that all students may learn and achieve well. Assumptions that only students with affluent parents can learn a high-challenge curriculum must be replaced with high expectations linked with high academic and social supports for all learners. Teachers who see colleagues as "lunch buddies" or "hall partners"—but not as collaborators with whom to engage in sustained professional learning—must now imagine and enact a different work model. Belief in keeping the status quo—because "that is the way we do things around here"—must make way for openness to innovation that best serves all children. These school culture factors can only be reshaped by teachers changing their beliefs and behaviors—and this is more likely to happen when teachers trust their principals to provide compelling reasons, role models, and a safe and encouraging climate for doing so—and when they trust their colleagues to help them learn and succeed.

Although relational trust among adults in school does not directly advance student learning, it does create the basic social frameworks, school cultures, and instructional practices that can. Whereas trust enables teachers to improve their professional performance and increase student learning, its absence can harm student learning. Distrustful teachers and students tend to engage in self-protective behaviors, unwilling to take risks to improve. Students, often keenly sensitive to teachers' feelings of discomfort, begin to feel unsafe, too; and they direct their attention to shielding themselves from embarrassment or harm by avoiding the inevitable mistakes that come with learning something new. Mistrustful people are apt to question even innocent actions or comments by those they doubt, constantly reconfirming their suspicions. And, once distrust takes hold, it tends to grow. Consequently, schools with declining trust undergo serious drops in teacher capacity, student-centered learning, and strong parent–school ties that are needed for effective school functioning and successful outcomes.

What principals do and say are very influential in nurturing relational trust. Principals initiate respect and personal regard when they come to understand their teachers as distinct persons, recognize their vulnerabilities, actively listen to and try to understand their concerns, and avoid making uninformed actions. When principals link this empathy to a persuasive school vision, and when teachers can see their behavior as advancing this vision, they find their work together more meaningful. And, when principals combine this vision and direction with competent school management—literally, ensuring that the buses and teacher paychecks arrive on time—an overall climate of respect and relational trust can emerge.

## BENEFITS OF DEVELOPING TRUSTING RELATIONSHIPS

Principals who deliberately cultivate increased trust across the school make an excellent investment. As faculty and staff come to respect and have confidence in each other's intentions and capacities to follow through, the school's emotional climate improves, and opportunities for school improvement that increases student learning gain traction. Relational trust assists the school in the following ways:[26]

- *Reduces individual vulnerability.* When teachers have strong relational trust, they can speak honestly with colleagues about which practices are working well and which aren't, without being judged as being negative, confused, or weak. Relational trust also reduces the risks associated with change. It fosters teachers' assurance that they can try out new strategies to increase student learning because "mistakes" are not "failures" but opportunities for improved practice and greater success.
- *Increases open communication.* People who trust each other are more likely to reveal more accurate, relevant, and complete information about school issues. Likewise, they are more likely to share the thoughts, feelings, and ideas needed to identify, diagnose, and correctly solve problems that interfere with student learning.
- *Increases mutual respect around controversial issues.* With high trust and mutual respect, faculty members don't have to mask their disagreements about "hot button" issues with fake politeness or avoidance. They can listen more thoughtfully and think more calmly during heated conversations. Even when their colleagues' voices grow louder and more passionate, having trust and respect for the speaker help the listeners keep listening even if they feel uncomfortable or disagree with what is said.
- *Increases commitment.* When relational trust is high, teachers believe their principals and colleagues will support them in rethinking and retooling their instructional practices. Similarly, parents believe the educators are looking out for their children's safety and learning despite the new ways of doing things.
- *Motivates efforts.* Upgrading schools asks teachers to take on the work of self- and organizational improvement and confront the inevitable conflicts that arise with change. Having confidence that their leaders and colleagues share their vision for better futures for all their students and will work to help each other accomplish this goal provides a powerful catalyst for action.
- *Increases collaboration.* When principals trust teachers enough to include them in school problem solving for improvement, teachers contribute valuable insights and information that improve decision quality. And, when teachers trust each other, they are more willing to work together as a professional community to improve their competence to increase student learning.
- *Enhances school climate and culture.* As the school climate becomes more open, it strengthens trust. Continued over time, the mutual confidence in each colleague's intentions and capacities becomes part of the school's culture, further reinforcing and sustaining the norm of honesty, collaboration, shared decision making, continuous learning, and improved practice.

- *Improves organizational citizenship.* When teachers trust their principals and respect their colleagues, teachers' actions are more likely to extend beyond the written job description, and they voluntarily act to improve their school without expecting extra recognition or reward. Personality traits such as altruism, courtesy, integrity, honesty, conscientiousness, team work, and ethical behaviors cannot easily be written into a job description—but these qualities make the work environment more satisfying and productive.

In addition to these anecdotal observations, years of studies conclude that teachers' trust in colleagues and their principal is related to school effectiveness[27] and positive school climate.[28] Research consistently finds that the principals' willingness to share responsibilities with teachers influences whether the faculty trusts the principals, while how well teachers treat each other shapes how much they trust their colleagues.[29] The principals' genuineness—openness in personal relations, respecting teachers as individuals, taking responsibility for mistakes and poor results, looking beyond stereotypes,

## REFLECTIONS AND RELEVANCE 6.5

# Building Trusting Relationships

**Principals who consciously cultivate increased relational trust are making a wise investment in their school's effectiveness.**

- In groups of four, identify a recorder and a reporter.
- Using your own experiences as teachers, give examples of how your principal did—or did not—develop strong relational trust before asking teachers to make major school improvement changes. What did the principal do—or not do—to develop this trust?
- Discuss the effect the presence—or lack—of strong relational trust had on teachers in the following dimensions:

  - individual vulnerability;
  - collaboration;
  - school climate and culture;
  - communications;
  - motivation;
  - mutual respect around "hot" issues;
  - organizational citizenship;
  - success of school improvement strategies as measured by student outcomes.

- After the groups have finished working, each will report to the class the example of how principals did—or did not—develop strong relational trust before initiating major school improvement initiatives and the effect on the teachers and student outcomes.

and acting in ways true to one's personal self—also makes a positive difference in how well teachers trust their principal and each other.[30] To flourish, trust needs direct links between individuals who interact in open and authentic exchanges.

Research findings suggest, too, that in schools where the relational trust level is high, teachers' orientation toward innovation and commitment, safety and order, and parent involvement continues to increase—and their professional practice improve—over the years. In contrast, where trust is low, data show weaker developments across the organization.[31] Other research conclusions offer persuasive evidence that the higher the faculty's trust in students and parents, the higher the school achievement in reading and mathematics, even after controlling for students' socioeconomic status.[32] And *teachers' collective sense of efficacy*—the extent to which they perceive that they and their colleagues can make positive contributions to student learning—having confidence and trust in their colleagues' intentions and effective practices—has also been strongly linked to student achievement.[33]

The evidence of relational trust's importance for a smoothly functioning and effective school is clear. Relational trust is positively related to school climate, to productive communications, to shared decision making, and to teachers' willingness to "go the extra mile" to help colleagues and students. Trust makes a measurable difference in student achievement, teachers' collective efficacy, and overall school effectiveness. In contrast, when relational trust is low or absent, teachers and administrators may not be willing to take the necessary risks to improve their performance. Ironically, in circumstances of low trust, the principal may feel the need to increase the school's rules, instructions, and oversight to enforce expectations for faculty behaviors—all of which further undermine relational trust.

## DEVELOPING TRUSTING RELATIONSHIPS

Interpersonal trust in schools does not simply happen. It often requires a nurturing climate, opportunities for respectful interactions, and models of appropriate behaviors. Principals play a key role in facilitating trust's growth and sustainability. Understanding its nature and how to initiate, sustain, and repair interpersonal trust can help school leaders foster its spread, maturation, and resilience.

### Levels of Trust

As a dynamic occurrence, trust displays different qualities at different stages of a relationship. The trust that a novice teacher has for a principal is not the same as the trust a veteran educator has for a principal who has been a cooperative and supportive colleague for a decade. In schools, several levels of trust can emerge:[34]

- *Provisional trust.* Appearing at a relationship's start, provisional trust assumes that each party will give the other at least the minimum respect and personal regard needed to keep their working relationship on track. In schools, trusting other educators at a basic level is reasonable: principals and teachers share backgrounds as educators, have employment contracts with the same school district, and are obliged to follow the district's policies and procedures. Nonetheless, provisional trust may be uneven and vary with the circumstances. For example, a principal who can commendably orient new teachers to the school's philosophy and program may not be able to give the best advice on how to teach a complex math lesson. If future interactions do not increase trust, relationships may remain rudimentary.

- *Knowledge-based trust.* As principals and teachers get to know each other as individuals and professionals, they become familiar with each other's intentions, competence, and integrity. Each becomes able to predict how the other party will act—and the degree of role competence each will show—in any given situation. Ongoing communication; respectful, pleasant exchanges; and keeping one's word help nurture this type of trust. And, like provisional trust, knowledge-based trust may be uneven and vary with the circumstance.

- *Identity-based trust.* In a mature relationship, parties develop empathy that strengthens their sense of identification with each other. Identity-based trust relies on such total understanding of the other's wishes and goals that each person can effectively stand in for the other when that other is not present. Identity-based trust tends to be unconditional.

In addition to having levels, trust in work relationships develops in stages: initiating, sustaining, and repairing. Educational leadership professors Megan Tschannen-Moran and Wayne Hoy have studied relational trust in schools extensively and find the following dimensions of organizational and interpersonal trust.[35] Principals and teachers who want to build and keep relational trust can see if they can identify these qualities in their own—and others'—actions.

## Initiating Trusting Relationships

Relationships have beginnings. Two people who do not know each other find themselves working together. Now they must quickly pinpoint the tasks where they must interact and assess the nature of the person with whom they are interacting. Characteristics that make people—including principals and teachers—willing to trust others include:

- *Willingness to risk vulnerability.* When principals invite teachers to participate in decision making, principals risk losing control of the outcome even though they are still responsible for it. Two parties are interdependent when a person's interests cannot be achieved without relying upon another person—and where interdependence exists, so does the need for trust. Where there is no interdependence and no risk, no trust is needed. When principals and teachers are willing to risk being disappointed (or worse) by depending on each other, they are ready to trust.

- *Confidence.* The extent to which a person can accept uncertainty in the face of risk is the degree to which that person can be said to have confidence. When principals believe that they can depend on their teachers working together to learn, practice, and use more effective instructional techniques, principals are willing to trust the teachers. And, when teachers feel secure that their principals will not assess them unfairly as they are learning to improve, they are willing to trust their principals.

While these qualities are essential if one is to trust another, their relative importance depends on the individuals' degree of interdependence and vulnerability in their relationship. For instance, if a heart patient goes to a cardiac surgeon for an aortic valve replacement, the patient's life or death literally depends on the surgeon's knowledge, skills, and experience performing this complicated operation (as well as on the hospital's attention to details and care during recovery). The patient is extremely vulnerable and depends almost totally on the physician's competence and the hospital employees' practices. To a much lesser degree, principals show vulnerability and dependence when they rely on their teachers to ensure that each child makes at least one year's worth of academic growth in a school year.

In addition to risking vulnerability and having confidence, several other qualities affect an individual's willingness to initiate trusting relationships. Principals can influence some, but not all, of these. These variables are worth considering when principals are deciding which persons to include on the school leadership team. These trust-engendering qualities include:

- *Emotions about the individuals they trust.* Principals' trust in teachers should be based on whether or not that teacher has the inclination, knowledge, and skills to get the job done correctly and well. When weighing trust, factors not related to getting the job done are irrelevant. The principal need not like the teacher personally in order to trust that teacher for his or her professional skills.
- *Assumed shared values.* It is easier for people who share common values to trust each other than for them to trust others who see the world very differently than they do. If new principals come into schools rip-roaring to "make their mark" by directly challenging the teachers' basic assumptions, norms, and ways of doing business, teachers' feelings of trust for their new leader may be very slow to develop—if at all.
- *Group diversity.* People tend to more readily trust those they perceive as similar to themselves in age, gender, social class, education, race, ethnicity, disability, or other factors. Trust is more difficult to establish among diverse members because people are unsure about others' cultural norms and may be unconsciously biased in favor of those who seem like themselves.
- *Rational calculations of the relative costs.* Deciding whether or not to invest a relationship with trust sometimes depends on "all things considered." For example, a principal expects all 9th grade English teachers to be part of the same professional learning community. But English teacher A does not get along with English teacher B, and English teachers C and D think both A and B are extremely weak instructors. Nonetheless, all the English teachers realize that they must trust each other enough to work together—and ensure their students make the expected learning gains—or they risk angering the principal and possibly receiving unfavorable evaluations.

- *Institutional factors.* Educators may start out with a basic level of trust in their administrators and colleagues because they all received the same basic professional preparation and have state-endorsed licenses or certificates attesting to their minimal levels of professional competence. Schools' norms, written rules, and procedures also clarify expectations and reinforce trust among their members.

Trust levels need to fit the context, the persons, and the situation. Principals and teachers do not need high levels of trust in every aspect of the other person's behavior in order to develop a trusting relationship. Rather, they only need trust in the areas in which they share an essential interdependence: where people rely on each other and bad things happen when expectations are not met. Ultimately, if a person's intentions and actions are perceived as benevolent, that person can be trusted even if his or her credibility is not perfect. Competence is the one factor that cannot be rationalized away, however. It is foolish to trust someone who clearly lacks the knowledge and skills to do the job well. Also, trust needs to be curbed by a willingness to stop or punish exploitive or incompetent behavior.

## Sustaining Trusting Relationships

Developing initial trust is only the first step in building a school climate and culture that allows improvements to enhance teaching and learning. By their words and actions, principals influence how well interpersonal trust is extended and reinforced throughout the school. School leaders need to consistently and visibly demonstrate those behaviors that make them appear trustworthy to others. When school leaders and teachers display the following behaviors, they influence others to see—and continue to see—them as trustworthy. These behaviors include:

- *Benevolence.* The belief in someone's good will breeds confidence that the person will protect—or at least, not harm—another's wellbeing or something he or she cares deeply about. Principals depend on teachers showing genuine concern for their students in ways that actively help them grow and learn, and teachers rely on their principals' fairness as they try out new teaching techniques and fine tune their practices.
- *Reliability.* The predictability of another person's behavior suggests that person will do as he or she says and will follow through on commitments. This consistency indicates trustworthiness. Principals who dependably make the time to listen to teachers' concerns—and teachers who continually perform with knowledge, skill, and care for children's wellbeing—are considered reliable.
- *Competence.* The person who demonstrates sufficient knowledge and skill to perform assigned tasks to the expected level of proficiency can be viewed as trustworthy. Good intentions without the capacity to back them up are not enough. Teachers are wise to feel uneasy when a principal who they believe lacks the requisite skills to accurately judge their instructional practices and provide a fair assessment observes their teaching. Likewise, principals have reason for worry when

teachers consistently fail to generate a year's worth of academic learning in their students in a school year.

- *Honesty.* A person's word—verbal or written—can be relied upon as a truthful and accurate statement of belief, fact, and intention (along with the absence of lying, cheating, or other self-serving behaviors). When principals and teachers accept responsibility for their own actions, admit their mistakes, and avoid twisting the truth to shift the blame elsewhere when errors occur, it validates their integrity.

- *Openness.* The extent to which individuals make relevant information available to others who need to know and the process by which people make themselves vulnerable to others by sharing personal information illustrates their sincerity. Principals who share complete, accurate, and timely information with teachers— even when it means acknowledging their own errors—shows openness. This candidness is a sign of the reciprocal trust between principal and teachers that neither the information nor the individual providing it will be misused.

Of these trustworthiness factors, principals tend to trust teachers based on their competence, reliability, and integrity while teachers base their trust of their principals on their perceived kindness, friendliness, and integrity.

Everyone who wishes to appear trustworthy needs to conscientiously exhibit these behaviors. But if teachers are to develop and sustain trusting relationships with their colleagues, they must perceive their peers as acting with benevolence, openness, honesty, and competence. Teachers see benevolence when they cover each other's classes in emergencies, when they take meals to families experiencing hardships, and when they voluntarily donate their sick days to give a seriously ill colleague more time to recover. They recognize openness when teachers share professional ideas, effective instructional practices, and materials and equipment to help colleagues better support students' learning. Teachers experience honesty when their peers tell the truth, even at risk to themselves, and when they refuse to participate in—or repeat—teachers' lounge gossip. Finally, teachers identify competence when they see their colleagues enacting effective practices with positive student results. Assurances of their colleagues possessing these interpersonal qualities make collaboration in professional learning communities possible and productive.

Although all school personnel are responsible for acting in ways that build and sustain relational trust, principals' unique position, formal authority, high visibility, and responsibility for leadership set the model for trustworthy behaviors. Research findings suggest that principals can effectively gain and keep their teachers' trust when administrators use behaviors that communicate consistency, integrity, concern, communication, and shared control.[36]

- *Consistency.* Principals are consistent when their personal beliefs, organizational goals, and work behaviors are in synch. When principals' words align with their deeds, teachers and staff rightly believe they can predict their principals' actions, thereby generating and sustaining trust.

- *Integrity.* Principals show integrity when they treat faculty and staff fairly, tell the truth, keep their word, accept responsibility for their actions, and avoid hiding or shading details to shift blame elsewhere.

- *Concern.* Principals exhibit caring and sensitivity to teachers' and staff's needs and interests when they listen to their worries, act to protect employees' rights, demonstrate kindness, and do not take advantage of them for personal or professional gain.
- *Communication.* Principals communicate well when they freely give teachers accurate information, adequate explanations, and timely feedback. They candidly express their school improvement ideas and qualms with teachers and encourage teachers to voice their own. They also invite teachers' feedback about the principal's decisions and actions (in an appropriate setting, naturally) without fear of repercussions.
- *Shared control.* Principals who share decision making with teachers increase teachers' views of the principal's trustworthiness and respect for the faculty. Distributive influence gives teachers greater occasions to give voice to their interests and grants them more responsiveness to students' needs.[37]

---

### REFLECTIONS AND RELEVANCE 6.6

## Initiating and Sustaining Trusting Relationships

To grow, relational trust requires a nurturing climate, opportunities for respectful interactions, and appropriate models of behavior.

- Working in groups of four, use the factors discussed above to describe your typical ease or difficulties in initiating and sustaining relational trust with colleagues in your school.
- Considering the *qualities that let others see you as trustworthy*, which do you think are your strongest (and give examples of your actions that you believe demonstrate each quality), and on which do you still desire more growth?
- From what your classmates have seen of your interactions with them and others in this class (or others), what does each member see as your top three qualities in sustaining relational trust?
- Discuss the overall experience and findings with the whole class.

---

### Repairing Broken Trust in Relationships[38]

Trusting another to protect one's interests is not always justified. A trusted person may behave in ways that hurt—rather than protect—a colleague's vulnerability. An insensitive comment, a broken confidence, a decision that offends the sense of care one expects from another can leave the offended person feeling surprised, puzzled, hurt, or fuming. In a few moments, a trusting relationship can be risked or ruined, and school functioning can be jeopardized.

In schools, violations of trust come from two sources: an injured sense of civil order (broken "rules" or norms) or a damaged identity. Broken rules include unkept promises, lying, evading work responsibilities, "borrowing" ideas from another then claiming them as one's own, revealing private conversations and secrets, and changing important expectations without enough lead time for others to successfully meet them. Coercive or abusive authority, corruption, sexual harassment, improper dismissal, and favoritism violate trust, too. Miscommunications and misunderstandings may feel like trust violations, and they can escalate out of proportion if not quickly corrected. Similarly, a damaged sense of self results from receiving public criticism, being the target of incorrect or unfair accusations, and being the object of slights or insults.

Violating someone's trust may be considered as an act of betrayal, and it can affect school functioning. When broken promises or publicly humiliating events lead to lost relational trust, teachers' performance erodes, and they more frequently express intentions to retire or transfer. Notably, betrayal's impacts may be long lasting. One study on betrayal in the workplace found that 50 percent of the incidents that participants remembered had happened more than 20 years earlier; 25 percent had happened more than 30 years before.[39]

People who feel betrayed are likely to respond in some manner. Whether the response leads to restored trust or retaliation depends on how they perceive the cause of the broken trust and the choices they make from that assumption. Does the injured party think the broken trust was accidental or deliberate? For instance, did the colleague miss this morning's conference with an angry parent because of a road mishap—a situation beyond the colleague's control—that delayed her timely arrival at school? Here, no forgiveness is necessary. Or did the colleague deliberately schedule a dentist appointment for that morning—an intentional act of unkindness or indifference to a coworker—so she would not be able to attend the meeting? If the harmed teacher concludes the colleague's absence was intentional, the betrayed teacher might want to "get even." A cycle of disappointment, reduced trust, revenge taking, and further disappointment, anger, and lost trust may result.

Revenge-seeking behaviors may be rational and deliberate or emotional and impulsive. Under the best conclusions, the offended person may choose to "let it go" (do nothing) or offer forgiveness. In contrast, betrayed individuals may become overly cautious and watchful, withdrawing from further contact with the offender. They may have revenge fantasies, try to punish the other in some way, arrange for private confrontations, or seek ways to restore their reputations. In schools, revenge-seeking teachers may sabotage each other or the principal, act uncooperatively, file union grievances, refuse to take on extra duties, and give as little effort as possible. They may prompt a self-reinforcing cycle of suspicion, competition, and retaliation which undermines school effectiveness. If the offense was public, observers may also lose trust in the offender, regardless of how the injured party responds.

Repairing trust is a complex and time-consuming process and requires several steps. To offer and receive forgiveness, each person must be aware of the breach and sincerely want to restore the relationship—or else any efforts to "make up" will seem phony or won't work. They must also believe that the short- or long-term benefits of rebuilding their trust are prized enough to invest the time and energy into fixing it. The individuals must then work cooperatively to find a win-win solution. But even to begin the repair, they need to have some measure of trust in reserve.

To begin repairing broken trust, the offending person must take the following steps:

- *Admit it.* Acknowledge (at least to yourself) that you have violated a colleague's trust—perhaps unintentionally—by your actions and, as a result, harmed the relationship.
- *Assess it.* Figure out exactly what you did that caused the other to feel broken trust in your relationship.
- *Apologize for it.* Take responsibility for the effects of your behavior on the other person and, as soon as possible, ask sincerely for forgiveness for the offending actions.
- *Listen and empathize.* Allow the offended person to express how they experienced the offending situation and what they want to do about repairing the relationship. Listen without interrupting or defensiveness, and try to understand the other's perspective.

In return, the offended person can choose one of four options to repair the trust:

- *Say "no."* Refuse to accept any actions, terms, or conditions for restoring the relationship.
- *Forgive, with unreasonable conditions.* Be willing to forgive but require unreasonable acts for making amends.
- *Forgive with qualifications.* Be willing to forgive and identify reasonable actions for making amends.
- *Forgive unconditionally.* Be ready to forgive with no further actions necessary.

Even seemingly small ("small" is in the eye of the beholder) actions can set off a series of trust-breaking and repairing actions. A high school assistant principal led the school improvement team and prepared an upcoming meeting's agenda with a list of reports to be given. Having heard indirectly about a new guidance department initiative, the AP listed the new program on the agenda without first speaking to the guidance director about it. Surprised and upset to see his pet project placed on the agenda without his prior knowledge or consent, the guidance director suspected that the AP was trying to take credit for the guidance director's idea and initiative. What seemed a "trivial" miscommunication to the AP was real enough to the guidance director to provoke feelings of surprise, hurt, and anger. Left untended, these emotions might have festered, creating unhelpful repercussions through the guidance department and beyond. Once aware of the guidance director's reaction, however, the AP promptly met with the director and apologized for the oversight. The AP admitted that rushing to complete the agenda without first speaking with the director was thoughtless, and the director would receive full credit for the program. But since the guidance initiative was school improvement, it rightfully belonged as an agenda item to announce another good thing the school was doing to help all students learn. The guidance director understood what had happened, accepted the apology, forgave the AP's haste, and proudly delivered the report. And, the positive relations and trust with the AP continued as before.

Constructive attitudes and actions can repair broken trust. Trying to understand and see the other person's viewpoint is a good start. Communicating clearly and genuinely in a conciliatory way with a sincere desire to reestablish trust without sacrificing either party's values or interests—and then reliably acting to do so—helps. Using persuasion rather than coercion creates a more trustful climate. It is wise to give the other party the benefit of the doubt: assume that no harm was intended. Nevertheless, extending trust blindly—accepting excuses that seem completely ridiculous given the information available—is ill advised. Instead of strengthening trust, it erodes it further.

If several attempts to restore trust fail, it is important not to overreact. Although principals have the authority to punish inappropriate behavior, they must use this power sparingly if they are to encourage and sustain trust within the school community. Usually, mutual benefit is gained by restoring trust and working together for their own benefit and in the best interests of the teachers and students. The principal is ethically responsible for acting in ways that best serve the interests of the school and the community.

## REFLECTIONS AND RELEVANCE 6.7

### Repairing Broken Trust

Trusting relationships can be risked—or ruined—and school functioning jeopardized, when relational trust is broken.

- In groups of four, each person will identify and describe an event at work in which someone's trust—perhaps yours—was betrayed. The event might appear "small" or "trivial," but still bothered the offended person a great deal. How did the offended person (or you) respond to the offender? To your colleagues?
- If you had been the offender, after reading the above section, what might you have done to make amends and try to repair the broken trust?
- Let the entire class give examples of broken relational trust and discuss the necessity—and the difficulties—of repairing it.

## BUILDING TRUSTING RELATIONSHIPS WITH PARENTS AND COMMUNITY

Since schools run better on trust, developing trusting relationships between educators, parents, and community partners is essential if the school is to succeed. Almost 40 years of research studies find family involvement is a powerful influence on student achievement—increasing students' grades, attendance, promotions, higher math and reading proficiency, better social skills, and fewer disciplinary referrals or placements in special education.[40] Likewise, varied studies find that trusting relationships among parents, teachers, and school leaders improves schools and students' achievement.[41] This holds true in urban schools between educational professionals and parents of low-income students,[42] in middle schools,[43] and in the social aspects of school improvement.[44] One longitudinal analysis of successfully restructuring schools concluded that trust and respect and other human factors were more essential than structural conditions to developing a professional community.[45] Similarly, an intensive, decade-long study of more than 400 Chicago elementary schools confirmed that schools with improving relational trust were more likely to have notable increases in measured student learning whereas schools with low relational trust had only a one-in-seven chance of showing improved academic outcomes.[46]

Trusting relationships between educators and parents brings the school reduced vulnerability and increased commitment and effort—on both ends. Parents depend on school leaders and teachers to keep their children safe and learning. When principals and teachers deliberately reach out to reduce parents' concerns—and make parents and guardians feel more secure about their children's safety and educational quality—educators nurture trust across the community. At the same time, teachers depend on parents to get their children to school every day, provide time and place at home for them to do homework and study, and problem solve around student behavior. When parents successfully meet these responsibilities, they strengthen the educators' trust in them. In addition, when parents and educators trust each other to do what is right and best for every student's learning, all parties feel increased commitment to work on behalf of every student's learning.

Trust between educators and parents (and, to a large extent, with educators and community partners) grows slowly, interaction by interaction, whether in person, in the school or community, by phone call, notes sent home, email or texting, or written comments on students' work. As teachers, principals, and parents interact, they come to discover each other's intentions around schooling. They notice each other's sincerity, actions, follow though, and student results. They observe and assess how well the other person is showing respect, personal regard, competence in their core role responsibilities, and personal integrity. They notice whether the other party is willing to "go the extra mile" for the child's wellbeing. And their conclusions influence how well—or if—relational trust develops. The same holds true for relationships between principals, schools, and community partners.

Building trust between educators and parents (and educators and community partners) may be challenging. As with all relational trust situations, unspoken assumptions about dependence, expectations, and obligations form the framework for assessing the actual social exchanges. But unlike educators who share professional norms and district-wide policies and procedures, parents, community partners, teachers, and principals usually have no personal history of interactions around schooling or other areas upon which to build trust. Parents, community partners, and teachers may not share the same socioeconomic, educational backgrounds, cultural norms, race/ethnicity, or language upon which to build trust. Instead, parents and community partners may rely on the educators' general reputation in the school or community or base their initial respect on commonalities of race, gender, age, religion, or other factors. Parents and community partners may even question principals' and teachers' assertion that "teachers know best" about how or what children should learn. Given these possible differences in expectations and obligations, principals and teachers must be acutely aware of what they say and how they act if they are to build strong interpersonal trust bonds with parents and community stakeholders.

Principals play a central role in engendering and maintaining interpersonal trust among teachers and parents as well as between their schools and their community partners. Many of the same behaviors that establish relational trust with teachers are those that foster relational trust with parents and with community associates. In addition, principals can advance teacher–parent trust when school leaders communicate clearly and often with parents about what their children are learning via newsletters, phone calls, emails, visitations, open room nights, student performances, class web pages, and parent conferences. Speaking with parents and community partners—in oral speech and in writing—works best when the language is clear and jargon-free. Occasions such as these give parents and community associates a chance to see the school in action and provide opportunities to interact with school leaders and teachers in informal and formal ways.

Principals can also encourage and support teachers' efforts to reach out to parents. First, principals need to let teachers know that improving teacher–parent relationships is a high-priority expectation that will help teachers be more successful. Since most teachers are prepared to work with students, and perhaps less so with their parents, teachers may need occasions to learn why and how to show respect for all parents, build personal regard for them as people, and appreciate parents' competence and assets in their core role responsibilities. Social class and racial/ethnic differences can create conditions for misunderstandings and distrust. Today's family structures vary far more than they did years ago, and teachers need to understand and accept these differences without adverse judgment. Teachers also need to appreciate the parents' perspective on educating their children and the circumstances that influence how well they can support their children's learning at home.

Teachers can learn how to sensitively and appropriately interact with parents in ways that help them to be more effective educational partners. For example, one successful principal worked with the faculty to build trust with parents. Any time a phone call went home about something "bad" that happened at school, the teachers found something "good" to call home about, thereby establishing a one-for-one balance of contacts with parents. And, if teachers do not feel respect, personal regard, and appreciation of parents' competence as their children's first educators, teachers need to look more deeply or "fake it until they make it" as a necessary step in building a more positive relationship that will aid their children's school success.

Sometimes, building educator–parent trust (or educator–community partner trust) requires more intensive actions. In a school with low levels of parent or community trust, the principal may need to reshape the faculty by filling staff vacancies with individuals who vocally and behaviorally support the school's vision and mission to educate every child to high levels—and to counseling out those teachers who resist working effectively with all students. Removing teachers who do not actively support educating every child and replacing them with teachers who do can rebuild parent and community trust. Not doing so undermines it.

## REFLECTIONS AND RELEVANCE 6.8

## Building Parents' and Community Partners' Trust

Relational trust between educators and parents (and between educators and community partners) is essential for a school to succeed. For the purpose of this activity, we will consider only educators and parents; many factors make developing relational trust with parents challenging.

- Working in groups of four, identify what you think are your own biggest challenges in developing relational trust with parents.
- Using ideas from the other group members, what experiences or suggestions can you use to effectively overcome these challenges to strong trusting relationships with your students' parents?
- As a class, discuss the major challenges to developing relational trust with your students' parents—and possible ways to overcome these.

## CONCLUSION

As a people business, education's success largely depends on the quality of its relationships. Ethics—how we act in our relationships—lies at the heart of school leadership. Ethical principals are individuals whose actions reflect integrity, who shows respect and fairness towards all others, and who consistently make decisions that are in every child's "best interests." Ethical behaviors form the basis for relational trust.

Relational trust is a reciprocal process. Principals, teachers, students, parents, and community partners depend on each other to accomplish school's ends. High relational trust makes all interactions and problem solving easier and more successful. But when trust is low, the school is unlikely to be effective. And, once distrust takes hold, it is difficult to undo.

One of principals' leadership challenges is developing a more sophisticated set of people skills so they may influence their colleagues' task and affective behaviors in useful ways. More than any other factor, high levels of ethical behavior and interpersonal trust provide the foundation for professional talk, openness, and work necessary to increase educators' capacity and improve students' academic outcomes.

## NOTES

1   Bryk, A. S., Sebring, P. B., Allensworth, E., Luppescu, S., & Easton, J. Q. (2010). *Organizing for school improvement. Lessons from Chicago* (p. 145). Chicago, IL: University of Chicago Press.

2.  Ciulla, J. (Ed.). (2008). *Ethics: The heart of leadership*. Westport, CT: Praeger.

3.  *Ethics* denotes the theory of right and wrong actions whereas *morals* indicate those ethical ideas in action. Ethics and morals are theory and practice, respectively; and the terms are often used interchangeably.

4.  Friedman, T. L. (2008). *Hot, flat, and crowded. Why we need a green revolution—And how it can renew America* (p. 192). New York, NY: Ferrar, Straus, & Giroux.

5.  Plato in Freakley, M., & Burgh, G. (2000). *Engaging with ethics: Ethical inquiry for teachers* (p. 97). Queensland, AU: Social Science Press.

6.  Hitt, W. D. (1990). *Ethics and leadership: Putting theory into practice*. Columbus, OH: Battelle Press.

7.  Spaemann, R. (1989). *Basic moral concepts*. London, UK: Routledge.

8.  Kanungo, R. K., & Mendonca, M. (1996). *Ethical dimensions of leadership*. Thousand Oaks, CA: Sage.

9.  Kaplan, L. S., & Owings, W. A. (2013). *Culture re-boot* (pp. 70–74). Thousand Oaks, CA: Corwin.

10. Goodlad, J. (1990). Studying the education of educators: From conception to findings. *Phi Delta Kappan, 71* (9), 698–701.

11. Kanungo & Mendonca (1996), ibid.

12. For a fuller account of these and other ethical systems, see Owings, W. A., & Kaplan, L. S. (2012). *Leadership and organizational behavior in education. Theory into practice*. Boston, MA: Pearson, (pp. 451–488); Johnson, C. E. (2009). *Meeting the ethical challenges of leadership* (pp. 137–161). Los Angeles, CA: Sage.

13. Meilander, G. (1986). Virtue in contemporary religious thought. In R. J. Neuhaus (Ed.), *Virtue: Public and private* (pp. 7–30). Grand Rapids, MI: Eerdmans; Alderman, H. (1997). By virtue of a virtue. In D. Statman (Ed.), *Virtue ethics* (pp. 145–164). Washington, DC: Georgetown University Press.

14. Starratt, R. J. (1991). Building an ethical school: A theory for practice in educational leadership. *Educational Administration Quarterly, 27* (2), 185–202; Starratt, R. J. (1994). *Building an ethical school*. London, UK: Falmer Press; Shapiro, J. P., & Stefkovich, J. A. (2001). Ethical leadership and decision making in education: *Applying theoretical perspectives to complex dilemmas*. Mahwah, NJ: Lawrence Erlbaum; Shapiro, J. P., & Stefkovich, J. A. (2005). *Ethical leadership and decision making in education: Applying theoretical perspectives to complex dilemmas* (2nd ed.). Mahwah, NJ: Lawrence Erlbaum.

15. Delgado, R. (1995). *Critical race theory: The cutting edge*. Philadelphia, PA: Temple University Press.

16. Hollenbach, D. (1979). *Claims in conflict*. New York, NY: Paulist.

17. See, for example, Apple, M. W. (1998). *Teachers and texts: A political economy of class and gender relations in education*. New York, NY: Routledge & Kegan; Astuto, R. A., Clark, D. L., & Read, A. M. (Eds.), (1994). *Roots of reform: Challenging the assumptions that control education*. Bloomington, IN: Phi Delta Kappan; Freire, P. (1970). *Pedagogy of the oppressed*. (M. B. Ramos, trans.). New York NY: Continuum.

18. Kaplan, L. S., & Owings, W. A. (2015). *Educational foundations* (2nd ed.) (pp. 284–288). Belmont, CA: Cengage.

19. See, for example: http://www.aasa.org/content.aspx?id=1390; http://www.naesp.org/resources/1/Pdfs/LLC2-ES.pdf; http://www.nassp.org/Content.aspx?topic=47103; http://www.nea.org/assets/docs/Transformingteaching2012.pdf

20. These are some of the leadership functions in Standard 4 in the 2015 ISLLC Standards (Draft). See: The Council of Chief State School Officers (2015). *Educational leadership policy*

*standards: ISLLC 2015*. Washington, DC: Council of Chief State School Officers. Retrieved from: The Draft for Public Comment is available at: http://www.ccsso.org/Documents/2014/Draft%202014%20ISLLC%20Standards%2009102014.pdf The final version of the 2015 ISLLC Standards are available at http://www.ccsso.org/Resources/Programs/Developing_and_Supporting_School-Ready_Leaders.html

21. Shapiro & Gross (2008), op. cit.
22. Shapiro, J. P., & Stepklovich, J. A. (2005). *Ethical leadership and decision making in education: Applying theoretical perspectives to complex dilemmas* (2nd ed.). Mahwah, NJ: Lawrence Erlbaum.
23. Definition adapted from Hoy, W., & Tschannen-Moran, M. (1999). Five facets of trust: An empirical confirmation in urban elementary schools. *Journal of School Leadership, 9* (3), 184–208 (p. 189).
24. Kaplan & Owings (2013), op. cit.
25. Bryk, Sebring, Allensworth, Luppescu, & Easton (2010), op. cit.
26. Kaplan & Owings (2013), op. cit. (pp. 77–80).
27. Hoy, W. K., Tarter, C. J., & Witkoskie, L. (1992). Faculty trust in colleagues: Linking the principal with school effectiveness. *Journal of Research and Development in Education, 26,* 38–45; Tarter, C. J., Sabo, D., & Hoy, W. K. (1995). Middle school climate, faculty trust and effectiveness: A path analysis. *Journal of Research and Development in Education, 29,* 41–49.
28. Hoy, W. K., Hoffman, J., Sabo, D., & Bliss, J. (1996). The organizational climate of middle schools. *Journal of Educational Administration, 34,* 41–59; Tarter, C. J., Bliss, J., & Hoy, W. K. (1989). School characteristics and faculty trust in secondary schools. *Educational Administration Quarterly, 25,* 294–308.
29. Hoy, W. K., Tarter, C. J., & Kottkamp, R. (1991). *Open schools/Healthy schools: Measuring organizational climate*. Beverly Hills, CA: Sage; Tartar et al. (1989), op. cit.; Tartar et al. (1995), op. cit.
30. Hoy, W. K., & Kupersmith, W. J. (1986). Principal authenticity and faculty trust: Key elements in organizational behavior. *Planning and Change, 15,* 81–88.
31. Bryk, Sebring, Allensworth, Luppescu, & Easton (2010), ibid.
32. See, for example, Bryk, A. S., & Schneider, B. L. (2002). *Trust in schools: A core resource for improvement*. New York, NY: Russell Sage; Bryk, Sebring, Allensworth, Luppescu, & Easton (2010), op. cit.; Goddard, R., Tschannen-Moran, M., & Hoy, W. (2001). A multilevel examination of the distribution and effects of teacher trust in students and parents in urban elementary schools. *The Elementary School Journal, 102* (1), 3–17; Hoy, W. D., Tarter, C. J., & Witkoskie, L. (1992). Faculty trust in colleagues: Linking the principal with school effectiveness. *Journal of Research and Development in Education, 26* (1), 38–45; Hoy, W. D., & Tschannen-Moran, M. (1999). Five faces of trust: An empirical confirmation in urban elementary schools. *Journal of School Leadership, 9* (3), 184–208; Tarter, C. J., Sabo, D., & Hoy, W. K. (1995). Middle school climate, faculty trust and effectiveness: A path analysis. *Journal of Research and Development in Education, 29* (1), 41–49; Tschannen-Moran, M. (2004). *Trust matters: Leadership for successful schools* (1st ed.). San Francisco, CA: Jossey-Bass.
33. See, for example, Bandura, A. (1993). Perceived self-efficacy in cognitive development and functioning. *Educational Psychologist, 28* (2), 117–148; Bandura, A. (1997). *Self-efficacy: The exercise of control*. New York, NY: Freeman; Goddard, R. D., Hoy, W. K., & Woolfolk Hoy, A. (2001). Collective teacher efficacy: Its meaning, measure, and impact on student achievement. *American Educational Research Journal, 37* (2), 479–508.
34. Lewicki, R. J., & Bunker, B. B. (1996). Developing and maintaining trust in work relationships. In R. M. Kramer, & T. R. Tyler (Eds.), *Trust in organizations: Frontiers of theory and research* (pp. 114–139). Thousand Oaks, CA: Sage; Bryk, A. S., & Schneider, B. (2003). Trust in schools: A core resource for school reform. *Educational Leadership, 60* (6), 40–44.

35. Tschannen-Moran, M., & Hoy, W. K. (2000). A multidisciplinary analysis of the nature, meaning, and measurement of trust. *Review of Educational Research, 70* (4), 547–593.
36. Tschannen-Moran & Hoy (2000), ibid.
37. Kaplan & Owings (2015), op. cit. (pp. 85–86).
38. Kaplan & Owings (2015), op. cit. (pp. 88–92).
39. Jones, W., & Burdette, M. P. (1994). Betrayal in relationships. In A. Weber, & Y. J. Harvey (Eds.), *Perspectives on close relationships* (pp. 242–262). Boston, MA: Allyn & Bacon.
40. For example, see Epstein, J. L. (2005, September). *Developing and sustaining research-based programs of school, family, and community partnerships. Summary of 5 years of NNPS research.* Johns Hopkins University, National Network of Partnership Schools (NNPS). Retrieved from: http://www.csos.jhu.edu/P2000/pdf/Research%20Summary.pdf; Henderson, A. T., & Mapp, K. L. (2002). *A new wave of evidence. The impact of school, family and community connections on student achievement, Annual synthesis 2002.* Eric Document No. ED 474521. Austin, TX: Center of Family and Community Connections with Schools. Southwest Educational Development Laboratory. Retrieved from: http://www.sedl.org/connections/resources/evidence.pdf; Jeynes, W. H. (2007). A meta-analysis of the relation of parental involvement to urban elementary school student academic achievement. *Urban Education, 42* (1), 82–110; Muller, C. (1993). Parent involvement and academic achievement: An analysis of family resources available to the child. In B. Schneider, & J. S. Coleman (Eds.), *Parents, their children, and schools* (pp. 77–113). Boulder, CO: Westview Press.
41. Bryk, A. S., & Schenider, B. (2003, March). Trust in schools: A core resource for school reform. *Educational Leadership, 60* (6), 40–45; Comer, J. P., Haynes, N. M., Joyner, E. T., & Ben Avie, M.(1996). *Rallying the whole village: The Comer process for reforming education.* New York: Teachers College Press; Meier, D. (1995). *The power of their ideas: Lessons for America from a small school in Harlem.* Boston: Beacon Press; Malloy, K. (1998). *Building a learning community: The story of New York City Community School District #2.* Pittsburgh, PA: Learning Research and Development Center, University of Pittsburgh.
42. Comer, Haynes, Joyner, & Ben Avie (1996), ibid.
43. Meier, 1995, op. cit.
44. Malloy, 1998, op. cit.
45. Kruse, S., Louis, K. S., & Bryk, A. S. (1994). *Building professional communities in schools.* Madison, WI: Center on Organization and Restructuring of Schools.
46. Bryk & Schneider (2003), op. cit.

# CHAPTER 7

# Communicating Effectively

The single biggest problem in communication
is the illusion that it has taken place.
—George Bernard Shaw

---

## LEARNING OBJECTIVES

7.1   Explain how interpersonal communications is a highly complex, intensive, and time-consuming relational and transactional process.

7.2   Describe how context factors can influence one-way and two-way communications.

7.3   Discuss three reasons why communications may break down and ways to avoid it.

7.4   Summarize how principals can make good use of formal and informal communication in schools.

7.5   Assess the relative importance of credibility and basic communication skills to a principal's leadership effectiveness and explain your rationale.

7.6   Identify some of the communications challenges and barriers principals and teachers face in working successfully with today's parents and community members.

7.7   Explain the benefits to principals, students, and schools when they build partnerships with local leaders to "scan" and "seed" the environment.

---

**2015 ISLLC STANDARDS: 1, 2, 3, 5, 6, 7, 8, 9, 10, 11**

## INTRODUCTION

Schools run on communication. Teachers instruct by speaking to their students and listening to (or reading) students' responses to check for accurate understanding. Principals communicate with teachers when they share a vision for all children's academic success, when they lead discussions at faculty meetings, and when they meet in formal and informal conferences. They communicate as they direct, monitor, and evaluate their management and operational systems. They communicate with central office supervisors, parents, and the community when they post newsletters on their school's website; when they meet for school conferences; when they contact one another by phone, text, or email; and when they keynote at the Kiwanis Club Breakfasts. Some might say that school administrators spend most of their time talking with others.

Communication can be viewed as a "bridging activity" that builds links with stakeholders.[1] Communications can be a means to improve school practices and student outcomes, manage conflict and reduce the interpersonal tensions among teachers, and generate and sustain community good will. In short, communications in schools—as in other organizations—can be a means to build bridges of cooperation that bring like-minded people in instead of moats to keep others out.[2]

Being an effective communicator is so essential to leading a successful school that a principal's weaknesses in this area may be career ending. A California study found that poor interpersonal communications is the major reason that most principals are fired.[3] In another study, teachers identified principals' mistakes as occurring in human relations and interpersonal communications—especially what teachers perceived as a lack of trust and an uncaring attitude.[4] In a Tennessee study, superintendents ranked "works cooperatively with faculty and staff" as "number 1" in their list of principals' career-threatening skill deficiencies.[5] Adding to this concern, the National School Public Relations Association's surveys and interviews of leading superintendent search firms find that the "lack of communication and the failure to keep people informed" is the primary factor affecting the superintendents' failure.[6] Research across many industries indicates that leaders often fail because of "communicative incompetence."[7]

This chapter will discuss communications issues that affect principals' leadership effectiveness. The communication process, one- and two-way communications, formal and informal communications, improving principals' communication skills, and communicating with parents and community all receive attention. When future principals learn to appreciate effective communications skills as an essential leadership capacity, they can begin to strengthen their own abilities in this vital domain.

## THE COMMUNICATION PROCESS

*Communication* is sharing ideas or attitudes in ways that produce an understanding between two or more people.[8] It is a relational and transactional process of expressing or exchanging information with another person by using words, symbols, behaviors, and contextual cues. Through their expressions and exchanges, people impart information and attitudes, convey expectations, give directions, ask questions, influence behavior, and receive feedback in ways that generate a degree of understanding between themselves and others.

In more technical terms, *communication* is the "transmission and/or reception of signals through some channel(s) that humans interpret based on a probabilistic system that is deeply influenced by context."[9] *Senders* with a particular purpose in mind transmit signals by speaking, writing, or drawing (along with demonstrating, touching, texting, FaceTime-ing, and other means) through a *channel* (such as a broadcast, email, letters, or speech). Typically, senders are individuals, groups, and organizational units that distribute messages to other individuals, groups, and organizations. *Messages* are usually verbal or nonverbal cues or symbols that stand for ideas and information that the sender intends to transfer to others. *Encoding* is the process by which the sender uses cognitive structures to turn the intended message into symbolic form. *Receivers* are those who accept the message, *decode* it (using cognitive structures to interpret the sender's message so it makes sense to them), and act on it. *Feedback* is the return message the receiver sends to the sender in response to the initial message that allows corrections to be made. Successful exchanges do not happen unless both parties agree on what the communication means. Each must accurately interpret the message.

As a relational and transactional process, communication allows people to construct meaning and develop assumptions about what is happening around them by exchanging *symbols*, that is, words that stand for ideas, intentions, emotions and other objects. Our alphabets and languages give community members a common symbol system with which to share their experiences with others. As children mature, they learn to use these symbols—words and gestures—by watching and listening to their parents speak and read stories to them and by responding back to their parents for affirmation or correction.

Communicating well is not easy. It is a time-intensive and costly process. In addition, language is highly complex and often ambiguous, influenced by the speakers' intentions, the organization's culture, and the listeners' prior experiences. Unless principals clearly think through what they want to say, express it simply—and with an appreciation for the range of possible listeners' agendas or unconscious biases—misunderstandings are not only possible, but also likely. As a result, high quality communication does not happen by accident. It is intentional, carefully planned, and reinforced—or undone—by daily interactions across the school. Although misinterpretations cannot always be avoided, principals who have a more sophisticated understanding of the communications process and how to strengthen their own language skills make miscommunications less probable. Understanding the strengths and limitations of one- and two-way communication is a useful place to begin.

## ONE-WAY COMMUNICATION

Communication can occur as an expression (one-way) or as an exchange (two-way). *One-way communication* happens when one person tells something to another person. This type of communication is unilateral: speaker to receiver. One-way communication occurs, for instance, when announcements resound over the school's public address

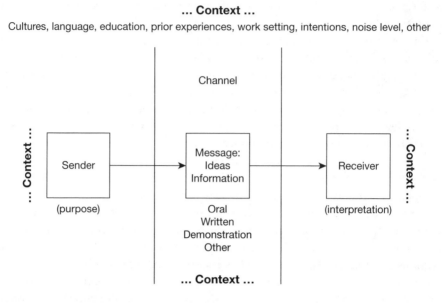

**FIGURE 7.1** One-Way Communication
Source: Kaplan, L. S., & Owings, W. A., 2014.

system, when teachers lecture their students on the day's lesson, when physical education coaches explain new athletic plays to their intramural teams, and when principals describe new school district programs to parents at Back-to-School Nights.

Figure 7.1 depicts basic, one-way communication between a sender and a receiver. The sender has a purpose—ideas or information—to convey to the receiver and transmits that purpose through a message. The message may take a variety of formats: a memo, an oral face-to-face meeting, a demonstration, email, or some other channel. The receiver must accept and accurately interpret that message. Ideally, the receiver will understand the message the same way the sender intends it to be understood. Meanwhile, the context surrounding both sender and receiver influences how the sender shapes, elaborates, and transmits the message and also influences how the receiver interprets its meaning. Context—the individuals' education and prior experiences, their family and social cultures, their facility with the language used, the workplace climate, and other factors—all influence how the message is prepared and how it is interpreted.

One-way communication in school may have several advantages.[10] First, it highlights the message sender's expressive and articulation skills. It encourages principals and teachers to think through their ideas and express them clearly with detailed directions, explanations, and descriptions. The less vague and ambiguous their message, the more likely the receivers will understand it as the sender intends and will correctly perform the proposed actions. Second, one-way tactics usually assume a strong and efficient link between communication behavior and goal achievement. Ideally, the receiving individual or group's focus is on the message rather than on collegial chatter or other off-task behaviors.

This one-way approach has a down side, too. Because it lacks the feedback loop from receiver back to sender, it is often an insufficient communication method. This is especially true in schools where teachers and administrators rely on shared under-standings in order to enact appropriate and effective actions. Simply because a sender expresses a highly polished message does not guarantee that the receiver understands it as the speaker intends. Here lies one-way communication's basic weakness: message sent does not always equal message received. An efficient correction loop is missing.

Nonetheless, many educators continue to rely on this one-way format. Two flawed assumptions help explain why. First, senders see receivers as passive information pro-cessors rather than as active constructors of the messages they receive. Senders don't recognize that receivers create their own meaning as they filter the sender's message through their own context-derived perceptual screens. Second, senders assume that their words carry their intended meaning. Instead, however, language varies its meaning with its usage and its contexts. For example, if a teacher announces to colleagues that his recently assigned 10th grade English essays made him "see red," did he mean he was angry at their poor quality, did he print the pages in red ink or on red paper, or did he give so much constructive feedback on each sheet that the pages were covered with red-pen edits? Words' meanings depend on how they are used, the people involved, and the context in which they are spoken (or read).

As Wayne Hoy and Cecil Miskel, two educational leadership professors, observe, "Words do not serve so much as containers of meaning as stimulators of meaning."[11] It would appear, therefore, that communication in complex organizations such as schools would need to be more sophisticated and allow for receiver feedback to sender to assure that message sent equals message received.

## TWO-WAY COMMUNICATION

*Two-way communications*—a reciprocal, interactive process in which all participants initiate and receive messages—makes this improvement. In comparison with one-way communication, two-way communication requires continuous exchanges—and feedback—between message senders and receivers. Each messages influences the next one. Examples of two-way communication include conversations, questioning and answering, debate, and classroom discussions in which teachers and students interact to exchange information.

Two-way communication begins at birth: babies (the message senders) cry and parents (the message receivers) struggle to figure out what the infant is trying to communicate and respond accordingly. Anxious parents run through mental checklists of possible information that the baby is straining to convey: Is the child hungry? Is a clean diaper necessary? Is the child frightened by a sudden loud noise? Does the child simply want to be held and cuddled? But since days- and weeks-old babies have yet to develop the cognitive capacity for words and sophisticated encoding, their com-munications consist of shrill crying, physical gestures, or vocal cooing. Urgent or calm, babies without conventional oral language send messages that are often unclear and imprecise. Parents eventually learn to decode their babies' cries and bring them what they need or want. Over time, with maturing cognitive capacities, practice, and increasingly refined messages and feedback, young children learn to understand and use the symbols—words and gestures—to speak their parents' language. As children watch and listen to an ever-wider circle of family, friends, teachers, and acquaintances, they learn to construct meaning with language in ways that are reasonably similar to those around them. At the same time, they develop assumptions and expectations and learn to predict what these people will think and do. Children's communication skills—and their brains—mature as their interactions with the world prompt them to receive and send messages in a reinforcing cycle.

Figure 7.2 illustrates how two-way, person-to-person communication works. This model stresses the relationship, feedback and response, and the contexts that influence how each person receives and interprets the message. Given the range of contextual and personal factors that influence perceptions, what may seem clear and precise to one person may not always seem clear and precise to another.

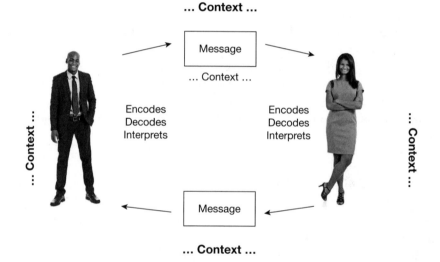

**FIGURE 7.2** Two-Way Communication
Source: Kaplan, L. S., & Owings, W. A., 2014. Images courtesy of Thinkstock.

Context plays an essential role in Figure 7.2 because it affects all aspects of communication. In schools, factors including the school climate and culture, the degree of bureaucratization, and the interpersonal trust and respect levels among administrators, teachers, students, and parents all impact what is said, how it is said, how the message is received and interpreted, and how the message sender will know if meaning sent equals meaning received. Positive contextual influences will facilitate effective and efficient communications. In contrast, negative climates and cultures, high degrees of bureaucratization, low trust and respect, and other adverse environmental factors can distort, limit, or even stop communication in schools. For instance, a smiling principal who frequently walks the halls during the school day, encouraging teachers and students to come over and have a chat, will hear and see more of what is really happening in the school than a principal sitting at a desk in an office with an "open door" guarded by a protective secretary.

Here is an example of how principals may use the school's contextual factors to benefit the message's purpose and improve the final outcome. In an effort to increase parents' involvement with their children's education, the school district has decided that all teachers, K-12, will be expected to post their coming week's classroom lessons and homework assignments on their school's website the prior Friday afternoon by 5 p.m. The program will begin in six weeks (at the start of the new grading period). The principal (sender) must inform (communicate) this message to the teachers (receivers). While deciding how to develop and deliver the message, the principal considers how context can shape the message and the teachers' responses to it. What desired effects or goals should the message have on the teachers? Should the principal limit the message to "the facts" about the central office's new program?

Should the principal paint a larger picture of how involving parents as allies can help teachers be more successful in generating students' learning? How can the principal explain this program in ways that will motivate teacher interest and involvement yet avoid teacher resentment and burnout? Is there a way teachers can meet this expectation by "working smarter, not harder"? Should the principal suggest the teachers select a planning committee with respected members from each department to design a school-wide format and procedures to meet this expectation? Or should the principal tell teachers "the facts" and how to address them?

After much thought, the principal decides that meeting this goal will require devising several communication strategies. The first step is recognizing that not all teachers will be happy with this extra set of work expectations, no matter how well intentioned. The principal will want to take a positive tone and frame the new program as a way to help teachers be more successful at increasing student learning. Next, the principal will need to get the teachers' attention by highlighting the importance of parent involvement in students' learning. The principal will need to provide information on how the proposed strategy reinforces the school's goals and values, how this expectation improves what they are already doing, or meets a need they have not yet successfully addressed. What changes, if any, will teachers need to make in their lesson-planning schedule or format?

Since most teachers will not enthusiastically welcome this extra responsibility, the principal will consider the best media for transmitting the information. The message will have to be widely distributed, well organized, with both formal and informal aspects. The principal may decide to use a logically developed, detailed memo given to teachers the day before a faculty meeting. The meeting will introduce the initiative and present the school's plan for teachers' collaboration to design a workable way to handle it. During the next two weeks, formal and informal face-to-face discussions, individual and small group meetings, and discussions will occur in regularly scheduled planning periods and department meetings. Teachers will work in these small groups to more fully and accurately decode the message, express their views about it, decide how their group would like to put the program into place, and give this feedback and "teacher-and-parent-friendly" suggestions to the principal. Positive teacher-talk and a teacher-designed solution will influence colleagues to accept this new responsibility. In this way, both principals and teachers are communicators and the process has become interactive and transactional. Each party is talking, listening, and cooperating to design a practical solution.

## PREVENTING COMMUNICATION BREAKDOWNS

Messages can be misunderstood. Communications can fail for any number of reasons. What is clear and precise to one person is not always received and interpreted in the way the sender intends.

Language is ambiguous. Problems may occur with encoding, decoding, and interpreting messages by senders and receivers for a variety of reasons. In the first place, words can have several meanings. One investigator found that the 500 most often used words in the English language had more than 14,000 definitions.[12] For instance, is a "fluke" a fish or a stroke of luck? Is a "bank" a place to deposit and withdraw money, the sides of a stream, or a cue shot in billiards? Even simple, everyday words can confuse the listener without more clarifying details. As a result, without additional specifics from the sender—adding context clues (a *finance* rather than a *fish* tale), clarifying the purpose of the message (for instance, "In regard to the new math curriculum ..."), and referencing the receiver's relevant prior experiences with the topic at hand (for instance, "As we discussed at our planning meeting last week ...")—misunderstandings are likely.

In the second place, people differ in their expectations and experiences, creating multiple realities to color the same received message. For instance, the superintendent might call a meeting to make a critical decision, the principal might view the same meeting as an opportunity to network, while the guidance director sees this as an opportunity to express an opinion. Each views the same meeting through a different orientation and may interpret the message through that perceptual filter.[13] Whether listeners interpret the message the way the sender intends depends on the context, the listener's expectations, and prior experiences. Different listeners may interpret the same message in idiosyncratic ways.

Additionally, many people are poor listeners who misunderstand what they hear or read. Moreover, understanding a message does not automatically mean the listener will agree or comply. Teachers may accurately understand the principal's request for them to meet with parents at school every evening for a week after report cards go home, but teachers may still resent doing it—or call in sick—because they are tired and have competing family commitments.

Third, because context affects language's meaning, it influences everything else in the communication models. The school's climate and culture, the role that teachers have in the schools' decision making, the number of bureaucratic levels separating teachers from their administrators and parents from educators, the openness granted educators to express their real ideas and concerns, the relational trust that teachers and administrators share, the frequency of occasions for teachers and principals to problem solve around actual issues all play roles in communications' efficiency and effectiveness. If these and other contextual factors are positive, mutual understandings and interpersonal relations are also more likely to be positive. In contrast, negative climate and culture, dense bureaucracy, low trust, and other unfavorable factors can limit, distort, or obstruct communications in schools.

Principals who understand that the most effective communication is a two-way interactive and relational process realize that sending a message is only the first step. Recognizing the many ways it may be misunderstood, receiving feedback, and clarifying

## REFLECTIONS AND RELEVANCE 7.1

## Communicating is Complex

Communicating effectively is not easy. It is a time-intensive and highly complex process with many factors affecting how well the message is sent and understood.

Working alone, think of the person with whom you have the easiest time communicating and the person with whom you have the most difficult time communicating. "Easy" and "difficult" refer to the amount of time spent preparing the communication and the likelihood it will be understood or misunderstood. Analyze your communications with these persons as you complete the table below. You may identify the individuals by name, relationship to you, or initials. Then work with a partner to explain your findings. What factors make your communications "easy" or "difficult"? Then discuss findings with the rest of the class. What factors make communicating easier or more difficult? What can you do to increase effective communication with difficult people?

| | "Easiest" Person | "Most Difficult" Person |
|---|---|---|
| *Setting*: home, work, other | | |
| *Message*: personal, professional, other | | |
| *Relationship*: between sender and receiver | | |
| *Channels*: fact-to-face, oral, writing, teleconference, other; long or short | | |
| *Context*: environmental, personal, social, cultural, educational, other | | |
| *One- or two-way*: feedback | | |

the message if needed are additional steps. Wise principals accept the importance of building rapport among stakeholders, creating a team environment of trust and mutual respect, and encouraging clarifying questions to generate useful feedback about how well the listeners are interpreting the message the way the sender intends. These are essential factors that reduce a message's ambiguity.

By soliciting questions and feedback, the principal's goal is not to increase teachers' productivity by making them feel happy and valued but rather to increase their accurate understanding and prompt their appropriate actions. In addition, building strong relationships, encouraging others to speak openly about their confusion or concerns, and providing constructive feedback actually fosters healthier employees. Researchers have found that positive social interactions at work are associated with instant and lasting effects on the cardiovascular, immune, and neuroendocrine systems.[14] Effective communication can literally lead to better health.

## FORMAL AND INFORMAL COMMUNICATION

Organizations such as schools are designed for communication. Communication is part of their administrative processes to manage and direct information. Status, power, and hierarchy tend to influence the direction of these flows. Traditionally, the messages and authority run from the top down, from supervisors to employees. "Make certain to go through proper channels" and "follow the chain of command" are two familiar phrases that reflect an organization's emphasis on using the regular communication pathway.

In schools, the superintendent reports to the school board, but since the superintendent is the district's leading educational professional, the superintendent advises the mostly amateur board members as well as sends messages to the central office directors and principals. In turn, the central office directors and supervisors send messages to the principals, and the principals send messages to the other building administrators, teachers, school staff, students, and parents.

For communication to work effectively, every organizational member must link to a communication channel (typically, the chain of command), and the channels must be known and be as short and direct as possible. In addition, most communication is expected to follow the hierarchical structure. It is unusual for teachers or principals to communicate directly with school board members about school-related issues unless they are friends, neighbors, or accidently meet in the checkout line at the local grocery store.

### Formal Communication

As with other organizations, people in schools communicate in both formal and informal ways. *Formal communication* is the use of official spoken or written language to relay or exchange ideas and information. It tends to occur in formal settings such as a work environment where people dress appropriately to the occasion. Usually planned, formal communications use certain prescribed channels organized by management along the lines of authority, and involve following specific procedures and rules. In schools, as in other organizations, formal communication networks or channels tend to follow the hierarchy of authority and status, from the top down.

Five types of formal communication travel downward from superiors to subordinates:[15]

- instructions about specific tasks;
- rationale about why the task needs to be done and how it relates to other tasks;
- information about the organization's procedures and practices;
- information about the organization's goals;
- feedback about individuals' performance levels.

Although sending communications downward through the organization is fairly easy to do, decoding them accurately remains complicated, and subordinates often misunderstand them. To be sure that the intended messages are correctly understood, administrators must use two-way communication channels and employ widespread feedback up and down the chain of command.

Meanwhile, upward communication from the lower organizational levels to the upper levels typically contains four types of messages:[16]

- routine operational messages;
- reports on problems;
- suggestions for improvement;
- information on how subordinates view each other and the job.

Upward communication is one way that superiors hold subordinates accountable. As a result, subordinates tend to stress the positive, hold back the negative, say what they think the boss wants to hear, or simply remain silent.[17] Since the accuracy and timeliness of information reaching the organization's top affects the quality of decisions made there, the more concrete and objective the information, the more likely that subordinates will communicate accurately with their superiors. Two-way exchanges will also improve communications' accuracy. This is why principals may prefer to give their reports to supervisors in person as well as in writing.

## Informal Communication

*Informal communication* is unofficial and follows no particular set of regulations apart from those belonging to the specific group or culture. Informal communication is usually spontaneous or casual, related to employees' social needs, does not flow along lines of authority, follows fewer rules and procedures, and is usually oral. It can occur in both formal and informal settings. Informal communication network members communicate easily and well among themselves. Facts, views, outlooks, worries, gossip and rumors, and orders travel freely from person to person.

While formal communication networks tend to follow an organization's hierarchy, informal networks—or "grapevines"—are active regardless of how complex and elaborate the formal networks tend to be. Built around teachers' and staff's social relationships, informal channels grow from links as simple as adjacent classrooms or desks, common free periods, shared departments, similar roles in separate schools, and friendships. They include conversations between teachers, between teachers and staff, and teachers' lounge or parking lot gossip. The informal communication language may include slang and colloquialisms that are not usually part of a formal communication. These social relationships and their communication channels occur at all levels of the organization, from the individual school to the central office and among principals leading separate schools.

Despite the potential harm that gossip and rumors can cause, informal networks have useful purposes. They monitor and express the school's quality of life. The "grapevine" provides information about the school's culture, its openness or rigidity, the collegiality or conflict among teachers, and the school's accessibility to parents and the community. In addition, messages coming from informal sources provide principals with essential feedback—the situational awareness of the school's undercurrents—that is one of principals' most important sources of information about how well the school is functioning. It brings school leaders opinions and sentiment about teacher, administrator, and student morale, information useful to preventing and solving problems. In fact, principals' level of situational awareness has an important relationship with student achievement.[18]

Principals and teachers also benefit from well-developed informal networks when in exchange for their insights and information, teachers gain opportunities to influence principals' thinking and actions. Veteran teachers, who understand their faculty and community, can advise principals on how to get things done, accurately identify what will or won't work in that school, or help resolve specific difficulties. Similarly, department chairs, school counselors, and teachers with specialized skills have valuable information that can help inform the principal's decisions.

Moreover, the informal "grapevine" provides information when no formal sources are available or adequate. Especially in times of change, the informal network carries information faster—and often more completely—than the formal channels can provide. For teachers who want to know what to expect and how to prepare themselves cognitively, emotionally, and professionally for new initiatives, the "grapevine" fills a necessary void. Plus, face-to-face message exchanges about new programs are often simpler and quicker than reading about them. Sometimes having some information about what lies ahead, even if incorrect, satisfies a "need to know" better than having no information and worrying about the unknown.

Likewise, informal communication channels may help teachers and staff meet their needs for affiliation and belonging that the school's formal channels cannot meet. Talking with other teachers about their family lives, sharing views on topics of mutual interest, expressing their opinions, and offering advice on issues having nothing to do with education or work brings personal satisfaction and enjoyment to the workplace.

Lastly, informal networks give meaning to activities within the school. Often, information given to teachers presents the facts but omits their implications. For instance, a principal announces to teachers that they will begin using new grading software by the start of the next school year. But what will that *mean* for each individual teacher's practices for compiling and entering student grades into a computer? Will they still need to maintain their gradebooks? How will the new software specifically affect each teacher's practices and workload? How and when will the teachers learn how to use the new system? How much more time will it take them to complete this accountability task? Although the principal may not have these crucial details in the announcements, the teachers will likely gain some version of it through informal sources.

In reverse, the principal might use the informal network to float a trial balloon to sample the teachers' receptiveness to a new program or procedure and check teachers' feelings about it—using the informal network as a "testing ground" for possible action.

For the most part, messages travelling through informal networks are highly accurate—translated with 75 to 90 percent accuracy for uncontroversial information.[19] Unfortunately, the grapevine's inaccurate 10 to 25 percent—even small distortions or errors—can cause principals and teachers big headaches.

Formal and informal communication networks tend to complement each other. Networks tend to overlap and interrelate.[20] The organizational chart cannot begin to identify the individuals who consistently interact with each other. Although the school and district's task networks—those people whose responsibilities require them to work together for a common purpose—are larger and better developed than the social networks, both are closely related and essential to organizational functioning.[21] In their content and reach to all organizational members, these networks are interdependent.

## REFLECTIONS AND RELEVANCE 7.2

### Formal and Informal Communications

Formal (official) and informal (the "grapevine") communications can each relay and exchange ideas and information in organizations. Each has advantages and disadvantages for the organization.

Working with a partner, identify and describe a time in your workplace when the informal communications network prevented or solved a problem for an individual or group. Also identify a time when the informal communications network created a problem for an individual or group. What do think should be the cautions about relying on the "grapevine" for information? After your discussion, meet with the entire class to identify the benefits and limitations of relying on the organization's informal communications networks.

# IMPROVING PRINCIPALS' COMMUNICATION SKILLS

Since effective communication skills are such a pervasive part of a principal's leadership repertoire—more than simply a role-related skill[22]—principal candidates benefit when they begin considering and consciously improving their own skills. Refining and expanding one's sending, listening, and feedback capacities are a must.

## Credibility

No matter how polished the language, teachers will not believe messages from a person who they do not see as credible. *Credibility* consists of the trust and confidence that the receiver has in the sender's words and actions. The principal's level of credibility—his or her reputation—with the teachers affects the teachers' responses to what the principal says and does. When a faculty views their principal as minimally competent or as someone who will often say one thing and then do another, or both, they are likely to distort or ignore most of the principal's communications.

## Trustworthiness, Integrity, and Openness

Similarly, the sender's trustworthiness, integrity, and openness are qualities that influence how receivers understand the message.[23] A principal's *trustworthiness*—the belief by others that the principal is an ethical person, one who is caring, honest, reliable, competent, and fair—is what makes the leader credible and believable. Principals with *integrity* act in ways that are honest and ethical, consistent with their stated values, and fair in their dealings with others. Principals who display *openness* express their true feelings and opinions. They are candid, frank, and plainspoken. The faculty notices these attributes. Their presence or absence in the principal—or in any communicator, for that matter—is a barometer for how accessible and collaborative the school's communication climate can be and the degree to which the leaders' messages will be received as intended.

For a principal to be credible, the teachers must believe that their leader's values and words are consistently aligned with good student outcomes. Although the principal can have formal authority, position, power, and expertise, teachers will be more likely to listen to the principal's messages without unnecessary distortions or misunderstandings if they trust their leader to have the children's best interests at heart and treat everyone in the school with respect and fairness. Only when the principal has established him or her self as a credible, trustworthy individual with integrity and openness can principals and teachers take the risks needed to openly discuss new ideas to improve teaching and learning.

Similarly, trust is especially important when discussing controversial topics. Before they speak, teachers need to know that if they express their honest views, their perspectives will be considered; and they will not be judged unfairly, humiliated, or punished.

One way that principals can maintain or enhance their credibility, trustworthiness, integrity, and openness is to say what they mean and mean what they say. They are congruent: genuine, receptive, and honest. Their verbal (words) and nonverbal (physical gestures) messages convey the same meaning, and their words and actions convey the same meaning. *Nonverbal communication* is all behavior that communicates that does not use words. Up to two-thirds of total communication is nonverbal.[24] Facial expressions and gestures such as raised eyebrows, restless leg bouncing, or impatient finger tapping are well-known nonverbal actions that express a particular meaning in our culture. Even voice tone, intonation, pitch, loudness, and speed of speaking can communicate about the person's emotional state as well as information about gender, age, place of origin, and social class.[25]

We express most of our feelings through our facial expressions, and six expressions are universal across cultures—happiness, sadness, anger, fear, surprise, and disgust.[26] In our mainstream American culture, eye-to-eye contact used for a short period is one of the most direct and potent ways people communicate nonverbally. Prolonged eye contact, by contrast, is perceived as threatening or, in a non-work setting, as romantic interest. Direct eye contact is also perceived as an indicator of honesty and credibility. People in our society learn that they can look directly at individual audience members to strengthen the impact of their presentation. Therefore, if the principal walks into the faculty lounge for morning coffee and greets teachers with a hearty, "Glad to see you!" but never smiles or looks directly at them, teachers will wonder what the principal really thinks. The words don't match the gestures; they are incongruent. Teachers may logically suspect that the principal does not enjoy mornings (or being around teachers).

The challenge for future principals who want to infuse relational trust, integrity, and openness throughout the school, therefore, is to prioritize developing positive and authentic relationships with teachers and staff, follow-through on promises made, take every opportunity to connect the daily business of running a school with the shared vision for improving teaching and learning, and ensure that their actions match their words.

## Congruence

Congruence also matches words to actions. For example, a principal tells teachers that his or her "office door is always open." But when they try to visit during the day to discuss an issue, the door may be ajar but the principal is out, or the door is closed and the principal is "in conference." In another example, a principal tells the faculty, "We treat each child the same" but then grants influential parents' requests for an honors class placement for their child. Again, the principal appears to be saying one thing but doing another. A principal announces, "The school's finances are open to the faculty," but when interested teachers visit the bookkeeper to review how the school is spending money, the records are never available. Incongruous verbal and nonverbal messages and incongruous words and actions can seriously undermine a principal's credibility and make his or her messages more likely to be distorted or disregarded.

## Nuts and Bolts

Certain mundane communication issues deserve attention, too. First-class public speaking skills convey principals' expertise and authority. Too many "and ums," "ahs," "you knows," and other crutch words impair presentations at faculty and PTA meetings. Recording one's presentations and replaying them privately can give school leaders a realistic idea of how they come across to listeners. (If you sound boring, unprofessional, or confusing, think of how these factors affect your faculty's reaction.) Likewise, high-quality writing skills are also important. Proofread all memos, and have a trusted associate who has excellent English usage and spelling read behind you to edit what you might have overlooked. Reread your emails and revise if needed before hitting "Send." Misspellings, typos, and subject-verb agreement errors in written communications lessen your credibility with the faculty, central office, and the community. But a principal's effectiveness in communication is more than having a facility with written and spoken words: it is a matter of personal character. So this is where future principals need to begin—with a look in the mirror.

---

**REFLECTIONS AND RELEVANCE 7.3**

## Your Credibility as a Communicator

Credibility is the trust and confidence that the receiver has in the sender's words and actions. Without credibility to listeners, the likelihood of your messages being distorted or ignored increases.

Assess your credibility for each item below on a scale of 1–5, with 1 meaning "needs improvement" and 5 meaning "excellent." Then provide an example from your work setting (past or present) for each quality. Share your findings with a partner. After you and your partner have finished, the whole class will discuss their findings. Also discuss as a class: How can you accurately assess your own credibility as a leader and as a communicator? How can you develop and refine your personal and communication skills in this area?

| Credibility Rating | Examples |
| --- | --- |
| Trustworthiness | |
| Integrity | |
| Openness | |
| Congruence | |

---

## IMPROVING BASIC COMMUNICATION SKILLS

In addition to having high credibility, transformational leaders' skill sets include *communication competence*—their messages are appropriate and effective within their organizational milieu.[27] Research finds that high job performers, especially those who supervise others, are very motivated to adapt their communication to the needs of the situation, develop more skills in communicating empathy, and manage interactions than listeners who are lower performing employees.[28] Able communicators can accurately "read" differing social situations, flexibly manage their interactions with verbal fluency and empathy, and adjust their messages accordingly. Through education, experience, and observing role models, they learn "how" to communicate, not just "what" to communicate.[29]

Future principals can strengthen their communication competence in sending, listening, and feedback skills by deliberately increasing their attention to the components of effective communication—and then by making occasions to practice doing them and requesting (and listening to) honest and detailed feedback about how well they did.

## Sending Skills

Sending skills are the abilities to make oneself understood. Five techniques can help educational leaders strengthen their sending skills. They are:[30]

- *Use appropriate language.* Speak directly to listeners, and use clear and relevant educational language to believably express ideas. Avoid using educational jargon or "fancy, complicated" words when simpler (and accurate) words will do. Correct grammar, usage, spelling, and neatness are always essential in formal letters, reports, and memos (as well as with graduate course assignments).
- *Provide clear and complete information.* Connect the new message to what the listeners already know so they can assimilate the new information and restructure their current knowledge to include the new content.
- *Minimize noise from the physical and psychological environment.* Any distraction interferes with the communication process. Meet in a setting that is free from random, loud, distracting sounds that interfere with listening (such as ringing telephones or construction), has good lighting, and comfortable temperature and seating. Providing cookies and punch or other light refreshments for attendees at after school meetings creates an inviting climate for tired and hungry teachers and helps them focus better on the topic at hand.
- *Use multiple and appropriate media.* Use graphics, pictures, audiovisual presentations—large enough to be clearly visible by those sitting farthest away— and provide regular opportunities for two-way dialogue to strengthen one-way communication.
- *Use face-to-face communication and repetition.* Especially when expressing complex or ambiguous ideas, listeners need vocal and visual cues along with repetition in order to fully receive, accurately interpret, and remember the message. Feedback to the speaker—checks for understanding—can also help ensure the message intended is the message received.

Effective communicators are sensitive to contextual factors that influence how listeners receive the message. Any form of noise—environmental, social, or personal— that interferes with communication can become more important to the listeners than the message. The time of day is such a factor. Especially in the afternoons, once students have left the campus, tired teachers need speakers with enthusiastic and engaging presentation styles (and food) if they are to pay attention. Social factors that create "noise" include such aspects as how teachers seat themselves for faculty meetings. Principals want to ensure that all the "detractors" do not routinely sit together in the back of the room, making comments under their breaths in response to the message. Personal factors that create "noise" include the sender being aware of his or her own biases and not allowing them to become barriers to communication. For example, in our multicultural society, principals will want to make sure that they are inviting questions and comments from teachers of each gender; every age, racial, and ethnic group; and each sexual orientation (rather than calling only upon those teachers who raise their hands to be heard or those with whom the principal is most comfortable). Since every message is filtered through listeners' or viewers' perceptual screens, predispositions, or cognitive schemas, it is crucial that principals present a message that avoids playing to these biases.

## Listening Skills

The old saying, "You have two ears and one mouth for a reason," suggests that it is more important to listen than to talk. *Listening* is the ability to accurately receive and interpret messages in the communication process. It is a form of behavior in which individuals try to understand what others are communicating to them through the use of words, actions, and things.[31] Hearing is easy; our auditory sense organs—ears—are part of our genetic endowment. We hear sounds around us as a primal alarm system to escape potential danger. Listening, where we connect meaning to what we are hearing, looking for the ideas beneath the words, amid all the possible distractions, is more complex. As Seth Horowitz, a Brown University auditory neuroscientist observes, "The difference between the sense of hearing and the skill of listening is attention."[32] Whereas hearing is a physical process, listening is a cognitive process.

For two-way exchanges to be relatively accurate, listening is needed. Listening means paying attention not only to the word but also to how the sender uses the language, voice, and body. Listening means being aware of both verbal and non-verbal messages. Paying attention, focusing on what the other person is saying and meaning, shows respect, interest, and concern for the other and his or her viewpoints.

According to counseling professors Allen Ivey, Mary Ivey, and Carlos Zalaquett (2013), effective listening depends on several essential elements: attending, observing, questioning, encouraging, paraphrasing, reflecting feelings, and summarizing.[33] *Attending* is the process of being alert to the conversation. It means putting aside other thoughts or environmental distractors that may sidetrack the listener from the speaker's message. Attending includes culturally, individually, and situationally appropriate eye contact and body language and remaining focused on the conversation. In our culture, making eye contact and looking at the person speaking expresses interest and attentiveness whereas looking away as the person is speaking indicates disinterest or indifference. Likewise, leaning forward, keeping an open posture, smiling, nodding one's head, and looking relaxed and receptive are nonverbal behaviors that express interest. Lastly, effective listening stays with the speaker, paying attention through the conversation.

*Questioning*—asking the speaker for greater clarification—is sometimes necessary in order to fully understand the speaker's intent and meaning. Some messages are vague or confusing, and questions can bring clarification. Allow the speaker to finish each point before querying. Certain factual questions are direct, clear, and simple: a "yes" or "no" is the only answer needed. With more abstract information, questions tend to be more open and call for speculation and further development. For instance, "What do you mean when you say you are 'confused'?" or "Could you give me an example of what you mean?" might bring the elaboration and details necessary to fully understand the speaker's concern. Skillful questions that clarify and elaborate are natural parts of thoughtful listening. The point of questioning, however, is to better understand the speaker's views and feelings about them, not to offer a rebuttal.

*Observing*—watching attentively—is another key aspect of listening. Is the speaker's demeanor friendly, angry, or stern? What is the voice tone and how does it change during the conversation? What topics prompt the change? Does the speaker make eye contact? Does the person's words and nonverbal behaviors match or does the person appear incongruent (and perhaps not telling you everything you need to know to understand the situation fully). Is the person constantly fidgeting and displaying possible anxiety? Looking for more information from what the speaker is saying, not saying, and doing can provide additional insights into what the speaker means. It is important to note, however, that the observer's interpretation of what the speaker's nonverbal gestures mean is opinion only (especially if the two do not share the same culture). The speaker alone can confirm their meaning (we can observe behaviors but cannot read minds).

*Encouraging* behaviors includes the listeners' actions that help advance the conversation. *Silence*—refraining from speech—is more than the absence of talk. It is a powerful nonverbal message. Saying nothing in response to a speaker's comments suggests that the listener is interested and wants to hear more. Empathic acknowledgements also facilitate communication with small verbal cues such as "yes," "I see," "uh-huh," and "tell me more"—especially when tied to nonverbal cues of smiling, leaning forward, and head nodding.

Silence may be an especially helpful tool for principals when listening to an angry or upset teacher or parent about a topic with which the listener and speaker disagree. The listener's purpose should be to fully and accurately understand the speaker's viewpoint and reasons for it—not to challenge, rebut, or argue against it. Remaining silent—rather than refuting the speaker's statements—can encourage the speaker to continue speaking. When interspersed with relevant questions to further clarify the situation, the silence may actually advance understanding, giving the listener time to think about what he or she is hearing and what it means. For principals, using encouraging silence to listen more carefully to teachers or parents who are angry or who disagree often provides valuable information and insights into why others see the situation as they do. This fuller understanding may help principals make better-informed—and more persuasive—rebuttals after the listening ends and the problem solving begins.

*Paraphrasing* means restating the message but with fewer words. Skillful listeners paraphrase to make sure they have interpreted the message correctly. Repeating the essence of the speaker's concern back to the speaker tests the listener's understanding of what has been heard and provides feedback to the speaker about what the listener is gaining from the conversation. When the listener accurately understands what the speaker has said, it advances the communication, and the speaker can continue. In contrast, if the listener's understanding is not accurate, the speaker can restate the message more clearly or differently.

*Reflecting feelings* occurs when the listener who has been closely attending, questioning, and observing the speaker accurately perceives the speaker's emotions and communicates that back to the speaker. "Sounds like you are disappointed with what happened" for instance, correctly reflects the speaker's emotions and creates empathy between the speaker and listener. Using the speaker's name at times during the conversation also helps deepen empathy and understanding.

*Summarizing*—when the listener creates a condensed version of what has been heard—occurs near the end of the conversation. Similar to paraphrasing, summarizing covers a longer period of time. The summary's purpose is to organize and integrate facts and emotions into a coherent, accurate, and brief synopsis. This recap provides the basis for further discussion or to move to the next step: solving the problem. Summarizing is a win-win situation: if the summary is accurate, the speaker will say so and feel understood. If the summary is off, the speaker will likewise say so, and clarify its meaning to make it more accurate. Either way, the conversation moves forward.

## Feedback

*Feedback* is the helpful information that the listener sends to the speaker to help them both know whether or not the message was received and interpreted as intended—and the listener's reaction to it. In turn, receiving feedback allows the sender to adjust, clarify, or repeat the message in order to improve its communication accuracy. Asking questions, describing behavior, and paraphrasing what the speaker said are all forms of verbal feedback.

Providing feedback includes both verbal and nonverbal messages and may be intentional or inadvertent. For instance, a listener who continually checks for new cellphone texts while supposedly paying attention to the speaker is sending feedback about where the listener's focus actually is. Ideally, the information offered in feedback should be helpful to the receiver: clear, emphasizing the positive, specific, descriptive (rather than evaluative), timely, and directed towards behaviors the person can control. Feedback is most useful when delivered within a trusting, mutually respectful relationship. It is then that both positive and negative feedback can be sent and received, accurately interpreted, and considered within a caring, helpful affiliation.

### REFLECTIONS AND RELEVANCE 7.4

## Improving Your Basic Communications

Leaders who have communication competence are able to send appropriate and effective messages within their organizations.

How effective are your basic communication skills? This activity gives you an opportunity to self-assess and receive feedback from a partner on your basic sending, listening, and feedback skills.

Using the table below, complete a self-assessment on each of these skills in your work setting on a scale from 1–5, with 1 meaning "needs improvement" and 5 meaning "excellent." Then, ask your partner to rate you on these same items after you have given a two-minute talk on "Why I chose a career in education and leadership." The listener is encouraged to ask clarifying questions, if needed. The listener will rate the sender on the sending skills, and the sender will rate the listener on the listening skills. They will rate each other on feedback skills. If you had no chance to observe a particular communication skill, place a dash (—) in the assessment column. If possible, have your partner or yourself provide an example from your mini-talk to support the rating.

After you have each had a turn self-assessing, speaking, listening, rating your partner, and giving your partner your feedback, the whole class will discuss their responses to this activity. Which aspects of basic communication did they find the easiest to do? Which aspects of basic communication are least familiar and used the least often? How will doing this activity affect the way they talk, listen, and give feedback in the future?

| Basic Communication Skills | Self-Assessment | Partner's Assessment | Example |
|---|---|---|---|
| *Sending Skills* | | | |
| • Uses appropriate language | | | |
| • Provides clear and complete information | | | |
| • Minimizes noise from physical and psycho/social environment | | | |
| • Uses multiple and appropriate media | | | |
| • Uses face-to-face communication and repetition | | | |
| *Listening Skills* | | | |
| • Attending | | | |
| • Questioning | | | |
| • Observing | | | |
| • Encouraging | | | |
| • Silence | | | |
| • Paraphrasing | | | |
| • Reflecting feelings | | | |
| • Summarizing | | | |

| Basic Communication Skills | Self-Assessment | Partner's Assessment | Example |
|---|---|---|---|
| *Feedback Skills* | | | |
| • Verbal and nonverbal | | | |
| • Intended and unintended | | | |

## COMMUNICATING WITH PARENTS AND COMMUNITIES

Actively engaging parents to partner with teachers in educating our children remains an essential school responsibility that pays dividends in increased student achievement. Research and anecdotal data both avow this as a given. At the same time, our local communities consist of more than our children's parents and grandparents. Nora Carr, a school public relations expert, observes that, "One of the great ironies of school leadership today is that you can do a great job of educating students and communicating with parents, and still miss 78 to 80 percent of the people upon whose support public education—and your livelihood—depend"[34] because most taxpayers do not have school-aged children. As our population ages, this lack of direct personal vested interest between community and school will become even more widespread.

Communities generate the resources to keep school doors open, instructional materials and technology available, new schools built, and educators paid. Although all school systems receive tax funding, many localities must pass public bonds and levies to fund operating budgets or support capital improvements. As a result, local schools depend on all voting residents' good will—many of whom do not have children or grandchildren enrolled in the schools. Increasingly, principals and teachers must reach not only their students' parents but also adults who lack any first-hand experiences with the local schools to persuade them to "invest" more of their tax dollars in someone else's children.

## WORKING WITH PARENTS TO IMPROVE STUDENTS' ACHIEVEMENT[35]

Although teaching quality is the most important in-school factor affecting student achievement, family and neighborhood variables matter more. At most, teaching accounts for about 15 percent of students' achievement outcomes while socioeconomic factors account for about 60 percent.[36] Although not everyone will agree with these numbers, it is clear that out-of-school factors—including generational poverty, family income, parents' education, and health care—usually influence students' academic success more than in-school factors. Research repeatedly affirms that the quality of home environments strongly correlates with students' academic achievement and school performance.[37]

More than 40 years of research confirms that family involvement is a powerful influence on student achievement. When schools and families work together to promote student learning, children tend to succeed in both school and in life as they attain the following outcomes:[38]

- Earn higher grades and test scores and enroll in higher-level academic programs;
- Attend school regularly and complete more homework;
- Pass classes, earn promotion to the next grade, earn more course credits;
- Show high math and improved reading proficiency;
- Receive fewer placements in special education;
- Have better social skills, show improved behavior, and adapt well to school;
- Receive fewer disciplinary referrals;
- Have higher graduation rates;
- Have greater enrollment in postsecondary education.

These evidence-based benefits of parents' involvement in their children's learning make communicating with families a worthwhile investment in students'—and teachers'—success. Notably, what a family *does* regarding education is more important to their children's academic attainment than what a family *earns*. Parent expectations and involvement at home have the most influence over student achievement while parents' attendance at school events has the least. And whether a family is financially struggling or affluent, whether parents completed high school or earned graduate degrees, families help their children do well in school when they can accomplish the following three conditions:[39]

- Create a home environment that encourages learning along with loving, supportive, and adequate discipline.
- Express high (but not unrealistic) expectations for their children's achievement and future careers.
- Become involved in their children's education in school and in the community.

Research also shows that when schools support families in these three areas, children from low-income families and varied cultural backgrounds earn the school grades and achievement test scores that approach those attained by middle-class students. They are more likely to avail themselves of the array of educational opportunities after high school graduation. Even when two of these conditions are present, children perform noticeably better in school.[40]

Effective communication matters here, too. Studies show that establishing regular and meaningful communication between school and home strengthens the parental involvement that is essential to children's academic success.[41] Communications stressing student achievement—rather than problems—create more positive and open dialogue between parents and school staff.[42] And when the school community provides welcoming outreach activities and programs to families—such as parenting workshops on helping their children at home, family nights in which children display and explain their school work, and student musical presentations—families feel empowered.

Reaching parents—in terms of media and what parents actually want to know— can be challenging, but new data can help principals in this effort. Informational fliers slipped into students' backpacks on their way to the departing school buses are not sufficient. A recent survey from the National School Public Relations Association (NSPRA) sampling 50 districts in 22 states asked parents their preferred delivery method for receiving school news. Instant and electronic media as school news sources are increasingly popular. The top five answers were: email from the district/school, online parent portal, district/school e-newsletters, district/school website, and the telephone/ voice messaging system.[43]

Parents also told investigators what they want to know from teachers, namely: updates on their child's academic progress or insight on how they can improve; timely notice when performance is slipping; information on what their child is expected to learn during this year; and homework and grading policies. In addition, they want to know: curriculum descriptions and information on instructional programs; a calendar of events and meetings; information on student safety (and quality of teaching, at the elementary level); educational program changes and updates (elementary level)/ curriculum updates and changes in instructional programs (secondary level); and information comparing their school's performance to others (elementary) and gradu- ation and course requirements (secondary). Parents would like to know these things as soon as the decisions are made.[44] Since no single means will reach everyone, many channels to spread the word are needed.

Throughout these media, the message to parents is consistent: the school values parents as partners in their children's education. They express the desire to build trusting collaborative relationships among teachers, families, and community members; convey recognition and respect for families; identify avenues to address families' needs as well as class and cultural differences; and offer a philosophy of partnership in which school and home share power and responsibility.[45]

To achieve effective school–home communications, principals can include parents in school decisions and develop parent leaders and representatives. Studies find that parents can play four roles in schools—as teachers, supporters, advocates, and decision makers—and all contribute to children's learning.[46] Knowledgeable and capable parents can serve on school advisory councils, school accountability teams, and governance committees. Principals will want to ensure that the roles and responsibilities for parent and community leaders on school committees are well-defined and reflected in job descriptions. These individuals need to clearly understand the benefits—and limitations—of their roles in the school if they are to work successfully with school personnel.

# WORKING WITH TODAY'S DIVERSE PARENTS AND COMMUNITIES

Today's student demographics present principals with additional communication challenges. Race, ethnicity, and social class are often undercurrents in schools where educators have difficulties developing trusting and mutually respectful relationships with parents and community members. Different spoken languages, interaction styles, social norms, and educational values—as well as teachers' comfort levels with parents—often create obstacles to communicating easily and working well together.

In addition, today's families reflect a wide array of configurations: children raised by two parents, single parents, same-gender parents, grandparents, or other surrogates, older children, foster homes, caretakers, and nannies, among others. The traditional definition of "parents"—a married mother and father living together with their children—is too narrow for today's realities and may inadvertently screen out those very individuals whom the school needs to involve as allies in increasing children's achievement and aspirations. Similarly, work schedules, caretakers' economic or health status, immigrant status, number of children at home, whether English is spoken at home, extended families, military families, families where the parents are in prison, and homelessness all complicate family relationships and communications with their children's schools.

Successful relationships that bridge cultures and languages usually require serious effort to create and maintain. What is more, principals and teachers need to learn about their families' *funds of knowledge and cultural assets*—ways of knowing, learning, and acting—if they are to recognize and use children's and families' strengths to deepen and accelerate learning. Principals may have to provide appropriate and on-going professional development for both teachers and parents because neither group may have the knowledge and skills needed to make these goals a reality.

At the same time, more parents are increasing their children's school readiness at home. Research suggests that today's parents—especially low-income parents—are more involved with their young children than they were a decade ago—reading, playing, eating dinner together, speaking with larger vocabularies and more complex syntax and structure—more like children will find in school.[47] Parents of all types are aware that their involvement with their children's learning is essential to their school success.

In short, making assumptions about today's families is problematic, and familiar suppositions may no longer hold. As a result, if principals are to develop trusting and mutually respectful relationships with parents and families, they and their teachers need to identify and remove an array of obstacles to their involvement with school. Table 7.1 illustrates the general barriers to parent–school communications and involvement: institutional, impersonal, and personal barriers as well as negative attitudes, lack of skills or means, and practical limits.

## Institutional Barriers

Institutional barriers include a school culture that is indifferent or hostile toward parent involvement, negative attitudes by school administrators and staff, insufficient personnel

**TABLE 7.1** General Barriers to Parent–School Involvement

| Negative Attitudes | Lack of Skills and Means | Practical Limits |
| --- | --- | --- |
| *Institutional* | | |
| School culture, school administration, and teachers are hostile toward increasing home involvement | Not enough staff are assigned to planning and implementing ways to enhance involvement: only a token effort to provide for different languages | School administration gives low priority to allocating space, time, and money resources to increase involvement with families |
| *Impersonal* | | |
| School administration is indifferent to increasing home involvement | Rapid increase of immigrant families overwhelms the school's ability to provide relevant home involvement activities | Schools lack resources; most homes have concerns related to work schedules, childcare, and transportation |
| *Personal* | | |
| Specific teachers and parents believe home involvement is not worth the effort or feel threatened by such involvement | Specific teachers and parents lack relevant language and interpersonal skills that could facilitate increased school–family involvement | Specific teachers and parents are too busy or lack resources to support increased school–family involvement |

Source: Adapted from the Center for Mental Health in Schools at UCLA (2011, December). *Enhancing home involvement to address barriers to learning: A collaborative process* (p. 7). Los Angeles, CA: Center for Mental Health in Schools. Retrieved from: http://smhp.psych.ucla.edu/pdfdocs/homeinv.pdf. Reprinted with permission.

assigned to planning and gaining parents' participation, and limited resources (usually money, space, and time) dedicated to parent and community involvement. The school may lack a parent-involvement policy, or its leaders and teachers may be pursuing this expectation half-heartedly. Teachers and staff may need upgraded awareness and skills if they are to communicate effectively with parents and caretakers who are different than they are.

## Impersonal Barriers

Impersonal barriers to home–school collaboration also limit school–parent collaboration. The rapid arrival of immigrant or ethnically diverse families may overwhelm the school staff's abilities to employ the qualified teachers needed to teach English-language learners, find appropriate classrooms, and gather instructional materials. Related issues including inconvenient work schedules, childcare, language, and transportation all may prevent school and families from building the relationships they need to help their children adjust and learn.

## Personal Barriers

Principals, teachers, and staff may not have the needed attitudes, skills, or temperaments for working with parents because developing these requires time, effort, and the willingness to jettison complex racial and cultural attitudes and overcome language differences. Without the view that family diversity brings potential assets and lacking persuasive information about the importance of home–school collaboration to successful learning, principals and teachers may lack the incentive to become involved with children's families.

## WORKING WITH THE LARGER COMMUNITY

As mentioned, people with school-aged children comprise only about one-fifth of the population. Principals need active support from the wider community if public schools are to continue educating neighborhood children for democratic citizenship and economic sufficiency.

*Community* refers to the neighborhood or places around the school, the local residents who may or may not have children in the school, and neighborhood groups. Principals and other school leaders need links with neighborhood members, district leaders, policy makers, and others to build a network of shared interests, foster wider understanding of schools' purposes and needs, and nurture the trust required to work constructively toward common goals. These extensive connections allow school leaders "to both *scan* the environment—to learn about issues, concerns and new developments outside the school—and *seed* the environment—to put insiders and advocates into positions of power and influence on the outside."[48] Effective communications are the essential underpinnings of this effort. Especially in an era of declining resources and increasing demand for public services, schools need partners who can leverage the strengths of many organizations to improve student outcomes.

Partnership between schools and communities may take a variety of formats, all focused on addressing students' needs. Examples of school–community partnerships, all of which rest on effective communications, include:

- *Occasions to educate and recruit community members.* Schools can use the traditional orientation meetings, open houses, and information nights to ensure that everyone understands the school's basic goals, philosophy, and work—and sees their students' accomplishments. Here is an opportunity to invite and enlist parents and other stakeholders for varied roles and responsibilities within the school. For example, starting a community relations committee consisting of teachers, parents, and local business representatives can bring the principal an early "heads up" to any emerging local issues or changes that will impact teaching and learning. This group can offer the principal valuable public support when needed.

- *Incentives to support students' success.* Working with neighborhood organizations, government agencies, churches, community groups, and businesses can gather incentives to motivate and reward student success. For instance, principals can work with local bankers to sponsor a Triple-A Club to provide students who earn all As or Bs, have perfect attendance (no unexcused absences), and no official discipline referrals for a marking period with a congratulatory breakfast and entry into a drawing for a U.S. Treasury Savings Bonds—all complements of the interested community leaders.

- *Opportunities for career development and relevant instruction.* If asked and given a compelling rationale, local business and industry might provide job shadowing and internships for students as part of their career exploration. These community CEOs might be willing to sponsor professional development for teachers—hiring them during the summer to work with experts in areas aligned with their teaching content to help the educators develop more high-interest and relevant links between the classroom and real-world applications.

- *Support for collective action.* Religious institutions offer existing relationships among congregation members who can be organized to support collective action infused with a moral purpose. Likewise, community organizations such as Kiwanis, Lions, and League of Women Voters can mobilize their members to act on behalf of important civic goals. Principals who educate these groups about the school's vision, its civic and social justice purposes and challenges, and who involve their key members with school leadership can gain important grassroots support for educational issues when needed.

- *Essential health, social, and protective services.* Partnerships with community health, recreation, social service agencies, the military services, and the police department are necessary to ensure students' academic success. Many children need a range of supplemental services to remedy problems that interfere with learning— from securing a pair of eyeglasses or tutoring to dealing with chronic illness or living apart from a deployed parent. Police and mental health officials can help principals develop policies and procedures to prevent cyber bullying and fake social network profiles, two forms of Internet harassment that can seriously disrupt a student's learning.

- *Learning beyond the classroom.* When teachers can blend professional expertise with pertinent community-based knowledge and practices, their students will learn more. Keeping the school–community boundaries permeable lets schools use educational experiences that their communities value. Principals can invite neighborhood leaders to help teachers better know their localities, resources, and histories so they can identify and use learning opportunities with their students.

More important than the actual community–school events, these collaborations can surround children with a culture of caring and achievement, repeating this message with varied activities in varied locales throughout the year. These school–community partnerships express to the children: "We, the larger community, believe in you, your ability, and your effort to achieve well in school and in life. And we are here to help you make it happen."

Despite the promise of education–community partnerships, a word of caution is in order. Principals working with community groups do well to recognize that all relationships have expectations. In exchange for essential assets, school leaders need to monitor the partners' expectations so as to not overextend the school personnel or sidetrack the school from achieving its essential goals. Principals will need to negotiate with external partners to shape their outlooks and demands in ways that actually benefit the school. Or principals may need to decide which partnerships expect too much in exchange for their involvement and resources and limit their participation.

Finding and enforcing this balance will require principals to communicate effectively. They will need to set and express clear ground rules for how they will use the relationship. They will outline a common vision in which partners can agree on the same goals. They will establish formal relationships and collaborative structures to accomplish more than scheduled ad hoc get-togethers. They will initiate and sustain open and respectful dialog about challenges and solutions, and provide data with clear information so all stakeholders can understand the current conditions, monitor progress, and hold each other accountable. Enlisting a central office contact person will demonstrate the district's commitment to developing and sustaining the community partnership. Principals will also need help from partners to maximize their resources to support programs and activities aligned with their shared values and goals.

Over time, regular contacts between schools and community persons can become long-term relationships with allies who understand the school, provide access to resources, and serve as public advocates for the schools with adults who may not have

## REFLECTIONS AND RELEVANCE 7.5

## Communicating With Parents and the Community

General barriers exist that make it difficult for principals and teachers to develop trusting and mutually respectful relationships with parents and community members.

Reread the descriptions in Table 7.1 (p. 206). Then consider the parent–school–community communications in your own workplace. Using the table below, fill in the grid with examples, icons, and words that accurately depict the extent to which your school is overcoming—or reinforcing—these communication barriers. Share results with a partner. When you and your partner have finished, discuss with the whole class the communication barriers that you hear or observe most often in your own school. Give examples. What do you think can be done in your school to remedy this? What do you think you can do in your own interactions with parents or community members to remedy this?

| | Negative Attitudes | Lack of Skills and Means | Practical Limits |
|---|---|---|---|
| Institutional | | | |
| Impersonal | | | |
| Personal | | | |

their own children enrolled. In the public arena, community and parent voices can speak more loudly—and persuasively—than educators. For instance, although a principal may spend a year trying to persuade the district office to rid the school of its rodent problem, an informed school's parent group can motivate the superintendent to send maintenance crews to fix the problem by the weekend. Such is the power in strengthening school–community communications.

## CONCLUSION

Education is a people business, and communication—inside and outside the classroom—lies at the heart of education. Excellent communication skills are an essential leadership component; they are a key to good relationships. Effective one-way and two-way exchanges are necessary for success at all levels of the school organization. School leaders must be excellent communicators if they are to develop the interpersonal trust and mutual respect needed for day-to-day work and for the positive school climate and culture essential to improved student outcomes.

Principals do themselves and their teachers a big favor when they work with parents and community members to develop communications strategies that meet teacher, student, and community needs. Learning to speak, write, and listen well are the building blocks for fostering the trust and mutual respect that will best serve the students and their communities.

## NOTES

1    Grunig, J. E. (2006). Furnishing the edifice: Ongoing research on public relations as a strategic management function. *Journal of Public Relations Research, 18* (2), 151–176 (p. 171).
2.   Lee, C. (n.d.). *Introduction: Why school communications matters. A matter of urgency.* Alexandra, VA: Porter and Carnes Communications. Retrieved from: http://www.porterfield andcarnes.com/P%26C/Introduction.html
3.   Davis, S. H. (1998). Superintendents' perspectives on the involuntary departure of public school principals: The most frequent reasons why principals lose their jobs. *Educational Administration Quarterly, 34* (1), 58–90.
4.   Bulach, C. R., Boothe, D., & Pickett, W. (2006). *Analyzing the leadership behavior of school principals.* CONNEXIONS (An electronic publication of the NCPEA) at www.cnx.org/content/m13813/latest
5.   Matthews, D. (2002). Why principals fail and what we can learn from it. *Principal, 82* (1), 38–40.
6.   Bagin, T. (2007). *How strong communications help superintendents keep their jobs.* Rockville, MD: National School Public Relations Association. Retrieved from: http://www.nspra.org/files/docs/strong_communication.pdfited
7.   Kowalski, T. J., Petersen, G. J., & Fusarelli, L. D. (2007). *Effective communication for school administrators.* Lanham, MD: Rowman & Littlefield Education.
8.   Lewis, P. V. (1975). *Organizational communications: The essence of effective management.* Columbus, OH: Grid.
9.   Clampitt, P. G. (2010). *Communicating for managerial effectiveness. Problems, strategies, solutions* (4th ed.) (p. 4). Thousand Oaks, CA: Sage.

10. Clampitt, P. G. (2001). *Communicating for managerial effectiveness* (2nd ed.). Newbury Park, CA: Sage.

11. Hoy, W. K., & Miskel, C. G. (2013). *Educational administration. Theory, research, and practice* (9th ed.) (p. 397). New York, NY: McGraw Hill.

12. Haney, W. V. (1979). *Communication and interpersonal relations: Text and cases.* Homewood, IL: Irwin.

13. Bolman, L. G., & Deal, T. E. (2013). *Reframing organizations* (5th ed.) (p. 309). San Francisco, CA: Jossey-Bass.

14. Heaphy, E. D., & Dutton, J. E. (2008). Positive social interactions and the human body at work: Linking organizations and physiology. *Academy of Management Review, 33* (1), 137–163; see also DiSalvo, V. S. (1980). A summary of current research identifying communication skills in various organizational contexts. *Communication Education, 29* (3), 283–290.

15. Katz, D., & Kahn, R. L. (1978). *The social psychology of organizations* (2nd ed.). New York, NY: Wiley.

16. Katz & Kahn (1978), ibid.; DeFleur, M. L., Kearney, P., & Plax, R. G. (1993). *Mastering communication in contemporary America.* Mountain View, CA: Mayfield.

17. Milliken, F. J., & Morrison, E. W. (2003). Shards of silence: Emerging themes and future directions for research on silence in organizations. *Journal of Management Studies, 40* (6), 1563–1566.

18. Marzano, R. J., Waters, T., & McNulty, B. (2005). *School leadership that works. From research to results.* Alexandria, VA: ASCD.

19. Clampitt (2001), op. cit.; Harris, T. E. (1993). *Applied organizational communications.* Hillsdale, NY: Erlbaum.

20. Jablin, F. M. (1980). Organizational communication theory and research: An overview of communication, climate, and network research. *Communication Yearbook, 4,* 327–347.

21. O'Reilly, C. A., & Pondy, L. R. (1979). Organizational communication. In S. Kerr (Ed.), *Organizational behavior* (pp. 99, 119–150). Columbus, OH: Grid.

22. Kowalski, T. J., Petersen, G. J., & Fusarelli, L. D. (2007). *Effective communication for school administrators.* Lanham, MD: Rowman & Littlefield Education.

23. Arlestig, H. (2008). In school communication: Developing a pedagogically focused school culture. *Values and Ethics in Educational Administration, 7* (1), 1–8. Charlottesville, VA: University Council on Educational Administration. Retrieved from: Rhttp://ucea.org/storage/VEEA/VEEA_Vol7Num1.pdf

24. Beale, A. E. (2004). Body language speaks: Reading and responding more effectively to hidden communication. *Communication World, 21* (2), 18–20.

25. Voice without words, facial expressions and gestures is a form of communication that accompanies speech called *paralanguage.* See Beale (2004), ibid.

26. Beale (2004), op. cit.

27. Spitzberg, B. H., & Cupach, W. R. (1984). *Interpersonal communication competence.* Beverly Hills, CA: Sage.

28. Payne, H. J. (2005). Reconceptualizing social skills in organizations: Exploring the relationship between communication competence, performance, and supervisory roles. *Journal of Leadership and Organizational Studies, 11* (2), 63–77. Retrieved from: http://jlo.sagepub.com/content/11/2/63.short

29. Spitzberg, B. H., & Cupach, W. R. (1989). *Handbook of interpersonal competence research.* New York, NY: Springer-Verlag.

30. Hoy & Miskel (2013), op. cit. (p. 397).

31. DeFleur, Kearney, & Plax (1993), op. cit.

32. Horowitz, S. S. (2012, November 11). Gray matter. The science and art of listening. Sunday Review. Opinion. *The New York Times.* SR10. Retrieved from: http://www.nytimes.com/2012/11/11/opinion/sunday/why-listening-is-so-much-more-than-hearing.html?

33. Ivey, A., Ivey, M., & Zalaquett, C. (2013). *Intentional interviewing and counseling: Facilitating client development in a multicultural society* (8th ed.). Belmont, CA: Cengage Learning.

34. Carr, N. (2005). The battle for democracy. The evidence is clear: It pays for public schools to spend more on communications. *NSPRA Counselor*. Rockville, MD: National School Public Relations Association. Retrieved from: http://www.nspra.org/files/docs/NSPRA_Counselor_article.pdfom

35. Kaplan & Owings (2013). *Culture Re-boot*, op. cit. (pp. 175–206).

36. Brill, S. (2011). *Class warfare: Inside the fight to fix American education*. New York, NY: Simon & Schuster, as cited in Goldstein, D. (2011, August 29–September 5). Can teachers alone overcome poverty? Steven Bill thinks so. *The Nation*. Retrieved from: http://www.thenation.com/article/162695/can-teachers-alone-overcome-poverty-steven-brill-thinks-so

37. Christenson, S. L., & Sheridan, S. M. (2001). *School and families: Creating essential connections for learning*. New York: Guilford Press.

38. See, for example, Epstein, J. L. (2005, September). *Developing and sustaining research-based programs of school, family, and community partnerships. Summary of 5 years of NNPS research*. Johns Hopkins University, National Network of Partnership Schools (NNPS). Retrieved from: http://www.csos.jhu.edu/P2000/pdf/Research%20Summary.pdf; Henderson, A. T., & Berla, N. (Eds.) (1994). *A new generation of evidence: The family is critical in student achievement*. Washington, DC: National Committee for Citizens in Education. Retrieved from: http://eric.ed.gov/ERICDocs/data/ericdocs2sql/content_storage_01/0000 019b/80/13/66/e0.pdf; Henderson, A. T., & Mapp, K. L. (2002). *A new wave of evidence. The impact of school, family and community connections on student achievement, Annual synthesis 2002*. Eric Document No. ED 474521. Austin, TX: Center of Family and Community Connections with Schools. Southwest Educational Development Laboratory. Retrieved from: http://www.sedl.org/connections/resources/evidence.pdf

39. Schargel, F. P., & Smink, J. (2001). *Strategies to help solve our school dropout problem* (pp. 52–54). Larchmont, NY: Eye on Education.

40. Schargel & Smink (2001), ibid.

41. National Council of Jewish Women (1996). *Parents as school partners: Research report*. New York: ERIC Clearing House on Urban Education/Columbia Teacher's College.

42. National Council of Jewish Women (1996), ibid.

43. O'Brien, A. (2011, August 31). What parents want in school communication. Teacher leadership. *Edutopia*. Retrieved from: http://www.edutopia.org/blog/parent-involvement-survey-anne-obrien

44. O'Brien (2011), ibid.

45. Henderson & Mapp (2002), op. cit.

46. Henderson, A. T., & Berla, N. (Ed.) (1994). *A new generation of evidence: The family is critical to student achievement*. Washington, DC: Center for Law and Education; Christenson & Sheridan (2001), op. cit.

47. Sparks, S. D. (2011, August 24). Census points to positive trends in parent involvement. *Education Week, 31* (1), 10.

48. Hatch, T. (2009, October). The outside-inside connection. *Educational Leadership, 67* (2), 18.

# CHAPTER 8

# Building Teacher Capacity

We get the leaders we create.

—Peter Block, organizational
development consultant
and author

---

## LEARNING OBJECTIVES

8.1   Explain what it means to "build capacity" in schools and how it affects teaching, leading, and learning.

8.2   Discuss four reasons why principals might want to build teachers' and schools' capacity.

8.3   Describe psychological contract theory, the mutual obligations it entails, and the consequences of violating them.

8.4   Explain how people's psychological contracts explain their attitudes and actions at work and how these might create difficulties for employers (or principals).

8.5   Analyze how principals can use teachers' desires for purpose, autonomy, and mastery to motivate them to build their capacities.

8.6   Describe the characteristics of professional learning communities and why they can help teachers build their capacities in instruction and leadership.

8.7   Summarize several ways in which principals can help teachers build their leadership capacities.

8.8   Identify the obstacles that prevent teachers from developing their leadership capacities.

---

**2015 ISLLC STANDARDS: 1, 2, 3, 4, 5, 6, 7, 8, 9, 10, 11**

## INTRODUCTION

In the folk tale, *Stone Soup*, a hungry stranger arrives in a village carrying only a cooking pot. The newcomer promises to make soup for everyone in the community using only a stone. Eventually, the stranger persuades everyone in town to add an ingredient—carrots, onions, seasonings—to the stewpot. Before long, a delicious and nourishing pot of soup is ready, teaching the villagers a lesson in cooperation.[1]

A contemporary version of this fable could cast principals as human capital managers who improve their schools by developing their teachers' capacity. For new principals to succeed, having innovative ideas or the "right" strategies to improve student outcomes is not enough. A 2013 RAND study found about 20 percent of principals new to a school—either first-year principals or experienced principals in a school new to them—leave that assignment within one or two years; and the school tends to continue its downward spiral. In contrast, principals new to a school who report higher levels of teacher capacity and higher levels of staff cohesiveness are more likely to remain in the school and more likely to generate student achievement gains. Also, the study analysis suggests that successfully implementing the principal's improvement strategies is related to the first-year principal's actions rather than to the teachers' original characteristics.[2] What the new principal does with the teachers makes a difference.

Leadership in today's schools does not focus solely on the principal. Schools rely on leadership throughout the organization to develop and share a vision, shape instructional practices, and generate successful student outcomes. Like the stranger who encourages townsfolk to contribute to the communal stew, principals lead by enlisting others to share their ideas, skills, and energies on behalf of the school's mission so, together, they may improve student outcomes. This chapter will consider why principals will want to develop teachers' professional capacity, how teachers' unvoiced expectations and "psychological contracts" influence their willingness to grow professionally and contribute to school improvement, how principals can develop teachers' competence in instruction and leadership, and how aspiring principals can expand their own capacities.

## CAPACITY BUILDING AS A LEADERSHIP RESPONSIBILITY

Understanding and developing people is a key leadership responsibility. Today's schools are complex organizations operating in a fast-paced society. The pressure of public accountability for principals and teachers to generate at least one year's worth of learning in each student during the school year is relentless. And since leaders work with and through other people, principals must ensure that every teacher and staff member has the knowledge, skills, and incentives to do the necessary work of helping every child reach high academic standards.

Effective principals encourage teachers to reflect and challenge their assumptions about teaching and learning and rethink their expectations about who can learn and how teachers might upgrade their own performance. Principals provide incentives, structures, and opportunities to advance individual adult learning and construct appropriate ways to monitor progress towards improvement. And, by their own actions, they set examples consistent with the school's values and goals for faculty and staff to follow. By providing intellectual stimulation, individualized support, and appropriate models,[3] effective school leaders develop capacity in their schools, enabling more teachers and staff to do their jobs well so more students will benefit.

*Capacity* is not a term that teachers tend to use when thinking about their professional development. For teachers, capacity usually means how many seats are available in the auditorium for a student drama performance or how many cars fit safely in the school's parking lot so families can attend the band concert. Lawyers use *capacity* to refer to a defendant's mental state or fitness to stand trial. A football coach may refer to a quarterback's physical capacity to throw the football with speed and accuracy as well as the mental toughness or capacity to stay calm despite the opposition's defense rushing to stop any pass.

*Capacity* was initially considered to be an individual's ability to accomplish work-related tasks, but it is also currently viewed as a collective organizational property. In a work context, *capacity building* means helping people to acquire skills and dispositions to learn new ways of thinking and acting so they may accomplish a particular work task. *Professional capacity* is the combination of teachers' knowledge, skills, beliefs, perspectives, and work arrangements that help them share responsibility for student learning and support their own and their colleagues' continuous improvement. *Capacity building*, then, can be understood as helping teachers to gain the knowledge, skills, and attitudes they need to better advance student learning and achievement. In school improvement, learning by the individual, the small group, and the entire school becomes the focus.

## REFLECTIONS AND RELEVANCE 8.1

## Building Teachers' Capacity

Capacity building means helping teachers gain the knowledge, skills, and attitudes they need to better advance student learning. How have you built your capacity? How do you continue to build your capacity?

Working in pairs, identify several pieces of knowledge, skills, and attitudes you learned since becoming a teacher that have helped you become more effective in generating student learning with diverse students. What student behaviors or outcomes let you know that you were successful? What knowledge, skills, and attitudes have you learned since becoming a teacher that have helped you develop your leadership capacity? Are you a recognized or "untapped" leader in your school—and how do you know? How do you plan to continue building your capacity?

After discussing in pairs, share your findings with the whole class.

Today, leadership is increasingly understood as an organization-wide phenomenon in which hierarchies flatten and leadership spreads over many people and roles. Increasingly, educators are becoming aware that informal instructional and organizational leaders can have a big impact on school practices and student outcomes. Many teachers have the professional expertise and willingness to make curricular and instructional decisions and can be invited to participate in relevant decision making. Likewise, many teachers have "untapped and often-unrecognized" talents for leadership.[4] When principals recognize teachers' skills and nurture their growth in instructional and leadership domains, schools increase their organizational capacity. And, as their members' capacities become more effective, the schools grow stronger. In a virtuous cycle, both teachers and students benefit.

## RATIONALE FOR BUILDING TEACHER CAPACITY

Among the school-related factors that affect student learning in school, leadership is second only to classroom instruction.[5] This is because leaders have the ability to build capacity and gather and direct the talents and energies in their organizations to address shared goals. Cultivating leadership in others is one of principals' five key practices.[6] But delegating responsibilities to others who function as leaders or distributing leadership throughout the school can only happen when those others have the knowledge, skills, and intentions to use their talents to help meet the schools' goals. A host of reasons persuade principals to build teacher and school capacity: principals cannot do it all alone, it increases and sustains school improvements, it advances student achievement, and it increases teachers' morale.

### Principals Cannot Do It All Alone

Schools are complicated organizations. With strategic planning, managerial, instructional, political, human resource, and symbolic roles to play, principals cannot do everything that needs to be done by themselves. To survive and thrive in these demanding environments, principals must adjust their leadership role to the needs, opportunities, and limits that their school context imposes.

Because schools vary, providing active leadership for teaching and learning looks different, school to school. For instance, it is practically impossible for the principal of a moderately large 2,000-student high school to have the same intimate knowledge of all pupils' reading and math levels and standardized test scores as an elementary school principal with 350 children might.[7] No matter how energetic, inspired, or knowledgeable, it is unrealistic to expect principals to be everywhere doing everything at once—or even during their extended work day and year. Instead, principals need to develop leaders down every hallway and in every classroom who nurture the commitment to enact desirable improvements every day and up close in the routine activities that make schools run. Studies of effective leadership are consistently finding that authority to lead need not be located only in the person of the leader but can be spread throughout the school among the faculty and staff.[8] To do less undermines organizational improvement.

At the same time, many secondary school principals have less instructional and curricular expertise than the teachers they supervise. And even if the principals have the necessary knowledge, skills, and desire to enact hands-on instructional leadership—frequently visiting classrooms and giving teachers detailed feedback on their instructional performances—their schools' basic structural and normative conditions—not enough time and "not the way we do things around here"—may work against it.

Similarly, teachers know their students and how they learn. Teachers have experiences inside and outside the classroom that can significantly add to improved student learning and achievement as well as to their own enhanced work-life quality. Many understand their school's needs, can identify their colleagues' concerns, and have good ideas of what strategies will and will not work with their students. What is more, in a classic "us vs. them" scenario, many colleagues will give peers' opinions more credence than they give administrators'. In short, teachers have perspective, information, and credibility that can notably contribute to school improvement planning, problem solving, and decision making. Likewise, teacher involvement in school decision making gives them a fuller appreciation of their interdependence and how their actions affect the whole enterprise.

It is also true that students now in U.S. classrooms are likely to be working with inexperienced teachers. Richard Ingersoll, a University of Pennsylvania educational leadership professor and researcher and his Ph.D. student, Lisa Merrill, find that at present, more first-year teachers head American classrooms than any other experience level, an eye-popping shift from a generation ago: in 1987, U.S. students were most likely to be in a classroom led by a 15-year veteran.[9] As enthusiastic and promising as these new educators may be, their principals will need to invest time, resources, and occasions for their continued growth so novice teachers can develop the capacity for both instructional effectiveness and school leadership.

## Increase and Sustain School Improvement

When all is said and done, teachers are the ones on the front lines, making school improvements happen every day in their classrooms. They need to know what they are doing, and they need to do it well. School improvement assumes that people and the organization have the knowledge, skills, and dispositions to enact the new initiatives—or have the willingness and ability to learn new approaches to teaching, put them into action, and solve the problems associated with change.

A growing body of evidence within the school improvement field identifies capacity building as a means to sustain improvements.[10] Teachers directly influence student learning when they create the appropriate *classroom* conditions—the learning environment, the adept instruction, the rigorous and relevant curriculum, and the procedures management—that impact student learning more than *school* conditions do.[11] Some investigators find that teacher leadership far outweighs principals' leadership in generating student engagement—their identification and involvement with school[12] —and a positive indicator of their motivation to achieve. So unless teachers have the necessary attitudes, knowledge, skills—and importantly, the desire—to use their talents and energies to improve student learning, it will not happen. Accordingly, building teacher capacity is foundational to conducting and sustaining school improvement.

## Increase Student Achievement

When teachers use rigorous, relevant, and coherent curriculum, effective instructional delivery, and in-time classroom management, student achievement increases. Both anecdotal and empirical studies confirm this, and the topic is more fully discussed elsewhere.[13] When principals nurture and sustain a culture of collaboration, trust, learning, and high expectations, they create the conditions and supports to help teachers develop and expand their pedagogical skills and become more able to help every child succeed academically.

The same holds true when principals help teachers develop their leadership skills: student achievement often increases. For example, one four-year study of nearly 200 elementary schools reported that shared leadership had a positive effect on students' math and reading achievement.[14] Another study involving 2,570 teachers from 90 elementary and secondary schools found that higher-achieving schools gave teachers and other stakeholders far more leadership roles than lower-achieving schools. Yet despite distributed leadership, principals were awarded the highest level of influence on schools at all achievement levels.[15] Noting this, investigators concluded that "influence seems to be an infinite resource in schools. The more those in formal leadership roles give it away, the more they acquire."[16] When principals deliberately make opportunities to develop their teachers' school leadership capacity, they can "grow-their-own" capable leaders.

## Increase Teacher Morale

*Morale* can be understood as the feelings of enthusiasm and loyalty that a person or group has about a task or job. Within the work context, it involves "being known and appreciated, having professional knowledge valued, and being given the freedom to act."[17] In addition, morale involves the willingness to endure hardship because one shares a common purpose and the sense of belonging and wellbeing with a group that has confidence in their future. It also includes learning, growing, making mistakes, reflecting, and continual improvement.[18] Teachers with high morale expect to satisfy their own needs while working in their organization. They look forward to going to work, feel satisfaction from being a member of their school's faculty and the teaching profession, show interest in the direction in which the school is moving, and willingly perform varied school tasks that go beyond their written job descriptions.

In contrast, low teacher morale results from professional lives that have little meaning, much frustration, limited ability to influence what is happening, unclear goals, and demands that push human and material resources to their limits.[19] Typically, teachers' perceptions of low status, low pay, and a lack of professional autonomy are three leading work environment factors that contribute to their low morale.[20]

It is no surprise that teacher morale in American public schools has been taking a beating. Surveys indicate that teachers' satisfaction has dropped 23 percentage points since 2008, from 62 percent to only 39 percent "very satisfied." On certain measures, teacher morale has fallen to its lowest level in the past 25 years.[21] Half of teachers (51 percent) report feeling under great stress several days a week, an increase of 15 percentage points over the proportion of teachers reporting that level in 1985. Notably, less-satisfied teachers are more likely to be working in schools that experienced drops in professional development and time for collaboration with their peers—even as 97 percent of teachers give high ratings to their school colleagues.[22] It is also difficult for teachers to love coming to work every day when they believe that policy makers, politicians, and editorial writers are making them into scapegoats for factors beyond their control, placing unfair and unrealistic expectations on them for raising students' test scores.

On the plus side, other studies find that giving teachers opportunities to enhance their knowledge and skills and providing school-based occasions to use them has positive effects on transforming schools as organizations and helps reduce teacher alienation and turnover.[23] Likewise, recent research seems to show that, generally speaking, low teacher turnover strengthens student achievement.[24] When schools create long-standing cadres of effective teachers who work together over time to improve their practice, not only does student learning and achievement increase, but so do teachers' positive feelings

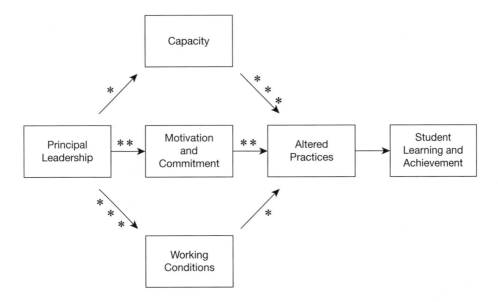

Key for the effects of school leadership on teacher capacity, motivation, commitment, and beliefs about working conditions: * = weak influence; ** = moderate influence; *** = strong influence

**FIGURE 8.1** How Principal Leadership Affects Teacher Capacity and Student Learning

Source: Adapted from: Leithwood, K., Harris, A., & Hopkins, D. (2008). Seven strong claims about successful school leadership. *School Leadership and Management, 28* (1), 33. Reprinted by permission of Taylor & Francis Ltd.

about themselves, their colleagues, and their schools. In another virtuous circle, when teachers build their capacities, they boost their morale and student achievement, too.

Principals play a direct role affecting teacher morale. When principals treat their teachers with respect and care as individuals and as competent professionals; give them a clear and important purpose for their work; provide the time and resources to support their growth as effective instructors and leaders; and give them opportunities to add their voices to school decision making about instruction, curriculum, and school climate, principals boost teachers' morale at the same time as they build school capacity. Figure 8.1 illustrates the principals' key influence on teacher capacity, motivation, commitment, and beliefs about the school's working conditions.

One school district superintendent put it this way: "Teacher morale . . . is not a function of practices designed to maintain or create it. It's a by-product of being treated as leaders . . . with respect. Teacher morale is the end product of empowering teachers to make decisions that affect their lives."[25]

## REFLECTIONS AND RELEVANCE 8.2

### Reasons for Building Teachers' Capacity

Principals have several strong reasons for wanting to build teachers' capacity.

Acting as teacher leaders, class members will form four groups to develop and deliver a persuasive talk to their faculties about how they should enthusiastically participate in a new school initiative for increasing their own skills in instruction and leadership. Each group's talk will include the four reasons: principals cannot do it all; capacity building increases and sustains school improvements; capacity building increases student achievement; capacity building increases teachers' morale. Each group will prepare and present a three- to five-minute talk, first by defining "capacity building" and then using a graphic to persuade their colleagues of the benefits to them and to their students if they build their capacity.

After the presentations, discuss the strengths and weaknesses of each presentation and make recommendations if they were to present it to their principals or colleagues.

## MOTIVATING TEACHERS TO BUILD THEIR CAPACITY

Persuading principals about the advantages of building their teachers' capacity is easy. The rationales are logical, bolstered by anecdotes and empirical research, and stand to benefit not only the principal but the teachers and students as well. Understanding how to motivate teachers to willingly and enthusiastically take on extra responsibilities for learning and leading is more challenging. Principals can use insights from the latest research on what motivates teachers, a brief revisiting of motivational theory (discussed in Chapter 2), and an introduction to psychological contract theory to help teachers become eager participants in their own professional growth.

Principals might begin by remembering why teachers chose their profession. A research consensus concludes that teachers enter an education career because they want to have a positive influence on students' lives and on the larger society.[26] This is especially true for our newest teachers, those with less than 10 years of experience who make up most of today's U.S. teachers.[27] Teachers with three to ten years of experience add their commitment to social justice and the belief that teaching can improve society.[28] These "second stage" teachers want to have a voice in education policy and practice. In addition, recent evidence suggests that high levels of interpersonal skills and emotional acuity displayed through a leader's personal attention to an employee and more fully utilizing the employee's capacities increase the employees' enthusiasm and optimism, reduce frustration, transmit a sense of mission, and indirectly increase performance.[29] Clearly, purpose, autonomy, and mastery are three important triggers for teachers' motivation, making them receptive to capacity-building opportunities.[30]

Offering opportunities to remain in their classrooms as well as exert influence and leadership to improve their schools and school systems give teachers occasions to learn and grow professionally in ways that improve student outcomes and enact social justice in their classrooms—and beyond.

## MOTIVATIONAL THEORY: REPRISE

Principals can use insights from motivational theory to promote teachers' commitment to capacity building and meeting school goals. Abraham Maslow's hierarchy of needs posits that once teachers meet their basic survival needs for salaried employment to support themselves and their families, they want to become accepted, respected, and valued members of their workgroups and larger community, have opportunities to accomplish important and meaningful work, be recognized for their contributions, and continue growing as individuals and as professionals. And, as expectancy theory asserts, teachers assume that if they teach their students well, they anticipate receiving respect, esteem, appreciation, autonomy, collegiality, and opportunities to grow and lead as a "fair" exchange for their efforts. Accordingly, building teachers' skills in instruction and leadership are a means to meet their needs for growth, community, autonomy, participation, and leadership opportunities.

Similarly, Theories X, Y, and Z offer perspective on building teachers' capacity. Unlike Theory X principals who believe that average teachers are lazy and avoid working hard whenever possible, Theory Y and Theory Z principals believe that teachers enjoy their work, and if they find it satisfying, they will commit their efforts to help the school reach its goals.

Likewise, principals who use Frederick Herzberg's motivation-hygiene theory incentivize their teachers by giving them opportunities for collegiality, achievement, recognition, responsibility, and advancement. Principals understand that although school district policies, interpersonal relations with colleagues, working conditions, salaries, and employment security may strongly affect teachers' feelings about their work, making these factors more attractive to teachers only prevents them from becoming dissatisfied with their jobs; they do not motivate them.

With these insights in place, along with understanding how teachers form an unspoken set of expectations about their employment relationship, discussed in the following section, principals can better prepare to help teachers develop their capacity.

## PSYCHOLOGICAL CONTRACT THEORY

Daniel Yankelovich, a leading interpreter of American social trends, observed that a person's commitment to an organization is the key to determining how much discretionary effort the person uses when given a choice in performance.[31] How employees decide how much effort to give to their jobs—when the option is theirs—depends on the implicit psychological contracts they have with their organization. Appreciating this phenomenon, accepting the mutual obligations it entails, and providing the "right" incentives to motivate individual teachers can help principals enlist their efforts and commitments toward the school's goals—and, at the same time, give teachers greater satisfaction in their work.

*Psychological contracts* are mental models that individuals use to frame events at work and color their expectations about how the organization will reward them for their contributions. Chris Argyris, the late professor emeritus at Harvard Business School, first originated the idea of psychological contract to refer to employer and employee expectations of the employment relationship—beyond the formal employment contract.[32] People's psychological contracts are influenced by their family upbringings, societal mores, past experiences; organizational documents, discussions, and practices; and individuals' cognitive and perceptual differences. These highly subjective models shape—and occasionally distort—our vision.

For example, a recruiter may comment, ambiguously, to a potential employee that promotions within their organization tend to come rapidly, often within three years. The employee perceives this statement as a promise to promote him or her within three years. When the promotion does not happen, the employee feels as if a promise has been broken and starts pulling back on the efforts invested at work. Our psychological contracts influence what we perceive and how we act at work.

Psychological contracts include the following:[33]

- *Based on beliefs or perceptions.* The employers' and employees' beliefs, perceptions, values, expectations, and aspirations, including ideas about *implicit promises* and *obligations*, the extent to which these are perceived to be met or violated, and how much trust exists within the relationship.
- *Implicit, not explicit.* Awareness that these expectations are not necessarily spoken or written. Each party must trust the other to fulfill this "contract."
- *Perceived, not actual.* Understanding that because the "contract" is based on individual perceptions, persons in the same organization or job may have different psychological contracts and may perceive and respond to organizational events in their own ways.

- *Based on exchange and reciprocity.* "Contract" holders believe an implied promise to behave in certain ways at work depends on the other party providing the "rest of the deal."
- *Ongoing and evolving.* Understanding that a psychological contract can be continually renegotiated, changing with an individual's or organization's expectations in shifting economic and social contexts

Similar to legal contracts—although rarely written or openly spoken—our psychological contracts imply mutual obligations. These implicit "contracts" describe the conditions that we see as fair, exciting, productive, and desirable; what we view as unfair, boring, and unpleasant; and include the limits of what we will do within our roles. Although they have no objective or enforceable meaning, the individuals' perceptions of what was understood become their reality. And, while usually undocumented and unspoken, we invest our psychological contracts with the power of our commitment; they are actively meaningful to us. Psychological contracts with the organization emerge, however, only when an individual perceives that his or her contribution *obligates* the organization to *reciprocate*—and that expectation is, or is not, met.

Lastly, psychological contracts serve both the employee and the employer. While they give employees a sense of control and security in their relationship with employers, they also give employers a way to manage and direct employee behavior without heavy-handed supervision.[34] But since these "contracts" are subjective constructs, the parties involved do not have to agree or even discuss the "contract's" terms. Given the "contract's" intuitive and changing nature, psychological contracts are challenging to handle. And, therefore, they are often breached.

## Breaking the Psychological Contract

Since psychological contracts are typically implicit and unspoken, they can easily be violated. The principal and the teacher, for example, may not consciously recognize that a psychological "contract" exists; or if aware, they may not agree about what it actually involves. Psychological contract violations may range from slight misunderstandings to outright disregard and lack of good faith. When a violation occurs, it can lead to feelings that promises have been broken or ignored. When this happens, trust breaks down and relationships weaken. The possible results are: teachers may want to give less time, energy, and commitment to their school, and principals may want to stop investing in the teachers' interests. Figure 8.2 depicts how people may experience violations of their psychological contracts. The ways that people interpret the circumstances of this failure to meet their expectations affects how they experience a violation—and how they respond to the breach.

An unintended "contract" violation occurs when both parties are able and willing to keep their agreement, but differing interpretations lead one to act in a way that disagrees with the other's assumptions and interests. For instance, a teacher forgets a rescheduled meeting and neglects to attend. When this error comes to light, the teacher apologizes for the mistake and promises to attend the next one.

| Types of Psychological Contract Violation | | |
|---|---|---|
| **Circumstance** | **Defined** | **How Perceived** |
| **Unintended** | Both parties willing and able. Differing interpretations. | Inadvertent actions made in good faith. Feel: disappointment, acceptance. |
| ↓ | | |
| **Disruption** | One or both parties willing but unable to satisfy "contract." | Unavoidable circumstance occurred without malice. Feel: frustration, acceptance. |
| ↓ | | |
| **Breach** | One party able but unwilling to fulfill "contract." | Intentional violation, betrayal. Feel: outrage, anger. |

**FIGURE 8.2** How People Perceive the Circumstances of Psychological Contract
            Violation

Source: Based on Harwood, R. (n.d.) The role of the psychological contract in the contemporary workplace. An interview with Prof. Denise M. Rousseau. Retrieved from: http://www.unfortu.net/~rafe/links/rousseau.htm

Disruption to the "contract" occurs when circumstances make it impossible for one or both parties to fulfill their end of the agreement. A principal schedules a classroom observation for the Monday after a teacher returns from an out-of-town conference, forgetting that the teacher will not have had enough time to prepare for the high-stakes lesson. When reminded of this dilemma, the principal cheerfully reschedules the observation to the teacher's preferred date.

Breach of "contract" occurs when one side, otherwise able to meet the contract's expectations, refuses to do so, and is perceived as reneging on an obligation owed. For instance, after doing an outstanding job for several years, an assistant principal expects to receive the principal's wholehearted endorsement for promotion to the district's next open principal position. Instead, the AP receives only the principal's lukewarm recommendation, and the principal glowingly endorses another administrator for the position.

## Responding to Psychological Contract Violations

Whether the "violated" party perceives the breach as unintended, a disruption, or deliberate has a big influence on the person's experience and reaction. Research affirms that people differ in their willingness to tolerate unfair or inequitable exchanges.[35] Personal and situational factors as well as available role models can influence how the injured person responds. For instance, individuals experience more intense feelings of violation when they attribute the breach to their employer deliberately reneging on a perceived obligation, and they feel unfairly treated in the process.[36] Offended teachers who have seen colleagues complain about "poor treatment" and get positive outcomes might successfully protest while those who have seen offended colleagues resign or transfer might favor this approach.

Persons who have experienced violations of their psychological contracts tend to respond in certain ways along two dimensions: active or passive and constructive or

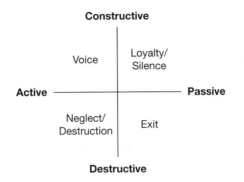

**FIGURE 8.3** Responses to Psychological Contract Violation

Source: Based on Harwood, R. (n.d.) The role of the psychological contract in the contemporary workplace. An interview with Prof. Denise M. Rousseau. Retrieved from: http://www.unfortu.net/~rafe/links/rousseau.htm

destructive. Figure 8.3 shows how they relate. Being alert to these behaviors may help principals more promptly resolve situations that threaten to undermine the relational trust essential to a well-functioning school.

*Voice*, actively taking constructive actions to remedy the violation—such as complaining to one's supervisor—is an effort to fix or make up for the "contract" violation while still remaining in the relationship. This approach is likely to fix the situation, reduce losses, and restore trust. Voice is most likely used when positive relationships and trust exist, a means is available to express the concern, other people in the organization successfully use this approach, and people believe that by speaking up they can influence the other person to act in the preferred direction.

*Silence*, a passive, constructive response to "contract" violation, also maintains the existing relationship. Seen as loyalty or avoidance, silence shows a willingness to endure or accept unfavorable circumstances—or can imply pessimism that no good alternatives for correcting the situation are available. Silence is a likely response to "contract" violations when no voice channels, established communication modes, or alternate means to address the violation exists.

*Neglect*, an active, destructive response to "contract violation," involves behaviors ranging from deliberate inattention to outright destruction. It can include not meeting one's responsibilities and harming other's interests. Negligent actions may involve not meeting work deadlines, not promptly returning emails or phone calls, or being rude or abrupt to colleagues or parents. Neglect may appear as an organization's failure to invest in certain employees while developing others. Neglect or destruction are most likely to occur when the organization has a history of conflict, mistrust, and "contract" violations, no voice channel exists, and most of the other employees behave with deliberate indifference or create outright damage.[37]

*Exit* is voluntary ending of the relationship; unhappy employees can quit an employer they view as an "untrustworthy" or "unreliable" who fails to deliver "promised" trainings, opportunities, or promotions. Exit is the most likely action following a violated psychological "contract" when the employee relationship with the employer is more job-focused than relationship-focused. Exit also is more likely when many other potential jobs or employees are available; the work relationship is relatively brief, other people are also resigning, and attempts to fix a broken "contract" have failed.

## What Research Shows

Studies show that widespread psychological contract violations harm the organization. Employees who experience these violations feel reduced trust in their employer, less satisfaction with their jobs and organizations, and increased intent to leave the employer and their position.[38] Frequent "contract" violations in an organization lead to increased numbers of people leaving the organization, increased whistle-blowing and grievance filings, decreased work effort, lower levels of loyalty to the organization,[39] and a reduced sense of mutual obligation to others in the workplace.[40] Additionally, employees with lower trust in their employers are more likely to look for incidents of violations while those with higher trust are apt to overlook, forget, or not recognize the contract violation.[41] Notably, the quality of the relationships between employer and employee is a mediating factor affecting the outcomes of psychological contract violations.[42] Employees who have a closer relationship with their employer—who believe they share more personal caring than simply a common workplace—are more disappointed by psychological contract violations than are employees who are "all business" with their employer, only focused on doing their jobs well.

Given the likelihood of psychological contract violations occurring, and the harmful consequences of their breaches to organizational health, principals would be well advised to encourage teachers and staff to use voice when breaches occur: "If a colleague in this school does something that makes you feel they broke your trust, find an appropriate time and place to speak respectfully to the 'alleged offender' about it. We all make mistakes, and we can all do better."

## PRINCIPALS CAN HELP TEACHERS FULFILL THEIR PSYCHOLOGICAL CONTRACTS

Principals can help teachers satisfy their psychological contracts in ways that advance both the teachers' and the organization's interests. The solutions revolve around strengthening the professional relationship, making the implicit expectations explicit, and following through on meeting the implied obligations.

To begin, principals need to understand that all the school's employees—including the principal and assistant principals—have certain assumptions and expectations about what they want to get from their work and participation in the school. Identifying some of the assumptions in each teacher's psychological contract with the school, for instance, will not only strengthen the principal–teacher relationship by showing genuine professional interest and concern, it will also give principals insight into the types of learning experiences and leadership opportunities that the school or district can provide to the teacher. In the best of all worlds, teachers' professional goals align closely with the school's improvement goals; and teachers can fulfill parts of their "contract" by meeting the school's most important needs, namely, generating better student outcomes.

Next, principals can make the implicit "contract" more explicit by asking teachers the right questions in the right settings and listening carefully to their answers. In a private location within the school, whether in the principal's office or the teacher's classroom, the principal can directly ask the teacher, "What led you to become a teacher?"; "What are your short- and long-term professional goals?"; "What opportunities, experiences, or benefits are you hoping to get from working in this school?" and "What do you want from me or from others in this school to help you meet your goals?" Then the principals must listen carefully, understand accurately, and find ways to follow through on helping the teachers satisfy their "contracts."

For example, does the teacher want to become a more effective instructor or help other teachers become more effective in generating student learning? Encouraging full participation in the school's professional learning community as a colleague or as a coordinator can be a productive avenue to meet this goal. Does the teacher want to have influence in school decision making? Inviting the teacher to serve on a school improvement committee and, eventually, co-chairing or chairing such a group helps the teacher gain a more complete view of the school as he or she develops organizational and leadership skills. Does the teacher someday aspire to have a central office position? Participating in relevant district-wide committees can give the teacher a better perspective on how a school district works, help them build a wider professional network, and gain access to potential supervisory or curriculum development opportunities. Listening carefully to teachers' answers and acting to meet the implied obligations to the extent possible (given resource and professional limits) builds trust, strengthens the relationship, and shows the principal as a person of integrity on whom others can rely. And, it helps ensure that teachers in the school find relevant occasions to meet their needs as they build capacity.

Then, too, the principal can show teachers respect and trust as professionals by offering them a degree of autonomy over instructional, curricular, and classroom management issues that directly affect them and are commensurate with their skill sets. Teachers with experience, expertise, and special talents can be invited to share in making decisions that affect the whole school. And, teachers who lack the experience, expertise, or special talents can be given frequent occasions in the school to develop, refine, and apply them.

Lastly, as discussed in Chapter 6, the principal is responsible for creating a school climate and culture of ethical behavior and interpersonal trust that encourages and supports teacher growth, leadership, and respectful, open exchanges. In such an environment, teachers know by watching others do it, that they can express their concerns appropriately and constructively in ways that identify and successfully resolve problems. And, if this is not the school's climate or culture, the principal is obliged to find resources to assist in making it happen. Otherwise, building teachers' capacity cannot occur.

## REFLECTIONS AND RELEVANCE 8.3

# Motivating Teachers to Build Their Capacity

Motivational and psychological contract theories offer useful perspectives that can help principals motivate their teachers to take on the work of building their capacities.

First, complete the communications web graphic by identifying the professional experiences that motivate you to work hard and invest your time, thought, and energies into your school. Write your biggest motivators on the longer lines and the lesser motivators on the shorter lines.

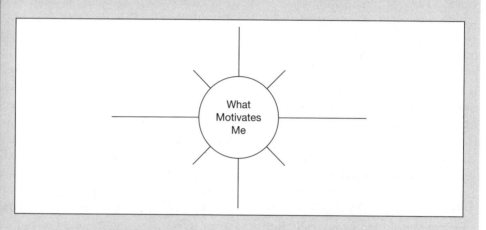

Next, working in groups of three, choose a facilitator, a recorder, and a reporter. Identify and discuss:

1.  What do principals need to understand about *your* motivations to persuade you to take on more responsibility for school leadership or instructional excellence?
2.  What do principals need to understand about teacher motivation in your school in order to persuade teachers to build their capacities?
3.  What might principals do or say to help teachers agree to work on building their professional capacities?
4.  What should principals avoid doing or saying to avoid undermining teachers' desires to build their capacities?

After identifying and discussing possible answers, share your findings with the whole class. What common ideas are being advanced? What are the most important ideas for you to remember when you become a principal?

# BUILDING TEACHERS' INSTRUCTIONAL CAPACITY

Principals have a profound impact on teaching effectiveness. One recent study determined that a highly effective principal raises student achievement by between two and seven additional months of learning in a single school year.[43] In another study over six years and 180 schools in nine states, investigators concluded that principals were the second most important school factor—next to teachers—in determining students' academic learning.[44] Principals are key players in student learning and achievement. If every classroom is to have a high-functioning and effective teacher, principals must recruit and hire, develop and retain them. And, because today's schools contain children from more diverse backgrounds and with more varied learning needs than ever before, improving teachers' capacities to be effective with each child pays off with academic success for more children. Clearly, preparing to lead schools means that aspiring principals need sufficient preparation to be instructional leaders.

Teaching well is a highly demanding skill set. Pedagogy matters. Regardless of how much content the teachers know, no evidence confirms that having subject knowledge, by itself, is sufficient to promote student learning.[45] Rather, effective teachers need a range of relevant instructional strategies, sound management techniques, a deep understanding of their curriculum, and first-hand knowledge about every student's learning needs. Teacher must understand the learning process and be able to adapt their instructional behaviors to meet the requisites of both students and curriculum. They must be able to recognize their students as individuals and as learners with background assets, interests, and learning preferences—and be able to use these insights to motivate students' efforts to learn. And, teachers must be able to manage their classrooms and provide safe and supportive learning environments if their students are to comprehend, practice, and master the material. In addition, teachers need to be able to help students acquire the complex knowledge, critical thinking, and communication skills needed in the 21st-Century economy. Accordingly, helping build teachers' instructional capacity is an essential school leadership challenge. Establishing and supporting professional learning communities with a focus on teaching and learning is an effective means to this end.

# PROFESSIONAL LEARNING COMMUNITIES

Teaching is a profession that expects its members to continue their specialized learning throughout their career if they are to remain effective. *Professional learning communities* (PLCs) are collaborative and collegial teams of teachers who focus on student learning. Instead of thinking of students as "your kids" and "my kids," teachers in PLCs expand their responsibilities and perspectives to consider all the students as "ours." According to Richard DuFour, a former school principal, district superintendent, and acknowledged leader of the PLC movement, these learning teams center on three big ideas: ensuring that all students learn; creating and sustaining a culture of collaboration for school improvement and removing barriers to student success; and a focus on results.[46] He also identifies four essential questions around which PLCs focus their efforts:[47]

1.   What do we want our students to learn?
2.   How will we know if our students have learned it?
3.   What will we do if our students don't learn?
4.   What will we do if they do?

PLCs have certain attributes and conduct a variety of collaborative, job-embedded professional learning activities that can improve teaching practices, increase student learning, and raise their achievement. These include the following:[48]

- *Collaborative teams.* Teachers who teach the same subject work interdependently on a near-daily basis to analyze and improve their classroom practices. Their goal is having all students learn to high standards. Each team member has access to the entire team's ideas, materials, techniques, assessments, and talents. They regularly visit one another's classrooms to monitor and evaluate students' (and teachers') progress and provide feedback and assistance. Research has found that building collective capacity—not merely individual capacity—can change teachers' practices, knowledge, and effectiveness and provide organizational growth.[49]
- *Collective inquiry.* Using open and reflective dialogue, teachers analyze student work together to determine how well their students are performing and identify the best practices around their students' existing achievement levels. Teachers have the chance to develop a common understanding of what high-quality student work looks like, identify common student misunderstandings, assess students' progress, and decide which instructional strategies are—or are not—working. Teams turn data into useful information to revise plans, target what students need, and inform later instruction.
- *Action orientation and experimentation.* Teachers accept that they may need to do things differently if they want different (that is, improved) outcomes. Involvement and informed experimentation with classroom practices and useful feedback are desirable ways to develop new understandings that lead to meaningful learning. Innovation for improved learning becomes "the way we do things around here."
- *Continuous improvement.* In their teams, teachers conduct on-going inquiry about what's working and what's not. They often use common assessments and student work to identify instructional strengths and correct weaknesses, refining teaching practices to generate more students learning. Changes occur as teachers describe, discuss, and adjust their practices to meet the collective standard of teaching quality and successful student outcomes. Teams may also introduce ceremonies, symbols, and celebrations to reinforce their community and socialize new members into the desired culture.
- *Focus on results.* Good intentions are welcome, but PLC members believe that their work quality will be judged by the outcomes. Teachers connect all initiatives to ongoing assessments linked to school and district goals and based on timely, concrete, relevant, and user-friendly feedback about student learning. In a virtuous cycle, these findings drive continuing improvement.
- *Study groups.* PLCs function as study groups in which members learn to improve their instructional and assessment practices, identify ways to raise expectations and

outcomes for all students (especially those who are traditionally underperforming), and design curricula that students will find relevant and engaging. Teams produce materials that reflect their learning focus, including lists of essential outcomes, varied assessments, analyses of student achievement, and strategies for improving results. Sometimes study groups focus on understanding their students' family cultures; consider how local, state, and national decisions are affecting their students' learning; and assess, analyze, and anticipate emerging trends so they may adapt their strategies.

In PLCs, teachers gain new ideas by reading and discussing professional journal articles or books, viewing commercially prepared and their own classroom instructional videos, observing effective classroom practices in their colleagues' rooms, or watching expert presentations in an area of relevance. Next, teachers transfer these skills to their own classrooms by planning and delivering lessons, producing materials, and conducting activities and assessments with their own students. Then, PLC members observe and reflect on the effects on student learning, asking themselves, "What worked? What is the evidence? What do I need to learn more about? Which students still need more instruction and support, and how am I/we going to provide it?" Lastly, PLC members meet with colleagues to discuss, solve problems, and create. They share what they learned, what they tried, what they observed, what happened with students, and what they might want to refine for use next time. And, they decide how and when to provide the extra time, attention, and supports to those students who did not master the lesson. Then they do it.

## WHY PROFESSIONAL LEARNING COMMUNITIES WORK

Several reasons explain why PLCs build teachers' capacity. First, they are based on verified principles of good professional development: theory, demonstration, practice, and feedback.[50] They give teachers the time, structure, and focus to understand how the new knowledge they seek improves their instructional practices and fits with what they already know and can do. They provide occasions to watch demonstrations and models of best practice so teachers see what it looks and sounds like, providing a platform upon which to draw. They give teachers opportunities to actively try out the new approaches through role play and in their actual classrooms. And, PLCs provide teachers with clear, accurate, and timely feedback on how well they accomplished their goals and reflected on what it means for their refined practice.

Additionally, PLCs build teachers' instructional (and for some, leadership) capacities because they respect and use the complex nature of teachers' classroom practice. In PLCs, teachers share an instructional system where their analysis of evidence from common practices presents a framework for refining and improving their teaching behaviors that are responsible for student outcomes. Importantly, teachers who may easily dismiss a principal's suggestions for a new instructional approach cannot as easily discount repeated evidence that his or her students are not being as successful as their peers in learning the knowledge and skills the teacher agreed were essential and as measured on many assessments that he or she agreed were valid.

When beginning a principalship, whether in a first assignment or in a later school, principals new to a school do well when they work closely with formal and informal teacher leaders to assess how teachers there continue their professional learning. Effective PLCs do not develop overnight, and no one size fits all. Whether it is time to create a study group to learn how PLCs can help teachers and students be more successful and report back with recommendations for starting them, or determining how to support and enhance the already-working PLC structure, principals' attention on creating a school-wide learning focus is a positive way to begin a leadership tenure.

## REFLECTIONS AND RELEVANCE 8.4

## Professional Learning Communities

Teaching well requires complex skills that continually need to be refined and expanded. Professional learning communities (PLCs) can help teachers work collegially to develop them.

You are teacher leaders. Working with your principal, your school leadership team has studied PLCs and decided to begin them in your school as a school improvement initiative. In groups of four, prepare a three- to five-minute persuasive talk to your faculty to introduce and explain the practice and why your colleagues should welcome the idea. Have one person in the group come up with reasons for arguing *against* PLCs. Include in your presentation a rationale for having PLCs in your school, its attributes, why they are an effective means to build teachers' instructional capacity—and include any anti-PLC concerns and ideas that might negate the opposition's view (anticipate opposing arguments). Give your talk to your class. After all groups have presented, discuss as a whole class the most important points—and the least important points—to use to persuade your peers that PLCs will help them be more successful and make them want to participate fully. Also discuss the value of including opposing ideas in your presentation to colleagues and administrators.

## TEACHERS AND LEADERSHIP

Teacher leaders are individuals with successful classroom experiences who influence others in their schools to improve their teaching practice and accept responsibility for realizing the school's goals.[51] Their colleagues recognize their effectiveness and hold them in high regard. Teachers attracted to leadership positions are achievement- and learning-oriented and are willing to take risks and assume responsibility.

Although principals hold legal responsibility for performing certain functions (including recommending faculty for hire, evaluating personnel, managing school resources, and implementing laws and regulations related to students, school programs, and curriculum), successful schools also need teacher leadership if their students are to learn and achieve well. In a role different than—but in conjunction with—the principal's leadership, teachers can strengthen their own and their principals' capacity to create successful school climates, cultures, and student outcomes. Such collective leadership is shown to have a stronger influence on student achievement than individual leadership. Plus, if teachers are to be held more accountable for student learning through a rigorous evaluation process, it makes sense to grant them more influence over their workplace as well as their work.

Despite the fact that principals and teachers might share certain school leadership roles, the principal remains *the* school's leader. Some responsibilities cannot—and should not—be shared. Whatever framework principals and teachers use to mutually enact leadership in their schools, principals remain central and responsible. They are the change agents. They shape, articulate, and continually communicate the school's vision, establish the school as an intellectual environment, align resources to support teaching and learning improvements, and perform additional key functions that protect the school's goals and work life. They hire, supervise, and evaluate (and occasionally dismiss) teachers to ensure that they are creating a safe and supportive learning climate and their children are making appropriate academic gains. At times, they act as buffers between the district and the school.

In a school with shared leadership, principals tend to enact less role-based authority and, instead, engage more in framing challenges and problems and providing space for inquiry to happen. Rather than telling teachers what to do, these principals ask "big-picture" questions, explore data, and involve faculty and the wider community in activities that can advance the school's interests. In turn, teachers provide the technical and motivational leadership to help the entire school organization reach children with improved practices and enhanced outcomes. Both principals and teacher leaders can show individual concern for teachers and staff and inspire all to do their best.

## AREAS FOR TEACHER LEADERSHIP

Schools have many avenues within which teachers can build their professional capacities for school-wide leadership. In formal roles, teacher leaders are visible as leaders of students or other teachers, such as coach, mentor, trainer, curriculum specialist, group facilitator, study group leader, or union representative. They can become leaders of operational tasks, including academic department heads, school improvement team members, or action researchers. In these roles, teachers can keep the school organized and moving towards its goals. They can also participate in decision making or partnerships as members of school committees or work with businesses, higher education, the local school district, and parent–teacher–student associations.

Teachers can also learn leadership by working in less formal leadership roles. They can operate collegially to shape school improvement efforts and guide others toward a shared goal; mediate by providing colleagues and parents with expertise and information about curriculum, instruction, and student learning needs; foster a collaborative culture by supporting colleagues' continuous improvement in ways that generate student learning and achievement; and cultivate outreach when they communicate and collaborate with families and community to enrich the student learning process.

When principals share leadership with teachers, principals do not give up their responsibilities. Rather, principals who expand leadership within the school view their colleagues as professional equals with valuable areas of expertise—and principals intentionally invite them to participate in the work of leading change.

## IDENTIFYING TEACHER LEADERS AND DEVELOPING CAPACITY

Teacher leaders tend to display certain personal capacities. They know schooling's "technical core"—what is required to improve the quality of teaching and learning—and have the "people skills" to work successfully with others. Moreover, teacher leaders tend to volunteer to help administrators gain a "ground-level picture" of how schools work. Allowing opportunities for teachers to volunteer to work with scheduling, committees, and planning sessions, for example, helps administrators identify teacher leaders and allows them motivational and growth opportunities.

A variety of characteristics indicate a teacher's readiness to take on leadership roles and responsibilities:[52]

- competent, credible, and approachable;
- excellent professional teaching skills;
- strong interpersonal skills, especially the ability to work well with colleagues;
- cognitive and affective depth and flexibility—enjoys thinking abstractly, connects theory to practice, shows sensitivity and receptiveness to others' thoughts and feelings;
- proactive, confident, assertive, and able to communicate clearly with adults from varied backgrounds and constituencies;
- visible in school and brings out the best in others;
- able to build trust and rapport among diverse individuals and groups;
- skilled in solving problems, resolving conflicts, negotiating difficult situations, and finding opportunities for "win-win" collaboration;
- strong organizational and management skills;
- has reached personal and career stages that enable them to give time, energy, and attention to others and to assume a leadership role.

Interestingly, a 2012 MetLife study found that most teachers (69 percent) say they are not at all interested in becoming a principal. Nonetheless, half (51 percent) of teachers are at least somewhat interested in teaching in the classroom part-time combined with other roles or responsibilities in their school or district, including 23 percent who are "extremely" or "very" interested in this option.[53] So principals will find that many teachers welcome the opportunities to develop and apply their leadership capacities—but most are not competing for the principal's job.

# DEVELOPING TEACHERS' LEADERSHIP CAPACITIES

Since each school has its own leadership style, climate, culture, policies, and practices, no one right way exists for developing and using teacher leadership. At its most basic, teacher leadership is about building collaborative relationships across all grades and academic departments and into the wider community. Principals can create opportunities at their schools—and find opportunities within the larger school district—in which teachers can participate and mature in leadership.

Much of this growth in leadership happens within caring professional relationships involving conversations, coaching, mentoring, and inducting new teachers into the school. At the same time, principals can structure their instructional program in ways that support teachers' professional learning for leading. Mature administrators and experienced teacher leaders may be able to assist principals in this endeavor.

## Conversations

In purposeful, informal, one-to-one talks with potential leaders, principals can help teachers increase their understanding of school leadership; reflect on and expand their beliefs and experiences about teaching, leading, and learning; discuss how to respond to or influence the political, social, economic, legal, and cultural contexts that impact the school and its students; practice leadership skills in actual situations; and identify increasingly skillful actions. They can share ideas about education, teaching, and learning; consider how they might adapt school practices to address emerging trends in education; review classroom and school data together; construct agendas for upcoming meetings; or discuss long-range planning. In thoughtful discussions, principals don't simply talk. Rather, they structure the conversation, listen carefully, and respond respectfully as teachers learn the perspectives and skills needed to lead successfully.

## Coaching

An interpersonal process of targeted analysis, reflection, and action that helps both experienced and inexperienced individuals grow in work effectiveness, coaching can build principals' and teachers' leadership capacities. Performance coaching includes clearly specifying what the teacher (or assistant principal) wants to learn, providing occasions to try out new leadership and instructional strategies, giving detailed and timely feedback on effectiveness, and keeping up a clear-eyed comparison between the present performance and the ideal one. A research consensus finds that teacher coaching is a more effective way of helping teachers turn knowledge into practice than "sit-and-listen" professional development.[54] Similarly, principals can ask questions that widen the teacher's (or assistant principal's) focus from self to others and outcomes. For instance, "What is your preferred end result for working with this team?"; "What role will you play?"; "What evidence will tell you that you have succeeded?" Throughout coaching, the principal as coach must be readily available for encouragement and practical guidance.

### Mentoring

Addressing a wider scope of behaviors than coaching, *mentoring* is a collegial and supportive relationship between experienced and inexperienced individuals to help the latter transition to more mature professional attitudes and behaviors. Mentoring aspiring leaders involves coaching, feedback, modeling, educating, encouraging, and providing opportunities to enact leadership behaviors in the school. Topics include any educational perspective or skill the pair agrees to work on—from considering how to evaluate and resolve potential moral dilemmas in the school to strategizing about how to advance the mentees' careers. As with coaching, both mentor and mentee benefit from this relationship: the mentee gains useful perspective, knowledge, and skill-building opportunities while the veteran educator gains increased job satisfaction, engagement with the school's professional community, and more leaders in the school to help it meets its learning goals.

### New Teacher Induction

Induction programs help teachers new to the job start their careers in a culture that supports adult learning and teacher leadership. Acculturating brand-new faculty to the school's vision, welcoming them into a community of adult and young learners, and identifying the varied opportunities for teacher leadership in classrooms and throughout the building helps sustain the school's teacher leadership culture. Placing new teachers in appropriate PLCs further ensures their successful transition to their classrooms and to the profession. Induction activities such as these can prompt new teachers to emerge as leaders early in their careers.

## REFLECTIONS AND RELEVANCE 8.5

## Building Teachers' Leadership Capacities

Schools need principals and teacher leaders if the school and its students are to be successful.

Working alone, assess yourself on a scale of 1–5 on the 10 characteristics (above) that indicate that a teacher is ready to take on leadership roles and responsibilities (1 = not ready today; 3 = have some characteristics but want/need more experiences; 5 = ready today). Then identify the experiences (or volunteer opportunities) noted in this section (or others that you can think of) that can help you more fully develop your leadership attitudes and skills. When will you begin? With whom would you like to work on this professional growth? After completing the individual assignment, find a partner to share your self-assessment and tentative plans. As a whole class, discuss your findings and discuss the ways you can increase your own leadership capacities.

# PREPARING THE PRINCIPAL FOR TEACHER LEADERSHIP

It may seem odd to introduce aspiring principals who expect to be their schools' "number 1" authority, control, and power center to the idea of sharing leadership— let alone sharing it with teachers whom they do not yet know. Sharing leadership and control with teachers is risky. Since principals are accountable for what others do, many principals hesitate to delegate responsibilities for important activities or decisions that might not meet their own or the school district's standards. Additionally, supporting teacher leaders takes time to advise, encourage, and "hand hold." It may seem safer and easier to do the job yourself. Or, it may seem that sharing power makes the principal appear weak.

At the same time, the idea of teacher leadership can reassure future principals that they are not carrying their school's burdens alone. Many teachers are competent to lead various kinds of instructional initiatives. Many are ready to help and willing to learn what they need to know so they can take on activities and responsibilities that they find stimulating and meaningful. In addition, teachers have the experiences and perspectives with these students and in their community that can inform the principals' own ideas and problem-solving efficacy. Most importantly, teachers are the only ones who can translate school improvement initiatives into the pedagogical behaviors that generate student learning.

By considering teacher leadership as an important vehicle to increase their morale as it improves student outcomes, future principals gain a valuable resource to help lead their schools to success. Research finds that total school leadership—including principals and teachers—has more positive impact on student achievement than either principals' leadership or teacher capacity alone,[55] and that stronger, more confident principals are more likely to share leadership with others than are weaker principals.[56] In short, principals lose no power or influence when teachers gain some—and students benefit.

Nonetheless, it is important to realize that not all teachers are willing to build their leadership capacity or take on leadership roles. Roland Barth, former teacher, principal, and founder of the Principals' Center at Harvard Graduate School of Education, identifies several reasons why: the leveling culture, teacher overload, and historically adversarial roles.[57] First, an "educational taboo" against teachers who elevate themselves above their peers may punish colleagues who "presume" to be "more important." Therefore, unless the principal and school's culture openly support teachers growing their leadership capacity, a principal's efforts to enlist faculty for leadership roles may not get far. Second, teachers already carry enormous responsibilities and public accountability for their students' learning. They may not have extra time beyond their immediate roles to take on more.

Third, the traditional distrust between teachers' unions and "management" tends to turn natural allies—principals and teachers—into adversaries; teachers who attempt to develop their leadership skills and become leaders may be accused of "consorting with the enemy." But, Barth admits, the need to share the educational load, the necessity for teachers to use their expertise to create relevant curricula to meet more rigorous standards, and the new models of school leadership evident in alternative schools (charter, pilot, and virtual, for instance) means "the time is ripe" to build teachers' leadership capacities.

Additionally, aspiring principals need to build their own leadership and instructional capacities. To do this well, future principals are advised to attend to both *what* and *how* they learn. Aspiring principals need to learn as much as they can about best practices for defining an instructional vision, identifying and recognizing what good and poor instruction looks and sounds like (from the teacher and from the students), collecting and using data wisely to assess organizational effectiveness and decision making, and involving families and the community in supporting student achievement. Even after becoming a principal of a school, continuing to learn and refine one's capacity should remain a career-long priority.

Likewise, aspiring principals need to fully engage all the opportunities available—formal coursework, readings and professional development programs, conferences, field-based practicums and internships, classroom observations, shadowing effective school leaders, and enlisting performance coaches and mentors—to learn how to be effective organizational and instructional leaders. The more hands-on and performance-based learning obtainable with high-quality and timely feedback, the deeper and more transferable the learning will be to real-world applications.

Finally, when seeking a position as principal, candidates can ask their interviewing school districts about the opportunities they provide their principals for continued growth and support. What means does the district use to formally and informally induct their new principals into their school district and leadership positions? What professional learning opportunities do they make available to principals, such as in-person or virtual coaching and collaborating with colleagues in private, confidential

## REFLECTIONS AND RELEVANCE 8.6

## Principals' Views about Teacher Leadership

Many principals are hesitant to share school leadership with teachers because they don't want to give up control since they retain all the responsibility.

Working with a partner after you have thoroughly reflected on the ideas, respond to the following questions:

1. What are your thoughts and feelings about teacher leadership?
2. What areas of school leadership do you think are appropriate for teacher leadership? Which areas do you believe are not appropriate for teacher leadership?
3. How has this chapter influenced your attitudes about teacher leadership or building teachers' capacity?

After working in pairs, discuss these questions as a whole class.

settings? What rigorous, on-going help does the school district provide to principals so they can continue to grow and improve their leadership effectiveness and student outcomes? What means and criteria do they use to evaluate principals' performance? And what resources do they provide to help principals improve? Along the same lines, do central office supervisors and directors view themselves as responsible for "compliance" or as resources to remove obstacles to principals'—and students'—success? Although the answers to these questions may not be "deal breakers" for principal candidates, they do offer a picture of the school districts' culture and the types of assistance principals can expect as they do—and grow in—their jobs.

## CONCLUSION

With the appropriate development and support, teachers and principals working together can improve schools. Together with their principals, teachers and staff can help create and express a vision for a school in which all children learn to high standards and all teachers are treated professionally. They can collaborate with colleagues to identify, refine, and expand their own instructional skills so they may engage more children in successful learning. Teachers can take on new leadership roles as department chairs, lead teachers, or school improvement committee members that introduce them to the "big picture" of what the school is doing with the student population it serves, recognize its challenges, and identify possible solutions. In the process, teachers mature in knowledge, skills, effectiveness, and job satisfaction, and principals gain additional leaders to make their schools—and their students' outcomes—better.

When teachers can nurture their commitment to educate all the community's children for responsible lives in a democratic republic, they can see their role in fulfilling the school's purpose. And, when teachers invest in their own—and their school's—success, they enact these attitudes and behaviors in their daily work, reshaping their school's culture and making these practices sustainable. To this end, Harvard's Roland Barth predicts that public education's future rests on the majority of teachers extending their work as educators to the entire school, not just in the classroom.[58]

## NOTES

1  Bambrick-Santoyo, P. (2013, October). Stone soup. The teacher leader's contribution. *Educational Leadership, 71* (2), 46–49.
2. Burkhauser, S., Gates, S. M., Hamilton, L. S., & Ikemoto, G. S. (2013). *First-year principals in urban districts. How actions and working conditions relate to outcomes.* Technical Report. Santa Monica, CA: RAND Education. Retrieved from: http://www.edweek.org/ew/articles/2012/03/02/23principals.h31.html; http://www.rand.org/content/dam/rand/pubs/technical_reports/2012/RAND_TR1191.pdf. Strategies that help accomplish teacher buy-in and cohesiveness for the principal's key strategies included promptly recruiting strong staff for their school improvement efforts, conducting one-on-one meetings with all staff to gain information on the school's perceived strengths and weaknesses, respecting and honoring prior effective instructional practices and culture by incorporating them into the proposed

school improvement strategies, being visible in the classrooms, and communicating clear and fair expectations.

3. Leithwood, L., & Riehl, C. (2003). *What we know about successful school leadership.* Philadelphia, PA: Laboratory for Student Success. Temple University. Retrieved from: http://csuphd.pbworks.com/w/file/fetch/62848668/what_we_know_about_school_leadership.pdf

4. Leithwood, K., & Mascall, B. (2008). Collective leadership effects on student achievement. *Educational Administration Quarterly, 44* (4), 529–561 (p. 530).

5. The Wallace Foundation (2013, January). *The school principal as leader: Guiding schools to better teaching and learning (Perspectives)* (p. 4). New York: Wallace Foundation. Retrieved from: http://www.wallacefoundation.org/knowledge-center/school-leadership/effective-principal-leadership/Pages/The-School-Principal-as-Leader-Guiding-Schools-to-Better-Teaching-and-Learning.aspx

6. The Wallace Foundation (2013), ibid.

7. Hallinger, P., & Murphy, K. (1986). The social context of effective schools. *American Journal of Education, 94* (3), 328–355.

8. Day, D., Harris, A., & Hadfield, M. (2000). Grounding knowledge of schools in stakeholder realities: A multi-perspective study of effective school leaders. *School Leadership and Management, 21* (1), 19–42; Harris, A. (2002). *School improvement: What's in it for schools?* London, UK: Falmer.

9. Ingersoll, R., & Merrill, L. (2012, April). *Seven trends: The transformation of the teaching force.* Paper presented at the annual meeting of the American Education Research Association, Vancouver, Canada.

10. Fullan, M. (2001). *Leading in a culture of change.* San Francisco, CA: Jossey-Bass; Hopkins, D., & Jackson, D. (2002). Building the capacity for leading and learning. In A. Harris, C. Day, M. Hadfield, D. Hopkins, A. Hargreaves, & C. Chapman (Eds.), *Effective leadership for school improvement* (pp. 84–105). London, UK: Routledge.

11. Bosker, R. J., Kremers, E. J., & Lugthart, E. (1990). School and instruction effects on mathematics achievement. *School Effectiveness and School Improvement, 1* (4), 233–248.

12. Leithwood, K., & Janzi, D. (2000). The effects of transformational leadership on organizational conditions and student engagement. *Journal of Educational Administration, 38* (2), 112–129.

13. See, for example, Barton, P. E., Coley, R., & Wenglinsky, H. (1998). *Order in the classroom: Violence, discipline, and student achievement.* Princeton, NJ: Educational Testing Service; Blair, J. (2000, October 5). ETS study links effective teaching methods to test-score gains. *Education Week, 20* (8), 24–25; Chetty, R., Friedman, J. N., & Rockoff, J. E. (2011, December). *The long-term impacts of teachers: Teacher value-added and student outcomes in adulthood.* NBER Working Paper 17699. Washington, DC: National Bureau of Economic Research. Retrieved from: http://www.nber.org/papers/w17699; Marzano, R. (2007). *The art and science of teaching: A comprehensive framework for effective instruction* (pp. 2–3). Alexandria, VA: Association for Supervision and Curriculum Development; Marzano, R. (2003). *Classroom management that works. Research-based strategies for every teacher.* Alexandria, VA: ASCD; Sanders, W. L., & Horn, S. P. (1995). Educational assessment reassessed: The usefulness of standardized and alternative measures of student achievement as indicates for the assessment of educational outcomes. *Education Policy Analysis Archives, 3* (6), 1–15; Wright, S. P., Horn, S. P., & Sanders, W. L. (1997). Teacher and classroom context effects on student achievement: Implications for teacher evaluation. *Journal of Personnel Evaluation in Education, 11,* 57–67.

14. Hallinger, R., & Heck, R. (2010). Collaborative leadership and school improvement: Understanding the impact on school capacity and student learning. *School Leadership and Management, 30* (2), 95–110.

15. Leithwood, K., & Mascall, B. (2008). Collective leadership effects on student achievement. *Education Administration Quarterly, 44* (4), 529–561.

16. Leithwood & Mascall (2008), ibid. (p. 529).

17. Koerner, T. F. (1990). Developing staff morale. *The Practitioner, 16* (4), 3.
18. Koerner (1990), ibid.
19. Koerner (1990), op. cit.
20. Evans, L. (1997). Understanding teacher morale and job satisfaction. *Teaching and Teacher Education, 13*, 831–845.
21. Harris Interactive (2013, February). *The MetLife survey of the American teacher: Challenges for school leadership.* New York, NY: MetLife. Retrieved from: https://www.metlife.com/assets/cao/foundation/MetLife-Teacher-Survey-2012.pdf
22. Harris Interactive (2013), ibid.
23. Mujis, D., & Harris, A. (2003). Teacher leadership—improvement through empowerment? An overview of the literature. *Educational Management, Administration, & Leadership, 31* (4), 437–448.
24. Ronfeldt, M., Loeb, S., & Wyckoff, J. (2013). How teacher turnover harms student achievement. *American Educational Research Journal, 50* (1), 4–36.
25. Strasser, D. (2014, February). An open letter on teacher morale. *Educational Leadership, 71* (5), 10–13 (p. 13).
26. Johnson, S. M. (2004). *Finders and keepers: Helping new teachers survive and thrive in our schools.* Indianapolis, IN: Jossey-Bass; Lortie, D. C. (1975). *Schoolteacher: A sociological study.* Chicago, IL: University of Chicago Press.
27. Coggins, C., & Peske, H. (2011, January 18). New teachers are the new majority. *Education Week, 30* (17), 21, 23. Retrieved from: http://www.edweek.org/ew/articles/2011/01/19/17coggins.h30.html
28. Coggins, C. (2010). Holding on to generation Y. *Educational Leadership, 67* (8), 70–74.
29. McColl-Kennedy, J. R., & Anderson, R. D. (2002). Impact of leadership style and emotions on subordinate performance. *Leadership Quarterly, 13* (5), 545–559.
30. Pink, D. (2010, April 1). Drive: The surprising truth about what motivates us. Retrieved from: http://www.youtube.com/watch?v=u6XAPnuFjJc; as cited in Peters, S., & Passanisi, J. (2012, December 5). What motivates teachers: It's more than money. *Education Week Teacher.* Retrieved from: http://www.edweek.org/tm/articles/2012/12/05/fp_passanisi_peters_motivates.html
31. Yankelovich, D. (1981). *New rules: Searching for self-fulfillment in a world turned upside down.* New York, NY: Random House.
32. Argyris, C. (1960). *Understanding organizational behavior.* Homewood, IL: Dorsey Press.
33. Conway, N., & Briner, R. B. (2005). *Understanding psychological contracts at work: A critical evaluation of theory and research.* Oxford: Oxford University Press; Owings, W. A., & Kaplan, L. S. (2012). *Leadership and organizational behavior in education. Theory into practice* (pp. 204–215). Upper Saddle River, NJ: Pearson.
34. Shore, L. M., & Tetrick, L. E. (1994). The psychological contract as an explanatory framework in the employment relationship. In C. Cooper, & D. Rousseau (Eds.), *Trends in organizational behavior* (Vol. 1, pp. 91–109). New York: Wiley.
35. Rousseau. D. M. (2001). Psychological contracts: Violations and modifications. In J. S. Osland, D. A. Kolb, & I. M. Rubin (Eds.), *The organizational behavior reader* (7th ed.) (p. 208). Upper Saddle River, NJ: Pearson; Rusbult, C. E., Farrell, D., Rogers, G., & Mainous, A. G. III (1988). Impact of exchange variables on exit, voice, loyalty, and neglect: an integrative model of responses to declining job satisfaction. *Academy of Management Journal, 31*, 599–627; Thomas, D. C., & Au, K. (2002). The effect of cultural variation on the behavioral response to low job satisfaction. *Journal of International Business Studies, 33* (2), 309–326; Turnley, W. H., & Feldman, D. C. (1999). The impact of psychological contract violations on exit, voice, loyalty and neglect. *Human Relations, 52* (7), 895–922.
36. See for example, Robinson, S. L., & Morrison, E. W. (2000). The development of psychological contract breach and violation: A longitudinal study. *Journal of Organizational Behavior, 21* (5), 525–546.

37. Sparrow, P., & Cooper, C. L. (2003). *The employment relationship: Key challenges for HR.* Burlington, MA: Butterworth-Heinemann.

38. Robinson, S. L., & Rousseau, D. M. (1994). Violating the psychological contract: Not the exception but the norm. *Journal of Organizational Behavior, 15* (3), 245–259; Grimmer, M., & Oddy, M. (2007). Violation of the psychological contract: The mediating effects. *Australian Journal of Management, 32* (1), 153–174; Kickul, J.(2001). Promises made, promises broken: An exploration of employee attraction and retention practices in small business. *Journal of Small Business Management, 39* (4), 320–335.

39. Turnley, W. H., & Feldman, D. C. (1999). The impact of psychological contract violations on exit, voice, loyalty, and neglect. *Human Relations, 52* (7), 895–922.

40. Robinson, S. L., Kraatz, M. S., & Rousseau, D. M. (1994). Changing obligations and the psychological contract: A longitudinal study. *Academy of Management Journal, 37* (1), 137–146.

41. Robinson, S. L. (1996). Trust and breach of the psychological contract. *Administrative Science Quarterly, 41* (4), 574–599.

42. Grimmer, M., & Oddy, M. (2007). Violation of the psychological contract: The mediating effect of relational verses transactional beliefs. *Australian Journal of Management, 32* (1), 153–175.

43. Branch, G. F., Hanushek, E. A., & Rivkin, S. G. (2013, Winter). School leaders matter: Measuring the impact of effective principals. *EducationNext, 13* (2), 62–69. Retrieved from: http://hanushek.stanford.edu/sites/default/files/publications/Branch%2BHanushek%2BRivki n%202013%20EdNext%2013%281%29_0.pdf

44. Louis, K. S., Leithwood, K., Wahlstrom, K. L., & Anderson, S. E. (2010, October). *Learning from leadership: Investigating the links to improved student learning.* Final report of research findings. Minneapolis, MN: Center for Applied Research and Educational Improvement/ University of Minnesota and Ontario Institute for Studies in Education/University of Toronto. Retrieved from: http://www.wallacefoundation.org/knowledge-center/school-leadership/key-research/Documents/Investigating-the-Links-to-Improved-Student-Learning.pdf

45. Berry, B. (2001, May). No shortcuts to preparing good teachers. *Educational Leadership, 58* (8), 32–36; Wilson, S., Floden, R. E., & Ferrini-Mundy, J. (2002).Teacher preparation research: An insider's view from the outside. *Journal of Teacher Education, 53* (3), 190–204.

46. DuFour, R. (2004, May). Schools as learning communities. *Educational Leadership, 61* (8), 6–11. Retrieved from: http://www.ascd.org/publications/educational-leadership/may04/vol61/num08/What-Is-a-Professional-Learning-Community%C2%A2.aspx

47. Jaquith, A. (2013, October). Instructional capacity. How to build it right. *Education Week, 71* (2), 56–61.

48. Kaplan & Owings (2013). *Culture Re-boot,* op. cit. (pp. 119–121).

49. Goddard, R. D., Hoy, W. K., & Woolfolk Hoy, A. (2000). Collective teacher efficacy: Its meaning, measures, and impact on student achievement. *American Educational Research Journal, 37* (2), 479–507; Leithwood, K., Louis, K. S., Anderson, S., & Wahlstrom, K. (2004). *Executive summary: How leadership influences student learning.* Learning from Leadership Project. New York: The Wallace Foundation; Seashore Louis, K., Leithwood, K., et al. (2010). *Learning from Leadership: Investigating the Links to Improved Student Learning. Final Report to the Wallace Foundation.* Minneapolis, MN: University of Minnesota. Retrieved from: http://www.wallacefoundation.org/KnowledgeCenter/KnowledgeTopics/CurrentAreasofFocus/EducationLeadership/Documents/Learning-from-Leadership-Investigating-Links-Final-Report.pdf

50. Showers, B., Joyce, B. R., & Bennett, B. (1987, February). Synthesis of research on staff development: A framework for future study and a state of the art analysis. *Educational Leadership, 45* (3), 77–87.

51. Katzenmeyer, M., & Moller, F. (2009). *Awakening the sleeping giant: Helping teachers develop as leaders* (3rd ed.). Thousand Oaks, CA: Corwin.

52. See, for example, Snell, J., & Swanson, J. (2000). *The essential knowledge and skills of teacher leaders: A search for a conceptual framework.* Paper presented at the annual meeting to the American Educational Research Association, New Orleans, LA; Harrison, J. W., & Lembeck, E. (1996). Emergent teacher leaders. In G. Moller, & M. Katzenmeyer (Eds.), *Every teacher a leader: realizing the potential of teacher leadership.* San Francisco, CA: Jossey-Bass; Leithwood, K., Jantzi, D., Ryan, S., & Steinbach. R. (1997). *Distributed leadership in secondary schools.* Paper presented at the annual meeting of the American Educational Research Association, Chicago, IL.

53. MetLife (2013, February). *The MetLife survey of the American teacher. Challenges for school leadership* (p. 5). New York, NY: MetLife. Retrieved from: https://www.metlife.com/assets/cao/foundation/MetLife-Teacher-Survey-2012.pdf

54. Joyce, B., & Showers, B. (2002). *Student achievement through staff development* (3rd ed.). Alexandria, VA: ASCD.

55. Leithwood, K., Harris, A., & Hopkins, D. (2008). Seven strong claims about successful school leadership. *School Leadership and Management, 28* (1), 27–42.

56. Barth, R. (2001). *The teacher leader.* Providence, RI: Rhode Island Foundation.

57. Barth, R. S. (2013). The time is ripe (again). *Educational Leadership, 71* (2), 10–16.

58. Barth, R. (2001). *The teacher leader.* Providence, RI: Rhode Island Foundation.

CHAPTER **9**

# Conflict Management, Decision Making, and Problem Solving

We cannot solve our problems with the same
level of thinking that created them.

—Albert Einstein

---

## LEARNING OBJECTIVES

9.1 Explain conflict as "incompatibility" and identify the ways it may appear in schools.

9.2 Discuss the meaning and implications of the statement: "The important point is not whether and to what extent organizational conflict exists but how well leaders manage it within their organization."

9.3 Describe how a cooperative orientation and norms, reframing, and mediation can aid conflict management and organizational performance.

9.4 Identify and explain Peter Drucker's steps in effective decision making.

9.5 Discuss the reasoning that underlies "bounded rationality" and examine how people in organizations use satisficing and simplifying to help them.

9.6 Analyze how teachers' zone of acceptance, the tests of relevance and expertise, and various decision-making formats can help principals decide when to use teachers in decision making.

9.7 Identify the cognitive, affective, and situational limits that can distort judgment and impair effective decision making.

9.8 Describe the conditions that tend to create groupthink, the symptoms that groupthink might be occurring, and what principals and other leaders can do to prevent it.

9.9 Summarize the main research findings on conflict in organizations, the influence of stress on group performance, and the factors that improve shared decision making, particularly in schools.

---

**2015 ISLLC STANDARDS: 1, 2, 5, 6, 7, 8, 9, 11**

## INTRODUCTION

Making complex decisions is a uniquely human capacity. As Harvard's Kennedy School's Peter Zimmerman observes, "Rats find their way through a maze and it appears that they decide to take one route over another . . . My dog Daisy gets up at 5.00 am every day and seems to know that it's time for breakfast and her walk. However, these behaviors are not decisions requiring the skills that leaders exercise. They are conditioned behaviors, simple patterns of stimulus and response, emerging from evolutionary and contemporary experience, automatic in character, and, as far as we know, in no way involving conscious thought and decision."[1]

Conscious and informed decision making is a distinctly human behavior. Making good decisions lies at the heart of successful leadership. Leaders make countless decisions—strategic, tactical, organizational, financial, and moral. Since many problems are complicated, the decisions to solve them are, too. Some choices affect thousands of people, others impact only a few. All require principals to have highly developed judgment and analytical skills. Making good decisions, and knowing when to decide alone and when to invite teachers' and community members' participation, can prevent problems that will need to be solved later. But our decision-making practices are not always reliable. We are all subject to predictable—and unpredictable—cognitive, affective, and situational limits that can distort judgment. But unlike rats and dogs, humans can learn, adapt, and improve their decision-making capacities.

This chapter focuses on how leaders address conflict, problem solving, and decision making in organizations, particularly in schools. We will discuss how conflict may positively and negatively impact organizations, the factors that influence decision making, and the real-world constraints on making "perfect" decisions. Rational decision making, shared decision making, and groupthink models and their implications for organizational effectiveness will be considered. Aspiring principals can gain perspective as well as practical steps for how they will manage conflict and make decisions in their schools.

## ORGANIZATIONAL CONFLICT

Conflict has been a fact of human life since the Garden of Eden, and its history and scientific research in the professional literature is more fully discussed elsewhere.[2] Since the schools in which principals work are complex organizations, meeting goals cooperatively brings the potential for conflict. Although school norms may celebrate teamwork, collegiality, and agreement in pursuit of shared objectives, no group can be totally harmonious all the time. Even straightforward school improvement strategies must take into account the many people with varied interests and needs they will affect.

Despite its inevitability, conflict is a condition that most leaders would rather avoid or end quickly rather than learn how to manage more successfully. Conflict is uncomfortable for many principals because—the specific issues aside—they typically see disagreement as situations in which one set of colleagues "win" while another set of colleagues "lose" (and good working relationships can be harmed). As a result, their organizations waste valuable resources as employees engage in dysfunctional conflict and miss occasions to use functional conflict to advance their interests. When principals understand their schools, their teachers, their communities, and the normal discord they contain—and develop the insights and skills to constructively manage them—leaders can actually use moderate conflict to benefit their schools.

# LEADERSHIP AND CONFLICT IN ORGANIZATIONS

*Conflict* is a process in which one party perceives that its interests are being opposed or negatively affected by another party[3]—whether individuals, groups, or organizations. In fact, social interactions may be seen as a process involving a struggle over claims to resources, power and status, beliefs, and other preferences. Conflict may stem from trying to persuade another to see things your way, trying to gain more resources, or, in the extreme case, trying to hurt or expel one's opponent from the field. When this happens between people who represent countries, war often results.

Although conflict may have many causes, Morton Deutsch, the Columbia University professor emeritus regarded as the founder of modern conflict resolution theory and practice, explains simply that conflict exists "whenever incompatible activities occur."[4] This incompatibility may be intrapersonal or interpersonal.

## Conflict as Incompatibility

Conflict can relate to incompatible preferences, goals, and activities. Generally, conflict may occur when:[5]

- A person is required to engage in an activity that does not align with his or her interests.
- A person wants to behave in certain ways that, if done, prevents another person from acting as he or she wishes.
- A person wants a mutually desired but limited resource; if the person gets what he or she wants, the others won't get what they want.
- A person has attitudes, values, skills, and goals that influence his or her behavior but that others perceive as preventing them from acting upon their own attitudes, values, skills, and goals.
- Two people partially disagree about how to conduct their common activities.
- Two people perform their functions or activities interdependently.

Incompatible goals produce a dilemma for the individuals or groups involved: one side gains at the other's expense. In these circumstances, conflict may produce a classic, zero-sum, "win-lose" situation that can potentially harm the individuals' relationships as well as organizational effectiveness. In conflict situations, everyone tries to avoid becoming a loser, and losers strive to become winners (or try to "score points" to even the tally). And, what may have started as a substantive, objective disagreement about a task rapidly becomes personal and emotional. This affective dynamic is a central quality of conflict in organizations. For instance, if teachers want their daily planning period for their own professional ends while the principal considers this time as a "duty period" for them to do what the principal assigns (often supervising students or performing "administrivia"), their goals are incompatible. If this situation continues, teachers are likely to become annoyed, creating ripples of resentment through the school and possibly harming student outcomes.

### Conflict as Intrapersonal or Interpersonal

Conflict may occur within the individual. Intrapersonal conflict occurs when a person feels torn between wanting to achieve two (seemingly) incompatible goals. For example, a principal wants to attend all the school's drama, choral, and sports events to support students and teachers and to be visible in the community. At the same time, the principal wants to spend every evening at home with family. Since the principal can only be in one place at a time, after a while, the conflicting goals lead to feelings of stress, stress-related behaviors such as indecisiveness, and occasionally to physical symptoms such as hypertension or ulcers.

Similarly, interpersonal conflict may occur between people or social units. For instance, both the English and physical education departments want to limit their class sizes to a "manageable" number of students to increase student engagement and boost learning. But because high-stakes standardized testing occurs in reading and writing, the administration closes the English classes at 24 students per teacher but closes the PE classes at 45 students per teacher. In the competition for resources (teachers per student), the PE teachers resent being treated as an "inferior" department. Arguments, sniping, gossip, absenteeism, or avoidance by members of each department toward the

### REFLECTIONS AND RELEVANCE 9.1

## Identifying Conflict in Schools

Conflict may stem from incompatible preferences, goals, and activities.

Working in groups of three, identify a facilitator, a recorder, and a reporter. Identify a possible school-based example for each of the bulleted statements in the section "Conflict as Incompatibility" (above). If the situation actually happened, identify how the school principal or other leader responded to the conflict and describe its aftermath. Next, have each person describe how conflict typically affects them, intellectually and emotionally.

After each group has finished, the class will share its examples of school-based conflict that started from incompatibility. Identify how your administrators typically respond to conflict and its aftermath. Discuss how conflict affects the class members intellectually and emotionally. What common elements are you finding about conflict in schools, its management, and how it affects teachers?

other—or toward the principal or school—may result. Conflict in organizational life usually involves interpersonal conflict and intergroup conflict.

From the school's perspective, leaders must learn to recognize and manage conflict to avoid or minimize hostility. When leaders can handle the conflict constructively in ways that solve the problem and prevent or reduce bad feelings, the school stands to benefit. Mishandled conflict can harm the school and student outcomes.

## CONTEMPORARY VIEWS ON ORGANIZATIONAL CONFLICT

Mid-19th-Century English naturalist, Charles Darwin, wrote of "the competitive struggle for existence" and "survival of the fittest."[6] Appreciating how conflict could raise difficulties for organizations, the classical organizational theorists preferred a smoothly functioning enterprise characterized by harmony, unity, coordination, efficiency, and order.[7] In their view, discord harmed operational efficiency and should be minimized. Managerial structures—hierarchies, lines of authority, rules, and procedures for reducing interpersonal friction—could lead the way for organizational success.

After World War II, conflict resolution emerged as an area of scholarship and professional practice. Unlike earlier views, contemporary scholars see conflict as inevitable, widespread, and often justifiable. Individuals and groups are interdependent and continually engaged in the dynamic process of defining and redefining the nature and extent of their interactions. Any well-led organization will experience conflict. Leaders' roles require gathering resources—people, money, time, facilities, and material—so the group may achieve its goals. Since resources are limited, competing ideas for how to use them (often along with other, unexpressed agendas) are likely. Conflicts result.

Today, conflict management is seen as the "essence of leadership,"[8] a way of confronting reality and creating new solutions to difficult problems. When well-managed, conflict can bring life and energy into our relationships, strengthen our interdependence, and improve outcomes. Conflict can make organizations more innovative and productive. In fact, conflict is essential for true involvement, empowerment, and democracy. By debating their varied viewpoints, people express their concerns and create a wider array of solutions. Conflict can even help people become united and committed to a common purpose. The important point is not whether and to what extent organizational conflict exists but how well leaders manage it within their organization. It has been said that when two persons in business always agree, one of them is unnecessary.[9]

## CONFLICT'S FUNCTIONAL AND DYSFUNCTIONAL OUTCOMES

Only moderate conflict can be helpful to organizational functioning. Opportunities for creativity, problem awareness, adaptation, and self-awareness can be better achieved through means other than generating discord. In truth, too much conflict is usually dysfunctional, generating significant negative effects, and running the risk of escalating in unanticipated and unproductive ways. Depending on how it's handled, conflict within organizations may have functional or dysfunctional outcomes.[10]

Functional outcomes of conflict include:

- stimulating innovation, creativity, and growth;
- improving organizational decision making;
- finding alternative solutions to problems;
- finding synergistic solutions to common problems;
- enhancing individual and group performance;
- giving individuals and groups occasions to search for new solutions;
- requiring individuals and groups to express and clarify their positions.

Dysfunctional outcomes of conflict include:

- causing job stress, burnout, and dissatisfaction;
- reducing communication between individuals and groups;
- developing a climate of distrust and suspicion;
- damaging relationships;
- reducing job performance;
- increasing resistance to change;
- affecting organizational commitment and loyalty.

Accordingly, the consequences of conflict may appear in the following helpful or harmful ways:[11]

- *Individuals.* Low levels of conflict may lead individuals to feel stimulated and energized. In contrast, high levels of conflict can lead to emotional distress, anxiety, tension, low job satisfaction, and reduced motivation.
- *Relationships.* Low levels of conflict may strengthen relationships by encouraging people to work together to reduce obstacles that interfere with their collaboration. In contrast, high levels of conflict can lead to perceived distrust, inability to understand an opponent's thinking or intentions, and weakened or broken relationships.
- *Communications.* Conflict may spur disputants to get their issues out in the open to permit effective problem solving. In contrast, conflict may lead to more hostile, distorted exchanges, misunderstandings, and increased communications with others not directly involved in the conflict—widening the dispute to include more parties.
- *Behaviors.* When successfully managed, conflict may lead to a stronger commitment to shared goals and more collaborative teamwork. In contrast, conflict may lead to avoidance, face-saving behaviors, venting emotions, confrontations, threats, physical force, harming others, increased absenteeism, and reduced productivity.
- *Organizational structures and norms.* Successfully managed conflict may lead to a more open and experimental culture and norms that encourage professional growth, innovation, and improved outcomes. In contrast, conflict may lead to decreased

interdependence and coordination, more "us" vs. "them" tensions, and more decision making by leaders with less shared input from members.

- *Issues.* Well-managed conflict can lead to a more complete identification of problems, more comprehensive and workable solutions, improved outcomes, and a culture that encourages on-going study, action, and improvement. In contrast, conflict may allow misunderstandings to increase and simple disputes to become stubborn "matters of principle."

- *Residues.* Well-managed conflict may lead to better decisions, "win-win" workable solutions, improved group efficiency, greater awareness of latent problems, and a culture that encourages open identification of issues needing improvement and effective problem solving. In contrast, conflict may lead to "winners" and "losers," undercurrents of unrest, resistance, increased absenteeism, and work sabotage.

Since organizational conflict has both positive and negative outcomes, if an organization is to benefit from it, leaders must find ways to limit conflict's harmful effects and strengthen its positive effects. Wisely managing conflict—not avoiding, denying, or suppressing it—is essential to advancing organizational health and effectiveness.

## FINDING THE RIGHT BALANCE

Organizations with little or no conflict stagnate, while high or uncontrolled levels of conflict are damaging. Organizational theorists agree that a moderate amount of conflict is needed for attaining an optimal level of organizational effectiveness. The relationship between too much and too little conflict appears as an inverted-U function, as illustrated in Figure 9.1.[12] In this view, conflict is a natural byproduct of

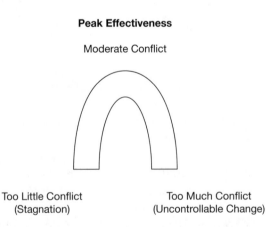

**Peak Effectiveness**

Moderate Conflict

Too Little Conflict          Too Much Conflict
(Stagnation)          (Uncontrollable Change)

**Low Levels of Organizational Effectiveness**

**FIGURE 9.1** Relationship Between Too Much and Too Little Organizational Conflict

Source: Based on Rahim, M. A., & Bonoma, T. V. (1979). Managing organizational conflict: A model for diagnosis and intervention. *Psychological Reports, 44* (3, Pt. 2), 1323–1344.

people working together. School improvement initiatives—and the moderate conflict that change generates—can keep educators continually learning to enhance their teaching and learning practices (and avoid getting stale and ineffective). If a conflict threatens to undermine problem solving, relationships, and positive outcomes, conflict management (namely, problem solving) become necessary.

### REFLECTIONS AND RELEVANCE 9.2

## How Low, Moderate, and High Conflict Affect Teachers

Conflict may be functional or dysfunctional to an organization, depending on its level and how it is managed.

In pairs, describe times in your school worksite when you (and teachers) experienced low, moderate, and high conflict. What was each conflict about? What indicators are you using to determine whether the conflict was low, moderate, or high? In which type of conflict did you feel excited and energized in a positive way? How did this affect your motivation, productivity, and relationships with colleagues? In which type of situation did you feel tense, angry, and resentful? How did this affect your motivation, productivity, and relationships with colleagues? How did your principal or other administrators respond to low, moderate, and high conflict situations—and what were the outcomes?

## CONFLICT RESOLUTION AND CONFLICT MANAGEMENT

Most conflicts eventually de-escalate, and opposing parties' intense feelings decrease. But that does not return parties to their earlier pre-conflict states any more than a three-alarm house fire returns a smoldering ruin into a comfortable home. Apologies, fatigue, conciliation, or finding the cost of conflict too high contribute to de-escalation. The most effective method for reducing conflict, however, is for one side to take a step that lessens the other's anger, shows a lack of malicious intent, or cuts the tension between the parties. Most conflicts benefit from attempts to manage them. In organizations, this can be accomplished through conflict resolution or conflict management.

Although the two terms are sometimes used interchangeably, *conflict resolution* and *conflict management* are not the same thing. *Conflict resolution* suggests reducing or ending conflict. In contrast, *conflict management* involves designing effective strategies to reduce the conflict's dysfunctions and boost the conflict's constructive functions to improve organizational learning and efficacy.[13] Rather than merely limit or end organizational friction, conflict management uses discord to fashion a more flexible, resilient, and productive organization. Either the individuals involved or third parties (such as principals, assistant principals, or teacher leaders) can initiate conflict management strategies.

In the 1970s, Kenneth Thomas and Ralph Kilmann, two business professors, proposed five main styles of dealing with conflict in organizations. These styles vary in their dimensions of cooperation (trying to satisfy the other person's concerns), assertiveness (trying to satisfy one's own concerns), and usefulness in different situations. These styles are:[14]

- *Competitive.* Individuals take a firm position; they know what they want and expect to get it by using their power position (such as rank, expertise, or persuasive ability). This style is useful in an emergency when a quick decision is essential, when the decision is unpopular, or when defending against someone who is trying selfishly to exploit the situation. When used in less urgent conditions, others may feel dissatisfied and resentful.
- *Collaborative.* Individuals try to meet the needs of all involved. Although these people may be highly assertive, they cooperate effectively and recognize that everyone is important. This style is useful when different viewpoints need to be brought together to find the best solution, when the group has experienced previous conflicts, or when the situation is too important to ignore other perspectives.
- *Compromising.* Individuals try to find a solution that will at least partly satisfy everyone. Everyone, including the leader, expects to give up something. Compromise is useful when the cost of conflict is higher than the cost of losing ground, when opponents with equal strengths are at a standstill, and when a deadline rapidly approaches.
- *Accommodating.* Individuals are willing to meet the needs of others at the expense of their own personal needs. This person is not assertive, is highly cooperative, and can be persuaded to give in to others' views even when it is not necessary. Accommodating is appropriate when the issues matter more to the other party, when "peace" is more important than "winning," and when the individual wants to be able to collect on the "favor" later. This approach is not likely to secure the best outcomes.
- *Avoiding.* Individuals seek to evade the conflict altogether. People who prefer this approach tend to delegate "hot" (controversial) decisions, accept default decisions (neglect to act and live with whatever happens), and want to avoid hurting anyone's feelings. Avoiding can be appropriate when winning is impossible, when the controversy is trivial, or when someone else is in a better position to solve the problem. In many situations, this approach is weak and ineffective.

At its roots, however, the conflict participants' orientations towards a cooperative or a competitive approach to solving the mutual problem typically determine the conflict's course and outcome. Goals, interpretations, past experiences, culture, and an assortment of other factors influence conflict-management strategies. The persons' characters and experiences, their social contexts, aspirations, social norms, desire for power and influence, and conflict orientations each play a role in directing the outcome. Typically, a cooperative stance leads to a constructive process in which the two parties successfully solve the problem. In contrast, a competitive stance often leads to a process in which the two parties enter into a contest or struggle to determine winners and losers.

Sometimes, both parties lose. Almost all conflicts contain both cooperative and competitive elements.

On the way to workable solutions, principals will want to maximize the cooperative elements and minimize the competitive ones. A cooperative or "win-win" orientation to resolving a conflict makes it easier to find a constructive solution. A competitive "win-lose" outlook makes it more difficult. Developing and keeping a cooperative attitude is easier if one has social support for this perspective from friends, colleagues, employers, the organizational culture, the media, and the larger community.

Nevertheless, it is important to remember that "win-win" is not always the best solution, unless it means better outcomes for students. In conflict management, "win-win" means that both parties have the opportunity for a fair, honest hearing in which they can fully and clearly express their views and have them considered. It does not necessarily mean that every party will walk away with the answers they want. A best solution is one that keeps the larger goals in mind.

## REFLECTIONS AND RELEVANCE 9.3

### Conflict Management Styles

**Kenneth Thomas and Ralph Kilmann identify five styles for dealing with conflict in organizations.**

Working in groups of four, select a facilitator, a recorder, and a reporter. Re-read the descriptions of the conflict management styles and identify possible school-based situations in which each style might be the most effective—and a situation in which each style might be the least effective. Which style is each member most comfortable using in this point of their careers? Which style does each member want to learn to use better?

After the small groups have completed their activities, the whole class will give examples of each type of conflict management style as it might appear in a school. Identify the commonalities and differences among the examples for each type and between types. Discuss the challenges for school leaders in addressing conflict management.

## Reframing the Conflict

Often, the key to gaining cooperative conflict management is *reframing* the conflict—placing a different perception around the discord as if inserting a familiar photo into a different picture frame to create a new appearance. Reframing the conflict as a mutual problem, for example, identifies it as one that can be solved through reciprocal efforts and establishes a cooperative outlook in which each party may still meet their needs. Reformulating the situation as a shared problem with a possible "win-win" outcome motivates each party to look for evenhanded procedures to resolve the conflict. And in the end, whatever the outcome, each party sees it as fair and acceptable.

For example, several academic departments like to use an empty media center conference room for after-school teacher–parent meetings. The room is clean, private, and comfortable (a limited, mutually desired resource). After the buses leave, teachers start appearing at the conference room door with families and students in tow, expecting the room to be vacant. Often, another teacher and family are already using it (one person's behavior prevents another from behaving in a desired way). After one or two scheduling conflicts, the principal hears grumblings and meets with the teachers. The principal identifies that the scheduling situation is "a mutual concern to help students and parents that needs a shared solution" (reframes the situation). Although frustrated, the teachers see their best interests require working together; they develop a fair-use procedure for using the conference room after school to which they all agree (they accept the reframed conflict as a problem-solving opportunity). And the scheduling conflicts end. Of course, not all conflicts are so easily understood, reframed, and resolved.

## Mediation

Sometimes, the principal is one of the parties to the conflict, and at other times, the principal can serve as a mediator to help engineer positive outcomes. *Mediation* is the process for bringing about an agreement or reconciliation between conflicting parties by the objective intervention of a neutral party. Principals may sometimes serve as mediator between teachers, between academic departments, and between teachers and parents. To be effective in this role, principals will want to have a reputation for fairness and integrity, gain knowledge of the specific conflict issues, establish a working relationship with the conflicting parties, instill a cooperative, problem-solving attitude between the parties, and facilitate the group problem-solving process.[15] This friendly, open-minded intervention approach is more effective than employing one's positional power unilaterally to "declare" a solution (unless the conflict situation is deemed an actual emergency).

In conflict management, the process can be as important as the solutions. The mediation process can help the parties improve their communications by focusing on listening and understanding rather than "scoring points." It can reduce disputants' stress by allowing them to air their concerns and give them the satisfaction of having been treated fairly. And ideally, experiencing the process and its outcomes may improve the parties' future problem-solving skills. Although research on mediation and its outcomes tends to look at non-school situations, most disputants express satisfaction with the process and accept the final agreements (77 percent),[16] even when they don't reach an agreement (75 percent).[17] It is likely that similar high levels of satisfaction with mediation may be true in school-based conflicts.

## Norms of Cooperation

Conflicts are not only about the problem to be "fixed" but also the interpersonal relationships to be maintained. Principals and teachers are more likely to reframe their conflict into a mutual and resolvable problem if they follow norms of cooperative behavior and develop the skills that facilitate its use. These cooperative norms resemble those for respectful, responsible, honest, empowering, and caring behaviors towards friends or fellow group members. They include:[18]

- *Value relationships as well as solutions.* Despite the stress the unresolved issue generates, be courteous, respectful, and constructive. People of good will can disagree without being disagreeable. In all likelihood, the parties involved will have to keep working together, and mutual respect as well as a track record of successful problem solving together will make future work relations easier and more productive.
- *Separate people from problems.* Recognize that frequently, the person on either side of the conflict is presenting real and valid differences; the person is not simply "being difficult." Separate the problem from the person, and address the issues without disparaging the other or impairing the working relationship.
- *Listen first, talk second.* Pay attention to the reasons for the other person's views. Understand why that individual is advancing that position. Is the problem scarce resources, incompatible goals, honest differences in how to best solve a mutual problem, or a misunderstanding? Only once you understand where the other person is coming from (and before you defend your own position), can you solve the problem effectively.
- *Present the "facts."* Agree to set out the objective, observable information that will influence the decision. Separating "facts" from emotions and opinions is a major challenge.
- *Find common ground.* Place disagreements into perspective by identifying common ground and common interests.
- *Build on others' ideas.* Listen to others' suggestions, fully acknowledge their value, and build on them.
- *Stress the positive.* Emphasize the positive and constructive ideas in the other person's suggestions for resolving the conflict. Limit and control expressing negative feelings to the other person's violation of cooperative norms (if that happens) or at the other's defeatism.
- *Empower the other.* Enable the other person to contribute effectively to the cooperative effort: ask the person for his or her facts and views and share information.
- *Consider options together.* Accept that the problem may have several ways of understanding it and several workable solutions that you can reach together. What disputants gain from shared problem solving may be more valuable and effective than what either position gives up.
- *Be appropriately honest.* Although being dishonest, misleading, or deceptive breaks cooperative norms, it is not necessary to be unnecessarily or inappropriately truthful. Unless the relationship has matured to a high level of intimacy, expressing every suspicion, doubt, fear, and sense of weakness about oneself or the other (especially in a blunt, undiplomatic manner) is likely to harm the relationship.
- *Be moral, caring and fair-minded.* Remain ethical, concerned, and evenhanded throughout the conflict. View the other person as a member of one's community and entitled to care and justice.

Resolving conflicts constructively requires mature and deliberate thought coupled with self-awareness and control over one's feelings. Sticking to the issues and speaking respectfully is challenging, especially when one is frustrated or upset, but it is essential. Carefully listening may mean a slight pause before responding, but momentary silence in the interest of a full and accurate understanding is OK. No matter how difficult, catching oneself in the act of being uncooperative, recognizing when this behavior starts, and then stopping, apologizing, and explaining what made one angry enough to want to hurt the other helps refocus the discussion on constructive engagement. It also helps maintain the interpersonal trust and strengthen the relationship. Likewise, becoming aware that each person has "hot buttons" that, once pressed, are likely to generate strong emotions, and *not* pressing them, will help the participants control their responses. Preventing disruptive emotions during problem solving can speed up movement toward a satisfactory resolution. Naturally, remaining calm and acting cooperatively is easier said than done, but it can be learned with practice and feedback.

## CONFLICT AND ORGANIZATIONAL PERFORMANCE

Whether a conflict is functional or dysfunctional depends on how it affects the organization's performance. In schools, conflict's outcomes can appear in the organization's health, adaptability, and stability.

Modern motivation theory confirms that people find challenge, meaning, and the need to solve problems as interesting, enjoyable, and galvanizing work qualities. Likewise, recognizing that many people in the organization have good ideas, divergent perspectives, and additional information that can contribute to better informed decisions helps make shared leadership effective. Rather than promote harmful discord, disagreements can jolt individuals into considering aspects previously ignored and help construct a more comprehensive understanding of the situation at hand. Managing conflict successfully also benefits organizational functioning by clarifying relationships, increasing collective understanding, and improving problem-solving practices.

Organizations that don't evolve become stale and out of step with the realities around them. Conflict within a group can often revitalize existing norms and prompt the emergence of new, more beneficial ones. In this way, social conflict offers an avenue for social norms to adjust to new conditions. Such friction benefits society, providing the flexibility needed to modify and create rules and behaviors that allow organizations to continue to thrive despite changed circumstances. For instance, federal and state laws and school regulations against student-on-student harassment (particularly regarding gender, disability, or sexual identity) are reasonable responses that show increased respect for diversity and an end to hostile teasing: student behaviors are reframed from "just teasing" to "assault." In contrast, rigid systems that suppress conflict actually kill the "canary in the coal mine," ignoring, denying, or avoiding the useful warning system that alerts members that change is needed. Ironically, rather than making conflict disappear, avoiding, denying, or suppressing it can actually increase the danger of catastrophic societal breakdown.[19]

Principals can help reduce conflict's destructive potential and increase its productive, creative, and useful possibilities when they understand conflict management, keep conflict within workable limits, and use it to strengthen their school's processes and outcomes. When handled effectively, conflict in schools can lead to a more vibrant school culture, increased understanding, and stronger group cohesion as well as personal and professional growth—all of which can be helpful in generating a more satisfying work environment and better student outcomes.

## REFLECTIONS AND RELEVANCE 9.4

## Using Reframing, Mediating, and Cooperative Norms

Reframing, mediating, and using cooperative norms can help principals manage conflict successfully.

In groups of four, select one of the school-based conflict management situations previously discussed—or create a new one. Each group will role play four parts: a principal as mediator, two teachers in a conflict situation, and an observer. Using the book or notes as a reference, the "principal" will reframe the situation and use the norms of cooperation to establish a cooperative outlook in which each party may meet their needs or at least see the solution as fair and acceptable. The "observer" will watch and listen for the reframing and cooperative norms, silently identify which cooperative norms are seen and/or heard during the role play, and give oral feedback to the "principal" and "teachers" immediately after each role play. The members can use the feedback to improve the mediation's effectiveness with each successive role play. Group members will role play four times, with an opportunity for each member to play each role.

After the groups have finished, members will discuss their experiences in each role with the rest of the class. How did they respond to the reframing, to the mediation, and to the norms of cooperation? When do class members think they will want to use these ideas?

## PROBLEM SOLVING AND DECISION MAKING

Leaders and subordinates both have a stake in problem solving and decision making. *Problem solving* is the mental process that involves discovering, analyzing, and solving difficulties (by making decisions). *Decision making* is the mental process of making choices among several alternatives. In a virtuous cycle, successful problem solving requires good decision making, and making good decisions avoids creating new problems.

For principals, one of the first decisions they make is whether they should solve a problem alone or whether to invite others to participate. Emergency situations require the principal's immediate, unilateral actions. An injury or a suspected "lock-down" situation must be handled straightaway without consulting a committee if lives are to be saved. In contrast, school improvement planning allows time for wider input, study, and discussion before making decisions. The varied ways in which leaders and employees work together—or apart—to solve problems in their organization affects the organization's functioning and productivity.

# MAKING EFFECTIVE DECISIONS

School improvement happens one decision at a time. How principals in schools make decisions depends, in part, on the schools' existing capabilities or the options available for decision making. As with other organizations, schools have a culture, mission, routines, and processes that affect how they identify goals, how they define problems, how they share information, and how they make decisions. School leaders must conceptually understand the decision-making process, how reality places limits on decision making, and how to decide when—and to what extent—to involve others in the process. Lastly, becoming knowledgeable about groupthink will help principals recognize when group decision making becomes dysfunctional.

## The Traditional Decision-Making Model

The traditional decision-making model assumes that decisions should be made rationally using an approach that seeks the best possible alternatives to get the best outcomes. The familiar model outlines the process as a series of sequential steps:

1. Identify the problem.
2. Establish goals and objectives.
3. Generate all possible alternatives.
4. Consider the consequences of each alternative.
5. Evaluate each alternative in terms of the goals and objectives.
6. Select the best alternative, the one that best accomplishes the goals and objectives.
7. Implement and evaluate the decision.

Most practitioners—and even scholars—see this traditional model as ideal, but unrealistic. People making decisions rarely have access to all the relevant information, and producing all the possible options and their outcomes is impossible. At the same time, people lack the cognitive information-processing capacities, knowledge, or time that this model assumes is available. And although our culture believes in *rationality*—the set of skills or aptitudes we use to find courses of action that lead to accomplishing our goals—rationality has its limits. People are humans living in complex environments, and they do what they have to do even if it is not objectively "rational." As the French philosopher Voltaire (1746) observed, "The best is the enemy of the good,"[20] suggesting that if one is too focused on achieving the "optimum," the problem will never be solved (because the "best" solutions may not be possible while the "acceptable" solutions are ignored). Consequently, the traditional decision-making model stands as an exemplar, rather than as a practical guide.

In the late 20th Century, business management specialists moved away from those who saw decision making as a mathematical model. Instead, they expanded the definition and practice of rationality to include the uncertainty that lurks beneath thinking and problem solving in the real world.

## Practical Steps in Effective Decision Making

Peter Drucker, an internationally renowned organizational scholar and consultant, believes that every decision is a risk-taking judgment. He sees the traditional decision-making model as the necessary—but not sufficient—steps in the effective decision-making process. Although principals are not business executives, they are in positions to make decisions that significantly affect large organizations. Drucker's steps for decision making offer principals a systematic approach for thinking through problem solving in their schools. These steps include:[21]

1. *Classify the problem.* Is this problem truly unique, a new type of problem for which no rule has yet been developed, or is it ordinary and routine? If it is ordinary and routine, applying the organization's principles, policies, or rules can solve it. Exceptions must be handled as they occur. Decision makers' common mistakes are to treat generic, typical situations as if they were exceptional events, and unique events as if they are a new example of an old problem. For instance, a high school student wants to take final exams one week early to be able to leave town on a family vacation during exam week. Is this a generic or exceptional situation? Most likely, it is generic, so the decision maker can use a policy manual or school rule to solve the problem.

2. *Define the problem.* What is the sum total of what we are dealing with? Errors happen at this step when decision makers pick the *plausible but incomplete* definition of the problem. For instance, when principals and teachers analyze test scores and consider only teaching factors—rather than curriculum alignment, low-scoring students' attendance or discipline records, or other intervening factor—they are overlooking essential variables in defining the problem.

3. *Specify the answer to the problem.* What are the "boundary" conditions? What are the minimum criteria—the goals and objectives—that the decision has to accomplish? What are the risks and trade-offs? This is decision making's most difficult step. For example, in test analysis, principals will want to ensure that every student subgroup is making appropriate learning and achievement gains—and if not, why not? Disaggregating data, therefore, is an essential step in analyzing student results and identifying the solution.

4. *Decide what is "right"—rather than what is acceptable—in order to meet the boundary conditions.* What will satisfy the specifications *before* giving attention to compromises, adaptations, and concessions needed to make the decision acceptable? In the end, compromise is always necessary, but the decision maker must be able to distinguish the *right* compromise from the *wrong* compromise. In the testing illustration, trying to raise all children's achievement, the principal decides that the school *will not accept* a lower pass rate or lower attendance rate for minority children in order for them to achieve "acceptable" academic progress. Any decisions about teaching, teacher assignments, schedule adjustments, class sizes, or other variables will have to begin from what is "right" in order to improve every student's achievement.

5. *Build the action to carry out the decision.* What does the action commitment have to be? Who has to know about it? Do the people who have to take the action have the knowledge and skills needed? This is the most time-consuming step in the decision-making process. Unless a decision includes specific steps for someone's work and responsibility, it is not a decision but only a good intention. And those who must carry out the actions assigned must have the capacity (attitudes, knowledge, behaviors, and habits) and resources (including time) to do it. For example, if the principal is focused on a third grade achievement goal, every second, third, and fourth grade teacher (and relevant administrators) must know about it (vertical articulation). Everyone will need to look at their students' prior measured achievement and know what types of learning must be done (which skills remain unmastered?). Everyone may take the just-in-time and relevant professional development to learn and practice the skills necessary to understand student achievement data, assesses individual students' needs, and design and deliver appropriate instruction. And everyone must be held responsible for addressing the learning issues and generating higher achievement.

6. *Test the decision's validity and effectiveness against actual events.* How is the decision being implemented? Is the decision based on appropriate or outdated assumptions? Gaining information and using feedback are essential parts of decision making, and they should be built into the decision to provide continuous testing of expectations against actual events. For the principal, this usually means finding out for oneself rather than relying on others' reports. In our example, the principal will want to see the professional development plan and calendar, determine whether the presenters and format fit with best practices for adult learning, attend several of the events, observe and speak with teachers who are trying out new instructional approaches to increase learning in their classrooms, and review ongoing data about student achievement. Principals will want to "trust, but verify."

Drucker believes that the specific role for executives—as compared with associates and managers—is to make important decisions that have a significant and positive impact on the entire organization. Effective leaders make decisions as a systematic process with clearly defined elements and in a distinct series of steps. Decision making faces many limitations, but Drucker's approach brings both practicality and shrewdness to the process.

## REFLECTIONS AND RELEVANCE 9.5

# Practical Steps in Effective Decision Making

**Peter Drucker developed a set of questions that organizational leaders can use to help think through problems in a systematic way.**

You are an organizational development consultant—and you are your own client. Your assignment is to conduct an after-action review of a "major" work-related decision you made during the past two years. First, think about the decision and recall the problem presented, the situation, the alternate options you considered, why you selected the option you did, and how well your decision worked in the real world. Then re-read Drucker's steps in effective decision making and think about your decision using his framework. Working with a partner from this class, relate the decision-making situation and answer the following questions as part of your after-action review:

1. Was the situation unique or generic? How can you tell?
2. What was the "plausible but incomplete" definition of the problem?
3. What was the complete definition of the problem?
4. What were the minimum criteria that the decision had to accomplish?
5. What were the risks and trade-offs?
6. What was the "acceptable" answer"? What was the "right" answer?
7. Did those who had to take the necessary actions to enact the decision have the knowledge and skills to complete it successfully?
8. How effectively did the solution work? By what measures can you determine this?

After you and your partner have conducted the after-action review, discuss Drucker's decision-making process with the class. What did you learn from conducting the process with your own decision? Which parts of Drucker's process is the most difficult for you to use? In what ways do you think this model of decision making may be helpful to you as a school leader?

## Limits on Rationality

Herbert Simon, a 1978 Nobel Prize-winning economist and Carnegie Mellon psychology professor, views decisions as not a single event but the product of a complex social process generally extending over a long period of time.[22] His interest in *how* people make decisions helped him realize that rationality in the decision-making process has its limits. As an economist, he sees decision making as rational behavior, but as a psychologist, he also recognizes its irrationality.[23] In addition, Simon understands the real world's ambiguity and uncertainty. Individuals have their own reasons (motives) for doing as they do. Organization's goals, technologies, and modern environments are highly complex. As a result, even the best decision-making models are over-simplifications.

In short, people's reasoning is fallible. The high number of possible options and unlimited amount of available information make it unrealistic for any individual to be highly rational. When making decisions, people conduct a limited search along familiar and well-traveled paths, usually selecting the first satisfactory alternative that appears and calling that a solution. Simon suggests that decision making in organizations is limited by the principle of *bounded rationality*—the adaptive behavior within the constraints imposed by three variables: the person's cognitive skills, habits, reflexes; the extent of the knowledge and information the individual has; and the values or sense of purpose which may differ from the organization's goals.[24]

As information processors, people have limits to which they must adapt: their perceptions, experiences, memories, knowledge, skills, aspirations, and competing goals. Subjective perceptions act as filters to actively exclude information from consideration. Their goals and values—which may be consistent or contradictory—depend on suppositions that may or may not be true and may create perceptual screens that distort or ignore data that disagree with what they actually want. Even "facts" may be real, supposed, or rest on certain assumptions. People's environment also imposes limits. The information about the alternatives may be incomplete. The instruments used to collect data and assumed accurate and representative may not be valid. Risk and uncertainty also affect rationality.[25] Additionally, people may not have all the information, time, and processes they need to make truly "rational" decisions.

As a result, rational behavior in the real world is as much a matter of people's inner environments and processes as their outer environments on which they act and which, in turn, act upon them.[26] The key to organizational effectiveness, Simon concludes, is overcoming each member's "bounded rationality," adding, "The resemblance of decision making to logical reasoning is only metaphorical . . . ."[27]

## Satisficing, Optimizing, and Simplifying

Satisficing, optimizing, and simplifying are labels that Simon assigns to two broad approaches to rational behavior in situations where complexity and uncertainty make complete rationality impossible. Satisficing means seeking an acceptable, good enough—as compared to optimal—solution. A plan of action is satisfactory if it is practical and exceeds some minimally acceptable threshold. Satisficing also means working on problems one-at-a-time rather than simultaneously and using standard, tried-and-true solutions. This solution-seeking behavior reflects the participants' education, experience, and goals. For instance, a principal wants to increase parent involvement with the PTSA and sets a goal of 50 percent increase in attendance at meetings but a 25 percent increase will satisfice.

In contrast, *optimizing* (like the traditional decision-making model) involves considering all the potential options and their relevant factors, identifying and balancing the pros and cons of each, and selecting the alternative that maximizes the individual's preferred outcome. Unlike satisficing that simplifies the cognitive task, stops at a satisfactory (if not the best) option, and reduces time invested, optimizing requires time and mental capacity that most individuals don't have and keeps going until the "best" solution is identified. Although the formal distinctions between optimizing and satisficing may be difficult—and impolitic—to draw, the practical differences may be very large.

Lastly, the individual in the organization may *simplify* the decision process by following well-practiced routines and learned "rules of thumb" to avoid uncertainty and to reduce complexity. For instance, a school may develop a handbook of procedures, or "performance programs," to spell out how to handle recurring situations. These directions and rules identify the paths to take to a satisfactory option and which to ignore. By restricting the range of situations and options available, these procedures greatly reduce decision making's cognitive and informational requirements. For instance, when a parent comes to the school office's front desk, a predefined series of actions occur: all front office employees must keep an eye on the counter, promptly look up from whatever they are doing when a parent or stranger arrives, greet them politely, and ask, "How may I help you?"

Because so many factors influence decision making in organizations, one of the leaders' tasks is to design the work environment so individuals will use rationality to the extent that it is practical so they may meet the organization's goals.

Figure 9.2 depicts two rational approaches to decision making in organizations: the traditional and the bounded rationality models. Principals, like other organizational leaders, tend to practice the bounded rationality model of decision making.

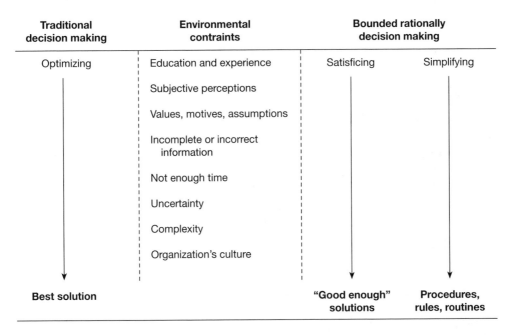

**FIGURE 9.2** Two Types of Rational Decision Making in Organizations
Source: Kaplan, L. S., & Owings, W. A., 2014.

**REFLECTIONS AND RELEVANCE 9.6**

## Limits on Rationality in Decision Making

Herbert Simon argues that people's reasoning is fallible, constrained by their cognitive skills, extent of knowledge, and sense of purpose. Instead of making rational decisions, they tend to satisfice and simplify.

Working in groups of four, each member will identify and describe a time in a work setting when they did—or saw someone else do something that—satisficed or simplified. When all the groups have finished, members will give examples of satisficing and simplifying in a school setting.

## WHEN AND HOW TO INCLUDE TEACHERS IN DECISION MAKING

Principals who want to involve teachers and others in decision making will need to decide which teachers, which decisions, and which situations are most appropriate for their participation. At the same time, teachers do not want to be involved in every decision. For certain issues, they trust—in fact, prefer—their principals make the choice. Teachers' preference for whether or not they want to give input to school-based decisions depends on which areas they see as inside—or outside—their zone of acceptance[28] (sometimes called the zone of indifference, as in, "It's not an issue I care about. Let the principal handle it."). Education professor Edwin Bridges as well as Wayne Hoy and John Tartar offer practical ideas to help principals in this arena.

### Zone of Indifference

Edwin Bridges, a Stanford University education professor, studied teachers' role in decision making and recognized that they have a zone of indifference[29] (or acceptance) within which they will accept an administrator's decision without question. He proposes two ideas about shared decision making to help principals decide when to involve teachers:[30]

1.  As the principal involves teachers in making decisions located in their zone of indifference (they will accept the principal making the decision), participation will be less effective.
2.  As the principal involves teachers in making decisions clearly located outside their zone of indifference (teachers expect to have their say in making the decision), participation will be more effective.

The challenge for the principal is determining which decisions fall inside and which fall outside the teachers' zone of indifference. Bridges suggests two tests to answer this question:

1. *The test of relevance*. Do teachers have a personal stake in the decision outcomes? For teachers, relevant decisions are those that largely deal with classroom matters, such as instructional practices, curriculum, assessment techniques for evaluating students' progress, and managing students. If the decision is relevant, teacher participation should be high. An example might be that math teachers will want a hand in writing a math curriculum because they will have to teach it, and they understand their students' learning needs.

2. *The test of expertise*. Do teachers have the expertise to make a useful contribution to the decision? For the teacher to be interested in participating in the decision, he or she must not only have some stake in the outcome but also be able to contribute to making a good decision. For example, a social studies teacher might be interested in helping to write the common core curriculum for reading, since students will be reading dense text in history, economics, and psychology as part of their English classes; but the social studies teachers might want to leave creating the rubric for grading the essays to the English teachers.

After deciding whether or not to involve teachers in making the decision—"Is the decision outside their zone of indifference?"; "Is the decision relevant to teachers' work?"; *and* "Do they have the expertise to make a meaningful contribution to an informed decision?"—the principal must then determine at what phase (or phases) in the decision-making process to include teachers and what their roles will be. The answers will set the amount of freedom that the teachers have to participate. Stages in the problem-solving process are:[31]

- *Problem-defining stage*. The principal spells out the objectives to be attained, gathers relevant information, identifies possible obstacles to reaching the goal, and decides whether—and how—to involve teachers.
- *Identify relevant action alternatives*. The principal generates a list of action alternatives either alone or with teacher input.
- *Predict the consequences related to each alternative considered*. The principal decides whether to involve teachers in predicting the outcomes of each alternative.
- *Choose from among the alternatives*. The principal weighs the alternatives and possible outcomes and selects the most appropriate course of action, or may involve teachers to recommend which alternative they prefer.

Bridges argues that if the decision to be made is clearly outside the teachers' zone of indifference, the principal should permit the teachers the maximum freedom to participate in all phases of the decision-making process as long as they don't make decisions beyond the principal's authority to carry out. In contrast, if the decision falls within the teachers' zone of indifference, the principal might ask teachers to suggest alternative options and their possible consequences but reserve the final choice of action for himself or herself. In either case, it is important to clearly express to the teachers the limits of their authority and the area of freedom in which they can operate—that is, what aspects or topics they can and cannot decide.

Bridges also describes how principals can facilitate the problem-solving group's functioning. Leaders can ensure that those with minority views have the opportunity to fully present their positions and give supporting facts. Leaders can also guide members to focus their attention on the same aspects of the problem at the same time as well as see the similarities and advantages of different arguments so they might move the group towards consensus.

## Model for Teacher Involvement

Extending Bridges' work, Wayne Hoy and John Tarter, professors at Ohio State University and the University of Alabama, respectively, build upon Bridges' ideas and develop a descriptive model to help principals decide when and how to involve teachers in decision making. In this model, as illustrated in Figure 9.3, when teachers (or other subordinates in the school) have both the expertise and a personal stake in the decision's outcome, the decision is outside their zone of acceptance and the principal should include them in the decision making. In contrast, if the teachers (or subordinates) have neither the expertise nor the personal stake, the decision is inside the zone of acceptance, and they do not need to be included in the decision making. In the event that teachers have the expertise but not the personal stake—or have a personal stake but not the expertise—Hoy and Tarter propose that involving them marginally in decision making will be marginally effective.[32]

Figure 9.3 depicts teachers' zone of acceptance in light of their expertise and personal stake in the decision's outcome and how the principal should—or should not—involve them in the decision making.

The issue of trust—when subordinates' personal goals conflict with organizational ones—also comes into play when deciding whether and to what degree to involve teachers in decision making. Principals need to be aware of subordinates' values and objectives and not put teachers into decision-making situations in which they do not have the organization's best interest in mind.

|  |  | **Do teachers have a personal stake?** | |
|  |  | **Yes** | **No** |
| **Do teachers have expertise?** | **Yes** | Outside zone of acceptance (Probably include) | Marginal with expertise (Occasionally include) |
|  | **No** | Marginal with relevance (Occasionally include) | Inside zone of acceptance (Definitely exclude) |

**FIGURE 9.3** Teachers' Zone of Acceptance and Involvement in Decision Making

Source: Adapted from Hoy, W. K., & Miskel, C. G. (2008). *Educational administration. Theory research, and practice*, 8th ed. Boston, MA: McGraw Hill, p. 365. Reprinted with permission.

Once the principal has decided to include teachers in decision making, Hoy and Tarter suggest five group decision-making formats to decide how much influence teachers will have in the final decision. These are as follows:[33]

- *Group consensus.* The principal involves teachers in the decision making and then the group decides. All members share equally as they generate and evaluate a decision, but the decision can only be made with total consensus.
- *Group majority.* The principal involves teachers in the decision making, and the group decides by majority rule.
- *Group advisory.* The principal invites the group members' opinions, discusses the implications of group suggestions, and then makes a decision that may or may not reflect the group members' wishes.
- *Individual advisory.* The principal consults individually with teachers who have expertise to inform the decision and then makes a decision that may or may not reflect the teachers' views.
- *Unilateral decisions.* The principal makes the decision without consulting or involving teachers in reaching a solution.

Finally, the principal can take on a variety of roles within the shared decision-making process. Within the group, the leader can serve as the *integrator* (who identifies the commonalities in varied positions to gain consensus); the *parliamentarian* (to promote open discussion that supports reflective group deliberation); the *educator* (who explains and discusses issues to help members better understand and accept a decision); the *solicitor* (who asks members for advice and information to improve decision quality); and the *director* (who makes unilateral decisions to achieve maximum efficiency).[34]

In addition, tactical and strategic concerns play roles in whether and how to involve teachers and others in decision making. Tactically, principals will act in each situation in ways that, ideally, solve the problem effectively and successfully so the schools meet their immediate goals within the time limits available. Strategically, however, principals may want to take the long view, identify those factors over which they have control, and develop their in-house leaders. They may also want input from parent and community leaders to better inform their discussions and decisions and to gain wider support for the eventual solution. Principals can provide knowledgeable, mature, and interested teachers with opportunities to learn more about key school improvement needs and gain real-world experiences in teamwork, group planning, and problem solving. In these ways, principals develop a leadership cadre of ready, able, willing, and responsible teacher leaders to help the school attain its goals and build school capacity.

Nevertheless, shared decision making is risky. Principals know that their superintendents and school boards hold them responsible for decisions coming from their schools, even if others make them. When the principal is always accountable, delegating decision making does not "pass the buck." At the same time, the amount of freedom that the principal gives to teachers, assistant principals, or community members to make decisions cannot be greater than the freedom the superintendents have given to the principal. The importance of the problem and the decision made—rather than the number of decisions allowed to teachers or other administrators—is a more accurate index of the principals' confidence in them and in the amount of freedom allowed for decision making.

Shared decision-making models are not a one-size-fits-all template, but they alert principals to the wide range of factors involved in the process. They offer useful guidelines for determining when and how principals, teachers, and community members might collaborate in decision making. The decision quality and the teachers' and the community's acceptance and commitment to put it into action are what determine the decision's effectiveness.

## REFLECTIONS AND RELEVANCE 9.7

## When to Include Teachers in Decision Making

Principals who want to include teachers (and others) in decision making will need to decide which teachers (and others), which decisions, and which situations are most appropriate to their involvement.

Working in groups of three, select a facilitator, a recorder, and a reporter. Using the concepts of Zone of Acceptance, Test of Relevance, and Test of Expertise, create three school-based scenarios: one that the principal *should* include teachers (and others), one in which the principal *should not* include teachers (and others), and one in which the principal might *marginally* include teachers (and others). After all groups have finished, each group will report their scenarios to the rest of the class by giving the relevant details, and allow the class to identify the appropriate decision about whether or not to include the teachers. The originating group will either confirm the class's decision or explain in their view, given the criteria in the situation, what the correct answer should be.

The class will discuss the usefulness—or not—of such a decision-making model.

## LEADERSHIP AND GROUPTHINK

*Groupthink*, a term coined by Yale research psychologist Irving L. Janis (1972), describes the worsening of a group's decision-making efficiency as a function of the leader's style, the level of group cohesiveness, and certain group norms.[35] For the past few decades, the groupthink phenomenon has been blamed for such decision-making calamities as the escalation of the Vietnam War, the 1986 NASA Challenger disaster, and the 2003 invasion of Iraq—in addition to flawed group problem solving in business and organizations. Lately, groupthink has been used to describe the cultural meme that "solitude is out of fashion" and only teamwork can generate creativity and achievement.[36] *Groupthink*, then, is a mode of thinking that people who are deeply immersed in a highly cohesive in-group use when their attempts to reach a unanimous agreement override their motivation to realistically appraise alternate courses of action.

Janis, with research professor Irving Mann, exhaustively studied the after-the-fact written records and interviews with top-level government and military persons involved in several high-pressure, momentous decisions that had potentially grave national consequences.[37] They speculated that making decisions about "hot," emotion-laden topics in stress-filled situations can lead to errors when scanning alternatives, distort meanings of warning messages, and produce selective inattention, forgetting, and rationalizing. A group that suffers from groupthink tends to reach a decision before they have realistically evaluated all available options, thus making a poor decision. Groupthink is not always bad, however; it can sometimes produce good decisions just as high-quality decision-making procedures can occasionally produce bad decisions.

## Conditions That Create Groupthink

Janis suggests that factors including leadership behavior, group cohesiveness, and the influence of group norms on group decision making interact in a unique way in any group making an urgent, crisis-filled decision. As a result, groupthink is likely to happen when the following conditions are present:[38]

- A decision-making group faces a crisis situation involving an outside threat.
- The group working together on a continuous basis forms a cohesive unit with esprit de corps. A moderate to high level of group cohesion—or the value that the group members hold for belonging to this group—is a necessary but not a sufficient condition for groupthink.
- The leader promotes a favored solution to a problem early in the discussion.
- The group lacks systematic procedures for generating and evaluating alternatives.
- The group shares similarities in social background and ideology and isolation from outside information.

Psychologically, Janis reasons that these conditions increase the group members' needs to reach a (premature) accord. By creating the shared perception of a secure social reality of respected individuals agreeing on a course of action, group members reduce their anxiety and uncertainty about their responsibility for making a very difficult decision in a high-stakes environment with the possibly of failure and catastrophic outcomes. Having a solution to which all these esteemed individuals agree reduces their stress and brings them the closure of "safety in numbers."

## Symptoms of Groupthink

Janis posits that the groupthink process generates identifiable symptoms that illustrate how group members try to reduce their angst associated with decision making and protect their self-esteems. Categorized into three types, the symptoms include:[39]

- *Type I symptoms: Overestimating the group.* Group members share the illusion that the group is invulnerable and the unquestioned belief that the group's cause is right.
- *Type II symptoms: Close-mindedness.* Group members collectively rationalize away information that does not fit with their preferred position and stereotype "enemies" as weak or stupid. As a result, they underestimate their opponents' capacities, do not discuss the pros and cons of alternate courses of action, and believe their own actions are inherently righteous and moral.
- *Type III symptoms: Pressure towards uniformity.* Members tend to censor their own misgivings about the group's position, adding to a shared illusion that the group unanimously accepts the majority position. Seeing itself as invulnerable to outside criticism, the group engages in excessive risk taking and non-reality thinking. It also puts direct pressure on any member who disagrees. Lastly, members may act as "mindguards" to protect the group from "problematic" or contradictory information that could undermine the members' confidence in the correctness of the group's stand.

When most or all of these groupthink behaviors are present, the group's decision-making process is likely to be seriously flawed.

## Defects of Groupthink

Janis argues that groupthink results in an array of outcomes that interfere with effective group decision making.[40] First, the group limits its discussions to only a few options, avoiding information that might generate new data for a more informed and effective decision. Second, after the group initially selects an option, members tend to ignore new information about its risks and drawbacks. At the same time, members avoid information about rejected alternatives' benefits; they fail to fully assess the "cons" and "pros." Third, members make little effort to invite experts to bring more precise and accurate information to inform their decision. Fourth, members neglect to consider what may go wrong and do not develop contingency plans.

At the end of this sequence, a poor-quality decision is more likely than in a more open, complete, and thoughtful decision-making process.

## Preventing Groupthink

Lastly, Janis suggests several approaches to prevent—or at least minimize—groupthink's dysfunctional outcomes.[41] Principals might use these suggestions:

- The group leader should encourage all group members to express their doubts and objections to any proposed solutions.
- The group leader should initially adopt an impartial posture rather than begin the group's discussions by stating his or her preferred solution.
- The group leader should encourage group members to discuss the group's deliberations with trusted associates who are not group members and report their responses back to the group.

- Outside experts should be invited to meetings and encouraged to challenge members' views with logical arguments, different perspectives, and relevant data.
- When a competitor is involved, the group should dedicate time to assessing the warning signs from the competitor and alternative scenarios of the competitor's intentions.
- When weighing alternatives, the group should occasionally separate into subgroups to meet separately.
- The group should hold a "second chance" meeting after reaching a preliminary consensus on a preferred alternative.
- The group should consider using dissonance-inducing group processes, such as asking and answering "Devil's advocate"-type questions.

The bottom line for principals: neither too much conflict nor too much harmony is useful in school improvement. Although collegiality is desirable, real conflict of ideas and information should not be avoided or suppressed in exchange for superficial teacher collegiality. Suppressing or disguising honest and constructive dissent in schools, especially during decision making, is likely to lead to reduced creativity, less innovation, and fewer positive student outcomes—and is likely to lead to a larger conflict in the long run. Groupthink is one of the highly undesirable outcomes of extreme consensus-seeking behaviors and should be avoided.

## REFLECTIONS AND RELEVANCE 9.8

### Groupthink Experiences

Groupthink is the worsening of a group's decision-making effectiveness as a function of the leader's style, the group's cohesiveness, and certain group norms.

Have you ever been part of a group that engaged in groupthink? Individually, reflect on a time you were a member of a problem-solving group in your work setting. Consider the leader's actions, the level of group cohesiveness, and the group's norms as identified in the section above. What conditions in your group worked to produce—*or prevent*—groupthink? Which symptoms of groupthink did—*or did not*—occur? What leadership actions fostered—*or prevented*—groupthink?

After considering your experience and deciding whether or not it engaged in groupthink, report your reflections to the class. Describe the group, its purpose (the nature of the problem you were to solve), and its members. Explain the conditions, symptoms, and behaviors that let you know whether your group was—*or clearly wasn't*—engaging in groupthink.

# RESEARCH ON LEADERSHIP AND GROUP DECISION MAKING

Conflict in schools can be beneficial. Research suggests that people in environments that contain some conflict, as compared with those in more consensual milieus, tend to ask others more questions and show a greater desire to understand their opponents' viewpoints.[42] They are also more able to remember opposing arguments, identify the reasoning their opponents used in the past, and predict their reasoning in the future. In addition, conflict in schools can promote and nurture individual creativity, develop respect for independent attitudes and thinking, improve the quality of group decisions, foster intragroup cooperation, and lead to better outcomes.[43] All these factors enable group members to pool the most reliable information to boost mutual understanding, collaboratively develop and support a vision and mission, support making high-quality decisions, and introduce innovative and sustainable approaches to benefit the school.[44]

How much conflict is helpful remains the issue, however. Despite the methodological matters that complicate its research,[45] the stress under which group decision making occurs can either increase or decrease performance quality, narrow attention to the more prominent task features, and generate more simplified information processing.[46] Within certain limits, groups seem able to adapt to higher levels of stress,[47] but when the stress increases to a certain level, group performance eventually deteriorates.[48] The impact of stress on group performance appears to vary with the specific circumstances (time, pressure, and the group members' perceptions about the initial task difficulty).[49] Groups working under stress display a stronger desire for uniformity of options and preferences. They are motivated to apply pressure to group members to accept the favored position, to reject members who disagree with that position, and to reach closure with a definite, unambiguous solution.[50]

As a result, a "closing of the group mind" appears to result from the stressful context in which group members make decisions, confirming that groupthink is present. Similarly, empirical studies on group decision making from the 1990s finds that groups are less-than-optimal users of information and frequently ignore data that is not widely shared among the members.[51] Notably, groupthink's main contribution to research is its evidence that descriptors usually viewed as positive aspects of groups—cohesiveness and collective effectiveness—do not always lead to improved group outcomes.[52]

Research on shared decision making in schools tends to be case studies occurring in specific settings. They confirm much of the best practices noted above. Factors found to strengthen shared decision making include members' confidence in themselves and in one another; essential resources provided at critical points (especially meeting time for face-to-face talks); the adoption of democratic rules and procedures (especially those that give the freedom for members to set agenda items, initiate discussions, and set attendance expectations); early, tangible accomplishments; and the principal's support (encouraging active participation, providing essential resources, providing training in group decision making, and providing information needed to make informed decisions about the issues under discussion).[53] In contrast, factors that limited group decision-making processes included inadequate time, lack of enthusiasm for involving teachers in decision making, teachers' lack of experience in debating issues in an open forum (difficulty presenting reasoned arguments without personal attacks), and the school community's distrust of the school district administration.[54]

## CONCLUSION

Conflict is endemic to wherever and whenever people live or work together. And problem solving in organizations is rarely purely rational. Problems in the real world do not appear in neat sequence or one at a time. Many organizational problems are poorly defined and not well understood at the time decisions must be made. School leaders typically face ambiguous circumstances in which several events are occurring at the same time, goals and values may conflict, many "right answers" are possible, and the time for making the decision always seems to be less than what is optimal. In short, schools are far too complex for simple lists of leadership "dos" and "don'ts" to guide conflict management or problem solving. Nonetheless, developing an informed awareness of the dynamics involved and ways to address them can be helpful.

Successful principals are insightful and flexible. They have accurate self-awareness, a sharp understanding of the individuals and groups with whom they are working and their readiness for growth. Successful principals have a deep understanding of their school, district, and the larger social environments in which they operate. Effective leaders maintain a high rate of accurately assessing the forces that determine the most appropriate behavior at any given time and are able to act accordingly. They recognize that teachers often respond to situational, personal, and psychological pressures that may not lead to the most effective problem solving. But wise principals act appropriately in light of these realities. Learning how to become such a leader takes time; understanding the dynamics of human motivation, conflict, and problem solving; practice; feedback; and reflection. And, as Dean Tjosvold, professor and international management expert concluded, "Well-managed conflict is an investment in the future."[55]

## NOTES

1. Zimmerman, P., as cited in Harvard University (2012, March 29–31). *Decision making for leaders. A synthesis of ideas from the Harvard University advanced leadership initiative think tank 2012* (p. 6). Cambridge, MA: Harvard University. Retrieved from: http://advancedleadership.harvard.edu/Portals/115252/docs/Decision_Making_ThinkTank_Final.pdf
2. See, for example, Deutsch, M. (1990). Sixty years of conflict. *The International Journal of Conflict Management, I,* 237–263; Lewis, C. T. (1995). Conflict and its management. *Journal of Management, 21* (3), 515–558; Pondy, L. R. (1967). Organizational conflict: Concepts and models. *Administrative Science Quarterly, I,* 296–320.
3. Wall, J. A., & Callister, R. R. (1995). Conflict and its management. *Journal of Management, 21* (3), 515–558.
4. Deutsch, M. (1973). *The resolution of conflict: Constructive and destructive processes* (p. 10). New Haven, CT: Yale University Press.
5. Rahim, M. A. (2002). Towards a theory of managing organizational conflict. *International Journal of Conflict Management, 13* (3), 206–235 (p. 207).
6. Darwin, C. (1959). *On the origin of species.* London, UK: John Murray.

7. See, for example, Fayol, H. (1949). General and industrial management. (C. Stors, trans. from French). London, UK: Pitman [originally published 1916]; Gulick, L. H., & Urwick, L. (1937). (Eds.). *Papers on the science of administration.* New York: Institute of Public Administration, Columbia University; Taylor, F. W. (1911). *The principles of scientific management.* New York, NY: Harper and Row; Weber, M. (1947). *The theory of social and economic organization* (A. M. Hendeson, & T. Persons, trans. from German). New York, NY: Oxford University Press.

8. Lewis, C. T. (1998). Conflict management as the essence of leadership. *Journal of Leadership and Organizational Studies, 4* (3), 20–31.

9. Wrigley, W. as cited in Tjosvold, D. (1997). Conflict within interdependence: Its value for productivity and individuality. In C. deDreu, & E. van deVliert (Eds.), *Using conflict in organizations* (p. 23). Thousand Oaks, CA: Sage.

10. See, for example, Cosier, R. A., & Dalton, D. R. (1990). Positive effects of conflict: A field assessment. *International Journal of Conflict Management, 1* (1), 81–92; Janis, I. J. (1972). *Victims of groupthink.* Boston, MA: Houghton Mifflin; Wilson, J. A., & Jerrell, S. L. (1981). Conflict: Malignant, beneficial, or benign? In J. A. Wilson (Ed.), *New directions for higher education: Management science applications in academic administration* (pp. 105–123). San Francisco, CA: Jossey-Bass; Rahim, M. A., Garrett, J. E., & Buntzman, G. F. (1992). Ethics of managing interpersonal conflict in organizations. *Journal of Business Ethics, 11* (5/6), 423–432; Rahm (2001), op. cit. (p. 7).

11. Walls & Callister (1995), op. cit.

12. Rahim, M. A., & Bonoma, T. V. (1979). Managing organizational conflict: A model for diagnosis and intervention. *Psychological Reports, 44* (3, Pt. 2), 1323–1344.

13. Rahm, Garrett, & Buntzman (1992), op. cit.

14. Thomas, K. W., & Kilmann, R. H. (1975). The social desirability variable in organizational research. An alternative explanation for reported findings. *Academy of Management Journal, 18* (4), 741–752; Kilmann, R. H., & Thomas, K. W. (1977, July). Developing a forced-choice measure of conflict-handling behavior: The "mode" instrument. *Educational and Psychological Measurement, 37* (2), 309–325; MindTools (n.d.). *Conflict resolution. Resolving conflict rationally and effectively.* London, UK: MindTools. Retrieved from: http://www.mindtools.com/pages/article/newLDR_81.htm

15. Deutsch, M. (1990). Sixty years of conflict. *The International Journal of Conflict Management, 1,* 237–263.

16. Roehl, J., & Cook, R. (1989). Issues in mediation: Rhetoric and reality revisited. *Journal of Social Issues, 41,* 161–178; McEwen, C. A., & Maiman, R. J. (1984). Mediation in small claims court: Achieving compliance through consent. *Law & Society Review, 18* (1), 1–39; McEwen, C. A., & Maiman, R. J. (1989). Mediation in small claims court: Consensual processes and outcomes. In K. Kressel and D. Pruitt (Eds.), *Mediation research: The processes and effectiveness of third-party intervention* (pp. 53–67). San Francisco, CA: Jossey-Bass; Wall, J. A., Jr., & Callister, R. R. (1995). Conflict and its management. *Journal of Management, 21* (3), 515–558.

17. For example, see Kelly, J., & Gigy, I. (1989). Divorce mediation: Characteristics of clients and outcomes (pp. 263–283). In K. Kressell, & D. G. Pruitt (Eds.), *Mediation research.* San Francisco, CA: Jossey-Bass; Pearson, J., & Thoennes, N. (1989). Divorce mediation: Reflections on a decade of research (pp. 9–30). In K. Kressell, & D. G. Priuitt (Eds.), *Mediation research.* San Francisco, CA: Jossey-Bass; Roehl & Cook (1989), op. cit.

18. Deutsch, M., Coleman, P. T., & Marcus, E. C. (2006). *The handbook of conflict resolution* (pp. 23–33). New York, NY: Wiley.

19. Deutsch, M. (1973). *The resolution of conflict: Constructive and destructive processes* (p. 9). New Haven, CT: Yale University Press.

20. Voltaire, F.M.A. (1746 [1973]). *Dicitonnaire philosophique.* Paris: Garnier.

21. Drucker, P. F. (2008). *Classic Drucker. Essential wisdom of Peter Drucker from the pages of Harvard Business Review.* Boston, MA: Harvard Business Review Publishing.

22. Simon, H. A. (1959). Theories of decision making in economics and behavioral science. *The American Economic Review, 49* (3), 253–283; Simon, H. A. (1965). Administrative decision making. *Public Administration Review, 25* (1), 31–37; Simon, H. A. (1993). Decision making: Rational, nonrational, and irrational. *Educational Administration Quarterly, 29* (3), 392–411.

23. Simon, H. A. (1986). Rationality in psychology and economics. *The Journal of Business, 59* (4), S209–S224.

24. Simon, H. A. (1985). Human nature in politics: The dialogue of psychology with political science. *The American Political Science Review, 79* (2), 293–304; Simon, H. A. (1976). *Administrative behavior: A study of decision-making processes in administrative organizations,* 3rd ed. New York, NY: Free Press.

25. Simon, H. A. (1956). Rational choice and the structure of the environment. *Psychological Review, 63* (2), 129–138.

26. Simon, H. A. (2000). Bounded rationality in social science: Today and tomorrow. *Mind and Society, 1* (1), 25–39.

27. Simon, H. A. (1959). Theories of decision making in economics and behavioral science. *The American Economic Review, 49* (3), 273.

28. Herbert Simon originated the term "zone of acceptance" as an alternate, more positive-sounding phrase to "zone of indifference." See: Simon, H. A. (1947). *Administrative Behavior.* New York, NY: MacMillan Publishing.

29. Chester Barnard originated the concept of "zone of indifference." See: Barnard, C. (1938). *The functions of the executive* (p. 167). Cambridge, MA: Harvard University Press.

30. Bridges, E. M. (1967). A model for shared decision making in the school principalship. *Educational Administration Quarterly, 3* (1), 49–61.

31. Bridges (1967), ibid.

32. Hoy, W. K., & Tarter, C. J. (1995). *Administrators solving the problems of practice: Decision making concepts, cases, and consequences,* 1st ed. Boston, MA: Allyn and Bacon.

33. Hoy, W. K., & Tarter, C. J. (2004). *Administrators solving the problems of practice: Decision-making concepts, cases and consequences,* 2nd ed. Boston, MA: Allyn and Bacon.

34. Hoy, W. K., & Miskel, C. G. (2008). *Educational administration. Theory, research, and practice* (8th ed.) (p. 368). Boston, MA: McGraw-Hill.

35. Janis, I. L. (1972). *Victims of groupthink.* Boston, MA: Houghton Mifflin; Janis, I. L. (1982). *Victims of groupthink* (2nd ed.). Boston, MA: Houghton Mifflin.

36. Cain, S. (2012, January 13). The rise of the new groupthink. *The New York Times Sunday Review.* The Opinion Pages. Retrieved from: http://www.nytimes.com/2012/01/15/opinion/sunday/the-rise-of-the-new-groupthink.html?pagewanted=all&_r=0

37. Janis and Mann studied historical records and interviews related to the 1960s Cuban Bay of Pigs invasion and the 1960s to 1970s escalation of the Vietnam War.

38. Janis, I. L. (1972). *Groupthink.* Boston, MA: Houghton Mifflin.

39. Ahlfinger, N. R., & Esser, J. K. (2001). Testing the groupthink model: Effects of promotional leadership and conformity predisposition. *Social Behavior and Personality. An International Journal, 29* (1), 31–41.

40. Janis (1972), op. cit.; Janis (1982), op cit.; Janis, I. L. (1989). *Crucial decisions: Leadership in policymaking and crisis management.* New York, NY: Free Press.

41. Janis (1972), op. cit.; Janis (1982), op. cit.; Janis (1989), ibid.

42. Tjosvold, D. (1997). Conflict within interdependence: Its value for productivity and individuality. In C. De Dreu, & E. Van De Vliert (Eds.), *Using conflict in organizations* (pp. 23–37). Thousand Oaks, CA: Sage.

43. De Dreu, C. (1997). Productive conflict: The importance of conflict management and conflict issue. In C. De Dreu, & E. Van De Vliert (Eds.), *Using conflict in organizations* (pp. 9–22). Thousand Oaks, CA: Sage.

44. Di Lima, J. A. (2001). Forgetting about friendship: Using conflict in teacher communities as a catalyst for school change. *Journal of Educational Change, 2* (2), 97–122.

45. Kerr, N. V., & Tindale, R. S. (2004). Group performance and decision making. *Annual Review of Psychology, 55* (1), 623–655. For a more complete discussion of the research on group decision making, see Kerr & Tindale.

46. Kaplan, M. F., Wanshula, L. T., & Zanna, M. P. (1993). Time pressure and information integration in social judgment: The effect of need for structure. In O. Svenson, & J. Maule (Eds.), *Time pressure and stress in human judgment and decision making* (pp. 255–267). New York, NY: Plenum; Karau, S. J., & Kelly, J. R. (1992). The effects of time scarcity and time abundance on group performance quality and interaction process. *Journal of Experimental Social Psychology, 28* (6), 542–571; Brown, T. M., & Miller, C. E. (2000). Communication networks in task-performing groups: Effects of task complexity, time pressure, and interpersonal dominance. *Small Group Research, 31* (2), 131–157; DeGrada, E., Kruglanski, A. W., Mannetti, L., & Pierro, A. (1999). Motivated cognition and group interaction: Need for closure affects the contents and processes of collective negotiations. *Journal of Experimental Social Psychology, 35* (4), 346–365.

47. Brown & Miller (2000), op. cit.; Hollenbeck, J. R., Sego, D. J., Ilgen, D. R., Major, D. A., Dehlund, J., & Phillips, J. (1997). Team judgment-making accuracy under difficult conditions: Construct validation of potential manipulations using the TIDE 2 simulation. In T. Brannick, E. Salas, & C. Prince (Eds.), *Team performance assessment and measurement: Theory, methods, and applications* (pp. 111–136). Mahwah, NJ: Erlbaum; Volpe, C. E., Cannon-Bowers, J. A., Salas, E., & Spector, P. E. (1996). The impact of cross-training on team functioning: An empirical investigation. *Human Factors, 38* (1), 152–172.

48. Adelman, L., Miller, S. L., Hendeson, D., & Schloelles, M. (2003). Using Brunswikian theory and a longitudinal design to study how hierarchical teams adapt to increasing levels of time pressure. *Acta Psychologica, 112* (2), 181–206; Entin, E. E., & Serfaty, D. (1999). Adaptive team coordination. *Human Factors, 41* (2), 312–325; Urban, J. M., Weaver, J. L., Bowers, C. A., & Rhodenizer, L. (1996). Effects of workload and structure on team processes and performance: Implications for complex team decision making. *Human Factors, 38* (2), 300–310.

49. Kerr & Tindall. (2004), op. cit.

50. Kruglanski, A. W., Shah, J. Y., Pierro, A., Mannetti, L., Livil, S., & Kosic, A. (2002). *The closing of the "group mind" and the emergence of group-centrism.* Paper presented at the Society for Experimental Social Psychology, Columbus, OH; Kruglanski, A. W., Webster, D. M., & Klem, A. (1993). Motivated resistance and openness to persuasion in the presence or absence of prior information. *Journal of Personality and Social Psychology, 65* (5), 861–876.

51. Stasser, G., & Titus, W. (1985). Pooling of unshared information in group decision making: Biased information sampling during discussion. *Journal of Personality and Social Psychology, 48* (6), 1467–1478.

52. Mullen, B., Anthony, T., Salas, E., & Driskell, J. W. (1994). Group cohesiveness and quality of decision making. *Small Group Research, 25* (2), 189–204; Whyte, G. (1998). Recasting Janis's groupthink model: The key role of collective efficacy in decision fiascoes. *Organizational Behavior: Human Decision Process, 73* (2/3), 185–209.

53. Weiss, C. H., Camboine, J., & Wyeth, A. (1992). Trouble in paradise: Teacher conflicts and shared decision making. *Educational Administration Quarterly, 28* (3), 350–367; Johnson, M. J., & Pajares, F. (1996). When shared decision making works: A 3-year longitudinal study. *American Educational Research Journal, 33* (3), 599–627.

54. Johnson & Pajares (1996), op. cit.

55. Tjosvold, D. (1997). Conflict within interdependence: Its value for productivity and individuality. In C. deDreu, & E. van deVliert (Eds.), *Using conflict in organizations* (pp. 23–37; p. 23). Thousand Oaks, CA: Sage.

# 10

# Data-driven Decision Making

In God we trust, all others bring data.
The most important things can't be measured.
—William Edwards Deming

---

## LEARNING OBJECTIVES

10.1 Discuss the factors that make students' achievement data "high stakes" for students, teachers, and principals.

10.2 Describe how principals and teachers can use varied formative, interim, and summative assessments to improve teaching and learning.

10.3 Explain the ethical and psychometric considerations of using multiple, relevant, and valid data sources in making high-stakes decisions.

10.4 Identify the benefits and limitations of using student growth model data to recognize learning gains even when students don't reach proficiency on standardized tests.

10.5 Describe the process of how principals can use their school's recent improvement data to assess their academic progress, identify current needs, and make school improvement plans.

10.6 Summarize and provide a rationale for the types of data needed for making informed and workable school improvement decisions.

10.7 Discuss several ethical issues and cautions involved in using data for decision making appropriately and effectively.

10.8 Compare and contrast the different qualities, types, and amounts of data needed for educators' professional growth decisions and for accountability decisions.

---

**2015 ISLLC STANDARDS: 1, 2, 3, 4, 5, 6, 7, 8, 9, 10, 11**

## INTRODUCTION

Most people want evidence that our schools are performing well. Student achievement has become *the* benchmark for judging school effectiveness, and schools have developed assessment and accountability systems to monitor student progress. As a result, data-driven decision making has become a hallmark of contemporary schooling. In fact, one of the principals' five key responsibilities includes managing people, data, and processes.[1]

Accordingly, contemporary principals and teachers are awash in data. *Data* are the facts and statistics collected for reference or analysis and assumed to be unbiased and objective. Data are central to today's schools. Schools collect and use data to monitor and evaluate student progress, identify goals, assess instructional effectiveness, and advance organizational learning. Student test scores guide school improvement strategies, determine school rankings, and factor in school accreditation. With the move to improved teacher and principal evaluations, student achievement data are now being used as a key aspect in deciding whether a specific educator is deemed successful.

Communities expect their principals to understand what data are available to improve teaching and learning, what these data mean, and how to use them appropriately in ways that improve outcomes for students and teachers. Managing and making sense of data from multiple sources in varied situations is an enormous leadership challenge.[2] Most principals are confident with people and ideas but perhaps feel less assured about working with "numbers." The large amount of information that principals routinely handle and use wisely may seem overwhelming.

What are the important data that principals need and use, and how do principals and teachers make sense of them? How can principals and teachers use these data appropriately to improve teaching and learning? Which data are suitable to use to increase teachers' and principals' professional growth and accountability—and which are not? Only as future principals become more data literate—and develop their administrators' and teachers' capacities for understanding and using data to make informed decisions—can they become more effective leaders.

## DATA THAT PRINCIPALS AND TEACHERS NEED

When the appropriate data are collected and used correctly as the basis for reasoning, discussing, and decision making, they can help educators answer questions such as these:

- How well are our (my) students learning?
- Is our school (my classroom) succeeding or failing—as compared to those across the school, state, nation, or world?
- What practices work best to help students learn—and how do we know?
- Am I an effective educator?

Schools run on data. Data are used to decide student placement into courses and academic programs (using students' measured skill levels, past grades, personal histories, classroom observations, pretests, and self-reports). Data are used for diagnosing students' learning needs (including specialized assessments to determine student's persistent misconceptions, identify and analyze missing skills, and identify specific problems). Student achievement data also are used to measure student attainment, see how well students are meeting the school's curricular and instructional goals, develop school improvement plans to close achievement gaps, and increasingly, as part of teacher and principal evaluations

Frequently, schools use their data for *high-stakes purposes*—outcomes with important consequences for students, teachers, principals, and schools—including public accountability. When significant consequences, such as rewards (promotions for students, performance bonuses or tenure for teachers, professional advancement for principals, positive school reviews in the local newspapers) or punishments (failure to be promoted to the next grade for students, poor performance evaluations for teachers, job termination for principals) become attached to testing as a means to incentivize teacher effectiveness and student achievement, testing becomes "high stakes."[3] Standardized tests themselves are not high- or low-stakes; the "stakes" refer to the purposes and decisions for which the test results will be used.

Because student achievement data are used for both everyday and high-stakes ends, principals need to clearly understand their purposes, strengths, and limitations if they are to make sense of their data and use them wisely to inform decisions.

## DATA FOR DETERMINING STUDENT ATTAINMENT

If principals are to improve their decisions by using relevant data, where should they begin to organize and make sense of them all? Which data are relevant to the decisions at hand? How much weight should any particular data have in shaping educators' choices? How much and what types of data are needed in order to make fair and accurate high-stakes decisions about students or educators? How can principals work with teachers to make sense of their data and use the findings to improve teaching and learning?

The answers to all these questions begin with student assessments. Principals and teachers routinely use a variety of formative, interim, and summative assessments to help determine the extent to which students are meeting the academic goals set in curriculum standards. Increasingly, teachers are also using formative and interim data to apprise their day-to-day teaching in ways that boost student learning. At the same time, states are using growth models to acknowledge students' learning gains even when they don't reach "proficiency" or mastery on objective measures. And value-added student achievement data are finding their way into teachers' and principals' evaluations. Principals and teachers benefit when they have a clear understanding of when and how they can—or *shouldn't*—use these data in decision making.

## FORMATIVE ASSESSMENTS

*Formative assessments* are assessments *for* learning. They include observations, questioning, discussions, exit/admit slips, think-pair-share, individual white boards, peer and self-assessments, and learning/response logs. Usually ungraded, they allow teachers to gauge student learning during the lesson instead of waiting until it ends. Embedded within the learning activities, formative assessments link directly to the current instructional unit and actively engage students in their own learning process. As learners begin to understand and apply their new knowledge and skills, teachers' formative assessments provide both with continuous and specific classroom feedback about the pupils' progress, their areas of mastery, and their knowledge gaps as they relate to curriculum goals and state standards. Teachers can use this information to gauge student progress, immediately modify instruction, and create appropriate work for individual students or groups of learners.

Assessing formatively in this manner advances—not simply monitors—student learning and achievement. Research studies affirm that:

- Feedback increases learning when teachers give students on-going information and guidance about how to improve their classwork and tests.[4]
- Students benefit more from feedback than from grades.[5]
- Consistent, formative practices are connected to significant achievement gains and a reduced achievement gap, especially for the lowest achievers.[6]
- Formative assessments motivate students in positive ways that reinforce successful learning.[7]

Formative assessments' limitations occur from their misuse.[8] Unfamiliar with their use as a tool to strengthen their teaching, many teachers mistakenly see formative assessment as time away from delivering their lesson rather than as an integral and essential part of it. If they rush the lesson to make time for the assessment, they turn an opportunity—to appraise each student's cognitive growth, generate and give constructive feedback, and adjust their lesson—into a shortcoming. Likewise, if students misunderstand formative assessment's lack of formal grade as meaning they are unimportant and do not perform at their best, teachers may misread the feedback from students and assume that re-teaching or providing extra assistance may be needed when in reality, the class should move forward.

Principals will want to assess their own faculty's familiarity and facility with formative assessment. These findings can support providing relevant and on-going professional development activities to help teachers learn about, further refine, and extend their instructional repertoire in this area to support student learning.

## SUMMATIVE ASSESSMENTS

*Summative assessments* are assessments *of* learning. These are the final tasks at a unit's or course's end used to evaluate students' performance against a defined set of content standards and make concluding judgments about their mastery. Historically, standardized tests for summative purposes have been used as measures of how students compare with each other (norm-referenced) or how much of a particular curriculum they have learned (criterion referenced). Summative assessments are intended to provide reliable total score and performance-level information for each student and groups of students across a wide range of content within a minimum of testing time, at a low cost, under standardized conditions. They are typically used to shape curriculum and instruction and as part of accountability programs or to inform policy.

To use summative data effectively, educators must know what cognitive content and skills their specific tests actually sample—and compare these to the types of cognitive demands and skills being taught and learned in their classrooms. The taught, learned, and tested curriculum must closely align or else the resulting data cannot logically or ethically be used to give a fair or accurate picture of the teaching, learning, and attainment occurring in that school.

For example, the Common Core State Standards (initially adopted in 46 states, the District of Columbia, and Department of Defense schools) aim at "fewer, higher, and deeper" standards in English language arts (ELA) and mathematics aligned with national and international standards.[9] To determine how well students are mastering these new, more rigorous, state-written curricula aligned with these standards, nationally developed assessments based on these standards will begin widespread use in 2014–2015. Whereas items on current state achievement tests mainly measure recall and recognition, the new Common Core assessments will include many more tasks that require students to think critically, reason from evidence, and solve complex problems. An analysis of the content specifications for these assessments finds that higher-level skills make up 68 percent of the ELA and 70 percent of mathematics targets.[10] Nonetheless, even these ambitious assessments do not measure all the skills identified in the Common Core standards, including extended writing and research, oral communications, using technology for investigating, modeling solutions to complex problems, and multimedia presentations.[11]

Ethically and psychometrically, principals must recognize that students and teachers can only be held accountable for the curricula they are teaching and students are learning. Ensuring a close match between curriculum, teaching, learning, and testing is essential if the data are to be used for high-stakes decisions—such as using achievement test results to assign students' report card grades, to justify or deny promotion, or as the basis for school improvement or teacher evaluation.

Assessment scholars agree. Although school accountability currently relies on annual appraisals of student achievement to make judgments about school quality, using such status measures for these purposes has been the focus of continuing criticism.[12] While student test results may be able to provided data for making judgments about students' achievement levels for a given year, by themselves, they are not appropriate for making high-stakes decisions about individual students or teachers' educational effectiveness. Likewise, summative achievement scores are blind to the reality that low-scoring students may be making real and measurable achievement gains from working with highly effective teachers in less-than-successful schools. As a result, summative test scores are not the only data points needed to make fair and accurate judgments about student learning and teacher effectiveness. Principals need to ensure that several meaningful measures of student achievement contribute to any decision with an important consequence for an individual student or teacher.

This means that whenever the stakes are high, test scores alone should not be the sole data influencing a decision. Decisions with high-stakes consequences attached require multiple pieces of relevant and valid information from an array of sources. In addition to standardized exams, end-of-the-year teacher-made tests as well as students' projects and portfolios illustrate students' achievement and progress. Students' capstone performances at science fairs, music recitals, or art also provide summative data that show how well a student has mastered a knowledge or skill.

To use standardized achievement test scores properly, principals also need to recognize standardized tests' limitations. The scores are generated in comparison to a norm group that may or may not resemble the students taking the test; this may make the results less valid and reliable for the current students although the data can still help teachers with long range planning. Next, end-of-year summative assessments are not designed to provide instructionally useful information. Students' learning gaps or errors cannot be remedied quickly. By the time the test results reach the school, students are gone for the summer and probably will have different teachers when they return in the fall. If the knowledge and skill gaps are major, the students may begin the next sequenced course academically behind classmates.

In addition, what a standardized test measures in three hours cannot compare in high-level thinking and cognitive rigor to student-designed and conducted science experiments, thoughtfully researched papers accompanied by oral presentations, or creative applications of learning in new, poorly defined situations. These work samples offer visible, in-depth, and extended students' products and performances that are hall-marks of high-quality education. Lastly, their high-stakes uses for school accountability often influence educators to narrow the curriculum to the tested subjects and "test prep"; these actions artificially inflate test scores rather than increase learning.

Nonetheless, standardized tests will always be an important part of teachers' assessment repertoire as a means to determine if they are teaching the standard course of study in ways that support many students' learning.[13] Given their weaknesses, however, many schools have begun using interim assessments to provide data to inform instruction during the school year.

## INTERIM ASSESSMENTS

Scheduled between formative and summative assessments, interim assessments are given several times a year (usually between two and six times) at course midpoints. Typically administered district-wide by individual teachers, they provide an objective, snapshot measure of student growth and progress to date towards a specific set of academic achievement goals throughout the school year. Interim data help everyone know which students are on track to meet the established goals—and which ones need additional help. Interim test results—such as teacher- or district-made end-of-chapter tests—can meaningfully be aggregated to the teacher, school, or district levels.

Interim assessments represent a hybrid that may be used for wide-ranging purposes. They may be formative if used to apprise teachers of a student's progress to date, motivate students with feedback about their learning, or to make instructional adjustments. They may be summative if used to assign students a grade, make evaluative decisions about the curricular or instructional choices, or to take actions to improve the program and later teaching. They may be diagnostic if used to identify and remediate gaps in student learning. Additionally, interim assessments may be used to predict a student's ability to perform well on a large-scale summative assessment. Depending on the particular test and the instructional strategies systematically employed in different classrooms, interim results may also help determine whether one pedagogical approach is more effective in teaching the material than another to a particular student group.[14]

Limitations exist with interim assessments, too. Since they are not directly connected to daily lessons, they tend to interrupt the flow of classroom instruction and learning. Other disadvantages include their inability to provide teachers or students with immediate feedback; even tests easily scored need at least one class period before any insights can be implemented. And since they do not "count" for promotion or accountability purposes, students may not take them seriously; results may not reflect their true academic progress. Since the interim assessment's quality (validity and reliability) is only as good as the items included, they are only useful to the extent that they accurately reflect the school's curricular goals.

Figure 10.1 illustrates the three levels of assessment typically found in schools. The triangle indicates that formative assessments are most often used and cover the narrowest curricular focus and the shortest cycle (often several times within a single class period). In contrast, summative assessments are administered the least often and have the largest scope and cycle. Interim assessments lie between these two other types on all dimensions.

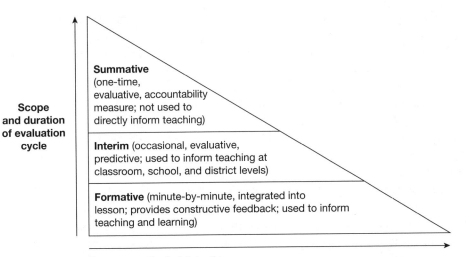

**FIGURE 10.1** Three Levels of Assessment Data

Source: Adapted from Perie, M., Marion, S., & Gong, B. (2009). Moving toward a comprehensive assessment system: A framework for considering interim assessments. *Educational Measurement: Issues and Practice, 28* (3), 5–13, p. 7. © 2009 National Council on Measurement in Education. Reprinted with permission.

## GROWTH MODELS

Teachers and principals know that students' lack of proficiency on formal assessments does not mean that they are not learning and growing academically. Pupils start the school year with different levels of understanding and readiness. For instance, a student who begins the school year reading four years below grade level may actually gain three school years' worth of learning—truly notable gains—and still not score "proficient" on an end-of-year test. Their growth and progress, as evidenced in available assessment data apart from the test score, may show real and measurable learning gains. And their improvement deserves to be recognized. Again, educators need multiple data sources before drawing a conclusion about an individual student's learning status.

As a result, states increasingly are using *growth models*—a variety of mathematical or statistical methods used to connect student scores over two or more points in time that supports interpretations about students, their classrooms, their educators, or their schools[15]—as a measure of student achievement for accountability purposes. *Growth* refers to an increase, expansion, or change over time. A growth model captures a student's score changes over more than one occasion, taking multiple snapshots of student achievement and focuses on the change itself.

The most accessible and intuitive growth model—a *gain-based model*—generates a *gain score*, the simple difference between a student's test scores from two points in time. The size of the gain indicates how much the student has changed, whereas the sign, plus or minus, indicates if the gain was positive (signifying improvement) or negative (signaling decline). Using gain scores requires understanding the underlying test score scale in order to interpret it meaningfully. For example, a gain score of 25 means different things on a test score scale of 75 than one of 350. The *student growth percentile model* that compares a student's current score with those of students with similar score histories, or "academic peers," is also becoming popular because it is explainable and uses visually appealing graphics. The student growth percentile model supports growth description and growth prediction.[16]

Some states uses growth model data to give information about individual student progress to parents, teachers, and administrators. States using growth models for No Child Left Behind (NCLB) compliance must be peer-reviewed and approved by the U.S. Department of Education. Similarly, most states are—or plan to—use student growth scores as part of teacher evaluations or as a measure of teacher effectiveness.[17]

Several reasons explain growth models' importance. First, they align well conceptually with the basic educational goal of student learning and are more effective than end-of-year achievement tests in measuring changes in students' learning over time. Second, because growth models connect scores from multiple assessments, they can provide more detailed information than a single score at one point in time about how well student learning is meeting academic goals. Third, unlike summative assessments, growth models focus on individual students' educational development rather than concentrate on the proportion of students meeting proficiency in a given school or comparing the school as a whole to other schools. In this way, growth models can reflect individual students' educational development, especially those who do not meet the proficiency level in a single academic year but who do show improvement over their earlier academic performance.[18]

Accurately interpreting growth model data is a major limitation for educators and parents. Mathematical or statistical in nature, they are more complicated and less intuitive to understand than are simple summative achievement scores. Complicating the matter further, since many different growth models are in use, accurately understanding one type does not necessarily generalize to other types. Next, growth models have difficulty providing accurate student growth information when students have missing data or when the model covers student achievement across curricula where course assumptions and concepts differ. Then too, growth models have difficulty capturing student growth because not all students develop academically in the same ways.[19] Lastly, because administrators and teachers can "game" and manipulate growth scores (such as by having less experienced teachers work with early tested grades to make impressive gains appear in later grades and misattribute improvements to more effective teaching by later teachers), they are not intended for use in a high-stakes accountability environment.[20]

Nonetheless, growth scores may help educators explain students' achievement test results under any new testing regimen. With the transition to the Common Core State Standards and their assessments, for example, the number of students rated "proficient" can be expected to drop for at least the first few years as educators implement the new curricula, adjust their teaching to the revised expectations, and administer the related assessments. Because academic growth data makes students' academic progress visible, they can help teachers and principals identify instructional needs and provide a more complete and accurate view of student learning despite the reality that "proficiency" numbers may drop by 20 or 30 percent.[21]

## DATA FOR CLOSING ACHIEVEMENT GAPS AND SCHOOL IMPROVEMENT PLANNING

Educational assessment is more than a culminating event: it is a collection of processes.[22] Gathering student achievement data is one step. Helping the school's leadership team select the most appropriate data and make sense of them to inform decision making is another.

Student achievement data do not exist in a vacuum. Rather, they are connected to other aspects of schooling: teaching effectiveness, curricular scope and rigor, content standards, assessments, the resources available for teaching and learning, other student-generated products or performances, the school climate, and the supports given students to reach the desired mastery levels. Likewise, student achievement is linked to student demographics (especially the percentage of students living in poverty and its related factors that undermine school learning and achievement),[23] attendance, children's prior academic and experiential knowledge that build vocabulary, comprehension, and cognitive capacity.[24]

An accountability system for student attainment or for principal and teacher evaluation that relies on standardized test scores alone is incomplete without information such as that listed above, and would be like a physician assessing health based on body temperature or blood pressure but ignoring age, weight, height, blood tests, or other medical indicators essential to a competent diagnosis.

## GATHER RELEVANT PROFESSIONAL LITERATURE

Likewise, using data intelligently requires gaining a frame of reference that will help select the most appropriate information, make it meaningful, and increase the likelihood that the school improvement strategies will be successful. To this end, principals and teachers will want to avail themselves of the advances in research knowledge for evidence about the indicators and predictors of student achievement and wellbeing before collecting and analyzing data.[25]

For example, a school that wants to improve student achievement would benefit from the research identifying the key indicators of potential academic failure: poor grades in core subjects, low attendance (especially unexcused absences), failure to be promoted, and disengagement in the classroom, including behavioral problems that prevent them from paying attention.[26] Then, using credible research sources,[27] the leadership team will have to ask and answer: "What instructional practices and policies are most likely to produce the desired student learning outcomes?"; "How do we know these practices and policies will lead to the results we want to accomplish?"; "How good or reliable is that evidence?"; "Were the students in the studies similar to our own?" With satisfactory answers in hand, this research information can guide the school improvement team to the appropriate data and their relative importance in effectively addressing this problem as well as to the points where well-designed interventions might be useful.

Despite the emphasis on data collection, review, meaning making, analysis, and problem solving, this book's goal is not to teach future principals how to analyze data or conduct school improvement. They will develop these insights and skills later in their graduate programs and refine them in their school leadership roles. Rather, the intent is to help future principals build the habits of mind that keep them aware of the key factors, related data, and processes they need to use as they lead their schools to improved student outcomes.

## USING DATA TO ASSESS WHERE YOU ARE

To manage data, principals must take on a researcher's perspective and systematically investigate their own school site. Working alone at first, the principal will bring together the applicable data (whole school and disaggregated by student subgroups), think through what they means for student achievement and teaching effectiveness, and identify what resources may be available to infuse new or enhanced approaches to improving student achievement in classrooms. Only after this initial step are principals ready to share these data with the school's leadership team.

Reviewing data from the school's own recent improvement history is the logical place for principals to begin. Start the data analysis by answering the following questions:

- How well did we as a school do last year?
- What were our improvement objectives?
- How do our improvement goals align with district and state standards?
- How well do our improvement goals align with local needs and interests?
- How well did we meet them? How do we know?
- What evidence can we use to assess the impact of our efforts?
- What unexpected problems or barriers appeared?
- What lessons did we learn? Knowing this, what would we do differently?[28]

Once the principal has identified, gathered, and studied the data to help answer these questions, the principal brings together the school's leadership team (consisting of assistant principals, lead teachers, department chairpersons, team leaders, and others) to examine the data (whole school and disaggregated) together, discern and discuss their meaning, and identify key improvement challenges.

Walking through the data piece-by-piece, the principal will:

- Help the administrators and teachers focus on the key points.
- Identify several data sources that appear to confirm the same meaning.
- Invite school leaders' accurate interpretations and evidence for what these data may indicate and to identify what other data may be available to confirm or refute these findings.
- Gain the team's insights into the data's meaning that contribute to a fuller and more accurate understanding.
- Develop a consensus for what the data suggest and how the school might best respond.

In reviewing these data, most schools identify an instructional problem or an achievement gap. Typically, certain groups of students are achieving noticeably better than others. Reviewing the previous year's data will provide school leaders with evidence of current needs. For example, the school's present achievement data may show the following:

- 93 percent of all students scored "proficient" on the state reading test.
- 96 percent of white students scored "proficient" on the state reading test.
- 91 percent of African American students scored "proficient" on the state reading test.
- 73 percent of Latino students scored "proficient" on the state reading test.

- 63 percent of students with special needs scored "proficient" on the state reading test.
- 45 percent of free- and reduce-price lunch students scored "proficient" on the state reading test.
- 33 percent of English language learners scored "proficient" on the state reading test.

These data suggest that many students are generally succeeding at a high level in reading, but an achievement gap exists between certain student groups and the school as a whole. In the example above, African American and white students have the highest reading achievement based on state results. Latino students, students with special needs, and students eligible for free- and reduced-price lunches are achieving much more poorly. English language learners fare the worst. Clearly, more needs to be done if all students are to perform at grade level (or above) in reading. More detailed and varied data are needed, however, for the school to identify reasonable and data-justified interventions.

## GATHERING RELEVANT STUDENT DATA

Working with the leadership team, the principal will gather a wider array of relevant data—the potential evidence—needed to more visibly and correctly diagnose the existing problems and identify possible solutions. Since educational problems are complex, leadership teams need a variety of data beyond test scores to help complete the picture and point to possible interventions. Accordingly, relevant data will include other information about student achievement, students' demographics, class placements, attendance, and discipline. Facts about the school climate and culture may also merit consideration.

Fortunately, the contemporary focus on school accountability, technology, and making data-informed decisions has made finding and gathering these data easier. Most school districts and schools have databases and computer spreadsheets that amass varieties of student data that schools can easily access. State achievement (summative) test results, district-required benchmark (interim) test results, student course grades, course enrollments, attendance, discipline records, and demographics often are the most easily retrieved.

It is always important to remember, however, that data points are information about children; and school improvement focuses on helping them. But not all students can be helped to the same degree at the same time. For example, concentrating on the *"bubble students"*—those whose scores put them "on the bubble" between passing and failing—may be a practical way to deal with limited time and resources. However this approach ignores those students whose mastery is far from proficient and who really need the extra attention and help if they are to have opportunities to earn a livable wage and support a modest quality of life. Deciding which students to address first—those who can more easily improve the school's achievement profile or those who need it the most—is an ethical one. In addition, these data must be used appropriately: only for educational purposes and in ways that safeguard the individual students' privacy.[29]

## DISAGGREGATING STUDENT ACHIEVEMENT DATA

According to the U.S. Census Bureau projections, children of color will represent a majority of children by 2018. By 2030, the majority of the U.S. labor force will be people of color.[30] Ensuring that minority students gain the high-level knowledge and skills essential for 21st-Century economic survival is an essential challenge facing today's educators. For this reason, it is especially vital that schools disaggregate student achievement data by subgroups—typically minority children, children receiving free- and reduced-price lunch, children receiving special education services, and English language learners—to ensure that members of every subgroup are making at least one year's worth of academic progress in a school year. While overall student scores give a global view, disaggregating the data (as shown above) provides a clearer picture of who are— or aren't—learning and performing well.

Our earlier example disaggregates student achievement scores by race and ethnicity, socioeconomic status, special education participant, and primary language. But since the percentages need a context if they are to be truly meaningful, school improvement teams will also want to determine the proportion of the total student population that each subgroup represents. For example, English language learners have the most ground to cover on their way to reading proficiency, but if they represent only 5 percent of the student body, the intervention for them might be different in scale and scope than an intervention for a group that represented 50 percent or more of the students in the school.

## CONDUCTING A ROOT CAUSE ANALYSIS

Principals and their school improvement teams who want to design the most effective ways to address an identified need will look intensively at the *root causes*—the initiating or underlying factors of the students' achievement—before identifying a solution. It is a natural tendency for leaders to want to act decisively and move quickly to problem solving. School districts expect written improvement plans by a set date, while states and communities impose their own time pressures to "fix it now."

Nonetheless, identifying a problem area—such as low reading achievement scores for certain students—does not identify the problem's causes or suggest avenues to remedy them. Performance gaps, low graduation rates, or high discipline referrals for certain student groups are *symptoms* of underlying conditions; they are not *causes*. Unless educators find these problems' primary causes, they will only be treating the symptoms, "putting lipstick on the pig," so to speak. This would be single-loop learning in action (see Chapter 5). The situation may improve temporarily because of the special attention—or "halo effect"—directed to it, but the problem will continue. The persistence of achievement gaps suggests that educators have not yet addressed the most important underlying factors. Root-cause analysis is an essential step in the improvement planning process.

Figure 10.2 depicts why searching for root causes of students' failure is so essential. Symptoms appear on the surface, warning us that a problem exists. The fact that only

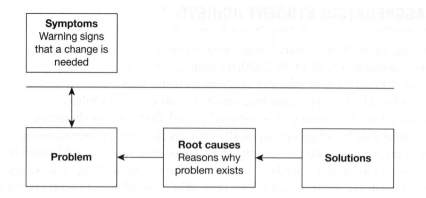

**FIGURE 10.2** Solutions Should Address Causes, not Symptoms

Source: Adapted from Bauer, S. C., & Brazer, S. D. (2012). *Using research to lead school improvement. Turning evidence into action* (p. 152). Thousand Oaks, CA: Sage. Reprinted with permission of Sage Publications.

45 percent of fifth graders receiving free- and reduced-price lunches score "proficient" on the state reading test is the symptom of an underlying problem. This score says nothing, however, about *why* these students are not succeeding. Faculty may have as many different "solutions" in mind as they have members: vocabulary building, after-school tutorials, more heterogeneous class groupings, a new reading series, and so on. But without looking at the problem more deeply—with more and different data as well as a review of the relevant professional literature and local best practices—the decision making is not informed and is likely to miss its mark.

To better understand root causes of student failure and select interventions that may remedy these, a serious review of the professional literature and successful local practices is the next step. In all likelihood, the students' achievement difficulties have many causes, some obvious and others not. If the goal is to address the causes rather than treat the symptoms, reading about how other schools of similar size, location, and student demographics successfully addressed similar issues will help school improvement teams more fully understand the causes and be able to select the evidence-based solutions that will fit their student population. This approach is more promising to problem solving than jumping to the "favorite" ("I used this before"), "favored" ("The superintendent likes this one"), or easily available ("We have a new reading series software") solution. The best practice to adopt depends on matching what the educators know about the cause of the performance gaps with what they know about which strategies work under what conditions with which types of students, teachers, and resources.

## USING MULTIPLE DATA SOURCES

Finding the underlying causes for students' academic failures often requires a look at these specific students in more detail. Teachers will want to review their failing students' data to see what patterns emerge within and across classrooms that point to root causes and possible interventions. Multiple data sources will be necessary, including the following:

- *Student achievement data.* Review past report cards, interim and benchmark assessments, and standardized tests to determine if this low achievement reflects a pattern of performance or a recent change. Do these students achieve well by teachers' grades but perform poorly on standardized tests? If yes, what accounts for the discrepancy? Are the taught and tested curriculum closely aligned? Is the degree of rigor—depth and scope—the same for both? Is the curriculum rigor the same in these students' courses as in courses in which most students perform well? Do students' teacher-assigned grades reflect academics only or do they also include "points for good behavior"? Does a difference in teacher expertise and experience exist between classes that achieve highly and those that don't? What do these data suggest might be an underlying cause (or causes)?

- *Students' attendance records.* Is poor attendance an issue with many of the failing students? A recent study of chronic absenteeism in school (missing 10 percent or more—18 days a year—of the school year for any reason) finds that poor attendance decreases learning and graduation rates while it increases achievement gaps and dropout rates.[31] Are failing students missing much class time—for instance, five or more days a marking period for whatever reasons—so that they cannot keep up academically? Is this true for this year and for previous years as well? What factors are keeping these children home? Are certain school factors pushing them out of school? What avenues does the school have to prevent or remedy these out-of-school absences? Being in school leads to succeeding in school.

- *Student discipline records.* How many days in a grading period is the student removed from regular classroom instruction? Do these failing students represent a certain student demographic by race, ethnicity, SES, gender, or gender identity? A 2014 series of reports concludes that schools across the country are assigning African American male students disproportionately harsher discipline penalties than white students for the same offenses. The report also documents discipline disparities for girls of color, students with disabilities, Latino students, and students who identify with the LGBT community. In addition, out-of-school suspensions are most often used for conduct that is not a threat to safety. These unnecessary suspensions can lead to lower academic achievement, higher dropout rates, and increased likelihood that students eventually will be arrested and jailed.[32] This report confirms earlier findings.[33] In turn, the U.S. Departments of Education and Justice have issued guidelines urging school leaders to rethink their zero-tolerance policies that have led to excessively high rates of suspensions and expulsions.[34] Reviewing your school's student suspension and expulsion data for failing groups of students, surveying teachers' views about their students' ability to succeed academically, identifying what teachers view as "threats to safety," determining how they perceive mutual respect, and reviewing their recent opportunities for professional learning and practice on these issues may point towards possible solutions.

- *Teachers and counselors.* Teachers and school counselors who work with students every day—often over several years—frequently have information and insights into their students' motivation to learn as well as the school and outside factors that interfere with their learning. Their insights may be idiosyncratic or they may point to root causes and possible interventions.

- *Surveys and focus groups.* Qualitative data from student, teacher, and parent surveys can give educators clues to root causes of student failure. What do students have to say about the school climate and culture that affects their school attendance, motivation, and performance? Do students complain about "boring" teachers or teachers who become easily frustrated when students ask questions or don't learn instantly? Does a particular group complain of bullying peers or disinterested educators? Well-written surveys can offer insights into student engagement, parent involvement, teacher attitudes and beliefs, and community perceptions—any of which may point to possible root causes of student failure as well as possible solutions. Similarly, conversations with students, parents, or teachers in focus groups can also identify trouble spots that need to be addressed if all students are to learn to high levels. In fact, research suggests that school climate can affect students' success in school:

  — A positive supportive, and culturally conscious school climate in high-risk urban environments can significantly shape urban students' degree of academic success.[35]

  — Positive school climate perceptions are protective factors for boys and give high-risk students a supportive learning milieu as well as prevent antisocial behaviors.[36]

  — Positive interpersonal relationships and optimal learning opportunities for students in all demographic environments can increase achievement levels and reduce maladaptive behaviors.[37]

  — Providing a positive and supportive situation for students is important for a smooth transition to a new school.[38]

- *Student demographic data.* Poverty affects students' learning and achievement and must be considered as a data source. Research has shown that growing up in chronic poverty contributes directly to stress that can affect children's health, brain development, and social and emotional wellbeing.[39] In 2013, at least one of every three African American, Latino, and Native American children lived in a home with an income below the poverty line.[40] To get a sense for how poverty affects students' learning and achievement, ask: Are issues of poor health, housing instability, frequent absences, or other circumstances a factor in many students' failure? It's ironic that getting a good education is children's only way to end their poverty, yet poverty and its related factors seriously undermine a child's ability to gain an education. Although the school cannot control poverty, principals can accept responsibility for enacting and supporting certain, research-supported ethical practices that may ameliorate its effects on children. Principals can ensure that their school and its personnel do not unconsciously practice racism by "tracking"[41] minority or low-achieving students into less rigorous courses, disproportionately assigning weak or novice teachers to low-achieving classrooms,[42] applying student discipline in unfair, nonobjective, or disproportionate ways,[43] hiring or keeping teachers who do not expect all their students to learn to high standards or who do not know how to develop mutually respectful relationships with all students,[44] or permitting their school climate to ignore or condone any type of student harassment.[45] In addition, principals can provide the professional development occasions to help teachers see low-income and minority students as having cultural assets and resources that can help them succeed in school.[46] The issue of how schools can effectively address poverty issues is discussed more fully elsewhere.[47] Finally, principals can develop alliances with community groups and businesses to offer local supports to help students and their families remove obstacles that interfere with the regular school attendance.[48] Principals can share relevant data with a wide range of school and community groups to help them understand the school's instructional needs and to actively support the school improvement efforts at the grass roots.

## MAKING THE DATA MEANINGFUL

To be meaningful, data must be understood and interpreted correctly. Collecting information from varied sources (such as state testing, teacher-made tests, district benchmarks) and of different types (including testing, attendance and discipline data, students' SES, student perceptions, and teachers' and counselors' information) helps the leadership team more fully understand patterns and trends within their school with greater clarity. Educators' challenge is to have these varied data make sense in ways that help accurately diagnose a school-wide learning need and point the way towards workable interventions.

*Triangulation*—the process of using data from multiple sources[49]—improves the trustworthiness of school improvement decisions. Any single piece of data has limited value. To assure it is not a random occurrence, it needs to be verified by other credible data. Therefore, when a fact is repeatedly confirmed through a range of data, they reinforce the validity of conclusions. The time invested in gathering and considering enough relevant and varied data to develop a complete understanding of the issue at hand is a wise way to begin planning and implementing solutions that will work (that is, address the root cause and not the symptom).

Talking knowledgably about student achievement data takes practice. At weekly or bi-weekly meetings within professional learning communities, working with colleagues who teach the same subject with the same assessments to similar students, teachers can learn how to read and make sense of their students' achievement data. They can triangulate data when they compare teacher-assigned grades to standardized achievement test results with rubric-scored student work samples to understand how their students are achieving in a variety of formats and interpret what it means for student progress, mastery, and teaching effectiveness. Similarly, they can review the achievement findings from their week's formative and interim assessments to focus on each student's learning progress, current status, and needs as they relate to state standards.

Thinking like detectives, teachers can reflect on what their own students' data may be telling them. Looking at the student errors, did many students miss similar questions? Perhaps the teacher did not teach this section effectively. Did the high achieving students answer certain questions correctly but the lower achieving students did not? If so, the teacher likely taught the relevant content but perhaps did not give the slower learners enough timely feedback and relevant practice so they could master the content or skill. Did the high-achieving students also make errors on this content or skill? If yes, perhaps the teacher did not instruct the material well—or cover it at all.

After making sense of the data and agreeing on their meaning, teachers can then plan for temporary regrouping for interventions in which all students—from advanced, to on-grade, to below-grade level—can expand their learning. As teachers become more comfortable reviewing student achievement data, they learn how to use test information: placing less emphasis on the actual numbers, more on where students are in their learning, and planning lessons accordingly.

## TWO CAUTIONS IN USING DATA

Because of the widespread use of student data for making decisions, words of caution are necessary. Educators who rely too heavily on achievement test data tend to narrow what they teach to what is tested, and the more consequential the testing outcomes for students or educators, the less valid the measure may be.

As the old saying goes, "What gets measured gets done." If educators test only basic skills—such as reading comprehension or arithmetic, that is what teachers will instruct students, and that is what students will learn. A recent study finds that standardized achievement tests that measure basic knowledge and skills influence teachers to spend more time and effort instructing students on basic skills—with considerably less attention directed toward helping students develop creativity and imagination.[50] This constricted focus on teaching only the tested content also means less time in the school day for students to make sense and personal meaning for what they are learning (factors essential to remembering and using the content and skills to build mastery), less time applying what they are learning to new situations (in ways that promote transfer of knowledge), and fewer occasions for students and teachers to develop strong, caring working relationships (that require talking about more than incorrect answers). Likewise, it means less time in the school day for non-tested subjects—social studies, sciences, the arts, physical education, foreign languages—which provide the information and perspectives needed to become a more fully aware person in a complex, global environment.

In addition, the data that educators use for high-stakes outcomes may not mean what teachers think they mean. In the 1970s, Donald Campbell, then the American Psychological Association president, warned about the perils of measuring effectiveness with a single, highly important indicator. "The more any quantitative social indicator is used for social decision-making," he observed, "the more subject it will be to

**REFLECTION AND RELEVANCE 10.1**

# Gathering and Analyzing Data for School Improvement

Educational assessment is a process, and student achievement data are connected to other aspects of schooling.

You and a partner are school improvement consultants. Using the steps and questions included in the section above, collect and analyze data in your own schools and bring your review and recommendations to this class in two weeks. (Professors can adjust the due date as needed).

1. *Identify an actual school improvement need in your school.* Check your school's improvement plan for a major focus—such as increasing student achievement in reading comprehension or math, reducing absenteeism, or improving student discipline.

2. *Read relevant professional literature.* Find three articles in the focus area from two different *credible* professional journals or sources. Identify the key points relevant to your focus area and cite their sources (name the journal and say why it is credible).

3. *Use data from your school to assess where you are.* Review the school's recent achievement history in your focus area and ask/answer the questions in the text.

4. *Gather relevant student achievement data for a root cause analysis.* Ask the school counselor to identify three students in the same grade who fail to meet achievement (*and* attendance or discipline) expectations. Ask if the students had any outside factors that the counselor suspects might have interfered with learning. Then, *using the student records in accordance with school regulations and student privacy rights*, find data from multiple sources to document their achievement, attendance, discipline, and demographic (SES) data for the past two or three years and identify possible factors contributing to their failure to achieve. Write down key data for each student in a format that permits comparisons, withholding student names of other privacy information.

5. *Triangulate the data to make it more meaningful.* Express how the data fit together to give a picture of these three students. What common patterns appear between student achievement and other factors? How long has this pattern been present? Relate your findings to the professional literature readings about interventions that worked successfully with students like these to improve their school learning and achievement.

6. *Make recommendations.* Prepare a statement of your recommended school intervention, including the intervention, the necessary professional development needed for teachers or others to enact the intervention, and how you will assess the intervention's effectiveness. Present your student factor comparisons, literature reviews, and school improvement recommendations to the class.

corruption pressures and the more apt it will be to distort and corrupt the social processes it is intended to monitor."[51] According to Campbell's Law, the higher the stakes attached to any measure, the less valid that measure becomes. For instance, even as the high-stakes NCLB achievement scores increased in many states, the states' low-stakes National Assessment of Education Progress (NAEP) scores remained flat,[52] leaving observers to wonder whether NCLB's learning gains were real.[53] This means that while high-stakes outcomes may cause test scores on a particular assessment to rise, the scores may not reflect true learning gains. Instead, they may simply reveal how well teachers improved students' test-taking skills or restricted the instruction to the content assessed on the test.

Thus, more and better tests do not guarantee better teaching or better learning. Rather, using multiple measures of performance to inform important decisions about students, teachers, principals, or programs is one way to prevent Campbell's Law from distorting judgments with suspect data.[54]

## DATA FOR TEACHER AND PRINCIPAL EVALUATIONS

Improving educators' performance has become a central focus of education reform. Research over the past 40 years shows that both instructional leadership and teacher quality are related to student achievement. Therefore, principals' and teachers' competence is essential to students' success and to society's wellbeing. Because student learning is a school's most important outcome, it makes sense to include student achievement data as part of teacher and principal evaluations as long as it is done fairly, accurately, and efficiently.

*Evaluation* is the process of defining, obtaining, providing, and applying descriptive and judgmental information about the merit and worth of some object's goal. Data for principal and teacher evaluation can be formative, benefitting the individuals' need for improvement and professional growth. And/or they can also be summative, meeting the organization's need for accountability and decisions about tenure, promotion, continued employment, or dismissal.

The data's low- or high-stakes uses influence how objective, standardized, and externally defensible the information must be. Generally speaking, data for teacher and principal professional growth can be richly descriptive narratives or phrases that highlight areas of strength, sources of difficulty, and avenues for upgrading knowledge, skills, and practices. In contrast, data for teachers' and principals' accountability—essentially, whether or not they keep their jobs—must be reasonably objective, standardized, valid, reliable, generalizable, include multiple data sources, and able to withstand credible challenge in a court of law. In addition, all principals in a school district must use the same formative and summative evaluation practices and protocols with their teachers—and likewise for central office administrators with principals—if results are to be perceived as fair, accurate, and believable.

In addition, the higher the stakes for the outcome, the more types of data are needed. Summative decisions require much mutually reinforcing data if the decisions are to be accurate, comprehensive, and credible. These data should be gathered throughout the year by regularly scheduled and unscheduled visits as well as by means other than formal observations. Qualitative performance data can come from first-hand anecdotes and informal performance observations, questioning (interviews with students, parents, teachers, peers, and self-assessments), and artifact analysis (from performance logs, service records, school improvement data, lesson plans, and portfolios). Quantitative data from student achievement or outcomes from leadership decisions will likely play a role. These varied sources give the evaluator and evaluatee a more complete, realistic, detailed, objective, valid, reliable, and defendable picture of actual job performance and provide a foundation upon which to develop realistic improvement plans.

Moreover, evaluation methods intended to support decision making about individuals must also consider the context in which the person performance occurs. Evaluating a principal requires superintendents to consider data such as the school's grade levels and total student enrollment, student and teacher demographic information, several years' worth of disaggregated student achievement and school climate statistics (including the attendance and dropout rates, discipline referrals, percentage of diplomas conferred) as well as school improvement plans if they are to make fair, credible, and defensible judgments about the principal's effectiveness.

## Teacher Evaluation

Teacher performance evaluations in 35 states and the District of Columbia now require student achievement data to be a "significant" or the "most significant" factor in the appraisals, up from 30 states in 2011.[55] States and districts are adopting new evaluation systems that combine evidence of student performance, direct measures of teaching, student input, and other relevant information. These reforms remain the subject of debate, however.

Although differing on how they define teacher effectiveness, policy makers and administrators generally agree that performance evaluation includes the degree to which teachers advance students' academic growth, encourage students' social, artistic, and physical development, and support the school's organization and functioning.[56] Teacher effectiveness measures include direct measures of teaching, incorporating classroom observations using locally adopted rubrics, value-added estimates based on student growth, and other information such as student and parent surveys of learning conditions.

## Classroom Observations

Principals' observations of teachers in their classrooms are a mainstay of teacher evaluation, but the traditional rating checklists have not always been useful or effective. Today, we have data affirming that effective teachers teach differently than ineffective teachers. Principals benefit when they engage in professional development on how to use research-affirmed *rubrics*—scoring tools that describe characteristics of practice at different levels of performance (or locally adopted versions of them)—to help look for specific teacher behaviors known to increase student achievement. Table 10.1 offers a sample of a teaching rubric.

A variety of studies from locations including Cincinnati, New York City, and Chicago have confirmed that teachers who tend to generate higher student achievement growth are actually teaching differently than teachers associated with lower student achievement growth. Intentionally observed teaching practices are connected with student achievement gains in real-world classrooms.[57] Trained evaluators, using an elaborate set of research-affirmed metrics (such as the Charlotte Danielson's Framework for Teaching, FFT, or the Robert Pianta and associates' Classroom Assessment Scoring System, CLASS)[58] that describe the behavioral practices, skills, and characteristics that effective teachers use, observed teachers in their classrooms and rated their pedagogy according to the rubrics. Investigators found that teachers with higher classroom observation rubric scores had students who learned more: the difference in student learning gains on state math tests between teachers in the top and bottom 24 percent of teachers' observation scores amounted to approximately 2.7 months of schooling.[59] The same studies found that students can perceive clear differences between more and less effective teachers.[60]

Table 10.1 illustrates how a teaching behavior rubric indicates levels of classroom effectiveness. These clear descriptors of effective teaching behavior with point values in two areas—for communicating learning objectives and expectations for students' performance—allow teachers to identify their own skills and plan for their own professional growth. At the same time, they give teachers and principals a common vocabulary and set of clear behavioral expectations for what effective teaching looks like.

**TABLE 10.1** Levels of Effectiveness for Teacher Observations

| Exemplary (4) | Proficient (3) | Needs Improvement (2) | Unsatisfactory (1) |
|---|---|---|---|
| All learning objectives and state content standards are explicitly communicated. | Most learning objectives and state content standards are communicated. | Some learning objectives and state content standards are communicated. | Few learning objectives and state content standards are communicated. |
| Learning objectives are: <br><br> a) consistently connected to what students have previously learned <br> b) known from life experiences, and integrated with other disciplines. | Learning objectives are connected to what students have previously learned. | Learning objectives are occasionally connected to what students have previously learned. | Learning objectives are rarely connected to what students have previously learned. |
| Expectations for student performance are clear, demanding, and high. | Expectations for student performance are clear. | Expectations for student performance are inconsistent. | Expectations for student performance are vague. |

Source: Adapted from Jason Culbertson, Putting the value in teacher education, *Phi Delta Kappan*, November 2012, p. 15. Reprinted with permission of Phi Delta Kappa International, www.pdkintl.org. All rights reserved.

Using teacher performance rubrics for classroom observations has its downside: they are highly labor intensive. Teachers and administrators must first learn and become fluent in the common language of behavioral expectations for effective teaching. Next, they must learn and practice using the rubrics accurately and to ensure interrater reliability. Additionally, conducting detailed observations and writing observation reports for 10 to 20 teachers (or more) per principal or assistant principal each year greatly increases administrators' workloads and the accompanying stress. No matter how beneficial to teacher growth, student achievement, and meaningful evaluations, schools and school districts must be realistic about the participants' capacities—time, knowledge, skills, and shared values—needed to thoughtfully engage with these evaluation procedures and tools.[61]

Yet, when teachers believe that evaluations of their performance are intended to help improve instruction, identify areas for professional growth, and determine whether they need additional support, most teachers view evaluation favorably. And when principals and other school administrators receive relevant and on-going training in observing teachers, using rubrics to guide and rate observations, and have occasions to develop interrater reliability in using rubrics, most agree that they are adequately prepared to provide feedback to teachers and to deal with challenging observation situations.[62]

## Value-added Models

Increasingly, value-added models (VAM) are providing data for teacher evaluations as a means of determining teacher effectiveness. *Value-added models* are statistical procedures that examine changes in student test scores over time by controlling for prior scores and certain student characteristics known to be related to achievement. VAMs estimate the contribution that each individual teacher (or school) adds to their students' learning during a given period of time. When linked to individual teachers, value-added scores are sometimes promoted as measuring teacher effectiveness. This conclusion, however, assumes that a particular test is a valid and reliable measure of student learning, that the teacher alone influences the score, that the score is independent from the growth of classmates and other aspects of the classroom environment. These assumptions are not justified.

In fact, researchers have found value-added scores as indicators of teacher effectiveness to be highly problematic. Briefly, several reasons explain why.[63]

- *Value-added models of teacher effectiveness are highly unstable.* Teachers' measured effectiveness ratings differ substantially from *class to class*, from *year to year*, from *test to test*, and from one statistical model to the next. For example, using data from five separate school districts, one study found that of the teachers who scored in the bottom 20 percent of rankings in one year, only 20 to 30 percent had similar ratings in the next year, while 25 to 45 percent of these teachers moved to scoring well above average. Meanwhile, of teachers scoring at the top of the distribution one year, only about 25 percent stayed at the same rating while most moved to lower ratings.[64]

- *Teachers' value-added ratings are significantly affected by differences in the students assigned to them.* As statistical models, VAMs require that students be assigned to teachers randomly; but they aren't.[65] The models cannot adjust fully for the fact that some teachers have a disproportionate number of students with greater challenges, and their scores on traditional tests may not reflect their actual learning. As a result, teachers are advantaged or disadvantaged based on the students they teach. For example, the same teacher who had won praise for her teaching excellence learned in 2012 that she was labeled the "worst teacher" in New York City. Later it was revealed that her ratings had failed to account for the fact that most of her students were English language learners.[66]

- *Value-added ratings cannot separate the many influences on student progress.* It is impossible to fully separate the influences of students' other teachers or school conditions on their reported learning. For instance, a student's essay-writing skills learned through a history teacher may be credited to the English teacher, and the math content and skills gained in physics class may be attributed to the math teacher. Factors such as home (parental education, SES), school (class sizes, curriculum materials, available instructional time, specialists and tutors, and learning resources), individual student needs and abilities (as well as health and attendance), and a range of other influences (such as peer culture and achievement, prior teachers and schooling, differential loss of learning during the summer, and specific tests which emphasize certain kinds of learning and not others) all affect student learning gains. These factors may matter more than the individual teacher in explaining changes in achievement scores.

- *Value-added scores are not available for every teacher.* Only educators who teach courses in which students take annual standardized tests can have VAM scores generated for them. This means that social studies, sciences, physical education, foreign languages, and the arts, for instance, may not receive value-added effectiveness ratings. In addition, if a teacher does not have enough years of teaching the tested course, insufficient data are available to generate an accurate value-added score or rating. This creates an unfair situation in which certain courses and teachers can receive effectiveness ratings—with whatever outcomes are attached—while their colleagues in the same schools teaching the same students cannot.

Using value-added data for teacher evaluation has both proponents and naysayers. Supporters assert that despite its flaws, data from VAM models are an improvement over the traditional teacher evaluation practices in which 99 percent of teachers are rated "satisfactory," 94 percent of all teachers are rate "good" or "great," and principals fail to respond to the real variations in teacher effectiveness.[67] Likewise, VAM models are cost effective. Proponents also argue that "perfect should not be the enemy of the good."[68] In contrast, detractors assert that although VAM scores based on student test scores are useful for looking at groups of teachers for research purposes—such as examining how specific teaching practices influence the learning of large numbers of students—professional consensus finds that value-added modeling data are not appropriate as a primary measure for evaluating individual teachers[69]—or schools.[70]

The VAM data are considered too unstable to be considered fair or reliable. Rather, VAM data can be beneficial when used for low-stakes decisions and when part of an integrated analysis of what the teacher is doing and who they are teaching.

Both sides agree that student achievement data are important components of meaningful teacher evaluation, and VAM data have a role to play; but it must be a limited one. Value-added data should not be the sole source of information in a teacher evaluation system. Educators must use it cautiously and combined with other data.

## Other Approaches to Teacher Evaluation

Additional teacher evaluation data are available to improve classroom practice and meet accountability needs. For example, standards-based performance assessments for licensure and advanced certification such as the National Board Certification, beginning teacher performance assessments, and district- and school-level instruments based on professional teaching standards have been shown to both predict teacher effectiveness and help improve teachers' practices. These standards have become the basis for assessments of teaching that produce ratings which are much more stable than value-added measures. They also incorporate classroom evidence of student learning and have recently been shown in large-scale studies to predict teachers' value-added effectiveness.[71]

In addition, effective teacher evaluation practices include data from on-the-job appraisal tools such as structured classroom observations or videotapes of teachers, classroom artifacts (such as lesson plans and assignments that can be scored according to a set of standards that reflect practices associated with effective teaching), evidence and analysis of student work and learning, student surveys about teaching practice, and frequent feedback based on professional standards; and each predict teacher effectiveness and improve teaching practice.[72]

Lastly, teacher evaluation systems are most effective when they use data that focus on improvement as well as on accountability. Teacher evaluation systems should be linked to professional development if the educators are to provide the essential feedback—the data—needed for teachers to analyze their own work and receive targeted support. In addition, teacher evaluation systems benefit from having well-trained evaluators (principals, administrators, and teachers' colleagues); frequent opportunities for targeted professional learning (to expand strengths and remedy weaknesses), evaluation, and feedback; available mentoring and coaching; and accessible processes such as peer assistance and review systems to support due process and timely decision making by an appropriate body. And the reminder of "multiple measures, multiple times, over multiple years" continues to make sense.

## Principal Evaluation

As James H. Stronge, an educational leadership professor at the College of William and Mary concludes, "The good news about traditional principal evaluation is that it doesn't hurt anyone," but "The bad news is that it doesn't help, either."[73] Even though research and experience recognize that principal performance is the second most important school factor (after teachers) influencing student achievement, schools rarely measure or document it effectively.[74] But despite the policy and community interest in evaluating principals' effectiveness, until recently, little systematic research has supported one approach over another.[75] At present, most principal evaluation overall does not differentiate among excellent, good, average, or poor principals. Nor does it offer a growth-oriented or accountability metric.

One comprehensive national study of principal evaluation practices finds that although states and districts evaluate principals on an array of performance areas—including management, external environment, and personal characteristics—they frequently ignore leadership behaviors related to rigorous curriculum and instructional quality. The study also confirms that principal evaluation is usually based on instruments that lack proven usefulness, psychometric properties, and accuracy.[76] Virtually all school districts continue to assess and evaluate principals using "home grown" evaluation tools of limited usefulness in appraising principals' instructional leadership skills: only about two-thirds of the instruments monitored curriculum, instructional quality, learning culture, or professional behavior.[77] They may or may not be aligned with existing professional standards.[78] And they often suffer from grade inflation. Principals are rated either "satisfactory" or "unsatisfactory," mostly the former.[79]

Recently developed standards offer a clear set of expectations for what principals as instructional leaders should be able to do. In 1996 (updated 2008, 2015), the Interstate School Leaders Licensure Consortium (ISLLC) published the ISLLC Standards for School Leaders.[80] Not meant to be all inclusive, these 11 research-based policy standards focus on indicators of traits, functions of work, and responsibilities that districts expect from their school leaders in order to increase student achievement. At least 43 states are using the ISLLC Standards for School Leaders as a whole or as a template for developing their own standards.[81]

But in our present accountability climate, simply identifying and measuring principals' behaviors is not enough. Communities and superintendents expect principals to produce results: higher achievement for all students. In some states and school districts, student achievement data can make up as much as 50 percent of the principals' total evaluation, even though studies find that the principals' influence accounts for about 10 percent or less of the variability in student learning.[82] Nonetheless, since principals hire, induct, support, and evaluate teachers—which some research finds accounts for as much as 30 percent of student learning[83]—principals' indirect effect on student learning is much greater than 10 percent. And if teachers are to be held accountable for student learning—with 30 to 50 percent of their evaluations based on their students' achievement data[84]—it is only fair to hold principals accountable, too. The debate continues about how to measure it and how much it should count, however.

Finally, as with teachers, valid and fair principal evaluation systems use multiple sources of information to document job performance. These include self-evaluation, observations, school site visits, document logs, surveys, and goal setting. With the school leaders' job so complex, only the proper use of multiple data sources can capture the broad range of responsibilities, increase the evaluation system's utility, and strengthen

## REFLECTIONS AND RELEVANCE 10.2

### Teacher and Principal Evaluations

Teachers' and principals' competence are essential to student success. It is logical to include student achievement data as part of teacher and principal evaluation as long as it is done fairly, accurately, and effectively.

You and two classmates are consultants invited by your local school board to give it guidance on how to develop teacher and principal evaluations that include student achievement data. Working together, prepare a five-minute informational talk for your school board about the factors to consider—and their rationales—when designing a teacher or principal evaluation program that is fair, credible, valid, reliable, and legally defensible. Include the pros and cons of using classroom observations with rubrics, value-added models of student achievement data, and types of quantitative and qualitative data to include Also discuss the merits to the school district of the evaluation system including opportunities for professional growth as well as for evaluation. Prepare a graphic to illustrate and help explain your points to the board. Present your talk to your class and receive their feedback about its effectiveness and why (or why not).

the processes' validity and reliability. And as with teachers, performance evaluation for principals works best when it balances growth with accountability, offering opportunities for self-assessment and professional learning as well as for high-stakes outcomes. Determining the appropriate data and their weights for principal evaluation remains a work in progress.

## CONCLUSION

In today's schools, data are used for school improvement, professional growth, performance evaluation, and public accountability. Principals and school leaders need to develop the habits of mind that allow them to recognize which data are important for which purposes and how to use them wisely to inform decision making. Data are only as effective as they are appropriate to the task, interpreted correctly, made meaningful, and used correctly and ethically.

As for the data themselves, the numbers are not the only things that matter; it is how we use and interpret the right data, enough data, and what we do with the findings that make the difference to improved practice and outcomes. Just as education is more than a test score, informed decision making in schools is more than data. Data do not drive school-based decisions about children's learning. They are necessary but not sufficient to leadership effectiveness. Rather, principals' leadership effectiveness depends on a widely shared set of values: a shared vision for learning; a school culture and instructional program that supports student learning and staff professional growth; efficient and safe management of resources; a collaborative faculty responsive to community interests and needs; a commitment to integrity, fairness, and ethical behaviors; familiarity with the advances in research knowledge on teaching and learning that help make the data and school improvement strategies meaningful; and an understanding of the political, social, legal, and cultural context in which schools find themselves.[85] Only within these contexts can educators make beneficial use of student data in decision making.

## NOTES

1   Wallace Foundation (2011). *The school principal as leader: Guiding schools to better teaching and learning.* New York NY: Author. Retrieved from: http://www.wallace foundation.org/knowledge-center/school-leadership/effective-principal-leadership/Pages/The-School-Principal-as-Leader-Guiding-Schools-to-Better-Teaching-and-Learning.aspx
2.  Principals need to remember to gather all relevant data before making *any* type of school-based decision. For example, when a teacher comes to a principal with a concern about a student, colleague, or parent—or a parent comes with a concern about a student's academics or behaviors—the first person to reach the principal is not always right. Principals need to collect *all relevant* data before drawing conclusions or making decisions about any issues brought to them for resolution.
3.  Herman, J. L., & Haertel, E. H. (Eds.) (2005). Uses and misuses of data for educational accountability and improvement. *The 104th Yearbook of the National Society for the Study of Education* (part 2). Malden, MA: Blackwell; Ryan, J. E. (2004). The perverse incentives of the No Child Left Behind Act. *New York University Law Review, 79* (3), 932–989.
4.  Black, P., & Wiliam, D. (1998, October). Inside the black box: Raising standards through classroom assessment. *Phi Delta Kappan, 80* (2), 141–151.
5.  Black & Wiliam (1998, October), ibid.
6.  See, for example, Bloom, B. S. (1984, May). The search for methods of group instruction as effective as one-to-one tutoring. *Educational Leadership, 41* (4), 4–17; Black, P., & Wiliam, D. (1998, March). Assessment and classroom learning. *Educational Assessment: Principles, Policy, and Practice, 5* (1), 7–74; Black & Wiliam (1998, October), op. cit., pp. 139–148; Meisels, S., Atkins-Burnett, S., Xue, Y., Bickel, D. D., & Son, A. (2003). Creating a system of accountability: The impact of instructional assessment on elementary children's achievement scores. *Educational Policy Analysis Archives, 11* (9). Retrieved from: http://epaa.asu.edu/epaa/v11n9; Rodriquez, M. C. (2004). The role of classroom assessment in student performance on TIMSS. *Applied Measurement in Education, 17* (1), 1–24.
7.  Danielson, C. (2007). *Enhancing professional practice: A framework for teaching* (2nd ed.). Alexandria, VA: Association for Supervision and Curriculum Development; Danielson, C. (2002). *Enhancing student achievement: A framework for school improvement.* Alexandria, VA: Association for Supervision and Curriculum Development.
8.  Black, P. (1993). Formative and summative assessments by teachers, *Studies in Science Education, 21* (1), 49–97; Black, P., & Wiliam, D. (1998). Assessment and classroom learning. *Assessment in education: Principles, policy and practice, 5* (1), 7–74; Stiggins, R. J., Griswold, M. M., & Wikelund, K. R. (1989). Measuring thinking skills through classroom assessment. *Journal of Educational Measurement, 26* (3), 233–246.
9.  For discussion of Common Core State Standards and their assessments and high-quality assessment systems, see: Darling-Hammond, L. (2010). *Performance counts: Assessment systems that support high-quality learning.* Washington, DC: Council of Chief State School

Officers. Retrieved from: http://www.ccsso.org/Documents/2010/Performance_Counts_Assessment_Systems_2010.pdf

10. Herman, J. L., & Linn, R. L. (2013). *On the road to assessing deeper learning: The status of Smarter Balanced and PARCC assessment consortia* (CRESST Report 823). Los Angeles, CA: University of California, National Center for Research on Evaluation, Standards, and Student Testing (CRESST).

11. Darling-Hammond, L., & Adamson, F. (2013). *Developing assessments of deeper learning: The costs and benefits of using tests that help students learn.* Stanford, CA: Stanford Center for Opportunity Policy in Education. Retrieved from: https://edpolicy.stanford.edu/sites/default/files/publications/developing-assessments-deeper-learning-costs-and-benefits-using-tests-help-students-learn_1.pdf

12. Linn, R. L. (2003, July). *Accountability: Responsibility and reasonable expectations (Tech. Rep.).* Los Angeles, CA: Center for the Study of Evaluation, CRESST; Linn, R. L., Baker, E. L., & Betebenner, D. W. (2002). Accountability systems: Implications of requirements of the No Child Left Behind Act of 2001. *Educational Researcher, 31* (6), 3–16.

13. English, F., & Steffen, B. (2001). *Deep curriculum alignment: Creating a level playing field for all children on high-stakes tests of educational accountability.* Lanham, MD: Scarecrow Press.

14. Perie, M., Marion, S., & Gong, B. (2009). Moving toward a comprehensive assessment system: A framework for considering interim assessments. *Educational Measurement: Issues and Practice, 28* (3), 5–13. Retrieved from: http://www.nwea.org/sites/www.nwea.org/files/aldocs/Perie%20-%20Moving%20Toward%20a%20Comprehensive%20Assessment%20System%20-%20A%20F_1.pdf

15. Castellano. K. E., & Ho, A. D. (2013, February). *A practitioner's guide to growth models.* Washington, DC: Council of Chief State School Officers. Retrieved from: http://scholar.harvard.edu/files/andrewho/files/a_pracitioners_guide_to_growth_models.pdf

16. Castellano & Ho (2013, February), op. cit.

17. Institute of Education Science (2012, July). *Growth models. Issues and advice from the states. A guide to the statewide longitudinal data systems grant program.* Washington, DC: Institute of Education Science, U.S. Department of Education. Retrieved from: http://nces.ed.gov/programs/slds/pdf/guide_growth-model.pdf

18. O'Malley, K. J., Murphy, S., Larsen, K., Murphy, D., & McBride, Y. (2011, September). *Overview of student growth models.* White paper. Iowa City, IA: Pearson Assessment and Information Group. Retrieved from: http://researchnetwork.pearson.com/wp-content/uploads/StudentGrowthWP083111.pdf

19. For a fuller description of the various types of growth models used for student achievement, see: Castellano & Ho (2013, February), op. cit.

20. Castellano & Ho (2013, February), op. cit.

21. Northwest Evaluation Association (2014, January). *The case for growth. Why measure student learning?* Portland, OR: Northwest Evaluation Association. Retrieved from: http://www.ndseed.k12.nd.us/files/2014/01/Catalyst-Series-Measuring-Growth-E-Book.pdf

22. Lambdin, D. V., & Forseth, C. (1996). Seamless assessment/instruction = good teaching. *Teaching Children Mathematics, 2* (5), 294–299.

23. A 2011 U.S. Census Bureau's report, "CPS 2011 Annual Social and Economic Supplement" (Table POV01), finds that over 20 percent of American children, ages 6–17 and more than 25 percent of children aged five and below live in poverty. Poverty is correlated with many challenges to student learning, including entry into school with severely reduced vocabularies, more schooling interruptions through absences and moving to new housing, higher dropout rates, and dropping out at earlier grades than children from non-poverty homes.

24. Marzano, R. J. (2004). *Building background knowledge for academic achievement: Research on what works in schools.* Alexandria, VA: ASCD.

25. Benjamin, S. (2014, April). Sifting from data to evidence for decision making. *Phi Delta Kappan, 95* (7), 45–49.

26. Kennelly, L., & Monrad, M. (2007). *Approaches to dropout prevention: Heeding early warning signs with appropriate interventions.* Washington, DC: National High School Center at the American Institutes for Research. Retrieved from: www.betterhighschools.org/pubs/usergd_dr.asp; Balfanz, R. (2009). *Putting middle grades students on the graduation path: A policy and practice brief.* Westerville, OH: National Middle School Association.

27. Credible research sources include, for example, the Education Resources Information Center (ERIC), an online library of educational research, and JSTOR, a digital library of academic journals, books, and primary sources. Look for refereed journals, where experts in the field have reviewed the articles for rigor and trustworthiness. See Guskey, T. (2014, May). Planning professional learning. *Educational Leadership, 71* (8), 10–16.

28. Bauer, S. C., & Brazier, S. D. (2012). *Using research to lead school improvement. Turning evidence into action* (pp. 77–79). Thousand Oaks, CA: Sage.

29. Student privacy as defined in the Family Educational Rights and Privacy Act of 1974 (FERPA) and the Children's Online Privacy Protection Act of 1998 (COPPA), both recently updated. See Molnar, M. (2014, May 14). Safeguard use of student data, White House report urges. *Education Week, 33* (31), 26.

30. U.S. Census Bureau (2012). *2012 National population projections: Summary tables.* Washington, DC: U.S. Census Bureau. As cited in Annie E. Casey Foundation (2014). *Race for results. Kids count policy report* (pp. 1–2). Baltimore, MD: Annie E. Casey Foundation. Retrieved from: http://www.aecf.org/m/resourcedoc/AECF-RaceforResults-2014.pdf

31. Balfanz, R., & Byrnes, V. (2012). *Chronic absenteeism: Summarizing what we know from nationally available data.* Baltimore: Johns Hopkins University Center for Social Organization of Schools. Retrieved from: http://new.every1graduates.org/wp-content/uploads/2012/05/FINALChronicAbsenteeismReport_May16.pdf

32. The Equity Project (2014, March). Discipline disparities series: Key findings. *Discipline Disparities: A research-to-practice collaborative.* Bloomington, IN: The Equity Project. Retrieved from: http://www.indiana.edu/~atlantic/wp-content/uploads/2014/03/Disparity_KeyFindings_031114.pdf

33. American Institutes for Research (2013, September). *Roundtable: The perspectives of youth affected by exclusionary school discipline.* Washington, DC: American Institutes for Research. Retrieved from: http://www.air.org/sites/default/files/Exclusionary_Discipline_Roundtable_Report_090613_pdf.pdf; Fabelo, T., Thompson, M. D., Plotkin, M., Carmichael, D., Marchbanks, M. P., & Booth, E. A. (2011). *Breaking schools' rules: A statewide study of how school discipline relates to students' success and juvenile justice involvement.* Retrieved from: http://justicecenter.csg.org/files/Breaking_Schools_Rules_Report_Final.pdf

34. Blad, E. (2014, January 15). Federal guidance urges schools to shift from 'zero tolerance'. *Education Week, 33* (17), 7.

35. Haynes, N. M., & Comer, J. P. (1993). The Yale School Development Program process, outcomes, and policy considerations. *Urban Education, 28* (2), 166–199.

36. Haynes, N. M. (1998). Creating safe and caring school communities: Comer School Development Program schools. *Journal of Negro Education, 65,* 308–314; Kuperminc, G. P., Leadbeater, B. J., Emmons, C., & Blatt, S. J. (1997). Perceived school climate and difficulties in the social adjustment of middle school students. *Applied Developmental Science, 1* (2), 76–88.

37. McEvoy, A., & Welker, R. (2000). Antisocial behavior, academic failure, and school climate: A critical review. *Journal of Emotional and Behavioral Disorders, 8* (3), 130–140.

38. Freiberg, H. J. (1998). Measuring school climate: Let me count the ways. *Educational Leadership, 56* (1), 22–26.

39. Shonkoff, J. P., & Phillips, D. A. (Eds.) (2000). *From neurons to neighborhoods: The science of early childhood development.* Washington, DC: National Academy Press.

40. Annie E. Casey Foundation (2013). *2013 Kids count data book: State trends in child well-being.* Baltimore, MD: Annie E. Casey Foundation.

41. See, for example, Children's Defense Fund (1988, January). *Making the middle grades work.* Washington, DC: Adolescent Pregnancy Prevention Clearinghouse.
42. See, for example, Oakes, J. (1985). *Keeping track: How schools structure inequality.* New Haven, CT: Yale University Press; Oakes, J., Ormseth, T., Bell, R., & Camp, P. (1990). *Multiplying inequalities: The effects of race, social class, and tracking on opportunities to learn mathematics and science.* Washington, DC: National Science Foundation; Finley, M. K. (1984). Teachers and tracking in a comprehensive high school. *Sociology of Education, 57,* 233–243.
43. See, for example, The Equity Project (2014, March), op. cit.; Barton, P. E., Coley, R. J., & Weglinsky, H. (1998, October). *Order in the classroom: Violence, discipline, and student achievement.* Princeton. NJ: Educational Testing Service, Policy Information Center, Policy Information Report; Myers, D. E. (1987, January). Student discipline and high school performance. *Sociology of Education, 60* (1), 18–33.
44. See, for example, Rosenthal, R., & Jacobson, L. (1968). *Pygmalion in the classroom: Teachers' expectations and pupils' intellectual development.* New York: Rineholt and Winston.
45. See, for example, Barton, P. E., Coley, R. J., & Weglinsky, H. (1998, October). *Order in the classroom: Violence, discipline, and student achievement.* Princeton, NJ: Educational Testing Service, Policy Information Center, Policy Information Report; Myers, D. E. (1987, January). Student discipline and high school performance. *Sociology of Education, 60* (1), 18–33.
46. See, for example, Baker, J. A. (1999). Teacher-student interaction in urban at-risk classrooms: Differential behavior, relationship, quality, and student satisfaction with school. *The Elementary School Journal, 100* (1), 57–70; Boykin, A. W., & Noguera, P. (2011). *Creating the opportunity to learn. Moving from research to practice to close the achievement gap.* Alexandria, VA: ASCD; Hamre, B. K., & Pianta, R.C. (2005). Can instructional and emotional support in the first-grade classroom make a difference for children at risk of school failure? *Child Development, 76* (5), 949–967.
47. See, for example, Annie E. Casey Foundation (2014). *Race for results. Building a path to opportunity for all children.* Policy report. Baltimore, MD: Annie E. Casey Foundation. Retrieved from: http://www.aecf.org/~/media/Pubs/Initiatives/KIDS%20COUNT/R/Racefor Results/RaceforResults.pdf; Kaplan, L. S., & Owings, W. A. (2015). *Educational foundations* (2nd ed.) (pp. 207–281). Belmont, CA: Cengage Learning.
48. Annie E. Casey Foundation (2013), op. cit.
49. Maxwell, J. (2005). *Qualitative research design: An interactive approach* (2nd ed.). Thousand Oaks, CA: Sage.
50. Faxon-Mills, S., Hamilton, L. S., Rudnick, M., & Stecher, B. M. (1923). *New assessments, better instruction? Designing assessment systems to promote more instructional improvement.* Santa Monica, CA: RAND.
51. Campbell, D. T. (1976). *Assessing the impact of planned social change.* Hanover, HH: Public Affairs Center, Dartmouth College.
52. Nichols, S. L., Glass, G. V., & Berliner, D. C. (2012). High stakes testing and student achievement: Updated analysis with NAEP data. *Education Policy Analysis Archives, 20* (20). Retrieved from: http://nepc.colorado.edu/files/EPSL-0509-105-EPRU.pdf
53. See, for example, Deans, E. (2010, September 8). *Examining the data: Using achievement data to compare state standards.* Washington, DC: New America Foundation. Ed Money Watch. Retrieved from: http://edmoney.newamerica.net/blogposts/2010/analyzing_the_data_state_performance_on_nclb_tests_vs_naep-36529; Lee, J. (2006). *Tracking achievement gaps and assessing the impact of NCLB on gaps: An in-depth look into national and state reading and math outcome trends.* Cambridge, MA: Harvard Civil Rights Project, Harvard Education Group. Retrieved from: http://www.civilrightsproject.harvard.edu; Olson, L. (2007, April 18). Gaps in proficiency levels on state test and NAEP found to grow. *Education Week, 26* (33), 12.

54. Goodwin, B. (2014, March). Better tests don't guarantee better instruction. Research Says. *Educational Leadership, 71* (6), 78–80.

55. Heitin, L. (2013, November 6). Teacher-evaluation policies becoming more rigorous. *Education Week, 33* (11), 4.

56. Stecher, B., Garet, M., Holtzman, D., & Hamilton, L. (2012, November). Implementing measures of teacher effectiveness. *Phi Delta Kappan, 94* (3), 39–43.

57. Grossman, P., Loeb, S., Cohen, J., Hammerness, K., Wyckoff, J., Boyd, D., & Lankford, H. (2010). *Measure for measure: The relationships between measures of instructional practice in middle school English language arts and teachers' value-added scores* (CALDER Working Paper No. 45). Washington, DC: National Center for Analysis of Longitudinal Education Data, The Urban Institute. Retrieved from: http://www.urban.org/uploadedpdf/1001425-measure-for-measure.pdf; Kane, T. J., & Staiger, D. O. (2012). *Gathering feedback for teaching. Combining high-quality observations with student surveys and achievement.* MET Project Policy and Practice Brief. Seattle, WA: Bill & Melinda Gates Foundation. Retrieved from: http://metproject.org/downloads/MET_Gathering_Feedback_Practioner_Brief.pdf; Kane, T. J., Taylor, E. S., Tyler, J. H., & Wooten, A. L. (2010). *Identifying effective classroom practices using student achievement data* (Working Paper 15803). Cambridge, MA: National Bureau of Economic Research. Retrieved from: http://www.danielson group.org/ckeditor/ckfinder/userfiles/files/IdentifyingEffectiveClassroomPractices.pdf; Sartain, L., Stoelinga, S. R., & Brown, E. R., with Luppescu, S., Matsko, K. K., Miller, F. K., Durwood, C. E., Jiang, J. Y., & Glazer, D. (2011). *Rethinking teacher evaluation. Lessons learned from classroom observations, principal-teacher conferences, and district implementation.* Research Report. Chicago, IL: Consortium on Chicago School Research at the University of Chicago Urban Education Institute. Retrieved from: http://ccsr.uchicago. edu/sites/default/files/publications/Teacher%20Eval%20Report%20FINAL.pdf

58. Danielson, C., Pianta, R., LaParo, K., & Hamre, B., cited in Kane & Staiger (2012), op. cit.

59. Kane & Staiger (2012), op. cit.

60. Kane & Staiger (2012), op. cit.

61. Strunk, K. O., Weinstein, T., Makkonen, R., & Furedi, D. (2012, November). Lessons learned. *Phi Delta Kappan, 94* (3), 47–51.

62. Stecher, B., Garet, M., Holtzman, D., & Hamilton, L. (2012, November). Implementing measures of teacher effectiveness. *Phi Delta Kappan, 94* (3), 39–43.

63. Darling-Hammond, L., Amrein-Beardsley, A., Hertel. E. H., & Rothstein, J. (2011). *Getting teacher evaluation right: A background paper for policy makers.* Washington, DC: American Educational Research Association and National Academy of Education. Retrieved from: http://tx.aft.org/files/gettingteacherevaluationright.pdf

64. Newton, X., Darling-Hammond, L., Haertel, E., & Thomas, E. (2010). Value-added modeling of teacher effectiveness: an exploration of stability across models and contexts. *Educational Policy Analysis Archives, 18* (23), 1–23.

65. Piro, J., Wiemers, R., & Shutt, T. (2011). *Using student achievement data in teacher and principal evaluations: A policy study.* Ypsilanti, MI: National Council of Professors of Educational Administration. Retrieved from: http://cnx.org/content/m41125/latest/

66. Sukin, T., Nicewater, W. A., Winter, P., Mitzel, H., Keller, L., & Schultz, M. J. (2014, April 2). Take the time to evaluate teacher evaluation. Commentary. *Education Week, 33* (27), 28–29.

67. Weisberg, D, Sexton, S., Mulhern, J., & Keeling, D. (2009). *The widget effect. Our national failure to acknowledge and act on differences in teacher effectiveness.* New York, NY: New Teacher Project. Retrieved from: http://carnegie.org/fileadmin/Media/Publications/widget.pdf

68. Ritter, G. W., & Shuls, J. V. (2012, November). If a tree falls in a forest, but no one hears . . . *Phi Delta Kappan, 94* (3), 34–38.

69. Darling-Hammond et al. (2011), op. cit.

70. McCaffrey, D. F., Koretz, D., Lockwood, J. R., & Hamilton. L. S. (2005). *Evaluating value-added models for teacher accountability.* Santa Monica: RAND Corporation.

71. Darling-Hammond et al. (2011), op. cit.
72. Darling-Hammond et al. (2011), op. cit.
73. Stronge, J. H. (2013, April). Principal evaluation from the ground up. *Educational Leadership, 70* (7), 60.
74. Weisberg, Sexton, Mulhern, & Keeling (2009), op. cit.
75. Ginsberg, R., & Berry, B. (1990). The folklore of principal evaluation. *Journal of Personnel Evaluation in Education, 68* (1), 58–74.
76. Goldring, E., Cravens, X. C., Murphy, J., Porter, A. D. Elliott, S. N., & Carson, B. (2009). The evaluation of principals: What and how do states and urban districts assess leadership? *Elementary School Journal, 110* (1), 19–39.
77. Goldring, E., Porter, A. C., Murphy, J., Elliott, S. N., & Cravens, X. (2007, March). *Assessing learning-centered leadership: Connections to research, professional standards, and current practice.* New York, NY: Wallace Foundation.
78. Heck, R. H., & Marcoulides, G. A. (1996). The assessment of principal performance: A multilevel evaluation approach. *Journal of Personnel Evaluation in Education, 10* (1), 11–28.
79. Weisberg, Sexton, Mulhern, & Keeling (2009), op. cit.
80. Council of Chief State School Officers (CCSSO) (2015). *Educational leadership policy standards: ISLLC 2015.* As adopted by the National Policy Board for Educational Administration. Washington, DC: CCSSO. Retrieved from: http://www.ccsso.org/Resources/Programs/Developing_and_Supporting_School-Ready_Leaders.html
81. Wright, G., & Gray, N. D. (2007, October 11–14). *The ISLLC standards: A unifying force in school administrators and counselor preparation.* Paper based on a program presented at the Association for Counselor Education and Supervision Conference, Columbus, OH; Retrieved from: http://counselingoutfitters.com/vistas/vistas09/Wright-Gray.doc
82. Waters, J. T., Marzano, R. J., & McNulty, B. (2003). *Balanced leadership: What 30 years of research tell us about the effect of leadership on student achievement.* Aurora, CI: McRel.
83. Hattie, J. (2008). *Visible learning: A synthesis of over 800 meta-analyses relating to student achievement.* New York, NY: Routledge.
84. Bill and Melinda Gates Foundation (2013*). Ensuring fair and reliable measures of effective teaching: Culminating findings from the MET Project's three-year study.* Seattle, WA: Bill and Melinda Gates Foundation. Retrieved from: http://www.metproject.org/downloads/MET_Ensuring_Fair_and_Reliable_Measures_Practitioner_Brief.pdf
85. Condon, C., & Clifford, M. (2012, January). *Measuring principal performance* (p. 2). Washington, DC: American Institutes for Research.

# Index

Note: 'F' after a page number indicates a figure; 't' indicates a table.